Azure Data Scientist Associate Certification Guide

A hands-on guide to machine learning in Azure
and passing the Microsoft Certified DP-100 exam

Andreas Botsikas, Ph.D.

Michael Hlobil

BIRMINGHAM—MUMBAI

Azure Data Scientist Associate Certification Guide

Publishing Product Manager: Aditi Gour

Senior Editor: David Sugarman

Content Development Editor: Nathanya Dias

Technical Editor: Sonam Pandey

Copy Editor: Safis Editing

Project Coordinator: Aparna Ravikumar Nair

Proofreader: Safis Editing

Indexer: Tejal Daruwale Soni

Production Designer: Vijay Kamble

First published: December 2021

Production reference: 1291021

Published by Packt Publishing Ltd.
Livery Place
35 Livery Street
Birmingham
B3 2PB, UK.

ISBN 978-1-80056-500-5

www.packt.com

Contributors

About the authors

Andreas Botsikas is an experienced advisor working in the software industry. He has worked in the finance sector, leading highly efficient DevOps teams, and architecting and building high-volume transactional systems. He then traveled the world, building AI-infused solutions with a group of engineers and data scientists. Currently, he works as a trusted advisor for customers onboarding into Azure, de-risking and accelerating their cloud journey. He is a strong engineering professional with a Doctor of Philosophy (Ph.D.) in resource optimization with artificial intelligence from the National Technical University of Athens.

I want to thank the people who have been close to me and supported me, especially my family. Moreover, I would like to thank the Packt team and the reviewers for the tremendous support throughout the book authoring process. Finally, I would like to thank Michael, who challenged me to co-write this book. The journey was long, full of adventures, full of discoveries, exactly as I was hoping it to be.

2c9d7257ca15856e46c7c35e30d138cf

Michael Hlobil is an experienced architect focused on quickly understanding customers' business needs, with over 25 years of experience in IT pitfalls and successful projects, and is dedicated to creating solutions based on the Microsoft Platform. He has an MBA in Computer Science and Economics (from the Technical University and the University of Vienna) and an MSc (from the ESBA) in Systemic Coaching. He was working on advanced analytics projects in the last decade, including massive parallel systems and Machine Learning systems. He enjoys working with customers and supporting the journey to the cloud.

I would like to first and foremost thank my grandparents: "Oma and Opa Danke für eure unermüdliche Unterstützung ohne euch wäre ich nicht das geworden was ich bin!". Moreover, I would like to thank my family. My wife and my three kids: "Danke für alles was ich lernen durfte und lernen darf!". A huge thank you to Andreas: "Ευχαριστώ για την υπομονή και τη φιλία σου!". Last but not least to the Packt team and the reviewers for the tremendous work they did throughout the book authoring process.

I have known Andreas and Michael from our FastTrack for Azure organization. Our core strategy is to meet customers wherever they are in their current cloud journey – primarily to accelerate and de-risk cloud deployments at scale while improving the Azure platform. Both are enabling customers all over the world to become successful with their Artificial Intelligence projects. AI plays a crucial role in the digital revolution we experience every day. There are challenges with every new technology, especially when it comes to building trust in the latest technology. This book covers both how to produce AI but also covers aspects of building responsible AI. I think these two aspects makes this book so valuable. I hope you enjoy it.

Juergen Daiberl, General Manager - FastTrack for Azure Lead

The exponential growth of data and the rapid evolution of cloud computing have put topics such as data science and machine learning on top of the agenda for many organizations. Andreas and Michael's long experience with hundreds of our customers comes together in this book, combining the concepts of AI with practical guidance on how to use it in real life scenarios, using the Microsoft Azure cloud. The insights and knowledge they share will help you find the right opportunities for AI in your organization and enable you to get started. I'm inspired by Andreas and Michael's work and how they live Microsoft's mission to empower every person and every organization on the planet to achieve more.

Ricardo Henriques, EMEA Lead - FastTrack for Azure

About the reviewers

Arianna Olivelli is a marine scientist based in London. She is currently undertaking a Ph.D. in chemical oceanography. In the past, she has worked on numerical, statistical, and machine learning models focused on marine and riverine plastic pollution. In her free time, she loves to play sports and spend time outdoors.

Maria Vrabie is an engineer working in the FastTrack for Azure team within the Engineering organization at Microsoft. She is currently helping various businesses implement Azure solutions focusing on Intelligent agents, Cognitive Services, as well as analytics. Community enthusiast and inclusion advocate, she has been volunteering at different events throughout years. In her spare time, she enjoys cycling and Latin dancing.

Table of Contents

3
Azure Machine Learning Studio Components

4
Configuring the Workspace

Section 2: No code data science experimentation

5
Letting the Machines Do the Model Training

6
Visual Model Training and Publishing

Section 3: Advanced data science tooling and capabilities

7
The AzureML Python SDK

8
Experimenting with Python Code

9
Optimizing the ML Model

10
Understanding Model Results

11
Working with Pipelines

12

Operationalizing Models with Code

Other Books You May Enjoy

Index

Preface

This book helps you acquire practical knowledge about machine learning experimentation on Azure. It covers everything you need to know and understand to become a certified Azure Data Scientist Associate.

The book starts with an introduction to data science, making sure you are familiar with the terminology used throughout the book. You then move into the **Azure Machine Learning** (**AzureML**) workspace, your working area for the rest of the book. You will discover the studio interface and manage the various components, like the data stores and the compute clusters.

You will then focus on no-code, and low-code experimentation. You will discover the Automated ML wizard, which helps you to locate and deploy optimal models for your dataset. You will also learn how to run end-to-end data science experiments using the designer provided in AzureML studio.

You will then deep dive into the code first data science experimentation. You will explore the **AzureML Software Development Kit** (**SDK**) for Python and learn how to create experiments and publish models using code. You will learn how to use powerful computer clusters to scale up and out your machine learning jobs. You will learn how to optimize your model's hyperparameters using Hyperdrive. Then you will learn how to use responsible AI tools to interpret and debug your models. Once you have a trained model, you will learn to operationalize it for batch or real-time inferences and how you can monitor it in production.

With this knowledge, you will have a good understanding of the Azure Machine Learning platform and you will be able to clear the DP100 exam with flying colors.

Who this book is for

The book targets two audiences: developers who seek to infuse their applications with AI capabilities and data scientists who want to scale their ML experiments in the Azure cloud. Basic knowledge of Python is needed to follow the code samples present in the book. Some experience in training ML models in Python with common frameworks such as scikit-learn will help you understand the content more easily.

What this book covers

Chapter 1, An Overview of Modern Data Science, provides you with the terminology used throughout the book.

Chapter 2, Deploying Azure Machine Learning Workspace Resources, helps you understand the deployment options for an **Azure Machine Learning** (**AzureML**) workspace.

Chapter 3, Azure Machine Learning Studio Components, provides an overview of the studio web interface you will be using to conduct your data science experiments.

Chapter 4, Configuring the Workspace, helps you understand how to provision computational resources and connect to data sources that host your datasets.

Chapter 5, Letting the Machines Do the Model Training, guides you on your first **Automated Machine Learning** (**AutoML**) experiment and how to deploy the best-trained model as a web endpoint through the studio's wizards.

Chapter 6, Visual Model Training and Publishing, helps you author a training pipeline through the studio's designer experience. You will learn how to operationalize the trained model through a batch or a real-time pipeline by promoting the trained pipeline within the designer.

Chapter 7, The AzureML Python SDK, gets you started on the code-first data science experimentation. You will understand how the AzureML Python SDK is structured, and you will learn how to manage AzureML resources like compute clusters with code.

Chapter 8, Experimenting with Python Code, helps you train your first machine learning model with code. It guides you on how to track model metrics and scale-out your training efforts to bigger compute clusters.

Chapter 9, Optimizing the ML Model, shows you how to optimize your machine learning model with **Hyperparameter tuning** and helps you discover the best model for your dataset by kicking off an **AutoML** experiment with code.

Chapter 10, Understanding Model Results, introduces you to the concept of responsible AI and deep dives into the tools that allow you to interpret your models' predictions, analyze the errors that your models are prone to, and detect potential fairness issues.

Chapter 11, Working with Pipelines, guides you on authoring repeatable processes by defining multi-step pipelines using the AzureML Python SDK.

Chapter 12, Operationalizing Models with Code, helps you register your trained models and operationalize them through real-time web endpoints or batch parallel processing pipelines.

To get the most out of this book

This book tries to provide you with everything you need to learn. The *Further reading* section of each chapter contains links to pages that will help you deep dive, into topics that are peripheral to the contents of this book. It will help if you have some basic familiarity with the Azure portal and have read some Python code in the past.

Software/hardware covered in the book	Operating system requirements
Azure portal	A modern browser on Windows, macOS, or Linux
Azure Machine Learning Studio	A modern browser on Windows, macOS, or Linux

In this book, we guide you to use the Notebooks experience available within the AzureML studio. If you want to execute the same code on your workstation instead of the cloud-based experience, you will need a Python environment to run Jupyter notebooks. The easiest way to run Jupyter notebooks on your workstation is through VSCode, a free cross-platform editor with fantastic Python support. You will also need to install Git in your workstation to clone the book's GitHub repository.

If you are using the digital version of this book, we advise you to type the code yourself or access the code from the book's GitHub repository (a link is available in the next section). Doing so will help you avoid any potential errors related to the copying and pasting of code.

If you face any issue executing the code, ensure that you have cloned the latest version from the GitHub repository. If the problem persists, feel free to open a GitHub issue to describe the issue you are facing and help you solve it.

Download the example code files

You can download the example code files for this book from GitHub at `https://github.com/PacktPublishing/Azure-Data-Scientist-Associate-Certification-Guide`. If there's an update to the code, it will be updated in the GitHub repository.

We also have other code bundles from our rich catalog of books and videos available at `https://github.com/PacktPublishing/`. Check them out!

Download the color images

We also provide a PDF file that has color images of the screenshots and diagrams used in this book. You can download it here: `https://static.packt-cdn.com/downloads/9781800565005_ColorImages.pdf`.

Conventions used

There are a number of text conventions used throughout this book.

`Code in text`: Indicates code words in text, database table names, folder names, filenames, file extensions, pathnames, dummy URLs, user input, and Twitter handles. Here is an example: "You can also change the autogenerated name of the pipeline you are designing. Rename the current pipeline to `test-pipeline`."

A block of code is set as follows:

```
from azureml.train.hyperdrive import GridParameterSampling
from azureml.train.hyperdrive import choice
param_sampling = GridParameterSampling( {
        "a": choice(0.01, 0.5),
        "b": choice(10, 100)
    }
)
```

When we wish to draw your attention to a particular part of a code block, the relevant lines or items are set in bold:

```
from azureml.core import Workspace

ws = Workspace.from_config()
loans_ds = ws.datasets['loans']
compute_target = ws.compute_targets['cpu-sm-cluster']
```

Any command-line input or output is written as follows:

```
az group create --name my-name-rg --location westeurope
```

Bold: Indicates a new term, an important word, or words that you see onscreen. For instance, words in menus or dialog boxes appear in **bold**. Here is an example: "Navigate to the **Author | Notebooks** section of your AzureML Studio web interface."

> **Tips or important notes**
> Run numbers may be different in your executions. Every time you execute the cells, a new run number is created, continuing from the previous number. So, if you execute code that performs one hyperdrive run with 20 child runs, the last child run will be run 21. The next time you execute the same code, the hyperdrive run will start from run 22, and the last child will be run 42. The run numbers referred to in this section are the ones shown in the various figures, and it is normal to observe differences, especially if you had to rerun a couple of cells.

Get in touch

Feedback from our readers is always welcome.

General feedback: If you have questions about any aspect of this book, email us at customercare@packtpub.com and mention the book title in the subject of your message.

Errata: Although we have taken every care to ensure the accuracy of our content, mistakes do happen. If you have found a mistake in this book, we would be grateful if you would report this to us. Please visit www.packtpub.com/support/errata and fill in the form.

Piracy: If you come across any illegal copies of our works in any form on the internet, we would be grateful if you would provide us with the location address or website name. Please contact us at copyright@packt.com with a link to the material.

If you are interested in becoming an author: If there is a topic that you have expertise in and you are interested in either writing or contributing to a book, please visit authors.packtpub.com.

Share Your Thoughts

Once you've read *Azure Data Scientist Associate Certification Guide*, we'd love to hear your thoughts! Scan the QR code below to go straight to the Amazon review page for this book and share your feedback.

https://packt.link/r/1-800-56500-3

Your review is important to us and the tech community and will help us make sure we're delivering excellent quality content.

Section 1: Starting your cloud-based data science journey

An Azure Data Scientist Associate is a subject matter expert with applied data science and machine learning knowledge, able to run machine learning workloads on Azure. The responsibilities for this role include planning and creating a suitable working environment for data science workloads on Azure. In this section, you will get an overview of the data science and machine learning terminology used throughout the book. You will also learn how to provision and configure the Azure Machine Learning services, the de facto environment for running machine learning experiments in the Azure cloud.

This section comprises of the following chapters:

- *Chapter 1, An Overview of Modern Data Science*
- *Chapter 2, Deploying Azure Machine Learning Workspace Resources*
- *Chapter 3, Azure Machine Learning Studio Components*
- *Chapter 4, Configuring the Workspace*

1
An Overview of Modern Data Science

Data science has its roots in the early eighteenth century and has gained tremendous popularity during the last couple of decades.

In this book, you will learn how to run a data science project within Azure, the Microsoft public cloud infrastructure. You will gain all skills needed to become a certified Azure Data Scientist Associate. You will start with this chapter, which gives some foundational terminology used throughout the book. Then, you will deep dive into **Azure Machine Learning (AzureML)** services. You will start by provisioning a workspace. You will then work on the no-code, low-code experiences build in the AzureML Studio web interface. Then, you will deep dive into the code-first data science experimentation, working with the AzureML **Software Development Kit (SDK)**.

In this chapter, you will learn some fundamental data science-related terms needed for the DP 100 exam. You will start by understanding the typical life cycle of a data science project. You will then read about big data and how Apache Spark technology enables you to train machine learning models against them. Then, you will explore what the **DevOps** mindset is and how it can help you become a member of a highly efficient, multi-disciplinary, agile team that builds machine learning-enhanced products.

In this chapter, we are going to cover the following main topics:

- The evolution of data science
- Working on a data science project
- Using Spark in data science
- Adopting the DevOps mindset

The evolution of data science

If you try to find the roots of the data science practices, you will probably end up discovering evidence at the beginning of civilization. In the eighteenth century, governments were gathering demographic and financial data for taxation purposes, a practice called **statistics**. As years progressed, the use of this term was expanded to include the summarization and analysis of the data collected. In 1805, Adrien-Marie Legendre, a French mathematician, published a paper describing the **least squares** to fit linear equations, although most people credit Carl Friedrich Gauss for the complete description he published a couple of years later. In 1900, Karl Pearson published in the *Philosophical Magazine* his observations on the **chi-square** statistic, a cornerstone in data science for hypothesis testing. In 1962, John Tukey, the scientist famous for the **fast Fourier transformation** and the **box plot**, published a paper expressing his passion for data analysis and how statistics needed to evolve into a new science.

On the other hand, with the rise of informatics in the middle of the twentieth century, the field of **Artificial Intelligence** (**AI**) was introduced in 1955 by John McCarthy as the official term for thinking machines. AI is a field of computer science that develops systems that can imitate intelligent human behavior. Using programming languages such as **Information Processing Language** (**IPL**) and **LISt Processor** (**LISP**), developers were writing programs that could manipulate lists and various other data structures to solve complex problems. In 1955, Arthur Samuel's checkers player was the first piece of software that would *learn* from the games it has already played by storing board states and the chance of winning if ending up in that state in a cache. This checkers program may have been the first example of **machine learning**, a subfield of AI that utilizes historical data and the patterns encoded in the data to train models and enable systems to mimic human tasks without explicitly coding the entire logic. In fact, you can think of machine learning models as software code that is generated by training an algorithm against a dataset to recognize certain types of patterns.

In 2001, William S. Cleveland published the first article in which the term **data science** was used in the way we refer to it today, a science at the intersection of statistics, data analysis, and informatics that tries to explain phenomena based on data.

Although most people correlate data science with machine learning, data science has a much broader scope, which includes the analysis and preparation of data before the actual machine learning model training process, as you will see in the next section.

Working on a data science project

A data science project aims to infuse an application with intelligence extracted from data. In this section, you will discover the common tasks and key considerations needed within such a project. There are quite a few well-established life cycle processes, such as **Team Data Science Process (TDSP)** and **Cross-Industry Standard Process for Data Mining (CRISP-DM)**, that describe the iterative stages executed in a typical project. The most common stages are shown in *Figure 1.1*:

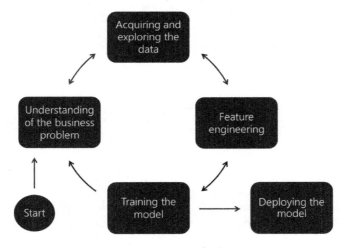

Figure 1.1 – The iterative stages of a data science project

Although the diagram shows some indicative flows between the phases, you are free to jump from one phase to any other if needed. Moreover, this approach is iterative, and the data science team should go through multiple iterations, improving its business understanding and the resulting model until the success criteria are met. You will read more about the benefits of an iterative process in this chapter's *Adopting the DevOps mindset* section. The data science process starts from the business understanding phase, something you will read more about in the next section.

Understanding of the business problem

The first stage in a data science project is that of business understanding. In this stage, the data science team collaborates with the business stakeholders to define a short, straightforward question that machine learning will try to answer.

Figure 1.2 shows the five most frequent questions that machine learning can answer:

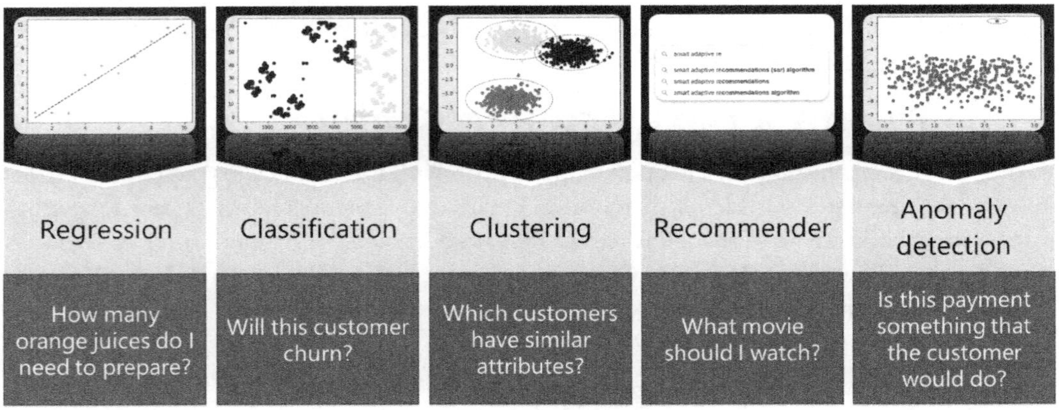

Figure 1.2 – Five questions machine learning can answer

Behind each of those questions, there is a group of modeling techniques you will use:

- **Regression** models allow you to predict a numeric value based on one or more features. For example, in *Chapter 8, Experimenting with Python Code*, you will be trying to predict a numeric value based on 10 measurements that were taken one year before the value you are trying to predict. Training a regression model is a **supervised** machine learning task, meaning that you need to provide enough sample data to train the model to predict the desired numeric value.

- **Classification** models allow you to predict a class label for a given set of inputs. This label can be as simple as a yes/no label or a blue, green, or red color. For example, in *Chapter 5, Letting the Machines Do the Model Training*, you will be training a classification model to detect whether a customer is going to cancel their phone subscription or not. Predicting whether a person is going to stop doing something is referred to as **churn** or attrition detection. Training a classification model is a supervised machine learning task and requires a labeled dataset to train the model. A labeled dataset contains both the inputs and the label that you want the model to predict.

- **Clustering** is an **unsupervised** machine learning task that groups data. In contrast to the previous two model types, clustering doesn't require any training data. It operates on the given dataset and creates the desired number of clusters, assigning each data point to the collection it belongs. A common use case of clustering models is when you try to identify distinct consumer groups in your customer base that you will be targeting with specific marketing campaigns.

- **Recommender** systems are designed to recommend the best options based on user profiles. Search engines, e-shops, and popular video streaming platforms utilize this type of model to produce personalized recommendations on what to do next.

- **Anomaly detection** models can detect outliers from a dataset or within a data stream. Outliers are items that don't belong with the rest of the elements, indicating anomalies. For example, if a vibration sensor of a machine starts sending abnormal measurements, it may be a good indication that the device is about to fail.

During the business understanding phase, you will try to understand the problem statement and define the success criteria. Setting up proper expectations of what machine learning can and cannot do is key to ensure alignment between teams.

Throughout a data science project, it is common to have multiple rounds of business understandings. The data science team acquires a lot of insights after exploring datasets or training a model. It is helpful to bring those gathered insights to the business stakeholders and either verify your team's hypothesis or gain even more insights into the problem you are tackling. For example, business stakeholders may explain a pattern that you may detect in the data but cannot explain its rationale.

Once you get a good grasp of what you are trying to solve, you need to get some data, explore it, and even label it, something you will read about in the next section.

Acquiring and exploring the data

After understanding the problem you are trying to solve, it's time to gather the data to support the machine learning process. Data can have many forms and formats. It can be either well-structured tabular data stored in database systems or even files, such as images, stored in file shares. Initially, you will not know which data to collect, but you must start from somewhere. A typical anecdote while looking for data is the belief that there is always an Excel file that will contain critical information, and you must keep asking for it until you find it.

Once you have located the data, you will have to analyze it to understand whether the dataset is complete or not. Data is often stored within on-premises systems or **Online Transactional Processing** (OLTP) databases that you cannot easily access. Even if data is accessible, it is not advised to explore it directly within the source system, as you may accidentally impact the performance of the underlying engine that hosts the data. For example, a complex query on top of a sales table may affect the performance of the e-shop solution. In these cases, it is common to export the required datasets in a file format, such as the most interoperable **Comma-Separated Values** (CSV) format or the much more optimized for analytical processing **Parquet** format. These files are then uploaded to cheap cloud storage and become available for further analysis.

Within Microsoft Azure, the most common target is either a Blob container within a storage account or a folder in the filesystem of **Azure Data Lake Gen 2**, which offers a far more granular access control mechanism. Copying the data can be done in a one-off manner by using tools such as **AzCopy** or **Storage Explorer**. If you would like to configure a repeatable process that could pull incrementally new data on a schedule, you can use more advanced tools such as the pipelines of **Azure Data Factory** or **Azure Synapse Analytics**. In *Chapter 4, Configuring the Workspace*, you will review the components needed to pull data from on-premises and the available datastores to which you can connect from within the AzureML workspace to access the various datasets. In the *Working with datasets* section of *Chapter 4, Configuring the Workspace*, you will read about the dataset types supported by AzureML and how you can explore them to gain insights into the info stored within them.

A common task when gathering data is the data cleansing step. You remove duplicate records, impute missing values, or fix common data entry issues during this step. For example, you could harmonize a country text field by replacing *UK* records with *United Kingdom*. Within AzureML, you can perform such cleansing operations either in the designer that you will see in *Chapter 6, Visual Model Training and Publishing*, or through the notebooks experience you will be working with from *Chapter 7, The AzureML Python SDK*, onward. Although you may start doing those cleansing operations with AzureML, as the project matures, these cleansing activities tend to move within the pipelines of **Azure Data Factory** or **Azure Synapse Analytics**, which pulls the data out of the source systems.

> **Important note**
>
> While doing data cleansing, be aware of **yak shaving**. The term *yak shaving* was coined in the 90s to describe the situation where, while working on a task, you realize that you must do another task, which leads to another one, and so on. This chain of tasks may take you away from your original goal. For example, you may realize that some records have invalid encoding on the country text field example, but you can understand the referenced country. You decide to change the export encoding of the CSV file, and you realize that the export tool you were using is old and doesn't support UTF-8. That leads you to a quest to find a system administrator to get your software updated. Instead of going down that route, make a note of what needs to be done and add it to your backlog. You can fix this issue in the next iteration when you will have a better understanding of whether you actually need this field or not.

Another common task is labeling the dataset, especially if you will be dealing with supervised machine learning models. For example, if you are curating a dataset to predict whether a customer will churn or not, you will have to flag the records of the customers that canceled their subscriptions. A more complex labeling case is when you create a sentiment analysis model for social media messages. In that case, you will need to get a feed of messages, go through them, and assign a label on whether it is a positive or negative sentiment.

Within AzureML Studio, you can create labeling projects that allow you to scale the labeling efforts of datasets. AzureML allows you to define either a text labeling or an image labeling task. You then bring in team members to label the data based on the given instructions. Once the team has started labeling the data, AzureML automatically trains a model relative to your defined task. When the model is good enough, it starts providing suggestions to the labelers to improve their productivity. *Figure 1.3* shows the labeling project creation wizard and the various options available currently in the image labeling task:

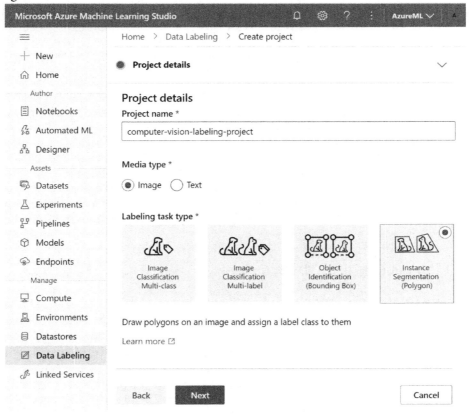

Figure 1.3 – Creating an AzureML labeling project

Through this project phase, you should have discovered the related source systems and produced a cleansed dataset ready for the machine learning training. In the next section, you will learn how to create additional data features that will assist the model training process, a process known as **feature engineering**.

Feature engineering

During the feature engineering phase, you will be generating new data features that will better represent the problem you are trying to solve and help machines learn from the dataset. For example, the following code block creates a new feature named `product_id` by transforming the `product` column of the sales dataset:

```
product_map = { "orange juice": 1, "lemonade juice": 2 }
dataset["product_id"] = dataset["product"].map(product_map)
```

This code block uses the **pandas** map method to convert text into numerical values. The `product` column is referred to as being a **categorical** variable, as all records are within a finite number of categories, in this case, `orange juice` or `lemonade juice`. If you had a 1-to-5 rating feature in the same dataset, that would have been a discrete numeric variable with a finite number of values that it can take, in this case, only *1, 2, 3, 4,* or *5.* If you had a column that kept how many liters or gallons the customer bought, that would have been a **continuous** numeric variable that could take any numeric value greater than or equal to zero, such as half a liter. Besides numeric values, dates fields are also considered as continuous variables.

> **Important note**
>
> Although the `product_id` feature is a **discrete** numeric variable in the preceding example, features such as that are commonly treated as a categorical variable, as you will see in *Chapter 5, Letting the Machines Do the Model Training.*

There are many featurization techniques available. An indicative list is as follows:

- **Scaling of numeric features**: This technique converts all numeric features into ranges that can be easily compared. For example, in *Chapter 8, Experimenting with Python Code*, you will be training a machine learning model on top of medical measurements. Blood glucose measurements range from 80 to 200 mg/dL, while blood pressure measurements range from 60 to 128 mm Hg. These numeric values are scaled down using their mean value, a transformation referred to as standardization or **Z-score** normalization. Their values end up within the -1 to 1 range, which allows machines to extract better insights.

- **Split**: Splitting a column into two new features is something very common. For example, the full name will be split into name and surname for further analysis.

- **Binning**: This technique groups continuous features into distinct groups or bins that may expose important information regarding the problem you are trying to solve. For example, if you have the year of birth, you can create bins to group the different generations. In this case, folks with a year of birth between 1965 and 1980 would have been the *generation X* group, and people in the 1981 to 1996 range would have formed the *millennial* bin. It is common to use the clustering models that you saw in the *Understanding of the business problem* section to produce cohorts and define those bins.

- **One-hot encoding of categorical features**: Some machine learning algorithms cannot handle categorical data and require all inputs to be numeric. In the example with `product`, you performed a label encoding. You converted the categorical variable into a numeric one. A typical example for label encoding is t-shirt sizes where you convert small to *1*, medium to *2*, and large to *3*. In the `product` example though, you accidentally defined the order between `orange juice` (1) and `lemonade juice` (2), which may confuse a machine learning algorithm. In this case, instead of the ordinal encoding used in the example that produced the `product_id` feature, you could have utilized one-hot encoding. In this case, you would introduce two binary features called *orange_juice* and *lemonade_juice*. These features would accept either *0* or *1* values, depending on which juice the customer bought.

- **Generate lag features**: If you deal with time-series data, you may need to produce features from values from preceding time. For example, if you are trying to forecast the temperature 10 minutes from now, you may need to have the current temperature and the temperature 30 minutes ago and 1 hour ago. These two additional past temperatures are lag features that you will have to engineer.

> **Important note**
> Making all those transformations in big datasets may require a tremendous amount of memory and processing time. This is where technologies such as Spark come into play to parallelize the process. You will learn more about Spark in the *Using Spark in data science* section of this chapter.

In *Chapter 10, Understanding Model Results*, you will use the `MinMaxScaler` method from the `sklearn` library to scale numeric features.

As a last step in the feature engineering stage, you normally remove unnecessary or highly correlated features, a process called **feature selection**. You will be dropping columns that will not be used to train the machine learning model. By dropping those columns, you reduce the memory requirements of the machines that will be doing the training, you reduce the computation time needed to train the model, and the resulting model will be much smaller in size.

While creating those features, it is logical that you may need to go back to the *Acquiring and exploring the data* phase or even to the *Understanding of the business problem* stage to get more data and insights. At some point, though, your training dataset will be ready to train the model, something you will read about in the next section.

Training the model

As soon as you have prepared the dataset, the machine learning training process can begin. If the model requires supervised learning and you have enough data, you split them into a training dataset and validation dataset in a 70% to 30% or 80% to 20% ratio. You select the model type you want to train, specify the model's training parameters (called **hyperparameters**), and train the model. With the remaining validation dataset, you evaluate the trained model's performance according to a **metric** and you decide whether the model is good enough to move to the next stage, or perhaps return to the *Understanding of the business problem* stage. The training process of a supervised model is depicted in *Figure 1.4*:

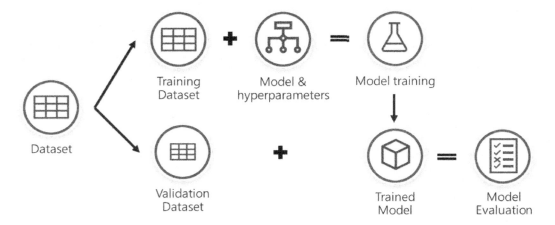

Figure 1.4 – Training a supervised machine learning model

There are a couple of variations to the preceding statement:

- If the model is in the unsupervised learning category, such as the clustering algorithms, you just pass all the data to train the model. You then evaluate whether the detected clusters address the business need or not, modify the hyperparameters, and try again.

- If you have a model that requires supervised learning but don't have enough data, the **k-fold cross validation** technique is commonly used. With k-fold, you specify the number of folds you want to split the dataset. AzureML uses **AutoML** and performs either 10 folds if the data is less than 1,000 rows or 3 folds if the dataset is between 1,000 and 20,000 rows. Once you have those folds, you start an iterative process where you do the following:

    I.   Keep a fold away for validation and train with the rest of the folds a new model.

    II. Evaluate the produced model against the fold that you kept out.

    III. Record the model score and discard the model.

    IV. Repeat *step I* by keeping another fold away for validation until all folds have been used for validation.

    V.   Produce the aggregated model's performance.

> **Important note**
> In the machine learning research literature, there is an approach called **semi-supervised** learning. In that approach, a small amount of labeled data is combined with a large amount of unlabeled data to train the model.

Instead of training a single model, evaluating the results, and trying again with a different set of hyperparameters, you can automate the process and evaluate multiple models in parallel. This process is called hyperparameter tuning, something you will dive deep into in *Chapter 9, Optimizing the ML Model*. In the same chapter, you will learn how you can even automate the model selection, an AzureML capability referred to as AutoML.

Metrics help you select the model that minimizes the difference between the predicted value and the actual one. They differ depending on the model type you are training. In regression models, metrics try to minimize the error between the predicted value and the actual one. The most common ones are **Mean Absolute Error (MAE)**, **Root Mean Squared Error (RMSE)**, **Relative Squared Error (RSE)**, **Relative Absolute Error (RAE)**, the **coefficient of determination (R^2)**, and **Normalized Root Mean Squared Error (NRMSE)**, which you are going to see in *Chapter 8, Experimenting with Python Code*.

In a classification model, metrics are slightly different, as they have to evaluate both how many results it got right and how many it misclassified. For example, in the churn binary classification problem, there are four possible results:

- The model predicted that the customer would churn, and the customer churned. This is considered a **True Positive (TP)**.

- The model predicted that the customer would churn, but the customer remained loyal. This is considered a **False Positive (FP)**, since the model was wrong about the customer leaving.

- The model predicted that the customer would not churn, and the customer churned. This is considered a **False Negative (FN)**, since the model was wrong about the customer being loyal.

- The model predicted that the customer would not churn, and the customer remained loyal. This is considered a **True Negative (TN)**.

These four states make up the **confusion matrix** that is shown in *Figure 1.5*:

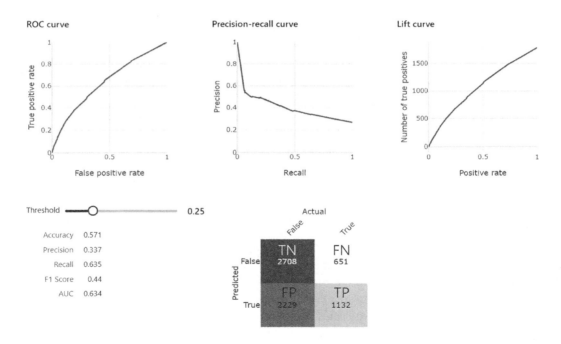

Figure 1.5 – The classification model's evaluation

Through that confusion matrix, you can calculate other metrics, such as **accuracy**, which calculates the total number of correct results in the evaluation test (in this case, **1132** TP + **2708** TN = 3840 records versus **2708** + **651** + **2229** + **1132** = 6720 total records). On the other hand, **precision** or **Positive Predictive Value** (**PPV**) evaluates how many true predictions are actually true (in this case, **1132** TP versus **1132** + **2229** total true predictions). **Recall**, also known as **sensitivity**, measures how many actual true values were correctly classified (in this case, **1132** TP versus **1132** + **651** total true actuals). Depending on the business problem you are trying to solve, you will have to find the balance between the various metrics, as one metric may be more helpful than others. For example, during the COVID-19 pandemic, a model that determines whether someone is infected with recall equal to one would identify all infected patients. However, it may have accidentally misclassified some of the not-infected ones, which other metrics, such as precision, would have caught.

> **Important note**
>
> Be aware when your model fits your data too well. This is something that we refer to as **overfitting**, and it may indicate that the model has identified a certain pattern within your training dataset that may not exist in real life. Such models tend to perform poorly when put into production and make inferences on top of unknown data. A common reason for overfitting is a biased training dataset that exposes only a subset of real-world examples. Another reason is target leakage, which means that somehow the value you are trying to predict is passed as an input to the model, perhaps through a feature engineered using the target column. See the *Further reading* section for guidance on how to handle overfitting and imbalanced data.

As you have seen so far, there are many things to consider while training a machine learning model, and throughout this book, you will get some hands-on experience in training models. In most cases, the first thing you will have to select is the type of computer that is going to run the training process. Currently, you have two options, **Central Processing Unit** (**CPU**) or **Graphics Processing Unit** (**GPU**) compute targets. Both targets have at least a CPU in them, as this is the core element of any modern computer. The difference is that the GPU compute targets also offer some very powerful graphic cards that can perform massive parallel data processing, making training much faster. To take advantage of the GPU, the model you are training needs to support GPU-based training. GPU is usually used in neural network training with frameworks such as **TensorFlow**, **PyTorch**, and **Keras**.

Once you have trained a machine learning model that satisfies the success criteria defined during the *Understanding of the business problem* stage of the data science project, it is time to operationalize it and start making inferences with it. That's what you will read about in the next section.

Deploying the model

When it comes to model operationalization, you have two main approaches:

- **Real-time inferences**: The model is always loaded, waiting to make inferences on top of incoming data. Typical use cases are web and mobile applications that invoke a model to predict based on user input.

- **Batch inferences**: The model is loaded every time the batch process is invoked, and it generates predictions on top of the incoming batch of records. For example, imagine that you have trained a model to identify your face in pictures and you want to label all the images you have on your hard drive. You will configure a process to use the model against each image, storing the results in a text or CSV file.

The main difference between these two is whether you already have the data to perform the predictions or not. If you already have the data and they do not change, you can make inferences in batch mode. For example, if you are trying to predict the football scores for next week's matches, you can run a batch inference and store the results in a database. When customers ask for specific predictions, you can retrieve the value from the database. During the football match, though, the model predicting the end score needs features such as the current number of players and how many injuries there are, information that will become available in real time. In those situations, you might want to deploy a web service that exposes a REST API, where you send in the required information and the model is making the real-time inference. You will dive deep into both real-time and batch approaches in *Chapter 12, Operationalizing Models with Code*.

In this section, you reviewed the project life cycle of a data science project and went through all the stages, from understanding what needs to be done all the way to operationalizing a model by deploying a batch or real-time service. Especially for real-time streaming, you may have heard the term **structured streaming**, a scalable processing engine built on Spark to allow developers to perform real-time inferences the same way they would perform batch inference on top of static data. You will learn more about Spark in the next section.

Using Spark in data science

At the beginning of the twenty-first century, the big data problem became a reality. Data stored in data centers was growing in volumes and velocity. In 2021, we refer to datasets as big data when they reach at least a couple of terabytes in size, while it is not uncommon to see even petabytes of data in large organizations. These datasets increase at a rapid rate, which can be from a couple of gigabytes per day to even per minute, for example, when you are storing user interactions with a website in an online store to perform clickstream analysis.

In 2009, a research project started at the University of California, Berkeley, trying to provide the parallel computing tools needed to handle big data. In 2014, the first version of Apache Spark was released from this research project. Members from that research team founded the **Databricks** company, one of the most significant contributors to the open source Apache Spark project.

Apache Spark provides an easy-to-use scalable solution that allows people to perform parallel processing on top of data in a distributed manner. The main idea behind the Spark architecture is that a driver node is responsible for executing your code. Your code is split into smaller parallel actions that can be performed against smaller portions of data. These smaller jobs are scheduled to be executed by the worker nodes, as seen in *Figure 1.6*:

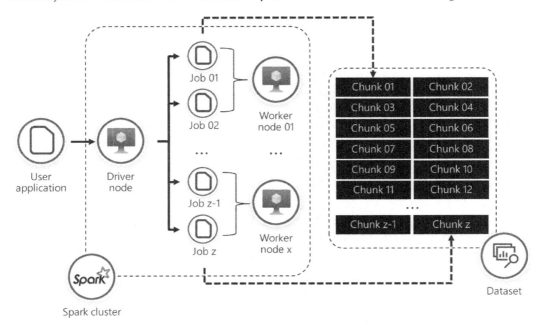

Figure 1.6 – Parallel processing of big data in a Spark cluster

For example, suppose you wanted to calculate how many products your company sold during the last year. In that case, Spark could spin up 12 jobs that would produce the monthly aggregates, and then the results would be processed by another job that would sum up the totals for all months. If you were tempted to load the entire dataset into memory and perform those aggregates directly from there, let's examine how much memory you would need within that computer. Let's assume that the sales data for a single month is stored in a CSV file that is 1 GB. This file will require approximately 10 GB of memory to load. The compressed **Parquet** files will require even more memory. For example, a similar 1 GB parquet file may end up needing 40 GB of memory to load as a `pandas.DataFrame` object. As you can understand, loading all 12 files in memory simultaneously is an impossible task. You need to parallelize the processing, something Spark can do for you automatically.

> **Important note**
>
> The Parquet files are stored in a columnar format, which allows you to load partially any number of columns you need. In the 1 GB Parquet example, if you load only half the columns from the dataset, you will probably need only 20 GB of memory. This is one of the reasons why the Parquet format is widely used in analytical loads.

Spark is written in the Scala programming language. It offers APIs for Scala, Python, Java, R, and even C#. Still, the data science community is either working on Scala to achieve maximum computational performance and utilizing the Java library ecosystem or Python, which is widely adopted by the modern data science community. When you are writing Python code to utilize the Spark engine, you are using the PySpark tool to perform operations on top of **Resilient Distributed Datasets** (**RDDs**) or `Spark.DataFrame` objects introduced later in Spark Framework. To benefit from the distributed nature of Spark, you need to be handling big datasets. This means that Spark may be overkill if you deal with only hundreds of thousands of records or even a couple of millions of records.

Spark offers two machine learning libraries, the old **MLlib** and the new version called **Spark ML**. Spark ML uses the `Spark.DataFrame` structure, a distributed collection of data, and offers similar functionality to the `DataFrame` objects used in Python pandas or R. Moreover, the **Koalas** project provides an implementation that allows data scientists with existing knowledge of `pandas.DataFrame` manipulations to use their existing coding skills on top of Spark.

AzureML allows you to execute Spark jobs on top of PySpark, either using its native compute clusters or by attaching to **Azure Databricks** or **Synapse Spark pools**. Although you will not write any PySpark code in this book, in *Chapter 12, Operationalizing Models with Code*, you will learn how to achieve similar parallelization benefits without the need for Spark or a driver node.

No matter whether you are coding in regular Python, PySpark, R, or Scala, you are producing some code artifacts that are probably part of a larger system. In the next section, you will explore the DevOps mindset, which emphasizes the communication and collaboration of software engineers, data scientists, and system administrators to achieve faster release of valuable product features.

Adopting the DevOps mindset

DevOps is a team mindset that tries to minimize the silos between developers and system operators to shorten the development life cycle of a product. Developers are constantly changing a product to introduce new features and modify existing behaviors. On the other side, system operators need to keep the production systems stable and up and running. In the past, these two groups of people were isolated, and developers were *throwing* the new piece of software over to the operations team who would try to deploy it in production. As you can imagine, things didn't work that well all the time, causing frictions between those two groups. When it comes to DevOps, one fundamental practice is that a team needs to be autonomous and should contain all required disciplines, both *developers* and *operators*.

When it comes to data science, some people refer to the practice as **MLOps,** but the fundamental ideas remain the same. A team should be self-sufficient, capable of developing all required components for the overall solution, from the data engineering parts that bring in data and the training of the models all the way to operationalizing the model in production. These teams usually work in an **agile** manner, which embraces an iterative approach, seeking constant improvement based on feedback, as seen in *Figure 1.7*:

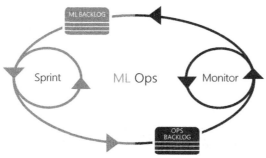

Figure 1.7 – The feedback flow in an agile MLOps team

The MLOps team operates on its backlog and performs the iterative steps you saw in the *Working on a data science project* section. Once the model is ready, the system administrators, who are part of the team, are aware of what needs to be done to take the model into production. The model is monitored closely, and if a defect or performance degradation is observed, a backlog item is created for the MLOps team to address in their next sprint.

In order to minimize the development and deployment life cycle of new features in production, automation needs to be embraced. The goal of a DevOps team is to minimize the number of human interventions in the deployment process and automate as many repeatable tasks as possible.

Figure 1.8 shows the most frequently used components while developing real-time models using the MLOps mindset:

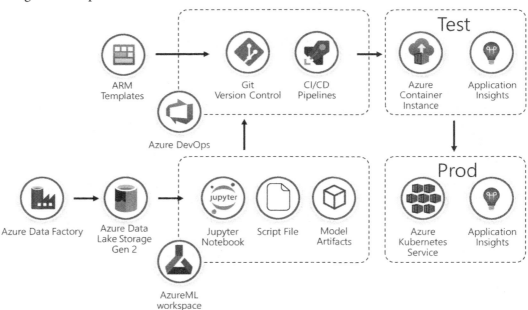

Figure 1.8 – Components usually seen in MLOps-driven data science projects

Let's analyze those components:

- **ARM templates** allow you to automate the deployment of Azure resources. This enables the team to spin up and down development, testing, or even production environments in no time. These artifacts are stored within Azure DevOps in a Git version-control repository. The deployment of multiple environments is automated using Azure DevOps pipelines. You are going to read about ARM templates in *Chapter 2, Deploying Azure Machine Learning Workspace Resources*.

- Using **Azure Data Factory**, the data science team orchestrates the pulling and cleansing of the data from the source systems. The data is copied within a data lake, which is accessible from the AzureML workspace. Azure Data Factory uses ARM templates to define its orchestration pipelines, templates that are stored within the Git repository to track changes and be able to deploy in multiple environments.

- Within the AzureML workspace, data scientists are working on their code. Initially, they start working on Jupyter notebooks. Notebooks are a great way to prototype some ideas, as you will see in *Chapter 7, The AzureML Python SDK*. As the project progresses, the scripts are exported from the notebooks and are organized into coding scripts. All those code artifacts are version-controlled into Git, using the terminal and commands such as the ones seen in *Figure 1.9*:

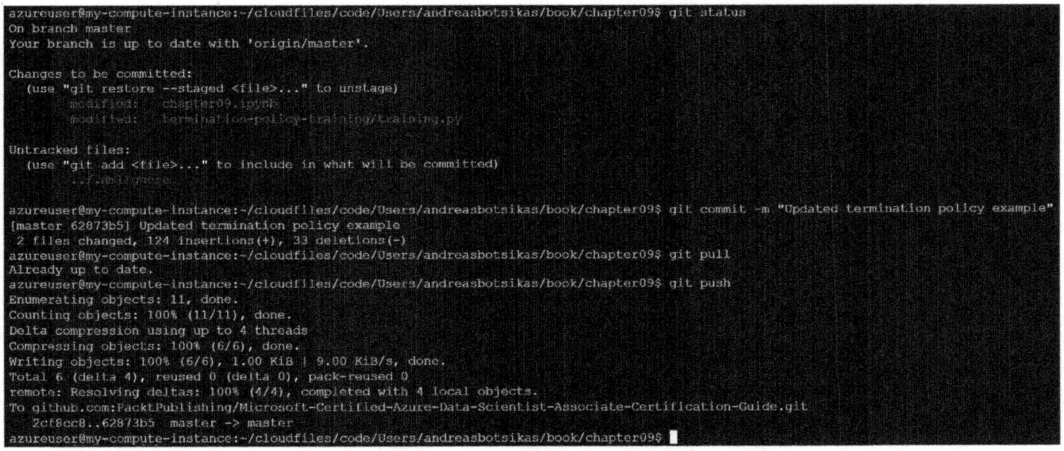

Figure 1.9 – Versioning a notebook and a script file using Git within AzureML

- When a model is trained, if it is performing better than the model that is currently in production, it is registered within AzureML, and an event is emitted. This event is captured by the AzureML DevOps plugin, which triggers the automatic deployment of the model in the test environment. The model is tested within that environment, and if all tests pass and no errors have been logged in **Application Insights**, which is monitoring the deployment, the artifacts can be automatically deployed to the next environment, all the way to production.

The ability to ensure both code and model quality plays a crucial role in this automation process. In Python, you can use various tools, such as Flake8, Bandit, and Black, to ensure code quality, check for common security issues, and consistently format your code base. You can also use the `pytest` framework to write your functional testing, where you will be testing the model results against a golden dataset. With `pytest`, you can even perform integration testing to verify that the end-to-end system is working as expected.

Adopting DevOps is a never-ending journey. The team will become better every time you repeat the process. The trick is to build trust in the end-to-end development and deployment process so that everyone is confident to make changes and deploy them in production. When the process fails, understand why it failed and learn from your mistakes. Create the mechanisms that will prevent future failures and move on.

Summary

In this chapter, you learned about the origins of data science and how it relates to machine learning. You then learned about the iterative nature of a data science project and discovered the various phases you will be working on. Starting from the problem understanding phase, you will then acquire and explore data, create new features, train a model, and then deploy to verify your hypothesis. Then, you saw how you can scale out the processing of big data files using the Spark ecosystem. In the last section, you discovered the DevOps mindset that helps agile teams be more efficient, meaning that they develop and deploy new product features in short periods of time. You saw the components that are commonly used within an MLOps-driven team, and you saw that in the epicenter of that diagram, you find AzureML.

In the next chapter, you will learn how to deploy an AzureML workspace and understand the Azure resources that you will be using in your data science journey throughout this book.

Further reading

This section offers a list of helpful web resources that will help you augment your knowledge of the topics addressed in this chapter:

- AzCopy command-line tool to copy blobs and files to a storage account: `http://aka.ms/azcopy`.

- Azure Storage Explorer is a free tool to manage all your Azure cloud storage resources: `https://azure.microsoft.com/features/storage-explorer/`.

- *The Hitchhiker's Guide to the Data Lake* is an extensive guide on key considerations and best practices while building a data lake: `https://aka.ms/adls/hitchhikersguide`.

- Optimizing data processing with AzureML: `https://docs.microsoft.com/azure/machine-learning/concept-optimize-data-processing`.

- The Koalas project: `https://koalas.readthedocs.io`.

- Guidance to prevent model overfitting and to handle unbalanced data: `https://docs.microsoft.com/azure/machine-learning/concept-manage-ml-pitfalls`.

- MLOps guidance for data scientists and app developers working in AzureML and Azure DevOps: `https://aka.ms/MLOps`.

2
Deploying Azure Machine Learning Workspace Resources

In this chapter, you will learn how to deploy an **Azure Machine Learning** (**Azure ML**) workspace through the Azure portal and the **Command-Line Interface** (**CLI**). You will also gain an understanding of the deployment parameters that you need to select while deploying the workspace. In the end, you will have a fully functional Azure ML workspace, and you will be able to navigate to all of the deployed Azure resources.

In this chapter, we're going to cover the following main topics:

- Deploying Azure ML through the portal
- Deploying Azure ML via the CLI
- Alternative ways to deploy an Azure ML workspace
- Exploring the deployed Azure resources

Technical requirements

To provision an Azure ML workspace, you will need an Azure subscription. You can get a free trial by visiting `https://azure.microsoft.com/free/`. If you want to use an existing subscription, you will need to request the owner of the subscription to provide you with the following **Resource Group** items:

- `packt-azureml-rg`
- `packt-azureml-cli-rg`

This book assumes that you have either a `Contributor` role or an `Owner` role on these resource groups. You are going to deploy an Azure ML workspace in both of those resource groups: one through the Azure portal and one through the Azure CLI.

Azure ML requires the following providers to be registered in the Azure subscription that hosts the resource groups you are planning to use:

- `Microsoft.MachineLearningServices`
- `Microsoft.KeyVault`
- `Microsoft.Storage`
- `Microsoft.insights`
- `Microsoft.ContainerRegistry`
- `Microsoft.Notebooks`

If you are the `Owner` of the subscription, Azure will automatically register the providers for you when you deploy the resources. Otherwise, you will need to request that the subscription owner registers these providers for you by following the instructions at `https://docs.microsoft.com/azure/azure-resource-manager/templates/error-register-resource-provider#solution-3---azure-portal`.

You will require a modern browser that has **JavaScript** enabled. This is required to access the Azure portal.

Optionally, you can download and install the Azure CLI from the official Microsoft documentation page at `https://docs.microsoft.com/cli/azure/install-azure-cli`. In this book, you will learn how to use the online version of this tool that is embedded within the Azure portal.

You can find all of the commands and code snippets of this chapter on GitHub at `http://bit.ly/dp100-ch02`.

Deploying Azure ML through the portal

In this section, you are going to deploy an Azure ML workspace through the Azure portal wizard. First, navigate to the Azure portal at `https://portal.azure.com`.

There are a couple of ways in which you can initiate the creation of an Azure ML workspace wizard. The following are the three most popular ones:

- From the home page of the Azure portal, you can select **Create a resource** from either the top of the page underneath the **Azure services** label or the **Azure portal menu** in the upper-left corner:

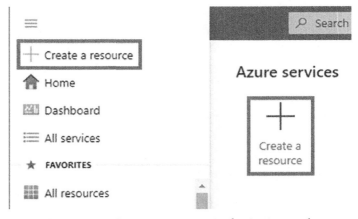

Figure 2.1 – Creating a resource in the Azure portal

This approach is the most generic one and will ask you to search for the service you want to create. Search for `machine learning` and select the first option from the **Marketplace** search results that are provided by Microsoft:

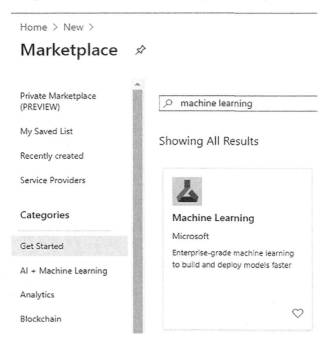

Figure 2.2 – ML search results in Azure Marketplace

You can review the service information. Then, when you are done, click on the **Create** button to start the wizard.

- Alternatively, you can search for `machine learning` in the top search bar of the Azure portal and select the **Machine Learning** option that appears under **Services**:

Figure 2.3 – The ML service showing in the Azure portal search results

This will navigate you to a list of already deployed ML workspaces that you have access to. If this is a new subscription, it will be empty; you can click on the **Add** button on the toolbar:

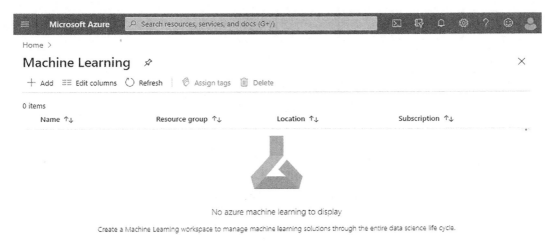

Figure 2.4 – The create buttons available in an empty service list

- The final popular approach is to navigate to the resource group where you want to deploy the Azure ML workspace and select **Add** from the toolbar:

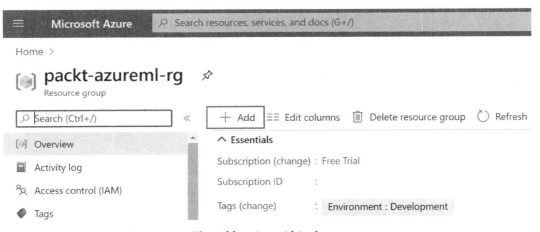

Figure 2.5 – The Add option within the resource group

Search for `machine learning` and select the first option in the Marketplace search result that is provided by Microsoft. Click on the **Create** button to start the wizard. This approach will prepopulate the resource group option of the wizard.

All three of these approaches will lead you to the deployment wizard:

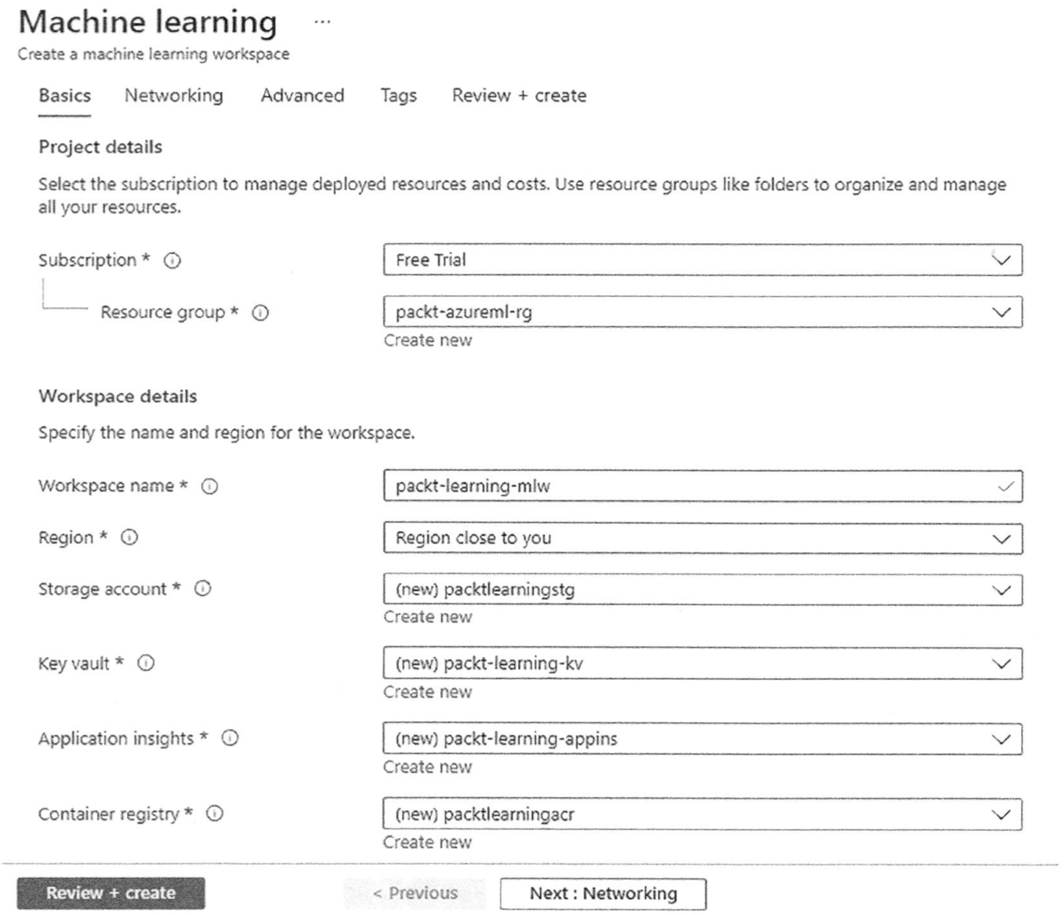

Machine learning   ···

Create a machine learning workspace

Basics   Networking   Advanced   Tags   Review + create

Project details

Select the subscription to manage deployed resources and costs. Use resource groups like folders to organize and manage all your resources.

Subscription * ⓘ	Free Trial ⌄
Resource group * ⓘ	packt-azureml-rg ⌄
	Create new

Workspace details

Specify the name and region for the workspace.

Workspace name * ⓘ	packt-learning-mlw ✓
Region * ⓘ	Region close to you ⌄
Storage account * ⓘ	(new) packtlearningstg ⌄
	Create new
Key vault * ⓘ	(new) packt-learning-kv ⌄
	Create new
Application insights * ⓘ	(new) packt-learning-appins ⌄
	Create new
Container registry * ⓘ	(new) packtlearningacr ⌄
	Create new

Review + create   < Previous   Next : Networking

Figure 2.6 – The ML workspace creation wizard

In the next section, you will learn how to use the wizard to deploy the Azure ML workspace.

Using the deployment wizard

The wizard consists of five steps or tabs:

1. **Basics**: This is basic information regarding the workspace you are about to deploy.

2. **Networking**: This refers to the advanced networking options you might want to configure.

3. **Advanced**: This includes the advanced identity and data security workspace options

4. **Tags**: This includes the associate tags within the workspace

5. **Review + create**: This is the last step of the wizard; after a short validation process, you can provision the workspace.

   In the next sections, we'll review all of the options available in the wizard along with the considerations you need to make before selecting them.

   > **Important note**
   > If you see the warning **The selected subscription doesn't have permissions to register the resource provider** in the **Basics** step of the wizard, please make sure you ask the owner of the Azure subscription to register the resource providers mentioned in the *Technical requirements* section of this chapter if the providers are missing. Failing to have those providers registered will cause a validation error in the **Review + create** step of the wizard.

Basics

The wizard starts at the **Basics** step:

1. The first thing you need to specify is the **Subscription** that is going to be charged by the Azure ML workspace.

   After selecting the subscription, a list of **Resource Group** options will populate. You can even create a new **Resource Group** by selecting the **Create new** button; this is something that requires, this is something that requires an access role like Contributor, at the subscription level, a `Contributor` access role at the subscription level. If you have started the wizard from the **Resource Group**, both the **Subscription** and the **Resource Group** are already filled in. Otherwise, select the one you created in the *Technical requirements* section, called `packt-azureml-rg`.

2. Type in a **Workspace name** that you will use to refer to the Azure ML workspace.
    The name is case-insensitive and should be unique within the resource group.
    The name can be up to 33 characters long and must only contain alphanumeric
    characters and hyphens.

    You can use `packt-learning-mlw`, which is a name inspired by the **Azure
    Cloud Adoption Framework (Azure CAF)** naming conventions.

3. You will need to select a **Region** to deploy the Azure ML workspace. The region is
    the Azure data center where you are going to deploy all of the resources required
    by the Azure ML workspace. The list is already filtered to include only the data
    centers that have the product available.

    There are three things you need to consider when selecting the Azure region
    to deploy your resources in. They include compliance and data residency
    requirements, service availability, and pricing. One example of such a requirement
    might be that you need to use some specialized **virtual machine** size that has
    a specific **Graphics Processing Unit (GPU)** such as the NV-series, which has the
    Tesla M60 – a virtual machine size that is not available in any Canada-based Azure
    region. For this book, you should select the region that is closest to you.

4. Optionally, you can modify the names of the **Storage account**, **Key vault**,
    Application insights, and **Container registry** that are going to be deployed within
    the Azure ML workspace. Each of those resources has different naming rules. For
    example, you cannot use a hyphen `(-)` in the storage account or the container
    registry names. Moreover, the names of the storage account, key vault, and
    container registry must be unique. You will learn more about those resource in this
    chapter's *Exploring the deployed Azure resources* section. If another resource exists
    with the same name, an error message will prompt you to change the name. *Figure
    2.7* shows how the basics wizard page looks like when it is filled in.

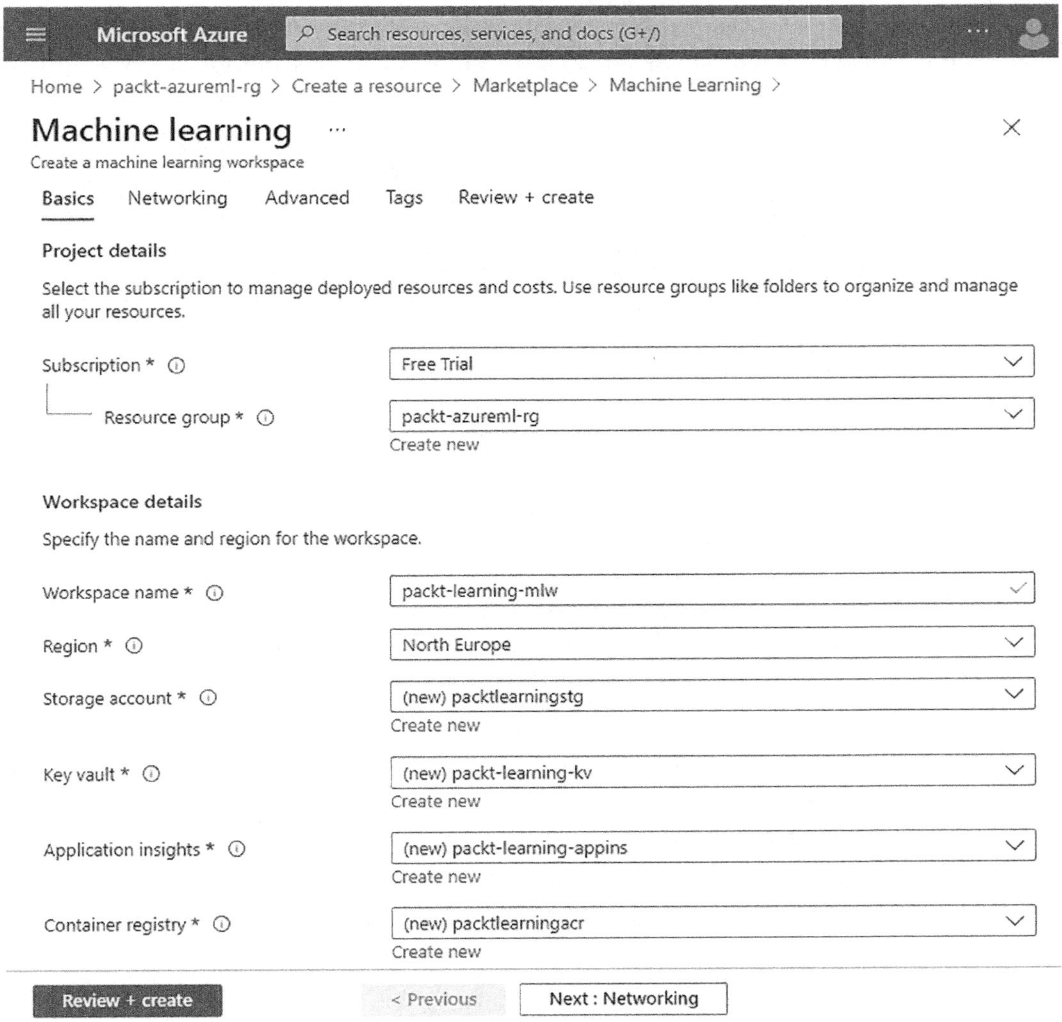

Microsoft Azure   🔍 Search resources, services, and docs (G+/)   ··· 👤

Home > packt-azureml-rg > Create a resource > Marketplace > Machine Learning >

Machine learning ···   ✕

Create a machine learning workspace

Basics   Networking   Advanced   Tags   Review + create

Project details

Select the subscription to manage deployed resources and costs. Use resource groups like folders to organize and manage all your resources.

Subscription * ⓘ | Free Trial   ⌄ |

    └─── Resource group * ⓘ | packt-azureml-rg   ⌄ |
                              Create new

Workspace details

Specify the name and region for the workspace.

Workspace name * ⓘ | packt-learning-mlw   ✓ |

Region * ⓘ | North Europe   ⌄ |

Storage account * ⓘ | (new) packtlearningstg   ⌄ |
                              Create new

Key vault * ⓘ | (new) packt-learning-kv   ⌄ |
                              Create new

Application insights * ⓘ | (new) packt-learning-appins   ⌄ |
                              Create new

Container registry * ⓘ | (new) packtlearningacr   ⌄ |
                              Create new

[Review + create]   [< Previous]   [Next : Networking]

Figure 2.7 – Information selected in the Basics step of the wizard

With all of the basic information filled in, you can now click on the **Review + create** button and skip all of the intermediate steps. This implies that you automatically accept the default options for the rest of the wizard's steps. However, for the purpose of learning, you should click on the **Next: Networking** button to navigate to the next wizard page.

Important note

Up until September 2020, the first page of these wizards asked for the **Edition** of the Azure ML workspace. There used to be a `Basic` edition and an `Enterprise` edition. The `Enterprise` edition was the one that provided the designer, and the Auto ML features you will see later on in the book. Since October 2020, all features are available in the `Basic` edition. The original certification had questions related to which feature belongs to what edition – something that you shouldn't encounter in your exam.

Networking

On this wizard page, you will need to decide how you are planning to connect to the data plane of the Azure ML workspace. The data plane consists of all data-centric operations within your workspace such as using the Azure ML studio web interface, triggering an ML pipeline, and making API calls through the **Software Development Kit** (**SDK**). There are two options, as follows:

- **Public endpoint (all networks)**: This is the default option that allows you to access the workspace from a publicly accessible endpoint.

- **Private endpoint**: A private endpoint reduces the risk of data exfiltration by reducing the attack surface to the Azure ML workspace. Once you decide to provide a workspace with **Private endpoint** connectivity, you will need to have a virtual machine or a **Virtual Private Network** (**VPN**) connection in order to access the private endpoint you will expose:

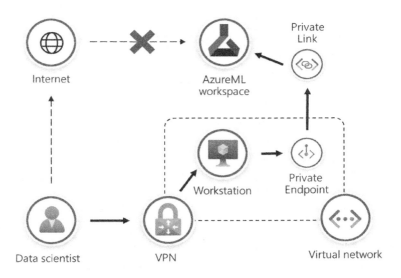

Figure 2.8 – The private endpoint secures access to the Azure ML workspace

For the purpose of this book, you will select **Public endpoint (all networks)**:

Network connectivity

You can connect to your workspace either publicly or privately using a private endpoint.

Connectivity method *   ⦿ Public endpoint (all networks)

                                 ◯ Private endpoint

| Review + create | | < Previous | Next : Advanced |

Figure 2.9 – Networking options in the creation wizard

On the next page, you are going to select the advanced options.

Advanced

On this wizard page, you can configure a few options regarding the security of the workspace and the metadata and metrics data privacy.

1. You can configure the **Managed identity** used by the AzureML workspace to authenticate and access other cloud resources. You can use either a **System assigned identity** or a **User assigned identity**. The system assigned ones will be automatically created when you deploy the AzureML resource. Instead, you can create a **User Assigned Managed Identity** resource within the Azure portal and use that during the deployment of the AzureML workspace. Using the user assigned option allows you to create the identity beforehand, configure access to various systems and data sources and then assign it to the workspace. You can even use the same identity in other services, like an Azure Automation account. You can read more about managed identities in this chapter's *Further reading* section. For this book, you will use the default option, which is the **System assigned identity**.

2. You can define how the AzureML workspace will be accessing the data stored in the default storage account. **Credential-based access** uses the storage account access key to read data. You can think of this approach as having a single password used by everyone who has access to the AzureML workspace to access the data within that storage account. In some organizations, the use of storage account access keys is forbidden for security reasons. In those cases, **Identity-based access** should be used. When you choose that option, AzureML uses its **Managed identity** to access the storage account data and write artifacts, like the trained models. Moreover, when the data scientists access datasets stored in the default storage account, their identity is passed through to the storage account to authenticate them and provide them with the data. You will use **Credential-based access** for the purposes of this book.

3. By default, Azure Machine Learning services store metrics and metadata in a Microsoft managed store using encryption keys managed by Microsoft. You can specify your own key to be used to encrypt the metrics and metadata. To do so, you will need to select a key stored within an existing **Key Vault**. This action will provision a couple of additional Azure resources, including a Cosmos DB, in a new resource group named based on the pattern <your-azure-ml-workspace-resource-name>_<GUID>, for example, packt-learning-mlw_ab07ab07-ab07-ab07-ab07-ab07ab07ab07. You do not have any control over those resources. Their lifecycle management is handled by the Azure Machine Learning workspace, meaning that they will be automatically deleted when you delete the workspace.

4. The last option of the wizard's step allows you to limit the amount of telemetry and metric data collected on your workspace. You can do that by selecting the **High business impact workspace** option.

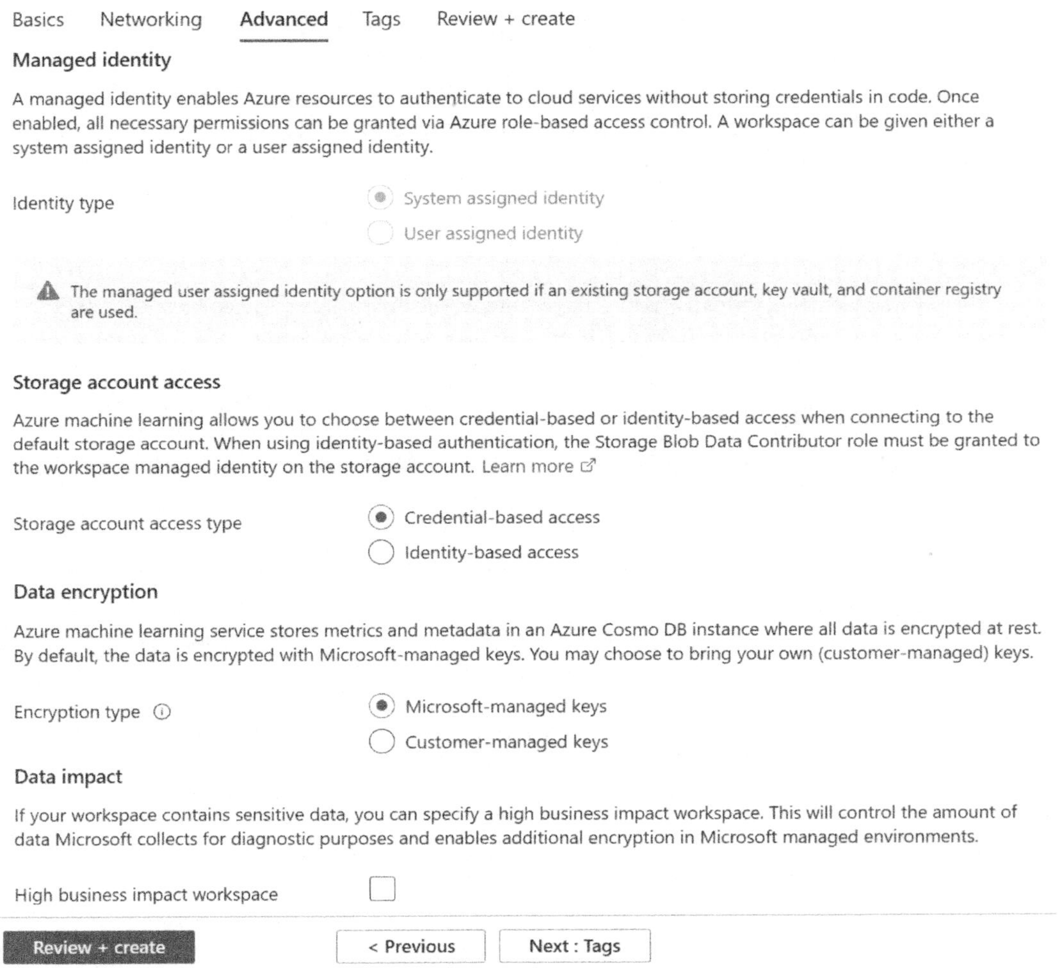

Basics   Networking   **Advanced**   Tags   Review + create

Managed identity

A managed identity enables Azure resources to authenticate to cloud services without storing credentials in code. Once enabled, all necessary permissions can be granted via Azure role-based access control. A workspace can be given either a system assigned identity or a user assigned identity.

Identity type   ◉ System assigned identity
                              ◯ User assigned identity

⚠ The managed user assigned identity option is only supported if an existing storage account, key vault, and container registry are used.

Storage account access

Azure machine learning allows you to choose between credential-based or identity-based access when connecting to the default storage account. When using identity-based authentication, the Storage Blob Data Contributor role must be granted to the workspace managed identity on the storage account. Learn more ☐

Storage account access type   ◉ Credential-based access
                              ◯ Identity-based access

Data encryption

Azure machine learning service stores metrics and metadata in an Azure Cosmo DB instance where all data is encrypted at rest. By default, the data is encrypted with Microsoft-managed keys. You may choose to bring your own (customer-managed) keys.

Encryption type ⓘ   ◉ Microsoft-managed keys
                              ◯ Customer-managed keys

Data impact

If your workspace contains sensitive data, you can specify a high business impact workspace. This will control the amount of data Microsoft collects for diagnostic purposes and enables additional encryption in Microsoft managed environments.

High business impact workspace   ☐

| Review + create | | < Previous | Next : Tags |

Figure 2.10 – Advanced options in the creation wizard

For the purposes of this book, you can leave both options with the default options and continue to the next step.

Tags

Tags are metadata that you can attach to any Azure resource, resource group, or subscription to help you locate and manage them. Throughout the Azure portal and the CLI, you can use these tags to filter the resource lists. Moreover, you can attach organizational information to the provisioned resources, for example, the business unit or even an email address that is responsible for the specific resource; this could be something that can give additional context to the IT teams if they need to modify something. Another common scenario is to use these tags to generate reports with usage and billing drill-downs.

For the purposes of this book, you should add a single metadata tag, that is, one to specify the type of the environment. The following tag can be used:

- `Environment`: Typically, you have multiple environments for your code base such as a development environment, a quality assurance testing environment, and a production environment. For the purposes of this book, you should specify the `Development` value.

You can add additional metadata tags if you want. The number can be up to 50, which is the current limit of tags per resource:

Figure 2.11 – The tags step in the creation wizard

When you are done, click on **Next: Review + create** to move to the last wizard step.

Review + create

This is the last step of the wizard. If you have forgotten to complete something or made an invalid selection in a previous step, you will get an error message and a red dot will indicate the step where the error is:

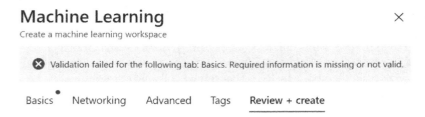

Figure 2.12 – An error validation indicating something is wrong in the Basics step

5. If everything is fine, a **Validation passed** message will appear and the **Create** button will be enabled:

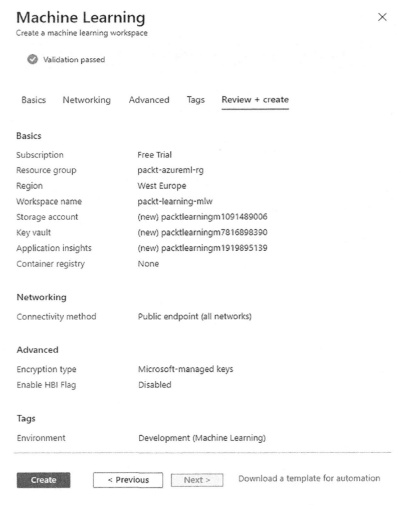

Figure 2.13 – Getting ready to provision the Azure ML workspace resources

> **Tip**
>
> Note the **Download a template for automation** link that appears at the bottom of the page. This link will generate an **Azure Resource Manager (ARM)** template for you that describes all the resources you have configured so far. You can then navigate to the **Parameters** tab and observe all of the parameters you have configured, including the `keyVaultName`, `storageAccountName`, and `applicationInsightsName` JSON values. This template can be deployed instantly from that view, or you can download it and use it to provision these resources in a different subscription. For example, imagine that you want to provision the production environment with the same resource structure. You can use this autogenerated ARM template, change the target **Resource Group**, the corresponding resource names and tag value, and deploy it in the production environment. Please note that the resource names you specify need to be unique, and you might need to experiment until you find a name that is available.

6. Click on the **Create** button to provision your Azure ML workspace resources. The resources will start deploying. This process could take a couple of minutes to complete.

   Finally, you should see a button called **Go to resource**, which you can use to navigate to the newly provisioned Azure ML workspace:

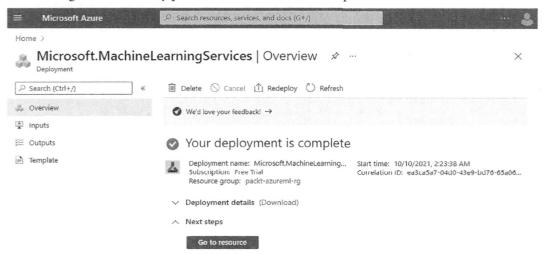

Figure 2.14 – The Go to resource button indicating the success of the Azure ML workspace deployment

In the next section, you will learn how to deploy the same Azure ML workspace using the Azure CLI, which is one of the most popular ways to deploy things in Azure.

Deploying Azure ML via the CLI

In this section, you are going to deploy an Azure ML workspace through the Azure CLI. You are going to use the `packt-azureml-cli-rg` resource group to deploy resources; you are going to use the Bash version of the **Azure Cloud Shell** that is built in the Azure portal – something that will require no installation on your machine. If you want, you can install the Azure CLI locally by following the installation instructions at `https://docs.microsoft.com/cli/azure/install-azure-cli`, and skip the provision of the Azure Cloud Shell.

> **Important note**
>
> You are going to use the Azure CLI in the next sections to manage various aspects of the Azure ML workspace. Although the book is going to assume you selected the Azure Cloud Shell, the syntax you will see is applicable for both the Azure Cloud Shell and the Azure CLI running within your local machine.

Deploying Azure Cloud Shell

Azure Cloud Shell is a browser-based shell that allows you to manage Azure. You can access it either by visiting the dedicated page at `https://shell.azure.com` or from within the Azure portal by clicking on the Cloud Shell icon in the top bar:

Figure 2.15 – The Cloud Shell icon in the top bar of the Azure portal

Let's begin!

1. The first time you invoke the Cloud Shell, you will see the welcome wizard. Select
    `Bash` to continue:

Figure 2.16 – The Azure Cloud Shell welcome wizard

2. Azure Cloud Shell requires a file share to save files. In this next step of the
    wizard, you can select a subscription; the portal will automatically deploy
    a storage account for you. Depending on your permissions at the subscription
    level, the wizard will either create a new resource group or use one where you have
    a `Contributor` role.

    If you want to fine-tune the process, you can select the **Show advanced settings**
    option and manually create new resource groups or define the name of the storage
    account and the file share name that is going to be used by your Cloud Shell:

Figure 2.17 – Advanced settings while provisioning Cloud Shell

3. For the purposes of this book, you should allow the wizard to automatically provision a storage account for you by selecting the **Subscription** you have, then clicking on the **Create storage** button without configuring the advanced settings:

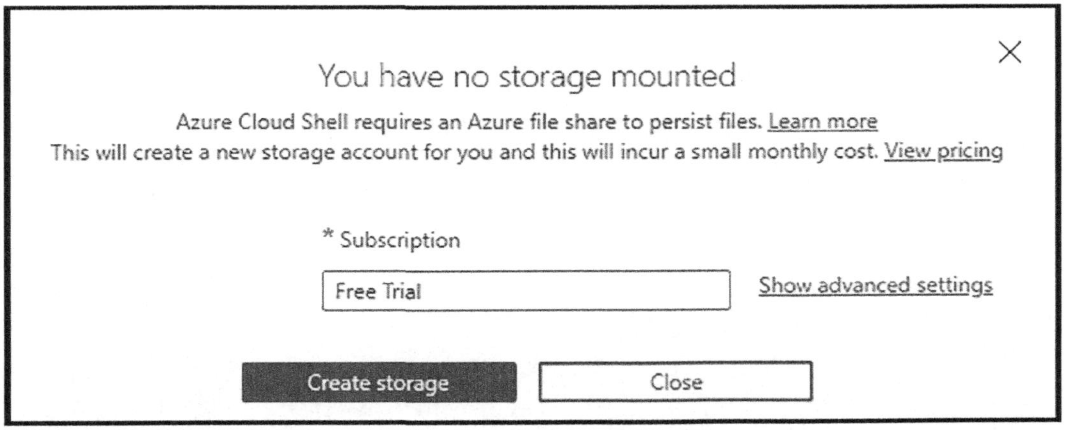

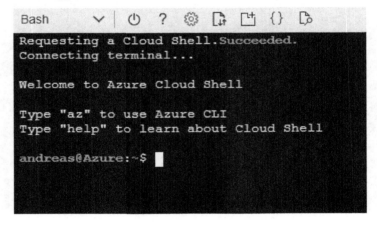

Figure 2.18 – Creating a storage account wizard page while provisioning Cloud Shell

After a while, a storage account will be provisioned, and your Cloud Shell Bash prompt should appear:

Figure 2.19 – The Bash prompt in Azure Cloud Shell

Now that you have a Cloud Shell, you can use the Azure CLI to manage your Azure resources; this is something that you will learn how to do in the next section.

Using the Azure CLI

The Azure CLI is a management command-line tool that you can invoke by typing in the `az` command. Through this tool, you can provision and manage your Azure resources. The easiest way to learn the Azure CLI is by using the `--help` argument at the end of any command. For example, you can start with `az --help`. This will list all of the available commands, such as the `login` commands, the `find` commands, and the subgroups, including the `storage` one:

```
Bash        ∨ | ⏻ ? ⚙ ⎚ ⎙ {} ⎙
Requesting a Cloud Shell.Succeeded.
Connecting terminal...

Welcome to Azure Cloud Shell

Type "az" to use Azure CLI
Type "help" to learn about Cloud Shell

andreas@Azure:~$ az --help

Group
    az

Subgroups:
    account                           : Manage Azure subscription information.
    acr                               : Manage private registries with Azure Container
                                        Registries.
    ad                                : Manage Azure Active Directory Graph entities needed
                                        for Role Based Access Control.
    advisor                           : Manage Azure Advisor.
    ai-examples           [Preview] : Add AI powered examples to help content.
    aks                               : Manage Azure Kubernetes Services.
    ams                               : Manage Azure Media Services resources.
    apim                  [Preview] : Manage Azure API Management services.
    appconfig                         : Manage App Configurations.
    appservice                        : Manage App Service plans.
    aro                               : Manage Azure Red Hat OpenShift clusters.
    backup                [Preview] : Manage Azure Backups.
    batch                             : Manage Azure Batch.
    billing                           : Manage Azure Billing.
    bot                               : Manage Microsoft Azure Bot Service.
    cache                 [Preview] : Commands to manage CLI objects cached
                                        using the `--defer` argument.
    cdn                               : Manage Azure Content Delivery Networks (CDNs).
```

Figure 2.20 – The az command's subgroups and commands

You can keep exploring the various subgroups and commands by appending them to the az command. For example, let's explore the group subgroup, by typing in az group --help. Then, we will investigate the list command, where you can discover all of the available options by typing in az group list --help:

```
Bash       ∨ | ⏻  ?  ⚙  ⎘  ⎗  { }  ⎙
andreas@Azure:~$ az group list --help

Command
    az group list : List resource groups.

Arguments
    --tag                              : A single tag in 'key[=value]' format. Use '' to clear existing
                                         tags.

Global Arguments
    --debug                            : Increase logging verbosity to show all debug logs.
    --help -h                          : Show this help message and exit.
    --only-show-errors                 : Only show errors, suppressing warnings.
    --output -o                        : Output format. Allowed values: json, jsonc, none, table, tsv,
                                         yaml, yamlc. Default: json.
    --query                            : JMESPath query string. See http://jmespath.org/ for more
                                         information and examples.
    --query-examples [Experimental]  : Recommend JMESPath string for you. You can copy one
                                         of the query and paste it after --query parameter within
                                         double quotation marks to see the results. You can add one or
                                         more positional keywords so that we can give suggestions based
                                         on these key words.
        This parameter is experimental and not covered by customer support. Please use with
        discretion.
    --subscription                     : Name or ID of subscription. You can configure the default
                                         subscription using `az account set -s NAME_OR_ID`.
    --verbose                          : Increase logging verbosity. Use --debug for full debug logs.

Examples
    List all resource groups located in the West US region.
        az group list --query ""

For more specific examples, use: az find "az group list"
```

Figure 2.21 – The az group list command help page

Another useful feature of Azure CLI is the az find command, which searches the Azure documentation for relevant information:

```
Bash       ∨ | ⏻  ?  ⚙  ⎘  ⎗  { }  ⎙
andreas@Azure:~$ az find "resource group"
Finding examples...

Here are the most common ways to use [resource group]:

Gets a resource group. (autogenerated)
az group show --resource-group myresourcegroup
```

Figure 2.22 – Using az find to discover Azure CLI commands

You can list all of the resource groups you have access to by issuing the `az group list -o table` command, where we have specified that we want to format the output as a table:

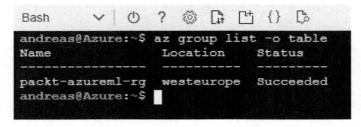

Figure 2.23 – Listing all of the resource groups you have access to through the Azure CLI

> **Tip**
> If you ever find yourself not understanding why the Azure CLI command you are typing doesn't work as expected, you can use the `--verbose` flag. If you need even more information, then you can combine that with the `--debug` flag.

In the next section, you will explore the most common actions that you can perform from the Azure CLI.

Authenticating in Azure CLI

If you get the error message **ValidationError: Please run 'az login' to set up account.**, then you will need to log in using your account. To do so, type in the `az login` command, which will prompt you to open a page and enter a code. This process is referred to as **interactive device authentication**. You will learn more about this process in section Authenticating from your device in *Chapter 7, The AzureML Python SDK*.

After visiting the web page and typing in the code, you will need to log in with the account that has access to the Azure subscription you want to control through the Azure CLI. Doing that will authorize the Azure CLI to act on your behalf. You can always log out from an Azure CLI by typing in `az logout`.

Selecting the active Azure subscription

If you have access to multiple Azure subscriptions, you will need to specify which one is the active one. To list your subscriptions, type in `az account list -o table`; you can activate a subscription by typing in `az account set --subscription "Subscription name or ID"` and passing either the name or the ID of the subscription you want to control from the Azure CLI.

Creating a resource group from the Azure CLI

One of the most well-documented Azure CLI commands on the internet is the one to create a resource group, which is a virtual folder where you can deploy Azure resources. The following command will create a resource group, called `packt-azureml-cli-rg`, and the record of this new resource group will be kept in the Western Europe Azure data center:

```
az group create --name packt-azureml-cli-rg --location
westeurope
```

A shortcut to the `--name` parameter is `-n`. Similarly, `-l` is a shortcut for `--location`. The preceding command can now be written as follows:

```
az group create -n packt-azureml-cli-rg -l westeurope
```

The `-n` and `-l` shortcuts are common across many Azure CLI commands.

> **Important note**
>
> You will need a `Contributor` role at the subscription level to be able to create a resource group. To be more precise, you will need a role that allows you to perform the `Microsoft.Resources/subscriptions/resourceGroups/write` operation, which you will read more about in the *Understanding Role-Based Access Control (RBAC)* section that appears later in this chapter.

In the next section, you will learn how to install an extension within the Azure CLI: the one that manages Azure ML workspaces.

Installing the Azure ML CLI extension

To manage Azure ML workspaces from the Azure CLI, you will need to install the **azure-cli-ml** extension. Install the extension by typing in `az extension add -n azure-cli-ml`.

To view the currently installed extensions and their versions, type in `az extension list -o table`:

Figure 2.24 – A list of all of the installed extensions including azure-cli-ml

To update the installed extension to the latest version, type in `az extension update -n azure-cli-ml`.

The extension you just installed has added the `ml` command subgroup to your Azure CLI. You can inspect the subgroups and the commands it contains by using the `az ml --help` command. In the next section, you will use these new commands to deploy an Azure ML workspace.

Deploying Azure ML using the az ml command

The goal of this section is to deploy an Azure ML workspace, named `packt-learning-cli-mlw`, in the resource group named `packt-azureml-cli-rg` and attach the `Environment` tag with the `Development` value.

To provision a new Azure ML workspace, you will need to use the `az ml workspace create` command.

The only required option is `--workspace-name` or `-w`, which is the workspace name. This will create a new resource group within your Azure subscription and deploy the new workspace there. This requires you to have at least a `Contributor` role at the subscription level; otherwise, you will get an authorization error.

In order to specify the target resource group where you want the new workspace to be deployed, you will need to either pass the `--resource-group` option or the `-g` option.

> **Important note**
>
> There are some common `az ml` parameters: the `-g` and `-w` parameters are common in all Azure ML CLI commands, and you will use them again later in this book.

To attach tags to the newly created resource, you can use the `--tags` parameter or the `-t` parameter, which uses the *key=value* syntax.

Type in the following command to deploy the requested Azure ML workspace:

```
az ml workspace create -g packt-azureml-cli-rg -w packt-
learning-cli-mlw -t Environment=Development
```

The result is displayed in the following screenshot:

```
andreasbotsikas@Azure:~$ az ml workspace create -g packt-azureml-cli-rg -w packt-learning-cli-mlw -t Environment=Development
Deploying AppInsights with name packtleainsightsa9d81e3d.
Deployed AppInsights with name packtleainsightsa9d81e3d. Took 3.69 seconds.
Deploying KeyVault with name packtleakeyvault5429d45f.
Deploying StorageAccount with name packtleastorage2e06e8216.
Deployed KeyVault with name packtleakeyvault5429d45f. Took 18.06 seconds.
Deploying Workspace with name packt-learning-cli-mlw.
Deployed StorageAccount with name packtleastorage2e06e8216. Took 21.11 seconds.
Deployed Workspace with name packt-learning-cli-mlw. Took 18.98 seconds.
```

Figure 2.25 – Deploying the Azure ML workspace through the CLI extension

In this section, you learned how to deploy an Azure ML workspace using the Azure CLI. For this book, you will only need the one you provisioned through the user interface, and you will delete the one you just provisioned in the next section.

Cleaning up the CLI resource group

For the purposes of this book, you are going to need a single Azure ML workspace. You are going to use the one you deployed through the Azure portal in the packt-azureml-rg resource group. If you want, you can delete the newly provisioned Azure ML workspace by issuing the following command:

```
az ml workspace delete -g packt-azureml-cli-rg -w packt-
learning-cli-mlw --all-resources
```

This will delete the Azure ML workspace and all of the related resources that were provisioned in the preceding steps.

So far, you have explored the most common ways to provision the Azure ML workspace, that is, through the portal and the Azure CLI. In the next section, you will learn about a few additional ways, including the ARM way, which is preferred by DevOps engineers.

Alternative ways to deploy an Azure ML workspace

There are additional ways in which you can deploy an Azure ML workspace:

- Create an ARM template. This is the Azure-native way of describing resources that you want to deploy in the form of a JSON file. An example of an ARM template for the Azure ML workspace can be found at https://bit.ly/dp100-azureml-arm.

The command to deploy such a template from the Azure CLI is as follows:

```
az deployment group create --name packt-deployment
--resource-group packt-azureml-rg --template-
uri https://bit.ly/dp100-azureml-arm --parameters
workspaceName=packt-learning-arm-mlw location=westeurope
```

You can also find an ARM template if you select the **Download a template for automation** link that appears on the left-hand side of the **Create** button in the last step of the Azure portal resource creation wizard.

- Through the Azure ML Python SDK, which you will learn about in *Chapter 7, The Azure ML Python.*

- Through the Azure management REST API as described in https://docs. microsoft.com/azure/machine-learning/how-to-manage-rest#create-a-workspace-using-rest.

In the next section, you will explore the Azure resources that have been deployed to the target resource group, and you will learn how to give workspace access to your colleagues.

Exploring the deployed Azure resources

Open the Azure portal and search for resource groups. Select the icon to navigate to the list of the resource groups you have access to, as shown in the following screenshot:

Figure 2.26 – Navigating to the list of resource groups

Select the **packt-azureml-rg** option and observe the resources that are deployed within this resource group:

- The ML workspace resource is named **packt-learning-mlw**. This is the main resource that you deployed. Through this resource, you can manage various aspects of the workspace.

- An Azure key-vault service named **packtlearningm<random_number>**. This key vault is used to securely store credentials and access keys that you will be using within the Azure ML workspace.

- A storage account with the name of **packtlearningm<random_number>**. This storage account was autogenerated during the provisioning process and is used to store files from the workspace, including experimental datasets and models.

- An application insight account named **packtlearningm<random_number>**. This is the monitoring service for all predictive endpoints that you will publish from within the Azure ML workspace.

These are the out-of-the-box components that get deployed within the Azure ML workspace:

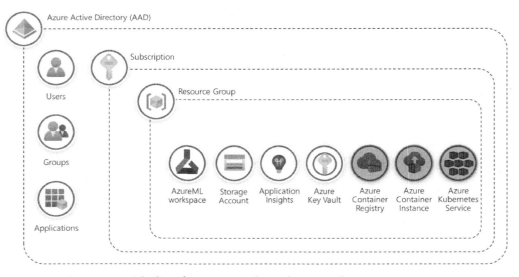

Figure 2.27 – The list of resources in the packt-azureml-rg resource group

There is actually one more resource that is going to be provisioned automatically when you run your first experiment: an **Azure Container Registry** (**ACR**). This will host various **Docker** container images, including the ones that are going to be exposing a web server that will make inferences with the **Artificial Intelligence** (**AI**) models you are going to train.

When you want to deploy a real-time endpoint for a model, you can deploy it in an **Azure Container Instance** (**ACI**) or **Azure Kubernetes Service** (**AKS**) from within the Azure ML studio. You will deploy an ACI for the first time in *Chapter 5, Letting Machines Do the Model Training*, of this book, and you will notice that an ACI resource will appear within this resource group next to the existing resources.

Understanding Role-Based Access Control (RBAC)

Azure provides RBAC, which allows you to define the operations each role can perform on specific resources. Each role is assigned according to a specific scope, for example, if you are assigned the **Contributor** role in a resource group, you will be able to provision resources only within that resource group and not at the subscription level. Out of the box, Azure provides three well-known roles:

- **Reader**: This allows you to browse through Azure resources, but you cannot modify or activate anything.

- **Contributor**: This builds on top of the **Reader** role and allows you to edit resources or create new resources within the scope of the role. This role doesn't allow you to modify the permissions that are attached to the resources. This means you cannot grant another user permission to the resources you might have provisioned.

- **Owner**: This role can do everything that the **Contributor** role does and can also assign and modify roles within the context that this role applies to.

Let's examine the roles that are assigned in the resource group where you deployed the Azure ML workspace. Click on the **Access control (IAM)** tab of the resource group and then select **Role assignments**. On this page, you will see a list of role assignments to the resource group level. Notice that your account has been assigned, at the very least, the **Contributor** role in this resource group to provision resources. If you don't see your account in the list, you are most likely an administrator, so take a look under the **Classic administrators** tab:

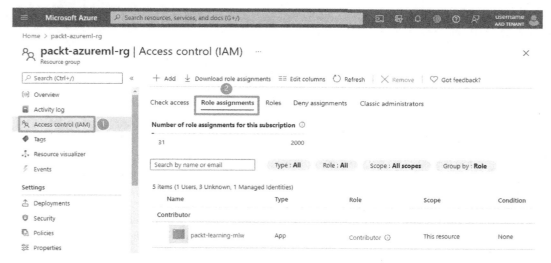

Figure 2.28 – Role assignments on the Access control (IAM) page
of the packt-azureml-rg resource group

When you provisioned the workspace, a new system-assigned managed identity was created with the name of the Azure ML workspace you provisioned. This was automatically assigned as a **Contributor** role for the resource group. This allows the ML workspace to deploy ACI resources within that resource group and access compute targets and data stores. Note that this identity is used by the platform itself and should not be used to assign access to external resources and so on.

Next, you will learn how this role assignment flows down to the resources.

RBAC inheritance

Open the **packt-learning-mlw** resource and click on the **Access control (IAM)** tab. Then, select **Role assignments**.

Notice that the roles that existed in the resource group are inherited down to the Azure ML workspace resource:

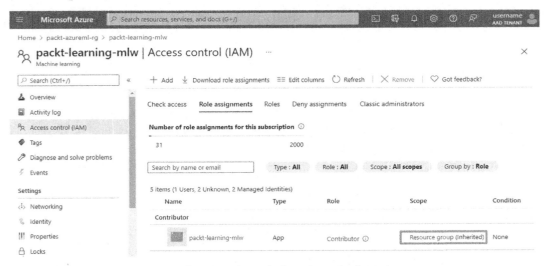

Figure 2.29 – RBAC inheritance in packt-learning-mlw from the resource group

The role assignments inherit from the subscription to the resource groups and from there to the resources. On top of the subscriptions, there is another grouping layer, called **Management Groups**, which allows you to build hierarchies that contain other management groups and or subscriptions. An example of the overall RBAC inheritance model is depicted in the following schema:

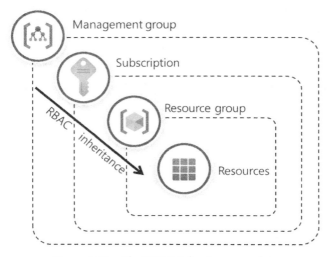

Figure 2.30 – The RBAC inheritance model

Now that you know how to assign out-of-the-box roles and have understood how inheritance works, in the next section, you will learn how to create custom roles for your Azure ML workspace.

Creating custom roles

Azure allows you to create custom RBAC roles where you can fine-tune what operations are allowed and what actions are not allowed; this is similar to an allow list and a block list. The portal provides a graphical experience that allows you to create custom roles at the resource group level or higher. The result of this experience is a JSON file, such as the following example:

```
{
    "Name": "ACI model deployer role",
    "IsCustom": true,
    "Description": "Can deploy registered model on ACI
resources",
    "Actions": [
```

```
"Microsoft.MachineLearningServices/workspaces/services/aci/
write"
    ],
    "NotActions": [ ],
    "AssignableScopes":["/subscriptions/<subscription_id>"]
}
```

This is a very simple custom role, named `ACI model deployer role`, which provides write access to the ACI service of the workspaces – an operation that is encoded in the literal `Microsoft.MachineLearningServices/workspaces/services/aci/write`.

A more complex example of a custom role is as follows:

```
{
    "Name": "Limited Data Scientist",
    "IsCustom": true,
    "Description": "Limited data scientist role",
    "Actions": ["*"],
    "NotActions": [
"Microsoft.MachineLearningServices/workspaces/computes/delete",
"Microsoft.Authorization/*/write"
    ],
    "AssignableScopes": [
"/subscriptions/<subscription_id>/resourceGroups/<resource_
group_name>/providers/Microsoft.MachineLearningServices/
workspaces/<workspace_name>"
    ]
}
```

Notice that in contrast to the previous role, which was explicitly allowing a single action, this role has a wildcard (`*`) in the allowed actions, meaning that it can do all available actions. To limit that effect, we use the `NotActions` sections, which indicate which operations are explicitly denied. In this example, we are explicitly disallowing the ability to delete compute resources (`Microsoft.MachineLearningServices/workspaces/computes/delete`) and cannot update any authorization aspect of this workspace (`Microsoft.Authorization/*/write`). Note that the wildcard can be used to match partial actions like in the `Microsoft.Authorization` action, where the wildcard matches action groups such as `lock`, `roleAssignments`, and `roleDefinitions`. In our case, we want the user who will have this role to not be able to add new users to the workspace, so we want to disallow the `Microsoft.Authorization/roleAssignments/write` action, which is covered by the wildcard expression we used.

Finally, `AssignableScopes` allows you to specify the scope of this role. This is a mandatory field. In the first example, you are limiting the scope of this role to the Azure subscription with an ID of `<subscription_id>`. In this case, you can assign this custom role to any resource group or resource that belongs to the subscription with ID `<subscription_id>`. In the second example, you are limiting the scope of this custom role to the Azure ML workspace, named `<workspace_name>`, that is deployed in the resource group named `<resource_group_name>`, which belongs to the `<subscription_id>` subscription. This means you cannot assign this custom role anywhere else as it has a very targeted assignable scope.

If you want to deploy a custom role in Azure through the Azure CLI, you can use the following command:

```
az role definition create --role-definition custom_role.json
```

Here, `custom_role.json` is a file containing the JSON role definition of the custom role that you want to deploy in Azure.

Once the role is deployed to Azure, you can assign that specific role to a user.

Assigning roles in the Azure ML workspace

Assigning a role to a user is a privileged operation that means you are modifying the permissions of a resource. To do so, you will need to have the `Owner` permission of the resource that you want to modify. To be more accurate, you will need a role that allows you to use the `Microsoft.Authorization/roleAssignments/write` operation – something that the built-in `Owner` role has.

If you do have the `Owner` permission, you can assign the **ACI model deployer role** that you created in the previous section to a user. You can do so in the following three ways:

- In the Azure portal, you can visit the Azure ML workspace you want and assign the role to the user through the **Access control (IAM)** tab that you saw in the *Understanding Role-Based Access Control (RBAC)* section.

- Through the Azure CLI by issuing the following command:

```
az role assignment create -assignee "user id"
--role "ACI model deployer role" --scope "/
subscriptions/<subscription_id>/resourceGroups/packt-
azureml-rg/providers/Microsoft.MachineLearningServices/
workspaces/packt-learning-mlw"
```

    Here, you assign the custom role to a user with an ID of `user id`. Then, you apply this assignment at the level of the Azure ML workspace. To get the user ID of the user with the email `username@organization.org`, you can use the following Azure CLI command:

```
az ad user list --query "[?mail=='username@organization.
org'].objectId" --output tsv
```

- Through the Azure ML CLI extension by using the following command:

```
az ml workspace share -w packt-learning-mlw -g packt-
azureml-rg --role "ACI model deployer role" --user
username@organization.org
```

With these steps, you can share the workspace with your colleagues by creating custom roles that fine-tune the allowed permissions.

Summary

In this chapter, you learned about the prerequisites for deploying Azure ML. You can work with either a trial subscription or you can request a resource group in your company's subscription, where you, at the very least, have contributor rights to the resource group. You also discovered, in depth, the two most common ways of deploying the Azure ML workspace in a development environment, and you also gained an understanding of the parameters that you need to specify. You also learned about the alternative ways you can deploy the workspace, including ARM templates, which are the more DevOps-friendly way of deploying in production environments. In the final section, you looked at the resources that are part of Azure ML workspace deployment, and you learned how RBAC works in Azure. Additionally, you learned how to use built-in or custom roles to give access to the Azure ML workspace you deployed.

In the next chapter, you will learn about the **Azure ML Studio** experience, which is a web environment that enables you to manage the end-to-end ML life cycle.

Questions

In each chapter, you should find a couple of questions that will allow you to perform a knowledge check on the topics discussed in this chapter:

1. Which of the following are applicable ways of deploying the Azure ML workspace?

    a. Azure CLI through the azure-cli-ml extension

    b. The Azure portal

    c. The deployment of an ARM template

    d. Azure ML Python SDK

2. You are creating a custom role and you want to deny the ability to delete a workspace. Where do you need to add the **Microsoft.MachineLearningServices/ workspaces/delete** action?

    a. To the `Actions` section of the JSON definition

    b. To the `NotActions` section of the JSON definition

    c. To the `AssignableScopes` section of the JSON definition

3. What do you have to install in the Azure CLI before you can deploy an Azure ML workspace?

Further reading

This section offers a list of useful web resources that will help you to augment your knowledge and understanding of Azure:

*   If this is the first time you are navigating to the Azure portal, you might want to read an overview of it at `https://docs.microsoft.com/azure/azure-portal/azure-portal-overview`. If you want to learn more about the features of Cloud Shell, you can visit `https://docs.microsoft.com/azure/cloud-shell/overview`.

*   You can learn more about selecting the proper region for your resources at `https://azure.microsoft.com/global-infrastructure/geographies/#choose-your-region`.

- If you are interested in learning how to create and deploy ARM templates by using the Azure portal, you can read the documentation at `https://docs.microsoft.com/azure/azure-resource-manager/templates/quickstart-create-templates-use-the-portal`.

- For a complete list of data centers that have an Azure ML service available, please visit `https://azure.microsoft.com/global-infrastructure/services/?regions=all&products=machine-learning-service`.

- You can learn more about the Azure resource name rules at `https://docs.microsoft.com/azure/azure-resource-manager/management/resource-name-rules#microsoftmachinelearningservices`.

- You can read more about the best practices for naming at `https://docs.microsoft.com/azure/cloud-adoption-framework/ready/azure-best-practices/naming-and-tagging`.

- You can also read more about how to use resource tags at `https://docs.microsoft.com/azure/azure-resource-manager/management/tag-resources`. The Microsoft Cloud Adoption Framework has a list of best practices related to metadata tags, which you can read at `https://docs.microsoft.com/azure/cloud-adoption-framework/ready/azure-best-practices/naming-and-tagging#metadata-tags`.

- For more information about the Azure ML private link feature, please refer to `https://docs.microsoft.com/azure/machine-learning/how-to-configure-private-link`.

- You can learn more about this system-managed identity concept that is infused in the Azure ML workspace at `https://docs.microsoft.com/azure/machine-learning/concept-enterprise-security#securing-compute-targets-and-data`.

- You can learn more about the default Azure roles (such as `Owner`, `Contributor`, and `Reader`) and how to create custom roles for the Azure ML workspace at `https://docs.microsoft.com/azure/machine-learning/how-to-assign-roles`.

- Learn more about Managed Identities: `https://docs.microsoft.com/azure/active-directory/managed-identities-azure-resources/overview`

- AzureML identity based data access: `https://docs.microsoft.com/azure/machine-learning/how-to-identity-based-data-access`

3
Azure Machine Learning Studio Components

In this chapter, you will explore the **Azure Machine Learning Studio** (**Azure ML Studio**) web interface, an immersive experience for managing the end-to-end machine learning life cycle. You will get an overview of the available components that allow you to manage your workspace resources, author machine learning models, and track your assets, including your datasets, trained models, and their published endpoints.

In this chapter, we're going to cover the following main topics:

- Interacting with the Azure ML resource
- Exploring the Azure ML Studio experience
- Authoring experiments within Azure ML Studio
- Tracking data science assets in Azure ML Studio
- Managing infrastructure resources in Azure ML Studio

Technical requirements

You will need to have access to an Azure subscription. Within that subscription, you will need a **resource group** named `packt-azureml-rg`. You will need to have either a `Contributor` or `Owner` **access control (IAM)** role at the resource group level. Within that resource group, you should deploy a **machine learning** resource named `packt-learning-mlw`. These resources should already be available to you if you followed the instructions in *Chapter 2, Deploying Azure Machine Learning Workspace Resources.*

Interacting with the Azure ML resource

In the previous chapter, you deployed the `packt-learning-mlw` machine learning resource within the `packt-azureml-rg` resource group. Navigate to the deployed resource by typing in its name in the top search bar and selecting the resource from the results list:

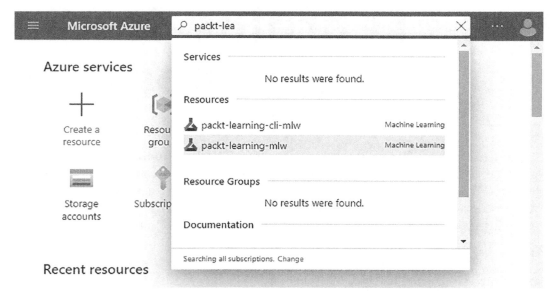

Figure 3.1 – Navigating to the Azure Machine Learning resource

This will land you on the overview pane of the resource, as shown in *Figure 3.2*:

1. On the left-hand side, you will see the typical resource menu that most of the Azure services have. This menu is also referred to as the left pane.

2. At the top, you will see the command bar, which allows you to download the `config.json` file, a file that contains all the information you need to connect to the workspace through the Python SDK, and to delete the machine learning workspace.

3. Below the command bar, you can see the working pane, which is where you can view information related to the workspace, including links to the storage account, key vault, container registry, and application insights resources that got deployed with this workspace:

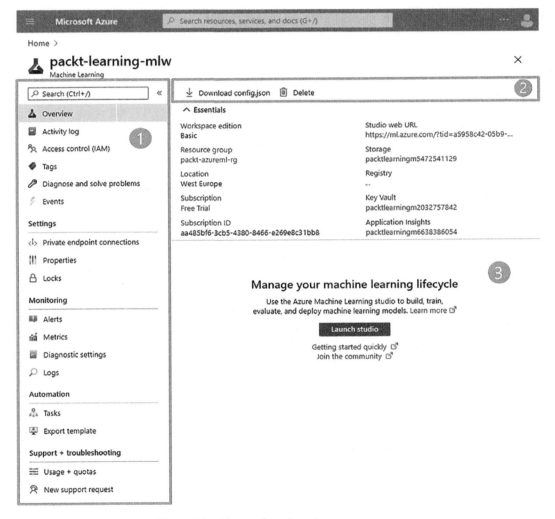

Figure 3.2 – The machine learning resource page

On the left pane, you will find all the common options you can find in all Azure resources. This includes the following indicative list:

- **Access control (IAM)**, which you can use to configure role access to the specific workspace, including assigning custom roles such as the ones you created in the previous chapter.

- **Diagnostic settings**, which enables you to configure streaming exports for the logs and metrics generated by the Azure Machine Learning workspace to the destination of your choice. Typically, this is **Log Analytics**, which is part of **Azure Monitor**.

- **New support request**, which allows you to easily request support if you ever face an issue with your workspace.

In the **Settings** section, you will also notice the **Private endpoint connections** option, which allows you to configure an Azure Private Endpoint. This is a virtual network interface that you can attach to a virtual network. It allows all the resources within that virtual network to connect to your Azure Machine Learning workspace privately and securely. Once you enable this option, all data plane operations, such as using Azure ML Studio, APIs (including published pipelines), or the SDK will need to go through this private endpoint.

Select the overview option from the left pane and click on the **Launch studio** button in the middle of the working pane. This will open a new tab in your browser, which will lead you to the Studio experience.

Exploring the Azure ML Studio experience

Azure Machine Learning comes with a dedicated web interface that allows you to implement both no-code and code-first data science initiatives. You can access the web interface either through the **Launch studio** button within the Azure portal resource, as you saw in the previous section, or by visiting the `https://ml.azure.com` page directly. With the latter approach, if this is your first time you've visited the Studio site, you will have to manually select the **Azure Active Directory** tenant, the **Subscription**, and the name of the **Machine Learning workspace** you want to connect to, as shown in *Figure 3.3*.

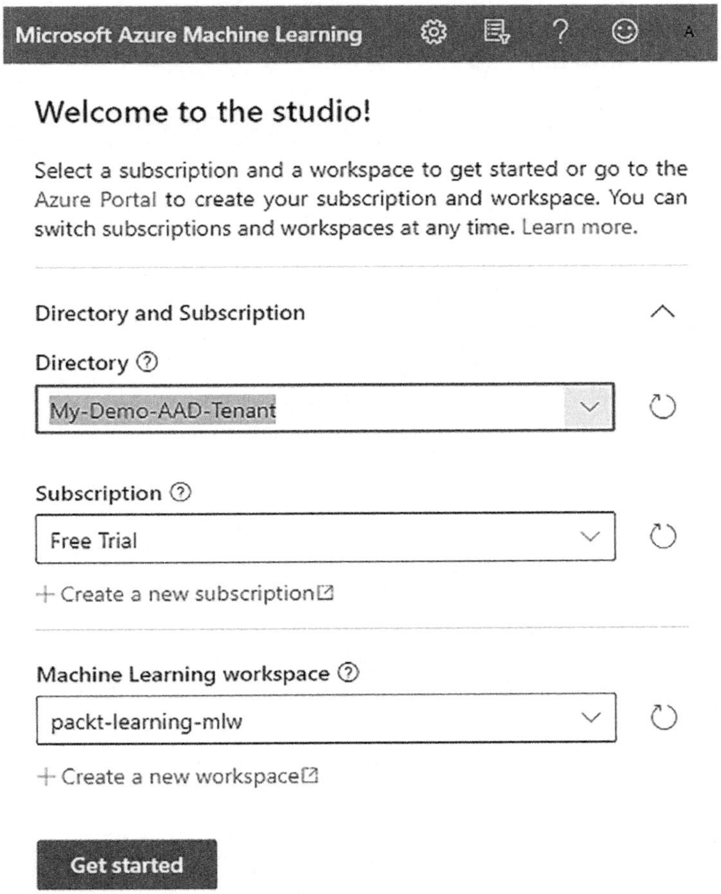

Figure 3.3 – Selecting the machine learning workspace in ml.azure.com

Once you've selected your workspace, you will land on the home page of Azure Machine Learning Studio, as shown in *Figure 3.4*.

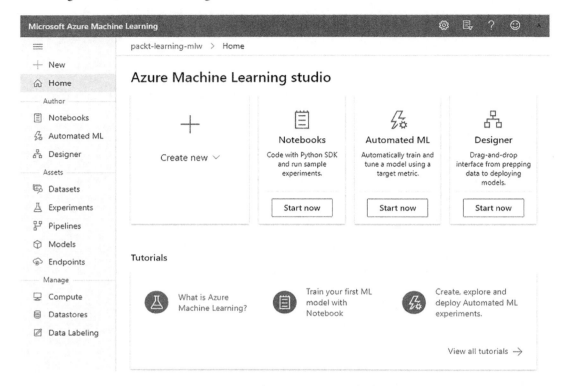

Figure 3.4 – Azure Machine Learning Studio home page

On the left-hand side, you have a menu that provides the following categories, all of which you will explore in the upcoming sections:

- **Author**: Build, train, evaluate, and deploy machine learning models using the authoring tools.

- **Assets**: Prepare your data, run and monitor your jobs, view and deploy models, and manage real-time and pipeline endpoints.

- **Manage**: View and manage resources for your workspace.

You can collapse the menu by clicking on the top-left icon, as shown in the following screenshot:

Figure 3.5 – Collapsed side menu

In the top-right corner, as shown in the *Figure 3.6*, you have the following options:

1. **Sign in info:** This displays information about the logged-in user and allows you to sign out.

2. **Workspace selector:** This allows you to change the active Azure Machine Learning workspace you are working on.

3. **Provide feedback:** This allows you to send a smiley or frowning face to the Azure Machine Learning team. This helps them improve on things that you don't like or highlight the things you do like.

4. **Help:** This provides links to help resources and documentation. This menu also allows you to run workspace diagnostics and identify potential configuration issues with your workspace.

5. **Settings:** From here, you can select the dark theme option and change your Studio's language and regional format.

6. **Notifications:** This menu option allows you to manage the workspace notifications you will be receiving. An example of such a notification is the one you receive when an experiment run has completed.

Figure 3.6 – Top-right menu

In the next section, we'll look at the various sections of the left menu, starting with the authoring ones.

Authoring experiments within Azure ML Studio

Azure ML Studio provides the following authoring experiences:

- **Notebooks** allows you to work with files, folders, and **Jupyter Notebooks** directly in the workspace. You will be working with notebooks in *Chapter 7, The AzureML Python SDK*, where you will see the code-first data science process.

- **Automated ML** allows you to rapidly test multiple combinations of algorithms against a given dataset and find the best model based on the success metric you define. You will read more about this in *Chapter 5, Letting the Machines Do the Model Training*.

- **Designer** allows you to visually design an experiment by connecting datasets and modules such as data transformation and model training in a flow. By designing this flow on a canvas, you can train and deploy machine learning models without writing any code, something that you will read more about in *Chapter 6, Visual Model Training and Publishing*.

- **Data Labeling** allows you to create labeling projects for curating datasets. This allows you to scale out your labeling efforts to multiple labelers, efficiently coordinate the labeling efforts, and augment the labelers' productivity using ML Assist, which automatically trains while you label data.

Both automated ML and designer are part of the no-code/low code approaches to data science, something you will explore later in this book.

> Important note
> Data labeling is currently under the **Manage** section, from the left menu. Nevertheless, it is logically part of the authoring experience that Azure ML Studio provides. Since the Studio experience is constantly evolving, this feature may move under the **Author** section in the near future.

Tracking data science assets in Azure ML Studio

Within the assets section, you can track all the components that are at the heart of machine learning operations. Every data science project has the following assets:

- **Datasets** is where you can find registered datasets. This is a centralized registry where you can register your datasets and avoid colleagues having to work on local copies of the same data or, even worse, subsets of this data. You will work with datasets in *Chapter 4, Configuring the Workspace*.

- **Experiments** is a centralized place to track groups of script executions or runs. When you are training a model, you are logging various aspects of that process, including metrics that you might need to compare performance. To group all attempts under the same context, you should submit all the runs under the same experiment name; then, the results will appear in this area. You will work with experiments in *Chapter 5, Letting the Machines Do the Model Training*.

- **Pipelines** allows you to create and manage workflows that orchestrate machine learning steps. For example, a very common machine learning training workflow contains three steps: data processing, model training, and model registration. Pipelines can be either ML training ones, like the ones shown in the previous example, or batch data inferencing ones – in other words, pipelines that use a machine learning model to make inferences for a dataset. In this section, you can view all registered pipelines, monitor their executions, and see the published endpoints, which allow you to trigger one of those pipelines ad hoc. You will be working with pipelines in *Chapter 11, Working with Pipelines*.

- **Models** is the registry for your machine learning models. It's where you keep track of their versions. It allows you to instantly deploy through the web interface. To publish a model, you will need to register it first in this registry. You will be working with this registry throughout this book, starting from *Chapter 5, Letting the Machines Do the Model Training*.

- **Endpoints** consists of two parts: the real-time endpoints and the pipeline endpoints. Real-time endpoints are web applications hosted either in **Azure Container Instances (ACI)** or **Azure Kubernetes Services (AKS)**, and they expose a REST API, which allows third-party applications to consume the machine learning model you have deployed. Pipeline endpoints, on the other hand, are the endpoints that allow you to trigger pipelines that have been registered in the corresponding sections mentioned previously.

All the preceding experiences are interconnected, and you will find yourself navigating from one section to the other while you are exploring the experiments you will be conducting:

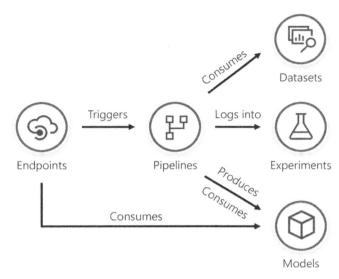

Figure 3.7 – Interconnected assets in Azure ML

A prerequisite for running a machine learning experiment is to have computational resources that will execute the training scripts. You will also need engines that will store, and give access to, the data that you register as datasets. These are the resources you will manage in the next section.

Managing infrastructure resources in Azure ML Studio

To conduct an experiment, you will need a couple of infrastructure resources to consume. You can configure and manage them through the following sections:

- **Compute** provides the managed compute infrastructure you can use in your experiments. This allows you to register and utilize virtual machines that may have multiple CPUs and GPUs and memory sizes that can load humongous datasets into them. Having those computes as a managed service means that you don't have to worry about installing the operating system or keeping it patched and up to date. You will learn more about the various compute options in *Chapter 4, Configuring the Workspace*.

- **Datastores** contains the connection information needed to get access to the data within various engines, such as **Azure Blob Storage** and **Azure SQL Database**. This information is used to access the datasets that you registered in the **Compute** section. You will learn more about the concepts surrounding datastores in *Chapter 4, Configuring the Workspace.*

- Linked services allow you to view the connections between external services and your workspace. For example, you can connect you Synapse Spark pools and run data preparation tasks with Spark.

- Environments allow you to specify the software requirements for your code to execute. For example, if you are training a PyTorch model, you will need the PyTorch library installed in the environment that will execute your training scripts. You will learn more about the environments in *Chapter 8, Experimenting with Python Code.*

Summary

Azure Machine Learning Studio provides a web environment where you can manage all the artifacts in your Azure Machine Learning workspace. You can view and manage your Jupyter notebooks, datasets, experiments, pipelines, models, and endpoints. You can also manage the compute resources and datastores that will be used in your experiments. Studio also offers interactive tools you can use to perform no-code data science experiments, something you will deep dive into in the next chapters of this book. The AutoML wizard is the first no-code experience that's baked into Azure ML Studio and allows you to run automated machine learning experiments. Azure Machine Learning designer is the next no-code experience and helps you graphically design pipelines and create workflows without writing code. This experience also enables low-code scenarios, where you can drop code snippets if needed. Finally, data labeling projects allow you to create, manage, and monitor tedious projects to label your data.

To start using these interactive tools, you will need to provision, at the very least, a compute resource. Moreover, you will need to register your data stores. These data stores will host the data you will be using in the model training phase.

In the next chapter, you will learn how to perform these actions through Azure ML Studio.

4
Configuring the Workspace

In this chapter, you will work inside the **Azure Machine Learning** (**ML**) Studio web interface and learn how to configure the infrastructure needed to run an experiment inside its workspace. Then, you will learn how to provision or attach to existing compute resources and establish the connection between the Azure ML workspace and the various datastores that host your data. With these resources configured, you will be able to register a dataset and explore the capabilities offered in Azure ML to monitor those datasets.

In this chapter, we're going to cover the following main topics:

- Provisioning compute resources
- Connecting to datastores
- Working with datasets

Technical requirements

You will need to have access to an Azure subscription. Within that subscription, you will need a **resource group** named `packt-azureml-rg`. You will need to have either a `Contributor` or `Owner` **Access control** (**IAM**) role at the resource group level. Within that resource group, you should deploy an ML resource named `packt-learning-mlw`, as described in *Chapter 2, Deploying Azure Machine Learning Workspace Resources.*

Provisioning compute resources

Compute resources allow you to execute code scripts during your data exploratory analysis, the training phase, and when operationalizing ML models. The **Azure ML** workspace offers the following types of compute resources:

- **Compute instances**: These are virtual machines dedicated to each data scientist that is working in the **Azure ML workspace**.

- **Compute clusters**: These are scalable computer clusters that can run multiple training or inference steps in parallel.

- **Inference clusters**: These are **Azure Kubernetes Service** (**AKS**) clusters that can operationalize Docker images, which expose your models through a REST API.

- **Attached compute**: These are existing compute resources, such as Ubuntu **Virtual Machines** (**VMs**) or **Synapse Spark pools**, that can be attached to the workspace to execute some of the steps of your training or inference pipelines.

When you visit the **Manage | Compute** section of Azure ML Studio, you will see and be able to manage each of these types by selecting the corresponding tab, as shown in the following screenshot:

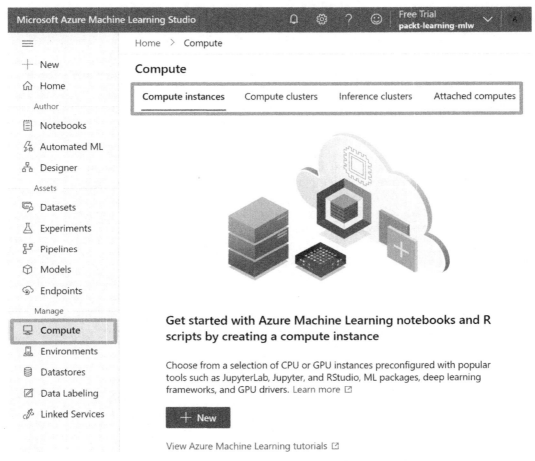

Figure 4.1 – Compute types in Azure ML Studio

In the following sections, you will discover each of these compute types and understand the important configuration parameters that you must be aware of.

> **Important note**
> Provisioning and attaching compute resources can also be done through the Azure ML CLI and the Azure ML Python SDK. You will see examples of provisioning the same resources via the Python SDK in *Chapter 7, The Azure ML Python SDK*.

Compute instances

A compute instance is a VM that will facilitate your daily work as a data scientist. This is a managed, Ubuntu-based workstation that comes preconfigured with data science tools such as Jupyter Labs, RStudio, and various deep learning frameworks such as **PyTorch** and **TensorFlow**. *Managed* means that you won't have to manually update the operating system or ensure that it is patched against the latest security vulnerabilities.

> **Important note**
>
> Compute instances are ideal for corporate users who may not be able to install Python on their corporate computers. Compute instances only require you to have a modern web browser and internet access. Once you are connected to a compute instance, you have access to all the software packages you will need to work with your Azure ML workspace.

All your files and preferences are securely stored within the /home/<username>/cloudfiles/code/ folder of the VM. This folder is not part of the VM's disk, but it is mounted from a remote file share located in your Azure ML storage account, as shown in the following diagram. This file share allows you to share code files and notebooks across multiple compute instances, and you can even mount that folder locally on your own computer:

Compute   /home/<user>/cloudfiles/code/   Compute
instance A   mounted from file share   instance B
                        in storage account

Figure 4.2 – Remote file share mounted on multiple compute instances

Compute instances primarily enable the **Notebooks** experience of the studio web interface, but they can also be used for training and inferencing at a small scale. In fact, compute instances provide job queuing capabilities and allow you to run up to two jobs per core, something that's very useful for testing and debugging scenarios. You will use your compute instance to perform data drift analysis in the *Data drift detection* section, later in this chapter. In the next section, you will learn how to provision your first compute instance.

Provisioning a compute instance

Let's learn how to provision an instance:

1. In the studio web interface, navigate to the **Manage | Compute** section and select the **Compute instances** tab. If no compute instances have been provisioned, you will see a short introduction to compute instances: you can click the **New** button to start the compute provisioning wizard, as shown on the left-hand side of *Figure 4.3*. If other compute instances have already been provisioned in the workspace, you can start the same wizard by clicking on the **New** button from the top menu, as shown on the right-hand side of the following screenshot:

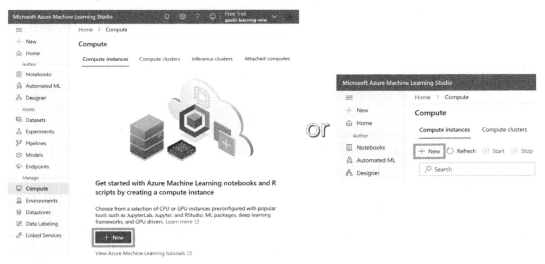

Figure 4.3 – Starting the compute instance provisioning wizard

2. The first thing you will need to select is the virtual machine's size. You can specify whether you need GPU-enabled machines or normal CPU machines. If you plan to run computer vision experiments or deep neural network training, a GPU machine can accelerate the training and inference process if the framework supports GPUs. Moreover, you can add filters to limit the list based on the minimum requirements you have for your workspace. In our case, we will select a CPU-only compute instance that has at least 14 GB of RAM and at least 4 cores, as shown in the following screenshot:

Create compute instance   ✕

Configure required settings
Select the name and virtual machine size you would like to use for your compute instance. Please note that a compute instance can not
be shared. It can only be used by a single assigned user. By default, it will be assigned to the creator and you can change this to a
different user in the advanced settings section.

✓ **Required Settings**

○ **Advanced Settings**

Compute name * ⓘ   👁

| my-compute-instance |

Location ⓘ

Your workspace region, like westeurope

Virtual machine type ⓘ

◉ CPU   ○ GPU

Virtual machine size ⓘ

◉ Select from recommended options   ○ Select from all options

Total available quota: 88 cores ⓘ

	Name ↑	Category	Workload types	Available quota ⓘ	Cost ⓘ
○	Standard_DS11_v2 2 cores, 14GB RAM, 28GB storage	Memory optimized	Development on Notebooks (or other IDE) and light weight testing	88 cores	$0.19/hr
✓	Standard_DS3_v2 4 cores, 14GB RAM, 28GB storage	General purpose	Classical ML model training, AutoML runs, pipeline runs (default compute)	88 cores	$0.27/hr
○	Standard_DS12_v2 4 cores, 28GB RAM, 56GB storage	Memory optimized	Training on large datasets (>1GB) parallel run steps, batch inferencing	88 cores	$0.38/hr
○	Standard_F4s_v2 4 cores, 8GB RAM, 32GB storage	Compute optimized	Real-time inferencing and other latency-sensitive tasks	88 cores	$0.19/hr

| Create | Back | Next: Advanced Settings | | Cancel |

Figure 4.4 – The first page of the compute instance provisioning wizard

In the results table, you can review the characteristics of each VM and get an estimation of how much it will cost per hour.

> **Important note**
>
> Virtual machines' costs depend on their size, but also on the region where they are provisioned. For example, while authoring this book, East US 2 had the lowest average price in USD per hour, while West Europe was among the most expensive regions.

The following table contains a bit more information about the first three virtual machine sizes that appear in the result list. The main difference between the **Standard_D3_v2** and **Standard_DS3_v2** virtual machines is the premium storage disk. This provides disk caching capabilities, something that allows the VM to achieve performance levels that exceed the underlying disk performance. Therefore, by default, the wizard suggests that you select the **Standard_DS3_v2** virtual machine size:

Size	vCPUs	Memory in GiB	Storage type	Temporary storage			Expected network bandwidth in Mbps
				Size in GiB	Max IOPS	Max read MBps	
Standard_D4_v3	4	16	Standard	100	6000	93	2000
Standard_D3_v2	4	14	Standard	200	12000	187	3000
Standard_DS3_v2	4	14	Premium	28	16000	128	3000

Figure 4.5 – Comparison of compute sizes based on the docs.microsoft.com site

3. Leave the **Standard_DS3_v2** size selected and click **Next** to configure the advanced settings for the compute instance:

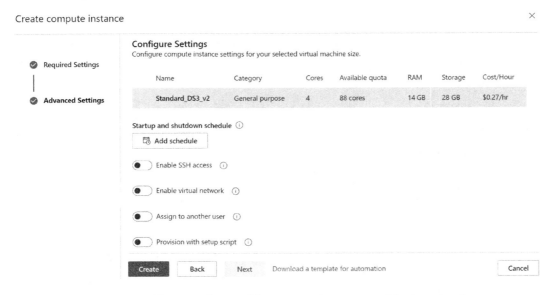

Figure 4.6 – The second page of the compute instance provisioning wizard

> **Important note**
> If you are on a free trial, then you have a fixed core quota, which you cannot change unless you switch to a pay-as-you-go subscription. You may need to select **Standard_DS2_v2** to reduce the number of cores your compute instance will be using. You will need at least two more cores for the computer cluster you will be provisioning in *Chapter 7, The Azure ML Python SDK*.

4. Now, you need to provide a computer name. This is the name you will be using to reference the specific computer. The compute name should be unique within the Azure region. This means that you may need to change the name to something unique, potentially by adding some numbers in the name; for example, `ds-021-workstation`.

5. Optionally, enable the SSH access flag. This option allows you to specify the public portion of the SSH key, which will give you remote access to the compute instance. The wizard allows you to generate that key directly within the wizard. Alternatively, you can generate one by following the instructions provided in the *Generating an SSH key pair* section. This option is not needed if you only plan to use the studio experience to conduct your data science experiments:

Figure 4.7 – Enabling SSH access to the compute instance

6. Click on the **Create** button to provision the compute instance. This will complete the wizard. At this point, the compute instance will be created and then start:

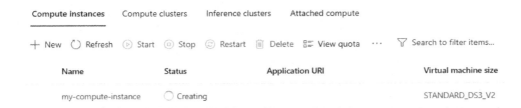

Figure 4.8 – Waiting for the compute instance to be created and transition to the Running state

In the following sections, you will be given a brief introduction to SSH key-based authentication and how to generate an SSH key if you are not familiar with the process. Moreover, you will explore the advanced options of the wizard, options we will not need for the purposes of this book.

Generating an SSH key pair

An SSH key pair consists of two files – a private key and a public key. This key pair allows end users to encrypt text using the public portion of the key. The encrypted text can only be decrypted by the private portion of the SSH key, as shown in the following diagram. The private portion of the SSH key needs to be stored in a secure place, while the public portion of the key can be freely distributed to anyone:

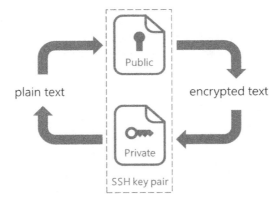

Figure 4.9 – A private key can decrypt information that's been encrypted with a public key

Using this property of the SSH key pair, you can configure your public key with a server so that it can use it for authentication. In a nutshell, when you try to connect to the server, the server will create a random challenge and encrypt it using the public portion of your key – the one you configured while provisioning the compute instance. You will have to decrypt that challenge using the private portion of the key, and then respond with an answer that will validate that you managed to decrypt the server's message. This flow will grant you access to the remote server over SSH.

There are multiple open source tools that can help you generate an SSH key pair on your local machine. Azure offers a very easy way to generate an SSH key pair on your browser, and then store the public portion of the key as a resource in the Azure portal. Let's take a look:

1. Navigate to `https://portal.azure.com` and click on the **Create a resource** button to add a new SSH key, similar to what you did in *Chapter 2, Deploying Azure Machine Learning Workspace Resources*, while provisioning the Azure ML workspace. Search for the SSH Key resource and click on **Create**:

Figure 4.10 – SSH key resource in the marketplace

2. Select the `packt-azureml-rg` resource group and provide a key-pair name, such as `azureml-compute`. Click on **Review + create** to navigate to the last step of the wizard:

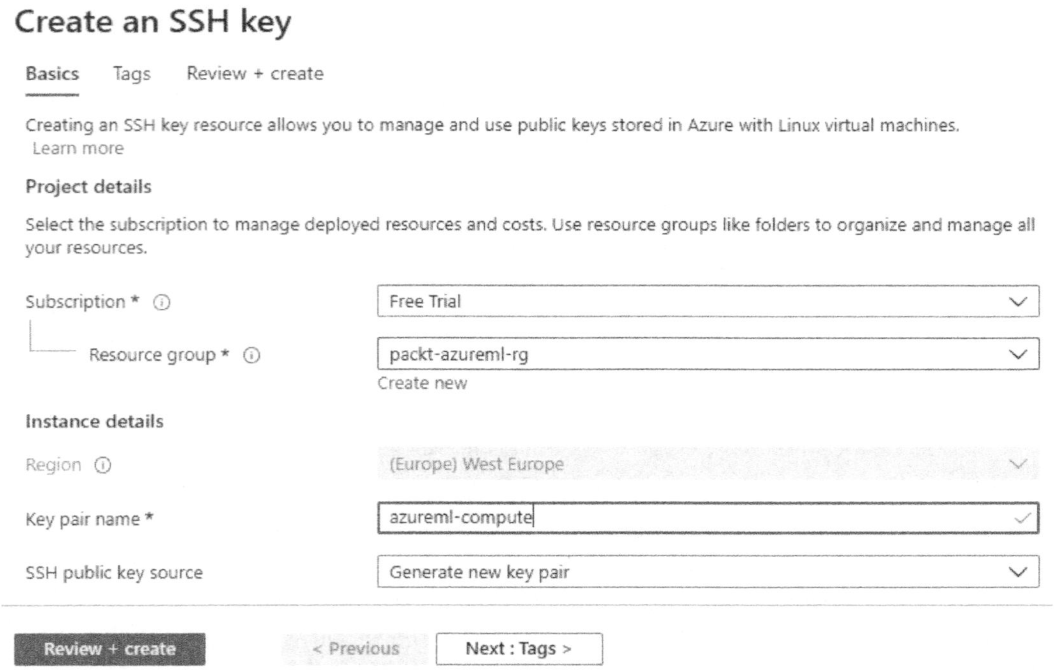

Create an SSH key

Basics   Tags   Review + create

Creating an SSH key resource allows you to manage and use public keys stored in Azure with Linux virtual machines.
Learn more

Project details

Select the subscription to manage deployed resources and costs. Use resource groups like folders to organize and manage all your resources.

Subscription * ⓘ	Free Trial ▾
Resource group * ⓘ	packt-azureml-rg ▾
	Create new

Instance details

Region ⓘ	(Europe) West Europe ▾
Key pair name *	azureml-compute|
SSH public key source	Generate new key pair ▾

Review + create   < Previous   Next : Tags >

Figure 4.11 – Generating an SSH key pair

3. Select **Create** to start the key generation process. The public and private portion of the key are generated in memory of your browser. A pop-up will prompt you to download the private key portion of the SSH key pair. Click on **Download private key and create resource** button. This will make your browser download a file named `azureml-compute.pem`. Make sure you store the file in a secure location:

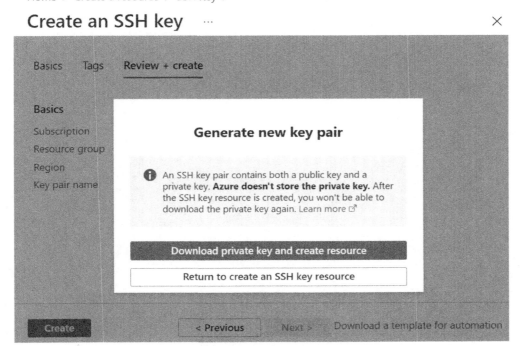

Figure 4.12 – Storing the private portion of the SSH key

Once this process is done, an SSH key resource will appear in the resource group you selected on the wizard:

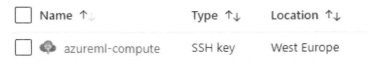

Figure 4.13 – The SSH key resource you deployed

In that resource, you can find the public portion of the SSH key, which you can copy and then paste into the compute instance provision wizard step you saw in the *Provisioning a compute instance* section:

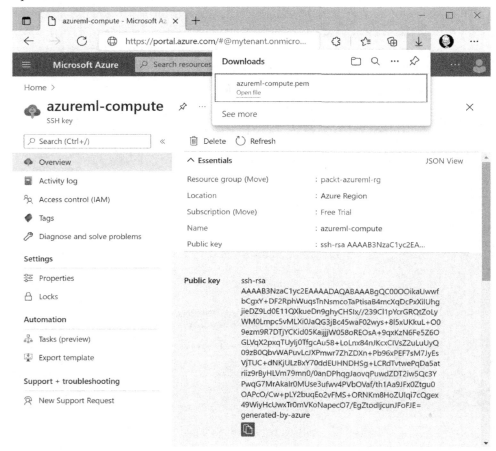

Figure 4.14 – The public portion of the generated key pair. At the top, you can see the downloaded private portion

> **Important note**
>
> The SSH key resource requires the `Microsoft.Compute` provider to be registered in the Azure subscription that you are planning to use. If you are the owner of the subscription, Azure will automatically register the providers for you when you deploy the resources; otherwise, you will need to request the subscription owner to register this provider for you while following the instructions provided in *Chapter 2, Deploying Azure Machine Learning Workspace Resources*.

So far, you have learned how to provision a compute instance and configure an SSH key, which will allow you to remote connect to that compute. You can also use this SSH key to connect to remote clusters, which you will provision in the next section, *Compute clusters*. In the following subsection, you will learn about the advanced configuration options of the compute instance provisioning wizard.

Advanced compute instance settings

In the compute provisioning wizard, you can optionally configure some advanced settings. One of them, is the **Enable virtual network** option, which allows you to attach the provisioned compute within a virtual network and to a specific subnet of that network, as shown in the following screenshot:

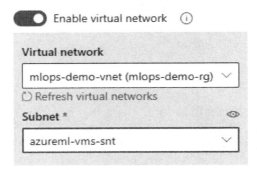

Figure 4.15 – Attaching the compute instance to a specific subnet

This feature unlocks multiple advanced networking topologies. The most common one is when you are planning to access data sources that are not accessible over the internet. For example, if you have a storage account that you have firewall-protected to deny access over the internet, you normally deploy a **private endpoint** in a specific subnet to allow access to that specific storage account. When you provision your compute instance and configure it to be on the same subnet using the preceding option, the compute instance will be able to access the protected storage account, as shown in the following diagram:

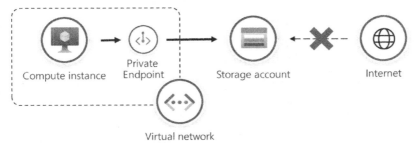

Figure 4.16 – Accessing a storage account that is only accessible through a private endpoint

Another advanced option shown in the wizard is **Assign to another user**. This option ties back to the *Creating custom roles* section of *Chapter 2, Deploying Azure Machine Learning Workspace Resources*, where you learned how to create custom roles for your Azure ML workspace. In enterprise environments, it is common to not allow end users to deploy whatever compute instance they want. This is done by creating a custom role and allowing only the following operations for the virtual machines:

- **Microsoft.Compute/virtualMachines/start/action**

- **Microsoft.Compute/virtualMachines/restart/action**

- **Microsoft.Compute/virtualMachines/deallocate/action**

In those environments, an administrator (or someone who has the **Microsoft.Compute/virtualMachines/write** permission) can provision compute instances and assign them to a specific person who may not be able to provision the compute instance on their own, as shown in the following screenshot:

Figure 4.17 – Assigning the provisioned compute instance to a fellow data scientist

Although this is a nice feature that the web interface wizard provides, it doesn't scale well when you need to provision multiple compute instances for multiple data scientists. Therefore, most of the time, administrators prefer to deploy compute instances through **ARM template** deployment. They can generate and download the template through this wizard and then deploy it for multiple users using the **Azure CLI** and pass the user ID as a parameter, as you saw in *Chapter 2, Deploying Azure Machine Learning Workspace Resources*.

So far, you have seen how to provision a compute instance. In the next section, you will learn how to manage compute instances.

Managing your compute instances

Once you have provisioned at least a single compute instance, the **Manage | Compute | Compute instances** interface changes to a list that shows the available instances in the workspace. By default, the list is filtered to show only the instances that you can use, meaning those that you provisioned on your own or someone else provisioned on your behalf:

Figure 4.18 – Compute instances list

From here, you can start, stop, restart, and delete the compute instances. When you start a compute instance, the resource's status changes to **Running** and the **Applications** column offers links to open a Terminal on the compute instance or open the Jupyter, JupyterLab, RStudio, and VS Code third-party authoring experiences.

Before you open any of those three editing experiences, you will have to accept an important notice regarding the code you can execute in those environments, as shown in the following screenshot:

Figure 4.19 – Warning message about the code you execute within Azure ML Studio

It is important for you to understand that if you download a random script from the internet, it may contain malicious code, which may enable others to steal data or even access tokens from your account, something that may enable them to access Azure resources on your behalf.

JupyterLab and Jupyter are very popular authoring experiences for Jupyter notebooks, Python script editing, and accessing the terminal to execute various commands, as shown in the following screenshot. When you click to open these editing experiences, a new browser tab will open. If you take a look at the URL on the new browser tab, you will notice that it consists of the compute instance's name, the region where this compute instance is located, and the suffix **instances.azureml.ms**. This is the reason why, in the previous section, *Provisioning a compute instance*, when you were provisioning a compute instance, you had to select a name that had to be unique within the Azure region where you are deploying the specific compute instance.

All these third-party authoring experiences have a strong community around them, and you can use them if you are already familiar with them. However, note that Azure ML offers the **Author | Notebooks** experience, an augmented editing experience on top of JupyterLab that adds capabilities such as IntelliSense, something you will be using from *Chapter 7, The Azure ML Python SDK*, onward:

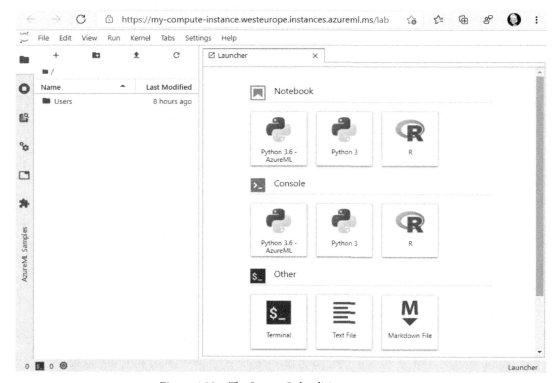

Figure 4.20 – The JupyterLab editing experience

Clicking on the **Terminal** link in the **Applications** columns will open a new browser tab. You will be transferred to the **Author | Notebooks** section. Here, a web-based terminal will open, allowing you to issue commands to the compute instance:

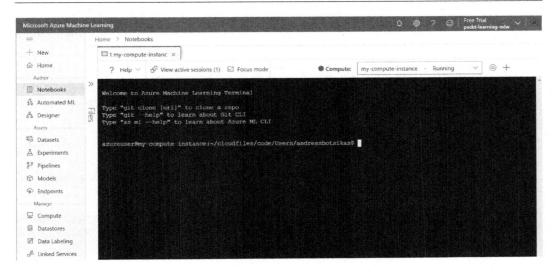

Figure 4.21 – Getting access to a terminal through the browser

When you don't need the compute instance, such as during the weekend, you can stop it to avoid incurring costs. The compute instance will transition to the **Stopped** status and the **Applications** links will be disabled. Starting a stopped compute instance takes some time.

If you have finished working with a compute instance, such as when the research phase of the project has been completed, you can **Delete** it to deallocate the reserved CPU cores that count against your subscription's quota. You can view the current quota by clicking on the corresponding **View quota** option from the menu shown in *Figure 4.18*.

For now, you can stop your compute instance. You will start it again in the *Data drift detection* section:

Name	State	Applications
my-compute-instance	⊘ Stopped	JupyterLab Jupyter VS Code RStudio Terminal

Figure 4.22 – Stopped compute instance

In this section, you learned how to provision and manage a compute instance that will provide you with the necessary computational power to author notebooks and scripts, as well as potentially execute small-scale training and inference pipelines. In the next section, you will learn how to provision a compute cluster, a compute resource that will be able to scale up and down to accommodate multiple training and inference pipelines in parallel.

Compute clusters

A compute cluster is a group of interconnected virtual machines that scale out and in to accommodate a queue of tasks. This means that the cluster can have only a few or even zero nodes in it to avoid incurring costs when it's not needed, and it can also scale out to multiple nodes when you want to run a lot of tasks in parallel or perform a distributed ML training process.

The creation process is very similar to provisioning a compute instance. Let's take a look:

1. Start by clicking the **New** button in the corresponding **Compute clusters** tab, as shown in *Figure 4.23*.

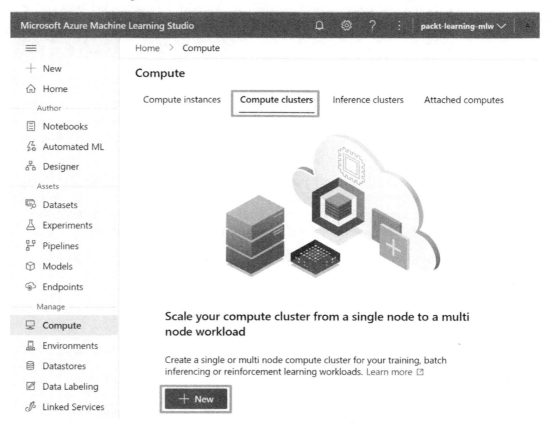

Figure 4.23 – Creating a new compute cluster

2. You will notice that the compute cluster provisioning wizard offers one additional option in comparison to the compute instances called **Virtual machine priority**, as shown in the following screenshot. Low-priority virtual machines take advantage of the surplus capacity in the Azure region where you want to provision a compute cluster. These virtual machines offer a significantly reduced price compared to dedicated VMs, but the compute nodes are not guaranteed to be available when you need them, or even if they will remain in your possession until the scheduled job is completed. This means that you may need to wait a long time until you can allocate such a VM, and a step in your training process may stop in the middle of its execution. Given these characteristics of low-priority VMs, you normally use this type of cluster when you have jobs that are not time-sensitive and consist of small running steps, or steps that automatically persist their state and can resume execution if they are evicted. For the purposes of this book, you can select the **Dedicated** option to avoid unexpected long waiting times when allocating compute nodes.

3. In the **Virtual machine type** option, select **GPU** and select the cheapest VM size available from the **Select from recommended options** list seen in *Figure 4.24*.

> **Important note**
>
> By default, free trial subscriptions do not allow you to provision GPU computes. Even if you change to a pay-as-you-go subscription, you will need to make a request through the Azure portal to increase your quota. If you run into a lack of quota issue, you can select CPU-based computes instead of GPU-based ones. For the purposes of this book, you do not need GPU-based clusters.

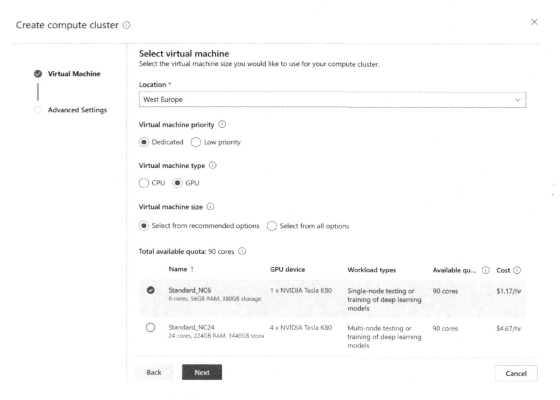

Figure 4.24 – The first page of the compute cluster provisioning wizard

4. Click **Next** to continue to the second page of the wizard:

5. On the second page of the wizard, you will need to specify a cluster name. This name is going to be how you reference this cluster in the web experience and through code, so make sure it's something that represents what this cluster is meant for, such as gpu-cluster:

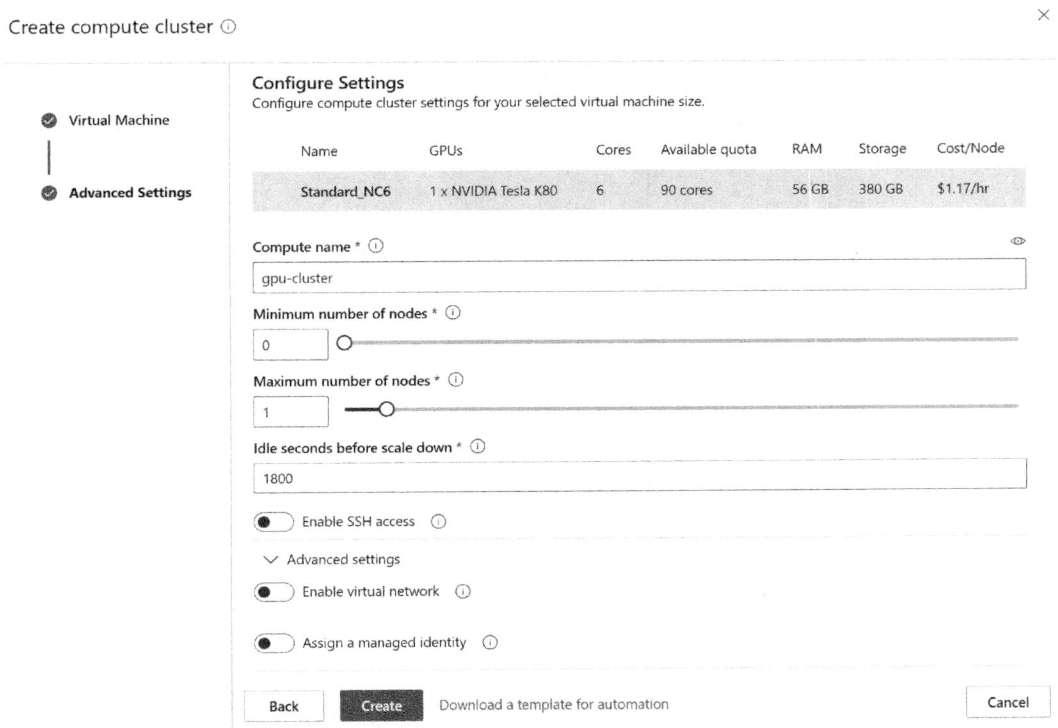

Create compute cluster ⓘ

Configure Settings
Configure compute cluster settings for your selected virtual machine size.

- ✓ Virtual Machine

- ✓ **Advanced Settings**

Name	GPUs	Cores	Available quota	RAM	Storage	Cost/Node
Standard_NC6	1 x NVIDIA Tesla K80	6	90 cores	56 GB	380 GB	$1.17/hr

Compute name * ⓘ

> gpu-cluster

Minimum number of nodes * ⓘ

> 0

Maximum number of nodes * ⓘ

> 1

Idle seconds before scale down * ⓘ

> 1800

(●) Enable SSH access ⓘ

∨ Advanced settings

(●) Enable virtual network ⓘ

(●) Assign a managed identity ⓘ

| Back | Create | Download a template for automation | Cancel |

Figure 4.25 – The second page of the compute cluster provisioning wizard

You can also tweak the minimum and maximum number of nodes and the idle seconds before the cluster scales down. Every time you request the cluster to perform a job, the tasks of the job are added to the cluster's scheduler. If the cluster doesn't have enough nodes to execute the scheduled tasks, it will scale out by adding a compute node to the cluster. Adding a node to the cluster takes some time, as you need to allocate the VM. Therefore, instead of deallocating the VM immediately once the scheduled tasks have completed, the cluster can wait for the defined idle period, just in case a new task gets scheduled.

Similar to the compute instances, you can **Enable SSH access** if you want to remotely connect to the compute cluster nodes to troubleshoot job executions. Due to the ephemeral nature of the cluster nodes, the wizard allows you to specify an **Admin password** if you want, instead of a **SSH public key**, as shown in the following screenshot:

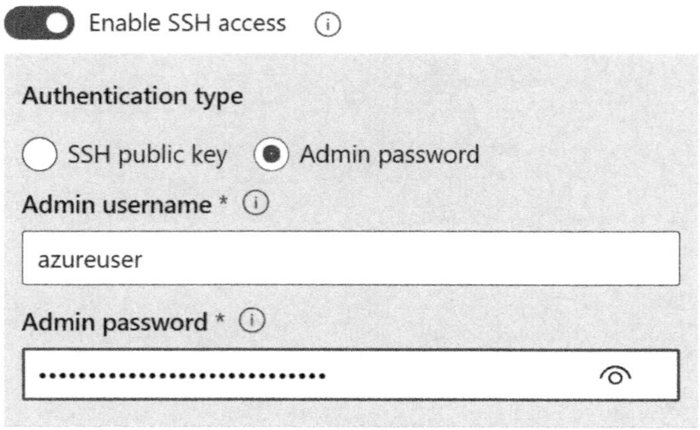

Figure 4.26 – Compute clusters allow you to use an Admin password instead of an SSH public key

Under **Advanced settings**, you can find the **Enable virtual network** option, which you saw when we looked at compute instances in the previous section. In addition to that option, you have the option to **Assign a managed identity** to the compute cluster:

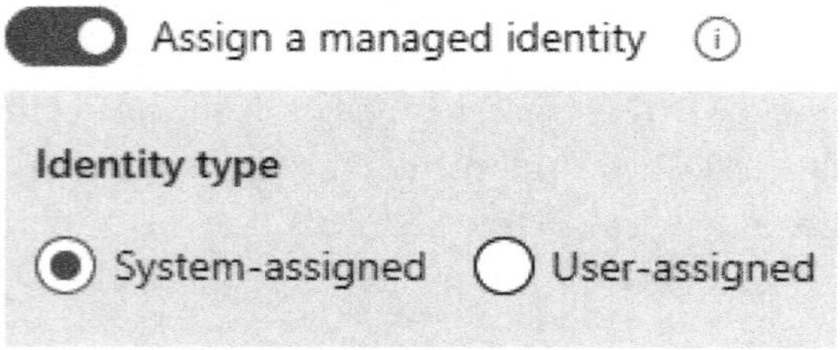

Figure 4.27 – Assigning a managed identity to the compute cluster

Azure allows you to attach an **Azure Active Directory (AAD)** identity to the compute cluster nodes, allowing the code that executes in those VMs to access Azure resources using that identity. **Managed identities** eliminate the need to have credentials stored within your scripts. The identity is attached to the specific VM, and your code can request AAD access tokens through the Azure Instance Metadata Service or through the Python SDK without a password, as long as the code is executed within that specific VM.

6. For the purposes of this book, you will not modify any option here. Name the cluster `gpu-cluster` and click on **Create** to create your first zero node, GPU-based compute cluster:

Compute

Compute instances   **Compute clusters**   Inference clusters   Attached compute

+ New   ◯ Refresh   🗑 Delete   ⬚⬚ View quota   ▽ Search to filter items...

Name	Provisioning state	Virtual machine size	Created on ↓	Idle nodes	Busy nodes	Unprovisioned nodes
gpu-cluster	✔ Succeeded (0 nodes)	STANDARD_NC6	6 Dec 2020 04:32	0	0	1

Figure 4.28 – Your first GPU-based compute cluster is ready to use

Notice that in the preceding screenshot, the compute cluster has been provisioned successfully but that there are 0 nodes in it, which means that it doesn't incur any cost. You can also see the following metrics in this list:

- **Idle nodes**: These are the nodes waiting for a task to be scheduled or to be de-allocated once the idle time has passed.

- **Busy nodes**: These are the nodes that are currently executing a task.

- **Unprovisioned nodes**: These are the nodes that haven't been allocated yet but can potentially be allocated if the number of scheduled tasks increases.

From this list, you can delete the cluster if you don't want it anymore.

If you click on the compute cluster's name, you will be able to see the cluster's details, as shown in the following screenshot. From this view, you can edit the minimum and maximum number of nodes, the idle seconds before the cluster scales down, and change how the managed identity that you configured previously is assigned. In fact, it is common for data science teams to modify their predefined compute clusters in the morning so that they have at least one node in them. It helps them avoid waiting for the first node to be allocated. When the day is over, they change the setting down to zero to save on costs:

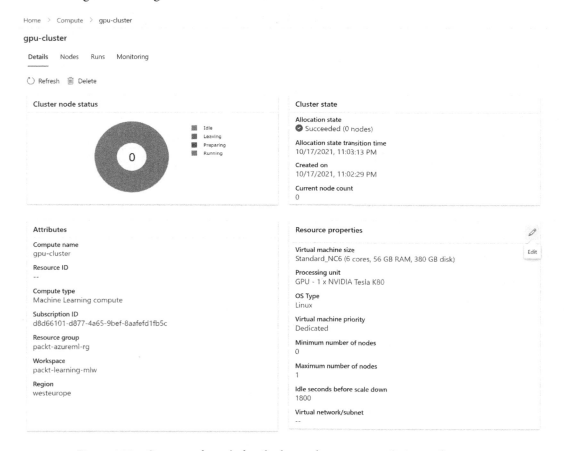

Figure 4.29 – Compute cluster's details about where you can edit its configuration

In this section, you learned how to provision a compute cluster. These clusters are used to perform training jobs and batch inferences. In the next section, you will learn how to provision an **Azure Kubernetes Service (AKS)**, which allows you to perform real-time inferences at a large scale.

Inference clusters

Kubernetes is a portable, extensible, open source platform for managing containerized workloads and services. It has been widely used to operationalize various forms of applications, from web applications to model inference REST APIs, due to its ability to auto scale and auto recover from failures. **Azure Kubernetes Service (AKS)** is the managed version of the Kubernetes cluster in Azure, a service that lets you focus on your workload and let Azure manage the operating bits of the cluster, such as its master nodes.

If you are not familiar with AKS, then don't worry – the following diagram provides a high-level overview of the components involved. In a nutshell, you can configure **Node pools**, a group of virtual machines that have the same configuration; for example, virtual machines with GPU cards on them. These pools can have one **node** (or more), which is a virtual machine. Within each node, you can host one or more **pods**. Each pod consists of a couple of **Docker images**, which form an application unit, one of which may be the model you want to operationalize. Each pod can be replicated into multiple nodes, either to accommodate increased load or for resiliency reasons in the case a node goes down:

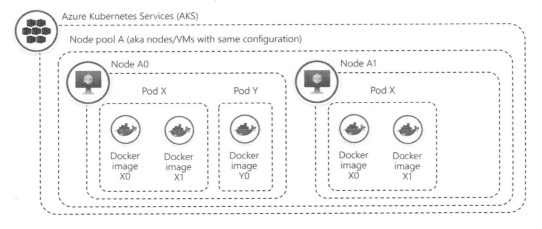

Figure 4.30 – High-level overview of AKS concepts showing Pod X being replicated in two nodes

From within Azure ML Studio, you can create or attach an existing AKS cluster to your workspace. You do *not* need to create an AKS cluster for the purposes of this book. Let's get started:

1. The creation wizard can be invoked by clicking on the **New** button in the **Inference clusters** tab, seen in *Figure 4.31*:

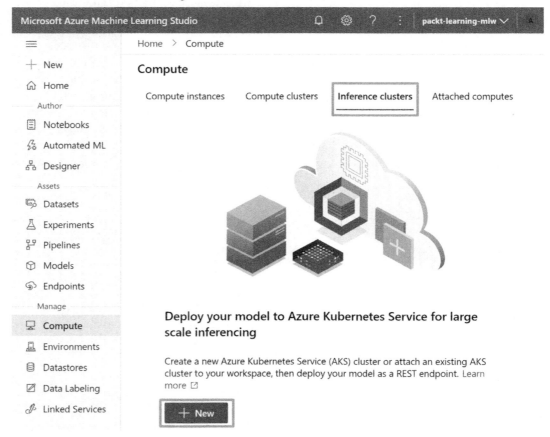

Figure 4.31 – Create or attach an AKS cluster to the Azure ML workspace

> **Important note**
>
> When you provision an AKS cluster, a new resource group is created within your Azure subscription that hosts all the components needed for AKS to work. This requires additional permissions at the subscription level. If you can't create resource groups, AKS cluster provisioning will fail.

2. In the first step of the wizard, you can either attach an existing AKS cluster or create a new one. If you choose to create one, you will have to specify the Azure region where you want the AKS cluster to be deployed. You will also need to specify the node pool's VM size, similar to what you did when you deployed a compute instance:

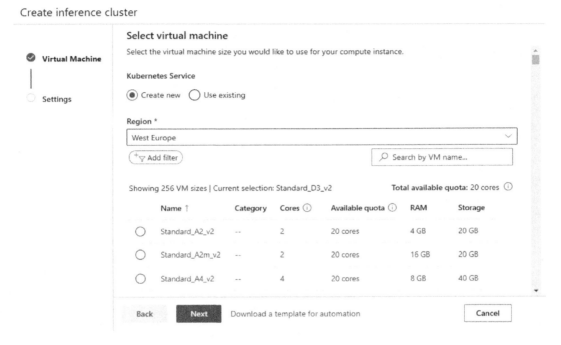

Figure 4.32 – Step 1 of provisioning an inference AKS cluster

3. Clicking **Next** will bring you to the **Settings** page, where you need to specify the name of the AKS cluster. You also need to specify the purpose of the cluster. If this is a production cluster, the number of virtual CPUs in the cluster must be more than 12; this means that if you selected a 4 core VM size, you will need at least three nodes to be able to provision a production-ready AKS cluster. If this cluster is for development and testing, you can provision just one node.

4. Besides the name and the number of nodes in the node pool, you can configure the networking options of the cluster and the SSL certificate that will be used to secure the connection to the applications, if you want to expose them through an HTTPS endpoint. For the purposes of this book, you do not need to modify any of those options:

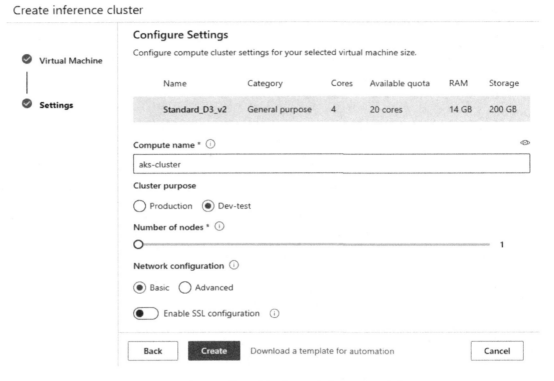

Figure 4.33 – Step 2 of provisioning an inference AKS cluster

5. Once your cluster has been created, you will be able to delete it or detach it from the workspace through the list shown in the following screenshot:

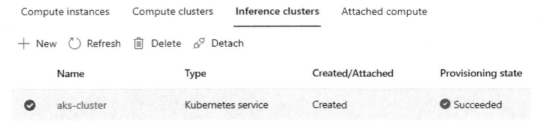

Figure 4.34 – List of AKS inference clusters

> **Important note**
>
> AKS is the production-ready way of deploying real-time endpoints. In the
> exam, when you are asked where you would deploy a production load,
> AKS should be the right answer. Nonetheless, because an AKS cluster is an
> expensive resource, this book will not use it in its examples. If you are using
> a free subscription, you will probably not have enough cores quota to be able to
> provision one. If you did provision one, make sure you keep an eye on the cost
> to avoid running out of credit.

In this section, you learned about how Azure ML can help you attach to or provision an
AKS cluster so that you can host your production real-time inference endpoints. In the
next section, you will learn how to attach existing compute resources to your workspace.

Attached compute

If you already have compute resources provisioned, not necessarily in the subscription
you have deployed your Azure ML workspace, you can attach them to your workspace.
Attaching those resources allows you to reuse them, especially in cases where they are
underutilized. A common scenario is for a department to have an Ubuntu-based **Data
Science Virtual Machine** (**DSVM**), which may be running 24 hours, 7 days of the week,
to serve a legacy web application. You can reuse this resource in your experiments by
attaching it to your workspace and then referencing it to execute various tasks, the same
way you would reference a compute cluster to perform a task.

The studio experience allows you to attach multiple types of computes, including the
following popular targets:

- **Virtual machines**: You can attach existing Ubuntu-based virtual machines that are
  publicly accessible over the internet. This option includes potential DSVMs you may
  already have.

- **Azure Databricks** and **HDInsights**: These options allow you to attach existing
  Apache Spark-based computes to your workspace.

- **Azure Data Factory**: The Azure Data Factory resource allows you to perform copy
  activities from one data source to another. For example, you can copy from a storage
  account to a SQL database using that resource. Azure Data Factory is currently only
  supported through the Azure ML SDK and not from the studio experience.

For the purposes of the DP100 exam, you will not need to attach any resources. The following screenshot shows how you can initiate the attach wizard from within the studio experience:

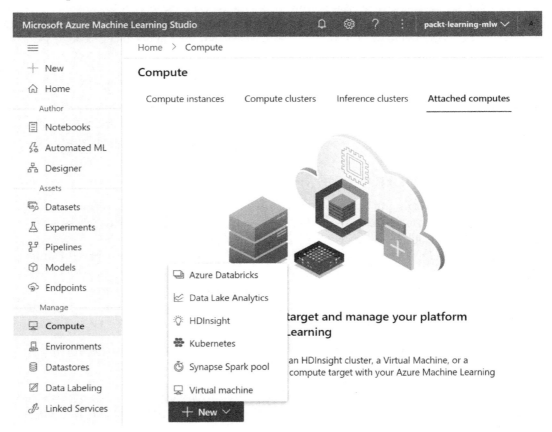

Figure 4.35 – Attaching existing compute resources to your workspace

In this section, you learned how to provision and attach compute resources to your Azure ML workspace. This allows you to execute code during the data exploration, model training, and model inference phases of your data science projects. In the next section, you will learn how to configure connectivity to various data sources, something that will enable you to access data.

Connecting to datastores

Datastores are the engines where your data resides and provide access to anyone authorized to do so. In most Python examples you see on the internet, there is a connection string that contains the credentials to connect to a database or a blob store. There are a couple of drawbacks associated with this technique:

- The credentials stored within these scripts are considered a security violation, and you can accidentally expose your protected datasets by publishing a script in a public repository such as GitHub.

- You need to manually update all the scripts when the credentials change.

Azure ML allows you to have a single centralized location where you define the connection properties to various stores. Your credentials are securely stored as **secrets** within the workspace's associated **key vault**. In your scripts, you reference the datastore using its name and you can access its data without having to specify the credentials. If, at some point in time, the credentials of a datastore change, you can centrally update them, and all your scripts and pipelines will continue to work.

You can view all the registered datastores by navigating to the **Manage | Datastores** section of the studio:

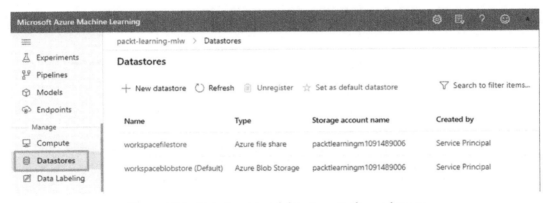

Figure 4.36 – List of registered datastores in the workspace

Note that, by default, you already have two datastores registered. The default one, named `workspaceblobstore`, is the default blob storage where all the pipeline metrics and artifacts are stored. Your workspace needs to have a default datastore. As you will see in *Chapter 7, The Azure ML Python SDK*, you can even reference that store very easily through the Python SDK. The other store, named `workspacefilestore`, is a file share datastore that you can mount on your local machine and upload files to.

From this list, you can do the following:

- Update the credentials of a datastore: You need to click on the name of the datastore, which will get you its registration details. From there, you can click on **Update credentials** to specify the updated value or change the type of authentication, something you will see in the next section.

- **Unregister** a datastore: You can unregister any datastore that is not marked as the default datastore.

- **Set as default datastore**: Change the default datastore to the one you selected from the list.

Finally, from this list, you can create a **New datastore** registration, an action that activates the new datastore wizard shown in the following screenshot:

Figure 4.37 – New datastore wizard

Here, you need to specify a unique datastore name within the Azure ML workspace. You must do this to reference this store in your scripts and the various components of the studio experience. The next thing you need to select is the datastore type. There are a couple of Azure-native datastores that are supported by the Azure ML workspace, something you will explore in the next section.

Types of datastores

Azure ML supports two categories of datastores: the ones based on files, such as blob storage, file shares, and data lake stores, and relational databases, such as Azure SQL and Azure PostgreSQL.

The currently supported datastores are shown in the following diagram:

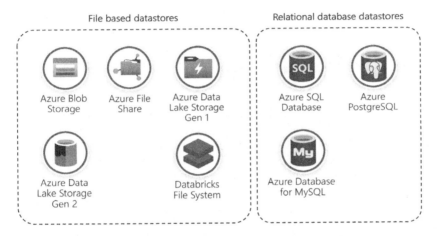

Figure 4.38 – Azure ML supported datastores

The recommendation is to use **Azure Blob Storage**-based datastores. These stores are the most cost-effective ones. They provide multiple tiers, such as the more expensive premium one, which provides you with increased throughput speeds, something that can reduce your training times if you are processing large volumes of data.

On the other hand, **Azure Data Lake Storage Gen 2** builds on top of **Azure Blob Storage** by adding hierarchical namespaces. This feature allows data lakes to assign access permissions at a folder level. Large enterprises usually structure their data lakes with various zones where they store their data. Each zone has its own **Access Control List (ACL)**, which gives permissions to specific groups of people. This means that you may be able to see the contents of one folder and not the contents of another, while in **Azure Blob Storage**, once you get access to a container, you can see all the data within it.

If your data resides in a datastore that is not supported out of the box by Azure ML, you can copy the data over to an **Azure Blob Storage** or **Azure Data Lake Storage Gen 2** easily using the copy tool from **Azure Data Factory**. **Azure Data Factory** allows you to copy data from almost anywhere, even if it resides within on-premises databases, as shown in the following diagram:

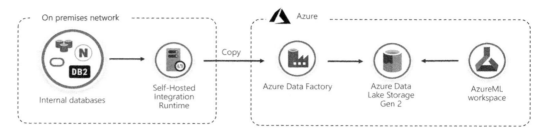

Figure 4.39 – Copying on-premises data to an Azure ML supported datastore using Azure Data Factory and the Self-Hosted Integration Runtime

> **Important note**
>
> In the *Attached compute* section, you saw that you can attach an **Azure Data Factory** (**ADF**) through the Azure ML SDK. Attaching ADF allows you to copy data between Azure ML supported datastores through code using `DataTransferStep`. Copying data from the on-premises network can be done in the same ADF, but you will have to author, execute, and monitor the data pulling pipeline from within ADF.

In this section, you look at the types of datastores supported by Azure ML. In the next section, you will learn about the various authentication methods supported by those datastores.

Datastore security considerations

Depending on the datastore, you will have to specify different type of credentials to register it in the Azure ML workspace. For the Azure Blob and Azure File Share datastores, you can use the following credentials:

- **Account key**: This gives access to the entire Azure Storage Account.
- **Shared Access Signature** (**SAS**) **token**: This is a more granular way to assign permissions to the various services of the storage account. Using the **Account key**, you can generate an SAS token that allows access to only a specific blob container and only for a limited amount of time.

For Azure Data Lake Storage datastores, due to their advanced security features, you will need to provide an **Azure Active Directory** identity, which will be accessing the data. This is a **service principal** that is uniquely identified by the **Azure Active Directory** Tenant ID (referred to as `tenant_id`) where this entity is registered and has a unique ID (referred to as `client_id`). This identity has a password (referred to as `client_secret`) that enables your code to access the datastores impersonating that identity.

For the relational database datastores, you will need to specify the database's name, the server's name, and the server port to connect to. For credentials, you can either provide a **service principal**, if the datastore supports it, or provide the necessary **SQL authentication** credentials, which consist of a database user ID and a password.

Some of the datastores allow you to use the workspace's managed identity for data preview and profiling. This option adds the system assigned managed identity that has been assigned to the workspace as a Reader to the specific resource, allowing the workspace to load a preview of the data within the studio experience. This option is available on the datastore registration page, as shown in the following screenshot:

Use workspace managed identity for data preview and profiling in Azure Machine Learning studio ⓘ

Figure 4.40 – Granting access to the workspace's managed identity

So far, you have learned how to register various datastores in an Azure ML workspace. In the next section, you will learn how to use these registrations to define datasets.

Working with datasets

In the previous sections, you were configuring compute and datastore resources under the **Manage** section of the studio. With this infrastructure configured, you can start pulling data into your registered datastores and register datasets in the **Assets** section of the studio:

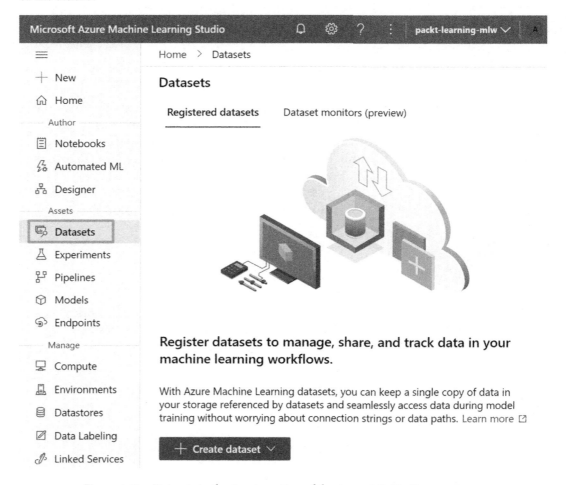

Figure 4.41 – Datasets in the Assets section of the Azure ML Studio experience

Datasets is an abstraction layer on top of the data that you are using for training and inference. It contains a reference to the physical data's location and provides a series of metadata that can help you understand their shape and statistical properties. When you want to access the dataset, you can reference it via its name, and you don't have to worry about credentials or exact file paths. Moreover, all the data scientists working on the same workspace can access the same datasets, allowing them to experiment on the same data in parallel.

There are two types of datasets – file-based ones and tabular ones. File datasets reference a list of files in a datastore. For example, if you are building a computer vision model, you will need images that can be downloaded or mounted to your compute as a `FileDataset`. The Tabular dataset represents tabular data residing in either file-based datastores or relational database datastores. For example, you can reference a couple of folders containing **Comma-Separated Value (CSV)** files and you can read all the records as a pandas **DataFrame** through the `TabularDataset` construct, without having to parse the physical files.

Another feature of datasets is that you can snapshot their properties and metadata using versions. Imagine that you have a folder structure that follows the `weather/<year>/<month>/` pattern. For example, you would find the weather measurements for January 2021 stored under `weather/2021/01/measurements.parquet`. As time flies, you will be getting more and more folders, each containing a single file under them. To reproduce your training results, you will want to reference the dataset that only contains files up to January 2021. This is exactly where dataset versioning comes in handy. While training a model, you register a version of the dataset that contains all the files you used for training. Later, you can refer to the dataset and request a specific version of it, which will give you a reference to all the files that used to be available back then.

> **Important note**
> Dataset versions do *not* copy the underlying data. They only store a reference to the actual files and the dataset metadata you will read about in the upcoming sections. This means that if you change the contents of a file instead of adding a new file, the dataset version will not load the same data.

Registering datasets

You can register datasets from various sources, as shown in the following screenshot, including from the datastore you learned how to register in the *Connecting to datastores* section:

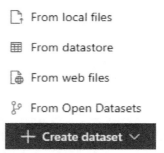

Figure 4.42 – Possible options for registering datasets

To get a better understanding of how the dataset registration process works, we are going to register two tabular datasets that are hosted on the web. These datasets consist of a single **parquet** file each. We will use these two datasets later in this chapter to understand the data drift detection feature. Let's get started:

1. Select **From web files** from the menu shown in the preceding screenshot to start the **Create dataset from web files** wizard.

2. On the first page of the wizard, provide the following information:

   • **Web URL**: https://bit.ly/survey-drift-base

   • **Name**: survey-drift-base

   • **Dataset type**: Tabular

3.   Click **Next**:

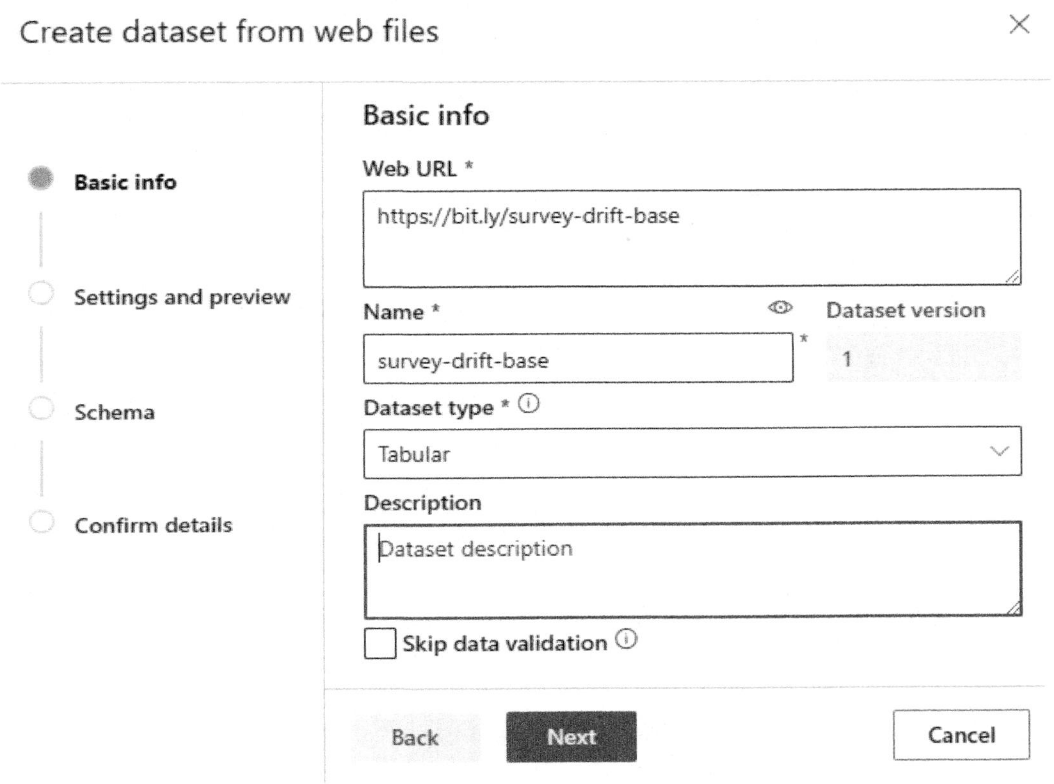

Create dataset from web files   ✕

Basic info

○ **Basic info**

Web URL *

https://bit.ly/survey-drift-base

○ Settings and preview

Name *   👁   Dataset version

survey-drift-base   1

○ Schema

Dataset type * ⓘ

Tabular   ⌄

○ Confirm details

Description

Dataset description

☐ Skip data validation ⓘ

Back   Next   Cancel

Figure 4.43 – The first step of the dataset registration wizard

4. The wizard will parse the file and figure out the file type and the schema of your dataset. You will need to validate the selection by clicking **Next**. Note that the wizard supports multiple file formats, as shown in the following screenshot:

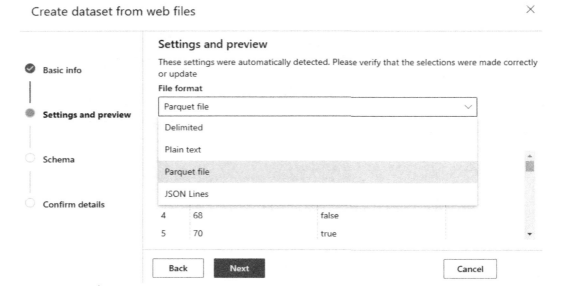

Figure 4.44 – The second step of the dataset registration wizard

5. In the next step, you can define advanced options regarding the schema. For the baseline dataset, leave the default options as-is. Click **Next**, which will lead you to the confirmation step.

6. In this step, you can review your selections in the previous steps, and you can also schedule your first data science analysis task – profiling the dataset. This process generates the profile that you will explore in the next section. Enable the option and select gpu-cluster, which you provisioned in the previous section, as shown in the following screenshot:

> **Important note**
>
> Within the **Select compute for profiling** option, you can select from both the compute instances and the compute clusters you provisioned in the *Compute instances* and *Compute clusters* sections. Selecting the compute cluster will force the cluster to scale from zero nodes to one node, analyze the dataset, and then scale down to zero nodes again. If you want, you can navigate to the **Manage | Compute** section and observe this scale out by clicking on the compute cluster's name. If you select the compute instance instead of the compute cluster, the job will be scheduled, and it will be executed when the compute instance starts.

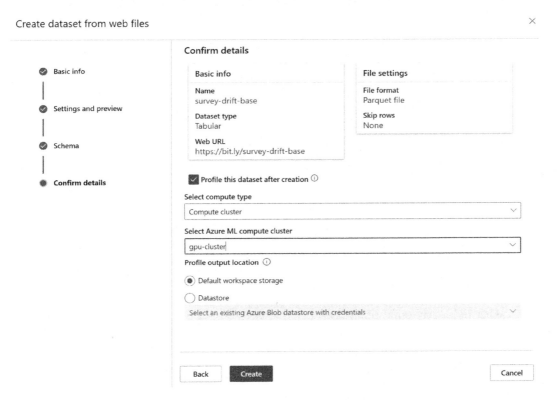

Figure 4.45 – Last step of the dataset registration process

You will need to register one more dataset. The process here is almost identical, only this time, you will mark the dataset as a time series one:

1. Click on **Create dataset** and select **From web files**, as shown in the following screenshot:

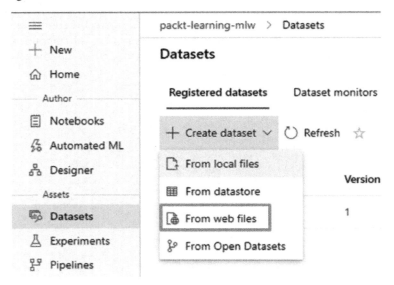

Figure 4.46 – Create dataset menu in the dataset list

2. Follow the same steps as you did previously and input the following information:

   - **Web URL**: `https://bit.ly/survey-drift-target`

   - **Name**: `survey-drift-target`

3. During the schema step, make sure that you select **Timestamp** from the **Properties** section of the **inference_date** column, as shown in the following screenshot. This option flags this tabular dataset as a **time series** dataset, something that allows you to perform additional analysis, as you will see in the *Data drift detection* section:

Create dataset from web files

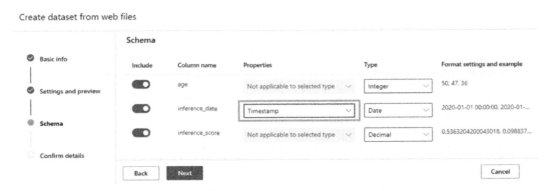

Figure 4.47 – Configuring a tabular dataset so that it becomes a time series dataset

4.   Schedule data profile analysis and complete the dataset registration process.

> **Important note**
>
> If you are following along, you may notice that for the **inference_date**
> column, you can specify either **Timestamp** of **Partition timestamp**. To mark
> your dataset as a **Time series** one, you will need to specify the **Timestamp**
> property in at least one **Date** column. In addition to that, if your data has
> been partitioned into a folder structure with time information, such as
> `year=2021/month=05/day=01/data.parquet`, you can create
> a virtual column through that path pattern and define that as your **Partition
> timestamp**. This improves the importance of time series functionality and
> allows you to load specific dates by selectively reading the required files only.

You should be able to see two registered datasets, as shown in the following screenshot:

Datasets

Registered datasets   Dataset monitors (preview)

+ Create dataset ∨   ↻ Refresh   ☆ Unregister   ▽ Search to filter items...

Name	Version	Data source	Created on	Modified on	Properties
survey-drift-target	1	URI	Dec 10, 2020 4:21 AM	Dec 10, 2020 4:21 AM	Tabular, Time series
survey-drift-base	1	URI	Dec 10, 2020 4:08 AM	Dec 10, 2020 4:08 AM	Tabular

Figure 4.48 – List of registered datasets in the Azure ML workspace

From this view, you can select a dataset and then click on the **Unregister** button to remove the registration. Upon clicking on a dataset, you can view more details about it, including the profile analysis you performed on top of the datasets, something you will see in the next section.

Exploring the dataset

In the dataset list, click on the **survey-drift-target** dataset to open its details. In the first tab, **Details**, you can modify the description of the dataset and specify tags that are associated with the dataset. Tags are name-value pairs. In the following screenshot, you can see that we specified **survey** as the value of the **experiment** tag:

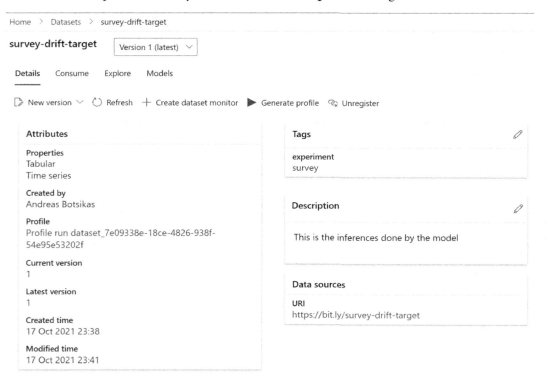

Figure 4.49 – Dataset details showing all the metadata associated with the specific dataset

In the **Consume** tab, you can copy the Python SDK code that you are going to use in *Chapter 7, The Azure ML Python SDK*, to get access to the dataset:

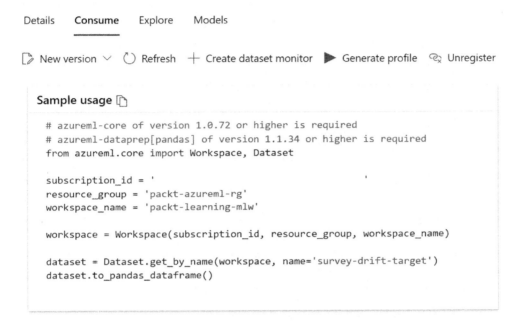

```
Details    Consume    Explore    Models
```

```
New version ∨    Refresh    + Create dataset monitor    ▶ Generate profile    Unregister
```

Sample usage

```
# azureml-core of version 1.0.72 or higher is required
# azureml-dataprep[pandas] of version 1.1.34 or higher is required
from azureml.core import Workspace, Dataset

subscription_id = '                                        '
resource_group = 'packt-azureml-rg'
workspace_name = 'packt-learning-mlw'

workspace = Workspace(subscription_id, resource_group, workspace_name)

dataset = Dataset.get_by_name(workspace, name='survey-drift-target')
dataset.to_pandas_dataframe()
```

Figure 4.50 – Consuming a snippet that gives access to the dataset

In the **Explore** tab, you will be able to preview a sample of the data that is included in the dataset, exactly as you saw during the registration process:

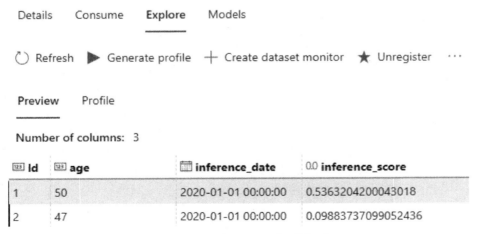

```
Details    Consume    Explore    Models
```

```
Refresh    ▶ Generate profile    + Create dataset monitor    ★ Unregister    ...
```

```
Preview    Profile
```

Number of columns: 3

Id	age	inference_date	inference_score
1	50	2020-01-01 00:00:00	0.5363204200043018
2	47	2020-01-01 00:00:00	0.09883737099052436

Figure 4.51 – Previewing a sample of the dataset

If you click on the **Profile** tab, you will be able to see the statistical analysis of the dataset, as shown in the following screenshot:

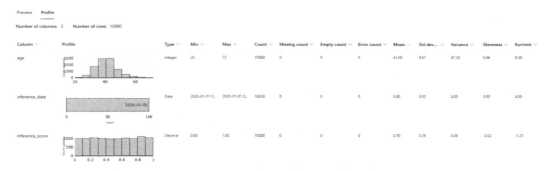

Figure 4.52 – Statistical analysis of the dataset

Important note

If your dataset contains fewer than 10,000 rows, profiling is done automatically for you, without you having to schedule the processing aspect for the dataset. If the dataset contains more than 10,000 rows, then Azure ML performs an analysis on the first 10,000 rows and shows a warning message that prompts you to schedule a complete profiling analysis, something you can do by clicking on the **Generate profile** button from the menu.

Finally, on the **Models** tab, you can see the models that relate to this dataset, something that you will do in *Chapter 5, Letting Machines do the Model Training*, when you will be registering the best model that you will be deploying as a web service.

Having registered a dataset, you can configure periodic monitoring for the dataset for data drifting, something you will learn about in the next section.

Data drift detection

Data drift detection is a technique that allows you to compare a time series dataset with a reference dataset, and then check whether the statistical properties of the features you are comparing have changed significantly. For example, let's assume that you trained an ML model that predicts if someone is going to participate in a survey based on their age. You used the `survey-drift-base` dataset to train that model. The following graph shows a density curve, which shows the distribution of age in the training dataset:

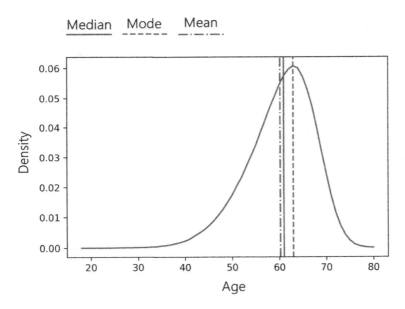

Figure 4.53 – Negative skewed unimodal distribution of the age feature in the training dataset

When you operationalized the model, you kept track of the inferences that it made on a weekly basis, and you logged this information in the `survey-drift-target` dataset, which you registered previously. This dataset contains the inferences that you did during the first 2 weeks of 2020. Data drift detection enables you to detect if the distribution of the input features changed over time. Let's take a look:

1. Navigate to **Assets | Datasets | Dataset monitors** and click on the **Create** button to start the dataset monitor wizard:

Figure 4.54 – Creating a new dataset monitor

2. On the target dataset, you will see all the registered time series datasets you want to monitor for data drift. This is the inference that your model has been doing in production. Select `survey-drift-target (Version:1)` and click **Next**:

Create new data drift monitor

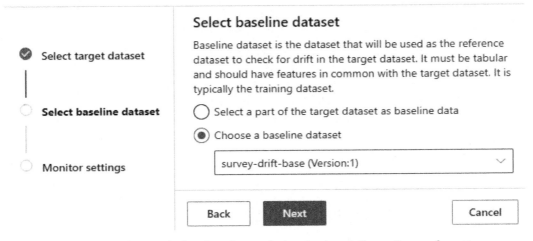

Select target dataset

Select target dataset

Select baseline dataset

Monitor settings

Target dataset refers to the dataset which will be monitored for drift. Every drift detection job that runs at a specified frequency (daily, weekly, or monthly) will compare the new data captured in respective the time interval to a baseline to detect drift.

Target dataset * (i)

survey-drift-target (Version:1)

Back   Next   Cancel

Figure 4.55 – The first step in data drift monitor configuration

3.   On the next page, you need to select your reference point. This can either be a specific point in time from within the time series tabular dataset or a specific dataset. In your case, select the `survey-drift-base (Version:1)` dataset, which is the dataset that was used to train the ML model:

Create new data drift monitor

Select target dataset

Select baseline dataset

Monitor settings

Select baseline dataset

Baseline dataset is the dataset that will be used as the reference dataset to check for drift in the target dataset. It must be tabular and should have features in common with the target dataset. It is typically the training dataset.

○ Select a part of the target dataset as baseline data

● Choose a baseline dataset

survey-drift-base (Version:1)

Back   Next   Cancel

Figure 4.56 – Selecting the baseline dataset during the data drift monitor configuration

4. In the last step of the wizard, you need to define the following information:

- **Name**: The name of the monitoring process you are about to configure. Name the process `survey-drift-monitor`.

- **Features**: Select one or more common features between the two datasets to monitor their distributions and whether there is data drift. In this case, the only common feature between the two datasets is the age feature.

- **Compute target**: The cluster that will be spinning up and down to perform the analysis.

- **Frequency**: The frequency specifies the time interval for the target data to be examined for drift. This property cannot be changed once the monitor has been created. You can choose between day, week, or month. Keep in mind that you need at fewer 50 samples per time interval to perform data drift analysis. This means that if you have less than 50 rows per day, you cannot use that as your frequency and you should opt for week, or even month, instead.

- **Latency**: It is common to have a delay between the actual scoring of a row and refreshing the target dataset. In this field, you specify how long to wait before assuming that the target dataset got the latest records; then, the monitor can perform data drift analysis.

- **Email address**: This is where to send an email if the dataset has drifted more than what's been specified for the **Threshold** parameter.

5. For the purposes of this book, you can disable the schedule, as shown in the following screenshot. You will manually run the data drift analysis.

6. Click on the **Create** button to create the monitor:

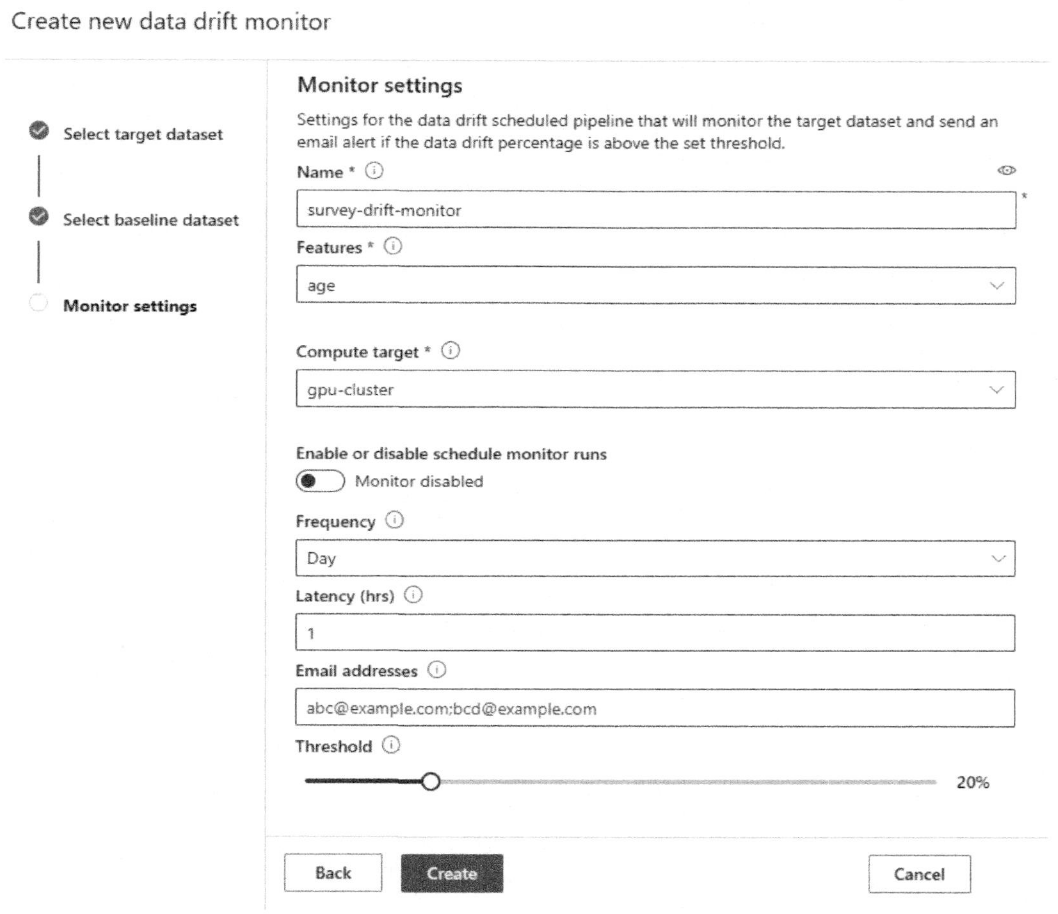

Create new data drift monitor

Monitor settings

Settings for the data drift scheduled pipeline that will monitor the target dataset and send an email alert if the data drift percentage is above the set threshold.

Name * ⓘ

survey-drift-monitor

Features * ⓘ

age

Compute target * ⓘ

gpu-cluster

Enable or disable schedule monitor runs

⬤ Monitor disabled

Frequency ⓘ

Day

Latency (hrs) ⓘ

1

Email addresses ⓘ

abc@example.com;bcd@example.com

Threshold ⓘ

20%

[Back] [Create] [Cancel]

Figure 4.57 – Data drift monitor settings

7. Click on the name of the new monitor you created from the monitor list:

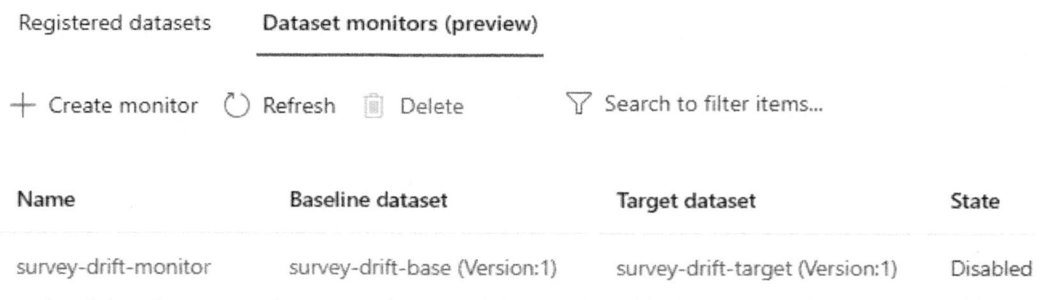

Registered datasets   **Dataset monitors (preview)**

+ Create monitor   ⟳ Refresh   🗑 Delete   ▽ Search to filter items...

Name	Baseline dataset	Target dataset	State
survey-drift-monitor	survey-drift-base (Version:1)	survey-drift-target (Version:1)	Disabled

Figure 4.58 – Data drift monitors list

The data drift monitor is meant to run on a schedule for new data. In your case, you want to analyze the existing data in the target dataset. Let's take a look:

1. Click on the **Analyze existing data** button, which will bring up the backfill wizard shown in the following screenshot:

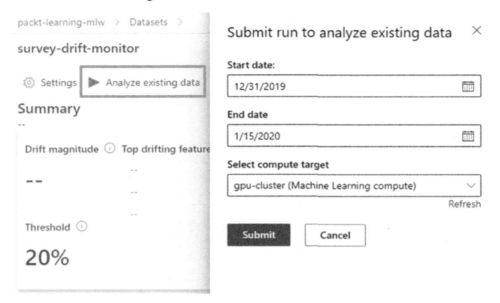

Figure 4.59 – Manually starting an analysis of past dates

2. Select from December 31, 2019 to January 15, 2020. This is the time range that contains all the records from the target dataset.

3. Select the compute cluster that will do the analysis.

4. Click **Submit**.

Once the analysis is complete, a process that will take some time, you will be able to see the data drift results, which indicate that a big data drift has been observed in our dataset. Note that the summary is referring to the latest inferences, which were done on January 5, 2020. You can manually select previous periods by clicking on the graphs for the corresponding dates:

Figure 4.60 – Data drift detected between the base dataset and the target one

If you scroll down to the feature distribution, you will be able to clearly see the distribution drift on the age feature. This indicates that the model is making inferences on a population that has different characteristics from the one it was trained on. This is a good indication that you may need to retrain the model, to bring it up to date with the new feature distribution:

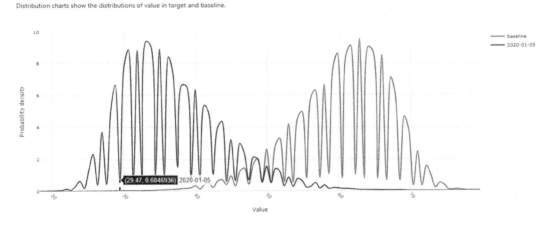

Figure 4.61 – The baseline is a negative skewed distribution, while the latest inferences follow a positive skewed distribution

In this section, you learned how to configure data drift detection, which you did by comparing the data that your model was observing in production against the dataset that was used to train the model. This is a powerful feature that allows you to determine whether you need to retrain the model with newer data, especially if the feature distribution has changed/drifted over time.

Summary

In this chapter, you learned how to provision and attach compute resources to your Azure ML workspace. You also learned how you can register various datastores so that you can access data in a secure manner. Finally, you explored the dataset registration capabilities of Azure ML Studio, something that allows you to easily access the data for your experiments. Having registered the datasets, you can configure data drift monitors, which warn you if the features' distribution changes over time, something that could indicate that the ML model that was trained on that dataset needs to be retrained. You should now feel comfortable configuring your Azure ML workspace, one of the key skills that's measured in the DP-100 certification.

In the next chapter, you will learn how to leverage the datasets that you registered in the workspace to perform **Auto ML** analysis, a process that will run multiple ML experiments on top of the compute clusters you provisioned to detect the best algorithm for your dataset.

Questions

In each chapter, you will find a couple of questions so that you can test your knowledge regarding what was covered in this chapter:

1. How many data scientists can work on a single compute instance that has 8 cores and 56 GB of RAM?

    a. Only one.

    b. Up to two.

    c. Up to five.

    d. As many as they want, as long as they don't deplete the compute resources.

2. What type of credentials do you need to provide to access a data lake store that's either Gen 1 or Gen 2?

    a. A **Personal Access Token (PAT)**

    b. A service principal's client ID and secret

    c. Your own AAD user credentials

    d. No credentials are needed

3. Which of the following Azure tools can help you orchestrate data moving from an on-premises environment?

   a. Blob storage

   b. Azure Active Directory

   c. Azure Data Factory

   d. Azure ML workspace

Further reading

This section offers a list of useful web resources that will help you augment your knowledge and understanding of the topics discussed in this chapter:

- You can learn more about how to use managed identity from within a compute cluster at the following link: `https://docs.microsoft.com/azure/machine-learning/how-to-create-attach-compute-cluster?tabs=python#managed-identity-usage`.

- The instance metadata service allows you to request tokens for Azure resources using the attached managed identity. You can learn more about this at `https://docs.microsoft.com/azure/virtual-machines/linux/instance-metadata-service`.

- You can learn more about the access control model of Azure Data Lake Storage Gen2 at `https://docs.microsoft.com/azure/storage/blobs/data-lake-storage-access-control-model`.

- You can learn how to easily copy data and configure regular data ingestions using Azure Data Factory's copy data tool at `https://docs.microsoft.com/azure/data-factory/quickstart-create-data-factory-copy-data-tool`.

- You can learn how to grant limited access to Azure Storage Accounts using SAS tokens at `https://docs.microsoft.com/azure/storage/common/storage-sas-overview`.

- You can learn more about service principals, which can be used to access Azure Data Lake datastores, at `https://docs.microsoft.com/azure/active-directory/develop/app-objects-and-service-principals`.

Section 2:
No code data science experimentation

Azure Machine Learning Studio offers various no-code/low-code wizards and designers that enable power users to perform end-to-end data science experiments. Experienced data scientists and machine learning engineers also use these experiences to kick start a project, verify a hypothesis, understand which model performs best on a given dataset and design data cleansing processes without writing any code. In this section, you will learn how to run data science experiments through the web designers and wizards provided in Azure ML Studio.

This section comprises of the following chapters:

- *Chapter 5, Letting the Machines Do the Model Training*
- *Chapter 6, Visual Model Training and Publishing*

5
Letting the Machines Do the Model Training

In this chapter, you will create your first **Automated Machine Learning** (**Automated ML** or **AutoML**) experiment. AutoML refers to the process of trying multiple modeling techniques and selecting the model that produces the best predictions against the training dataset you specify. First, you will navigate through the AutoML wizard that is part of the Azure Machine Learning Studio web experience and understand the different options that need to be configured. You will then learn how to monitor the progress of an AutoML experiment and how to deploy the best-produced model as a web service hosted in an **Azure Container Instance** (**ACI**) to be able to make real-time inferences.

The best way to go through this chapter is by sitting in front of a computer with this book by you. By using your Azure subscription and this book together, you can start your journey through AutoML.

In this chapter, we're going to cover the following main topics:

- Configuring an AutoML experiment
- Monitoring execution of an experiment
- Deploying best model as a web service

Technical requirements

You will need to have access to an Azure subscription. Within that subscription, you will need a **resource group** named packt-azureml-rg. You will need to have either a Contributor or Owner **Access control (IAM)** role at the resource group level. Within that resource group, you should then deploy a **machine learning** resource named packt-learning-mlw, as described in *Chapter 2, Deploying Azure Machine Learning Workspace Resources*.

Configuring an AutoML experiment

If you were asked to train a model to make predictions against a dataset, you would need to do a couple of things, including normalizing the dataset, splitting it into train and validation data, running multiple experiments to understand which algorithm is performing best against the dataset, and then finetuning the best model. Automated machine learning shortens this process by fully automating the time-consuming, iterative tasks. It allows all users, from normal PC users to experienced data scientists, to build multiple machine learning models against a target dataset and select the model that performs the best, based on a metric you select.

This process consists of the following steps:

1. **Preparing the experiment**: Select the dataset you are going to use for training, select the column that you are trying to predict, and configure the experiment's parameters. This is the configuration phase you will read about in this section.

2. **Data guardrails**: This is the first step of executing the experiment. It performs basic data guardrails on top of the provided training dataset. AutoML tries to identify potential issues with your data; for example, all the training data must have the same values in the column you are trying to predict.

3. **Training multiple models**: Train multiple combinations of data normalization and algorithms to find the best model that optimizes (maximizes or minimizes) the desired metric. This process continues until one of the exit criteria is met, either a time constraint or a specified model performance target.

4. **Creating an ensemble model**: Here, you train a model that combines the results of the best models trained so far and produces a potentially improved inference.

5. **Selecting the best model**: The best model is selected based on the metric you specified.

Azure Machine Learning provides a web-based wizard that allows you to configure such an experiment. In *Chapter 3, Azure Machine Learning Studio Components*, you explored the **Azure Machine Learning Studio** \ web experience.

In this chapter, you will create an AutoML classification model that will predict whether a customer will churn or not. This model will be able to predict whether a customer will continue being a loyal customer or whether they will terminate their active mobile phone contract. You will use a fabricated dataset from a fictional telecom company. The dataset shows, for each customer, information about how long they have been with the company and how much they are using their active subscription. Let's get started:

1. To start the AutoML experiment, you will need to open a browser and navigate to the Azure Machine Learning Studio. You will land on the home page, as shown in the following screenshot:

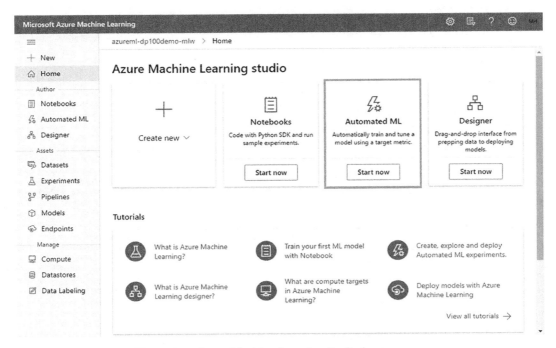

Figure 5.1 – Azure Machine Learning Studio home screen

2. On the Azure Machine Learning Studio home screen, navigate to the **Author |
   Automated ML** section by clicking the **Start now** button under **Automated ML**,
   as highlighted in the preceding screenshot. This will open the **Automated ML** home
   screen, as shown here:

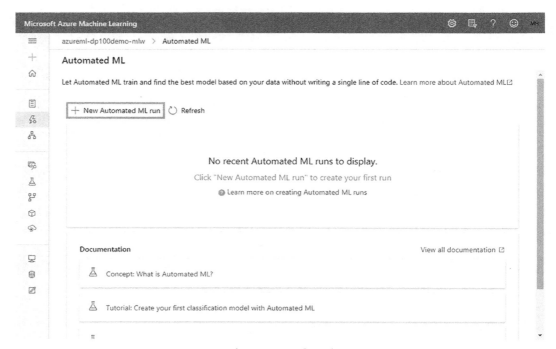

Figure 5.2 – The Automated ML home screen

On this home screen, you can find the recently executed Automated ML
experiments. Since this is the first time you are using this workspace, you shouldn't
find any runs listed here.

3. By pressing the **New Automated ML Run** button, you will start the **Create a New
   Automated ML** wizard, as shown here:

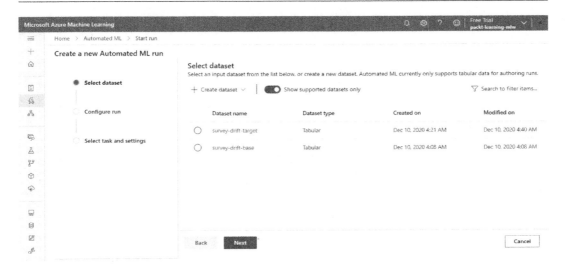

Figure 5.3 – Starting the Automated ML wizard

In this first step of the wizard, named **Select dataset**, you can either select an existing dataset or create a new one. From this list, you will be able to see the two datasets that you registered in *Chapter 4, Configuring the Workspace*. You will not need those datasets. In the next section, you will learn how to create a new dataset to use for the Automated ML experiment you are about to perform.

Registering the dataset

In the **Select dataset** step of the **Automated ML** wizard, you can register a new dataset to be used for the AutoML experimentation. Follow these steps to register the fabricated churn dataset:

1. Click on **Create dataset** on the top of the screen.

2. Select **From web files** from the drop-down menu that appears. This will start the **Create dataset from web files** wizard shown in the following screenshot.

3. On the first page of the wizard (**Basic info**), provide the following information:

   a) **Web URL**: https://bit.ly/churn-dataset.

   b) **Name**: churn-dataset.

c) **Dataset type**: `Tabular`. This is an option that you cannot change since AutoML currently only supports tabular datasets.

d) **Description**: `Dataset to train a model that predicts customer churn:`

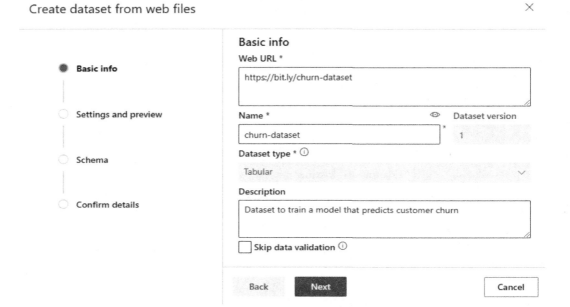

Figure 5.4 – Basic info when creating a dataset from web files

4. Once you've filled everything in, press **Next**. It will take a while to download and parse the file. The wizard will move to the **Settings and preview** screen:

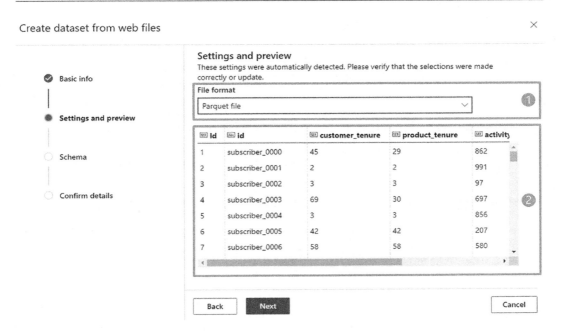

Figure 5.5 – The Settings and preview screen of the Create dataset from web files wizard

5. The steps shown in the preceding screenshot provide important information for the demo dataset. The file format of the sample file is automatically detected to be the **Parquet** file format. You can modify the selection if needed.

The demo dataset consists of seven columns:

- **ld** is a sequential record number that is not part of the original Parquet file. Auto ML generates this sequence number to let you validate the data you can see in the preview window. This column will not be part of the registered dataset.

- **id** is a string that uniquely identifies each customer in the dataset.

- **customer_tenure** is an integer value telling us how long each customer has been with the fictional telecom company. The value represents months.

- **product_tenure** is an integer value that tells us how long a customer has owned the currently active subscription. It is measured in months.

- **activity_last_6_month** tells us how many hours the customer has talked on the phone over the last 6 months.

- **activity_last_12_month** tells us how many hours the customer has talked on the phone over the last 12 months.

- **churned** is a flag that informs us whether the customer renewed the subscription or terminated the active contract. This is the column you will be trying to predict.

  From this fabricated dataset, the most relevant features for the classification model you are trying to build are **customer_tenure**, **product_tenure**, **activity_last_6_month**, and **activity_last_12_month**. The **churned** column is the **target** for the model you are trying to build. The **id** column allows you to link a model's prediction back to the actual customer who may churn.

6. Pressing **Next** will open the wizard's **Schema** screen, as shown here:

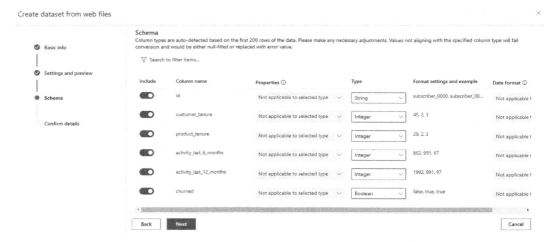

Figure 5.6 – Schema step of the Create dataset from web files wizard

This screen provides a detailed view of the schema of the dataset. On this wizard screen, you can exclude columns by switching the **Include** toggle for the specific column you would like to exclude.

The **Type** column allows you to specify the data types of the columns of the dataset. The supported types that are available are **String, Boolean, Integer, Decimal**, and **Date**. The dataset you are registering is stored in **Parquet** file format, as you saw back in *Step 4*. This file format stores additional metadata information regarding the type of each column. This information is read by the wizard and the right data types are selected for you. If you were using a file format that doesn't include the data types, such as **Comma-Separated Values** (**CSV**) files, the wizard would try to guess the types, but you would have to validate the selections.

The **Properties** column is enabled when you can specify additional details for the **Type** of data that a column stores. For example, if you select Date as the type of a column, you will be able to select whether this column is a timestamp, something that will mark the dataset as a time series one. **Date format** is also enabled when you select Date as the column's type. This allows you to define the date pattern that should be used to parse the specific column. For example, you can use %Y-%m-%d to specify that the date is stored in a year-month-day format.

7. Once you've finished exploring the wizard's **Schema** screen, press **Next**. The wizard's **Confirm details** screen provides you with an overview of the new dataset you want to register in your workspace, as shown here:

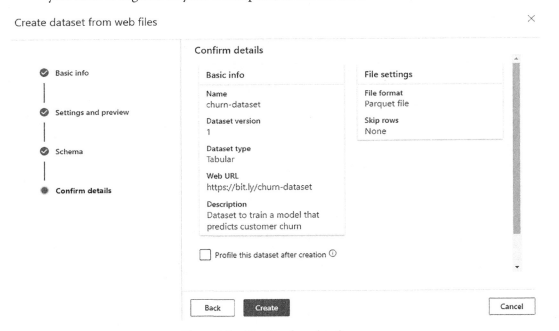

Figure 5.7 – The Confirm details page

This screen summarizes the dataset information you read about in the *Working with datasets* section of *Chapter 4, Configuring the Workspace*. If you select the **Profile this dataset after creation** checkbox, you can select a compute target to generate the profile of the newly created dataset. You do not need to generate the profile for this dataset since it only has 6,720 rows and Azure ML will automatically provide a full profile for you.

8. Click the **Create** button to complete the wizard.

Now that you have registered churn-dataset, you can continue with the AutoML wizard, where you will select the newly registered dataset, configure the experiment parameters, and kick off the AutoML process, something you will do in the next section.

Returning to the AutoML wizard

Now that you have created churn-dataset, you can continue with the AutoML wizard. The wizard contains three steps, as shown in the following diagram:

Select dataset   Configure run   Select task and settings

Figure 5.8 – AutoML wizard steps

Let's begin with the steps!

1. As the first step, select churn-dataset, which you created in the previous section, *Registering the dataset*, and click **Next**, as shown here:

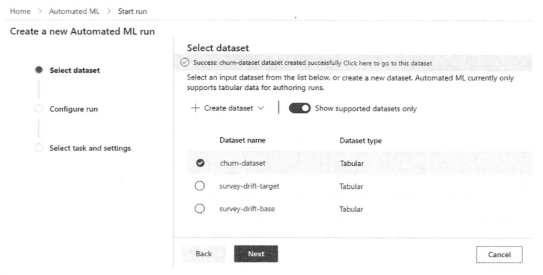

Figure 5.9 – The Select dataset step of the Create a new Automated ML run wizard

2. In the **Configure run** step, you can visualize the selected dataset and configure the basic experiment parameters:

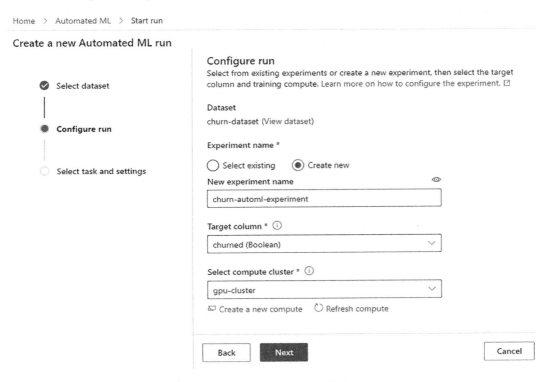

Figure 5.10 – The Configure run step of the Create a new Automated ML run wizard

The experiment options you need to configure are as follows:

- **Experiment name**: Every time you perform a data science experiment, you need to keep track of the various runs you have done to be able to compare the results. For example, you may end up running multiple AutoML attempts while trying out different wizard options. In this case, you would like to keep all the attempts under the same experiment to keep them grouped. From this wizard, you can **Select existing** experiment, or you can **Create new**. Create a new experiment and specify churn-automl-experiment for **New experiment name**, as shown in the preceding screenshot.

- **Target column**: This is the dataset column that the model will be trained to predict. Select the churned column. Based on the type of the target column, the wizard will automatically select the best task for this column, as you will see in the next wizard step.

- **Select compute cluster**: You will need to select the compute cluster that will be used to perform the AutoML runs. You can select `gpu-cluster` here, which you created in the *Compute clusters* section of *Chapter 4, Configuring the Workspace*. If you don't have a cluster registered in your workspace, you can use a compute instance or you can start the dedicated wizard by clicking on the **New** button shown in the preceding screenshot.

> **Important note**
> In *Chapter 4, Configuring the Workspace*, you were asked to provision a GPU-based cluster named `gpu-cluster`. By default, free trial subscriptions do not allow you to provision GPU computes. For this experiment, you can select CPU-based clusters instead of GPU-based ones.

3. Once you have configured the run details, click on the **Next** button.
4. The next page of the wizard is the **Select task and settings** page, as shown here:

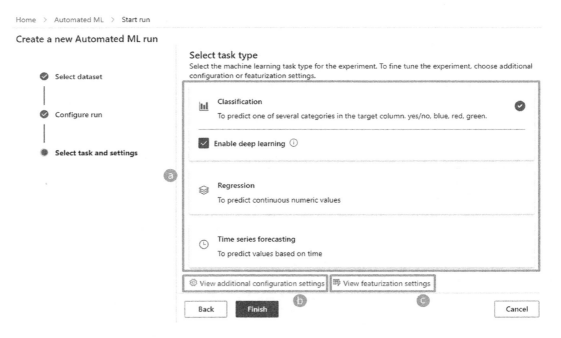

Figure 5.11 – The Create a new Automated ML run wizard – Select task type

In this step, you can configure the following:

a) **Select task type**: AutoML currently supports three types of tasks:

- **Classification**: The produced model can predict the category a record belongs to. A category can be anything, such as a yes or no **Boolean** value or a blue, green, or yellow color value. In our case, you are trying to predict if the customer is going to churn, which can be answered with a yes or a no.

- **Regression**: Use regression models when you want to predict a numeric value, such as the price of an apartment or the diabetes disease level. We will look at this in *Chapter 8, Experimenting with Python Code*.

- **Time series forecasting**: You usually use this type of model to predict time series values such as a stock's price while considering the progress of the value over time. This type of model is a specialization on top of the regression models. This means that all regression models can be used, but there are also a couple of more specialized algorithms such as Facebook's **Prophet** algorithm or the **Auto-Regressive Integrated Moving Average** (**ARIMA**) technique.

Depending on the target column you selected, the wizard will automatically guess the task you are trying to perform. In our case, it selected **Classification**.

b) **View additional configuration settings**: Depending on the task type you selected, you can configure various settings, including the target metric to be used to evaluate the models and the exit criteria that will terminate the search for the best model. Depending on the task's type, the options on that wizard page change. You can see some of these options in the following diagram. You will visit this part of the wizard in *Step 5*:

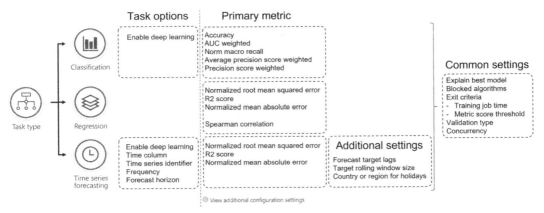

Figure 5.12 – Configuration settings depending on the selected task type.

c) **View featurization settings**: This allows you to configure various operations regarding the features that the model will use to make its prediction. In this section, you can exclude features such as row unique ID or irrelevant information to speed up the training process and reduce the size of the final model. You can also specify the type of each feature and the imputation function, which takes care of the missing values in the dataset. You will visit this section of the wizard in *Step 6*.

5.   By clicking on **View additional configuration settings**, additional configurations will appear for the classification task that you selected on the main wizard page:

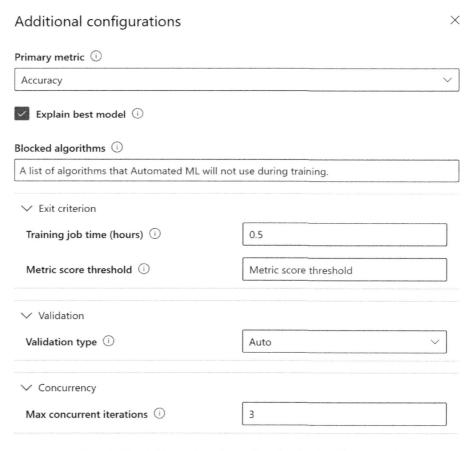

Figure 5.13 – Additional configurations for the classification task

In the **Additional configurations** section, you can set up the following parameters, which are common for all types of tasks:

- **Primary metric**: This is the metric that's used to monitor the training progress of the model and the metric that's used to compare the produced models so that you can select the best one. **Classification** tasks have different metrics from **Regression** and **Time series forecasting** ones, as shown in *Figure 5.12*.

- **Explain best model**: If checked, the best model gets explained and the results are stored within the run. You will learn more about model interpretability in *Chapter 10, Understanding Model Results*.

- **Blocked algorithms**: This is a list of algorithms that AutoML will not use during training. You can use this list to see the supported algorithms per task. You can exclude specific algorithms to avoid using one that is known to overfit for your scenario or focus the AutoML process to explore a small subset of the algorithms deeper.

- **Exit criterion**: This option allows you to specify the termination criteria of the best model search. You can specify the following exit criteria:

  - **Training job time (hours)**: The maximum amount of time, in hours, for an experiment to search for the best model.

  - **Metric score threshold**: When AutoML trains a model with a primary metric that's better than this threshold value, it will cancel all remaining jobs and exit.

- **Validation type**: You can modify the way you are validating the model's results by specifying a specific one, such as the famous **k-fold cross validation** one. For k-fold, the idea is that you split the dataset into k sets and then train with the k-1 sets and validate with the last one. Then, you rotate the sets and keep a new one for validation. You can use `auto` in most cases unless you have a reason to modify it. By default, 10-folds cross-validation is used if you have fewer than 1,000 rows, 3-folds is used if you have more than 1,000 and fewer than 20,000 rows, and if you have more than 20,000 rows, the dataset is split into 90% training data and 10% validation data.

- **Max concurrent iterations**: This represents the maximum number of iterations that would be executed in parallel. This option allows you to spin up multiple nodes in the cluster to search in parallel various models. Therefore, this option needs to be less than the max nodes your cluster can scale to.

  To save on cost and time, set **Exit criterion | Training job time (hours)** to 0.5, which is half an hour or 30 minutes. You can leave the rest of the options as is, as shown in the preceding screenshot. Click **Save** and return to the **Select task type** page of the wizard you saw in *Step 4*.

6. By clicking on **View featurization settings**, the **Featurization** screen will open, as shown here:

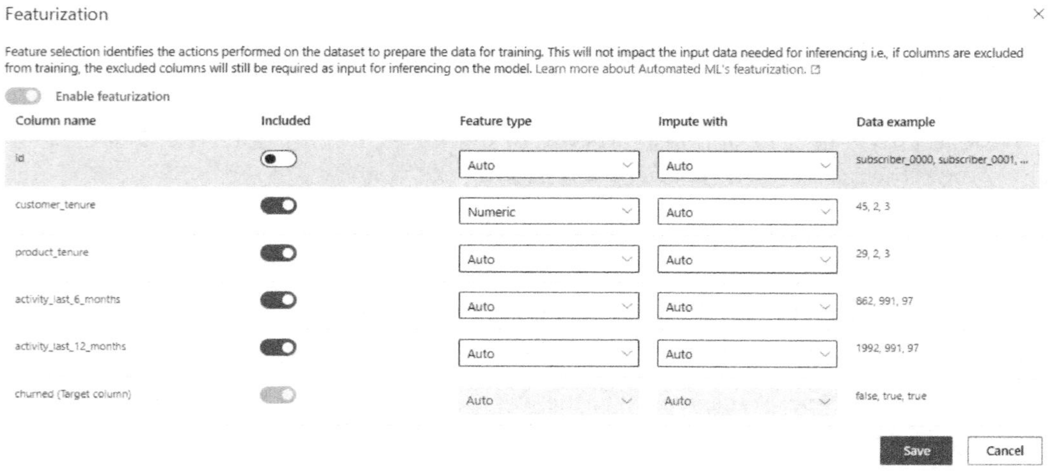

Figure 5.14 – The Featurization view on the create AutoML wizard

On this screen, you can define actions that influence the data preparation phase for the training process. The following options can be configured:

- **Included**: You can exclude columns that should not be considered by the algorithm. The target column cannot be excluded.

- **Feature type**: By default, the **Auto** value is selected, which will automatically detect the type of each column you have in the dataset. It can be one of the following types: **Numeric, DateTime, Categorical, Categorical hash,** or **Text**. If you want, you can manually configure a column to be one of the available types.

- **Impute with**: If you have missing values in your dataset, this option will do in-place imputation based on the selected methodology. The options you can choose from are **Auto**, which is the default one, **Most frequent**, and **Fill with constant**. Especially for **Numeric** features, you can also use the **Mean** or the **Median** imputation strategy.

> **Important note**
>
> Imagine that you had a product ID feature that explicitly mentioned the subscription product each customer is registered for. This feature would have numeric values, such as 1,055 and 1,060. This feature could accidentally be marked as a numeric feature, even though it is a categorical one. If you were missing values in the training dataset, the automatic approach may have imputed missing values with the average product ID, which doesn't make any sense. AutoML is smart enough to understand that if a numeric feature only has a few unique values repeating, this feature may be a categorical one, but you can explicitly assist the machine learning models by marking them as **Categorical** regarding **Feature type**.

7. On this wizard page, you should exclude the **id** feature. The **id** feature provides information on who the actual customer is. It doesn't provide any relevant information to the classification problem, so it should be excluded to save on computational resources. Click **Save** to return to the **Select task type** page of the wizard you saw in *Step 4*.

By clicking **Finish**, as shown in *Figure 5.11*, you can finalize the configuration of your AutoML experiment, and the run will automatically start. The browser will redirect you to the AutoML run execution page, which allows you to monitor the AutoML training process and review the training results. You are going to explore that page in the next section.

Monitoring the execution of the experiment

In the previous section, *Configuring an Automated ML experiment*, you submitted an AutoML experiment to execute on a remote compute cluster. Once you have submitted the job, your browser should redirect you to a page similar to the following:

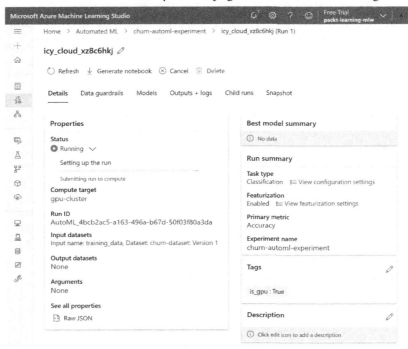

Figure 5.15 – Running a new Automated ML run for the first time since the run finished

At the top of the page, the name of the run of the experiment is autogenerated. In the preceding screenshot, it is called `AutoML_05558d1d-c8ab-48a5-b652-4d47dc102d29`. By clicking the pencil icon, you can edit this name and make it something more memorable. Change the name to `my-first-experiment-run`. Right below the run's name, you can click on one of the following commands:

- **Refresh**: This will refresh the information provided on the page. While running an experiment, you can get the latest and greatest information.

- **Generate notebook**: This will create a notebook with all the Python code that is needed to run the same experiment using the Azure ML SDK. You will learn more about the code needed to run an AutoML experiment through code in *Chapter 8, Experimenting with Python Code.*

- **Cancel**: This will cancel the current run. This option is only available if the experiment is still running.

> **Important note**
> When you cancel a run, it may take a while until the run is canceled. By clicking on the **Refresh** button, you can check the progress of the cancelation process.

- **Delete**: This deletes the selected run. It is only enabled if the run has been canceled or has finished executing.

The run experiment page provides a lot of information regarding the entire process and is structured using tabs. By default, you start from the tab called **Details**. In this tab, you will find the following important information:

- On the **Properties** box, which is located on the left of the preceding screenshot, the most important information is located in the following fields:

  a) **Status**, which describes the state of the current run. This can be running, canceled, errored, or completed.

  b) **Compute target** is where the run is executed.

  c) **Raw JSON** is a link that allows you to review all the configuration information of the current run in a machine-readable format.

- In the **Run summary** box on the right, you will find **Task type**, which is the type of model you are training. By clicking on **View configuration settings**, you can get a summary of the configuration parameters for the current experiment.

- The **Description** box allows you to document the hypothesis you are evaluating in the current experiment. By clicking the pencil icon, you can add a description of your experiment run, information that will allow you to recollect what you were looking for with this experiment and what the outcome was.

The second tab of the run page is named **Data guardrails**. This tab provides you with detailed qualitative and quantitative information on the dataset you are using in your experiment. Depending on the task type, you will have different types of validation being performed. The status of each validation is **Passed** if everything was OK, **Failed** if your dataset has an issue that needs to be resolved, or **Done** if AutoML found an issue with your dataset and fixed it for you. In the **Done** cases, you will be able to see additional information on what was fixed in your dataset by clicking on the **+View additional details** button.

The third tab is called **Model** and contains a list of all the models AutoML has trained so far, as seen in *Figure 5.16*. The model with the best metric score will be listed at the top. The table shows **Algorithm name**, the specific model's explanation results (if they are available) (**Explained**), the model's score (**Accuracy**, in this case), the percentage of the data used to train the model (**Sampling**), and information regarding when the model was trained and how long it took (the **Created** and **Duration** columns). If you select a model from the list, the following three commands will be enabled:

- **Deploy** initiates the deployment of the selected model, which you will learn about in the next section.

- **Download** allows you to download the selected model to your local disk. It is a ZIP file that contains `model.pkl`, which includes the actual trained model and all supporting files needed to perform inference.

- **Explain model** kicks off the **Explanations** wizard, where you need to select a **compute cluster** to calculate the model explanations for the specific model. By default, AutoML will explain the best model, but you may want to explain additional models to compare them. Once the explanations have been calculated, you can view them by clicking on **View explanation** in the **Explained** column. This will open the **Explanations** tab of the selected model, which has populated the report. You will learn more about model interpretability in *Chapter 10, Understanding Model Results*.

The fourth tab on the main page, called **Outputs + logs**, displays the outputs and log of the specific run in a simple files explorer. These logs are the ones of the overall AutoML process. If you want to view the logs of a specific model training process, you will need to select the model from the **Models** tab and then visit the **Outputs + logs** section of that child run. The files explorer that's available in this tab allows you to navigate through the folder structure on the left-hand side. If you select a file, its contents will be displayed on the right-hand side.

So far, you have managed to train a couple of models and see the best model to predict whether a customer will churn or not. In the next section, you will learn how to operationalize this model with only a couple of clicks.

Deploying the best model as a web service

In the previous section, you navigated around the run experiment page while reviewing the information related to the run execution and the results of the exploration, which are the trained models. In this section, we will revisit the **Models** tabs and start deploying the best model as a web service to be able to make real-time inferences. Navigate to the run's details page, as shown in *Figure 5.15*. Let's get started:

1. Click on the **Models** tab. You should see a page similar to the one shown here:

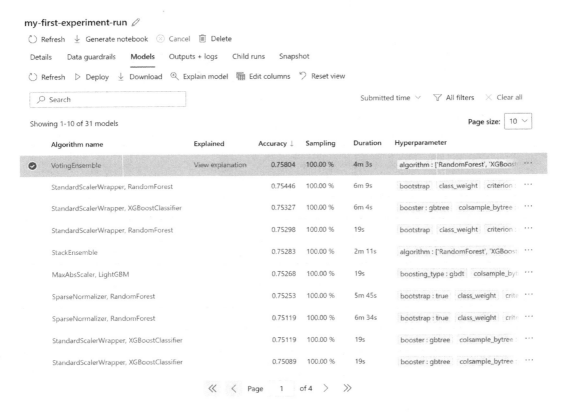

Figure 5.16 – The Models tab as a starting point for deploying a model

2. In this list, you can select any model you want to deploy. Select the row with the best model, as shown in the preceding screenshot. Click the **Deploy** command at the top of the list. The **Deploy a model** dialog will appear, as shown here:

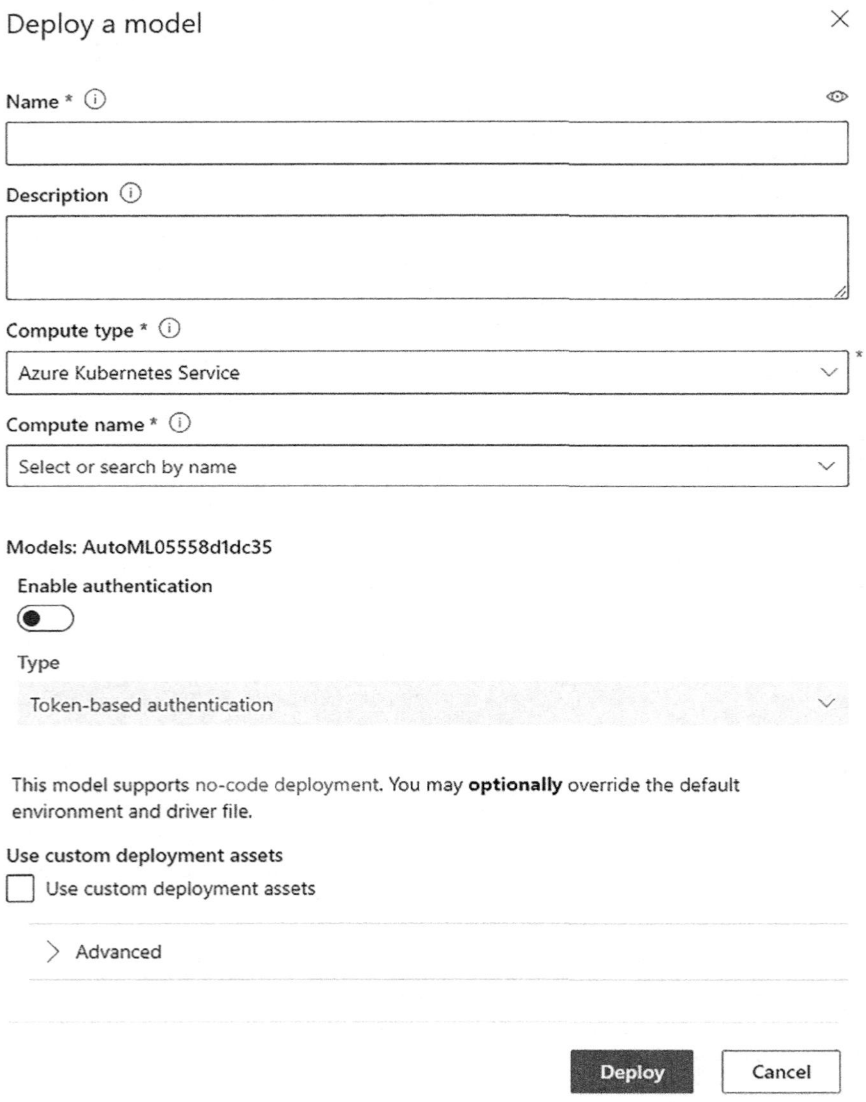

Deploy a model   ✕

Name * ⓘ   ◉

Description ⓘ

Compute type * ⓘ

Azure Kubernetes Service   ∨   *

Compute name * ⓘ

Select or search by name   ∨

Models: AutoML05558d1dc35

Enable authentication

（●   ）

Type

Token-based authentication   ∨

This model supports no-code deployment. You may **optionally** override the default environment and driver file.

Use custom deployment assets

☐ Use custom deployment assets

＞ Advanced

[Deploy]   [Cancel]

Figure 5.17 – The Deploy a model dialogue

3. In the **Deploy a model** dialog, you will be able to define a deployment name and the compute type to be able to proceed:

-   **Name**: The name of the service that will expose the model. Type in `myfirstmlwebservice`.

-   **Compute type**: There are two types you can choose from:

    -   **Azure Kubernetes Cluster (AKS)**: This option should be selected when you want to deploy your model for a production workload and are handling multiple requests in parallel. This option allows for both key-based and token based authentications if you want to protect the endpoint. It also supports using **Field Programmable Gate Arrays (FPGAs)** for even faster model inferences. In this case you would also need to specify the **Compute name** property of the AKS cluster where you want to deploy the model. The list should contain all inference clusters you may have registered in *Chapter 4, Configuring the Workspace.*

    -   **Azure Container Instance**: If you plan to do functional testing or you want to deploy a model for the development environments, you can deploy the web service as a single Azure Container Instance. This compute type is cheaper, but it doesn't scale and it only supports key-based authentication. For this book, you can select this type to deploy the model.

4. By pressing **Deploy**, you can start deploying the model.

    In the top-right corner of your browser, a popup window will appear, as shown in the following screenshot, letting you know that your model has started being deployed:

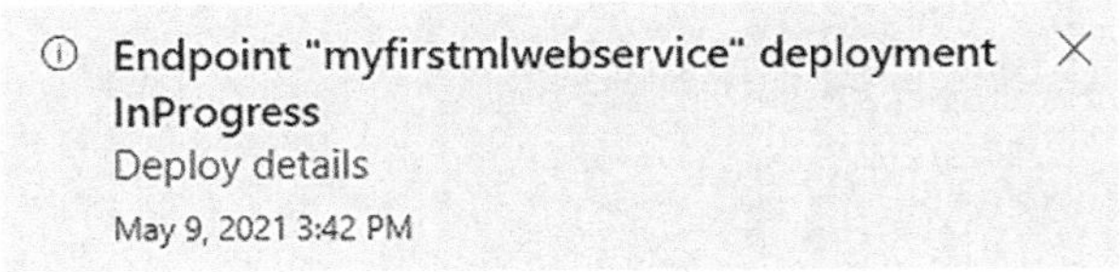

    ⓘ **Endpoint "myfirstmlwebservice" deployment** ✕
        InProgress
        Deploy details
        May 9, 2021 3:42 PM

Figure 5.18 – Endpoint deployment window – deployment InProgress

5. The pop-up window will quickly disappear, but you can revisit it by clicking on the notification **bell** icon in the top-right corner, as shown here:

Figure 5.19 – Azure Machine Learning Studio taskbar in the top-right corner

6. The model will take a couple of minutes to deploy. By looking at your notifications, you can check the progress of your deployment. If the notification turns green, as shown in the following screenshot, then the deployment is completed:

Figure 5.20 – Endpoint deployment window – deployment Completed

7. By clicking on the **Deploy details** link in the notification, your browser will redirect you to the endpoint page of the deployed model, as shown here:

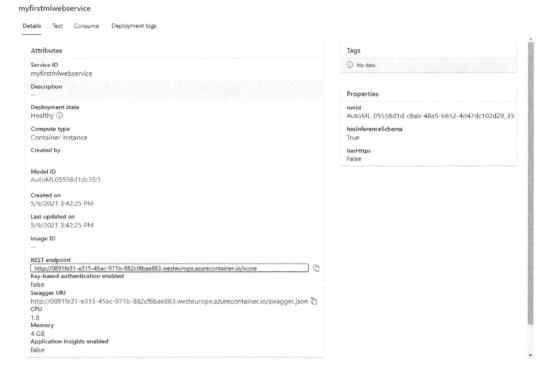

Figure 5.21 – Endpoint page of the deployed model

> **Important note**
>
> There are multiple ways you can reach the endpoint page of your model. For example, you can see a list of all the published endpoints by going to the **Assets | Endpoints** menu in Azure ML Studio. To reach the same page, select the endpoint you want to inspect.

The endpoint page of the deployed model has a similar tab-based structure to the run experiment page. The first tab is called **Details** and provides information regarding the deployment of the model. Out of them, the most important ones are located in the **Attributes** box shown in the preceding screenshot. They are as follows:

- **Service ID** is the name of the service you specified in *Step 3* of the deployment wizard.

- **Deployment state** provides the state of the deployed or to-be-deployed model. There are five states the endpoint can be in. You can find more information regarding states and potential issues in the *Further reading* section of this chapter.

- **Rest endpoint** is the link you can copy into an application's code to call the deployed model via a REST API.

8. The second tab is called **Test** and allows you to test the deployed model. By default, you get the **Fields** mode, which is a form containing all the inputs your model is expecting, as shown here:

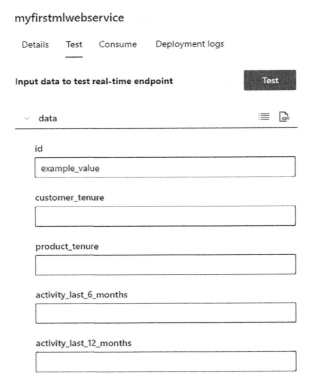

Figure 5.22 – The endpoint page of the deployed model

9. If you want to perform a mini-batch inference, meaning that you want to send multiple records at once, you can switch to **CSV** from the top-right corner. In that mode, you can copy the contents of a CSV file into the text box that will appear and hit the **Test** button.

   In either mode, once you hit the **Test** button, the input data will be submitted to the REST API and results will be provided.

10. The third tab of the endpoint page is called **Consume**. On that page, you can find basic code for the consumption of the REST API in **C#**, **Python**, and **R**. This code is automatically generated using a file called swagger.json, which is automatically generated in the endpoint. This file describes the expected inputs and outputs of the REST APIs and is commonly used by web developers to provide documentation on the REST endpoints they produce.

11. Finally, the **Deployment logs** tab shows a detailed log of the deployment of the model. You can troubleshoot potential deployment issues using this tab.

Congratulations – you have successfully deployed your very own real-time endpoint that makes inferences on whether a customer will churn or not! In the next section, you will learn about the artifacts that are created when your model is deployed.

Understanding the deployment of the model

In the previous section, you deployed a model as a REST endpoint. In this section, you will understand what happened behind the scenes and discover the artifacts that were generated in the process.

You started from the list of models that the AutoML process has trained. In that list, you selected a model and clicked on the **Deploy** command. By doing that, you registered the selected model in the Azure ML workspace and once that was done, the process continued with deploying the endpoint, as shown in the following diagram:

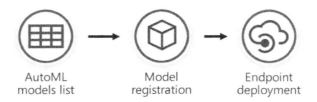

Figure 5.23 – From AutoML model list to endpoint deployment

Model registration creates a versioned record within the Azure ML workspace that allows you to keep track of what datasets were used to train the specific model and where the specific model was deployed. You will learn more about model registration in *Chapter 12, Operationalizing Models with Code*. Let's take a look:

1. To see this model registration, in Azure ML Studio, navigate to **Assets | Models**. You will end up on the **Model List** page, as shown here:

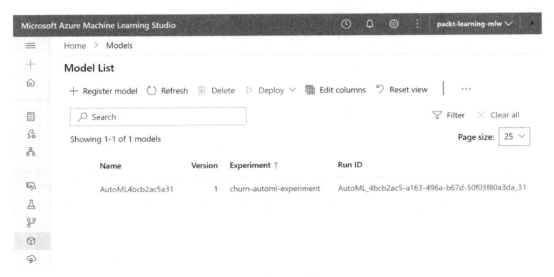

Figure 5.24 – The Model List page

The **Model List** page lists all registered models within the Azure ML workspace. These are the models that are being tracked by the workspace. Each model has a unique name. You can have multiple versions of the same model, something that automatically happens when you try to register a model with the same name. The model list allows you to select a model and perform various actions on it, such as deleting and deploying it.

> **Important note**
> You can only delete a registered model if it is not being used by any endpoint.

2.   By clicking on the **Name** property of a model, you will end up on the details page of the selected registered model, as shown here:

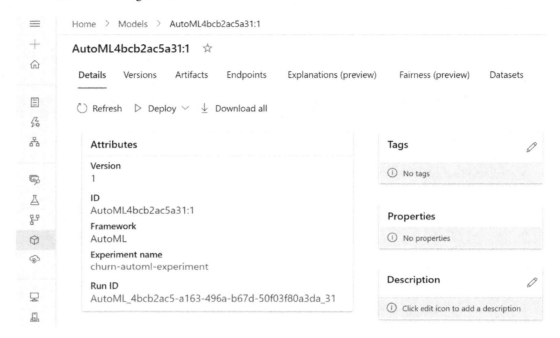

Figure 5.25 – Registered model details page

Here, you can get the general details regarding the model, such as which run trained the specific model, what framework was used, and the experiment name where this run is registered. Note that since this model was trained using AutoML, the framework is the generic AutoML one. In *Chapter 12, Operationalizing Models with Code*, you will be able to register your own models and specify the framework you used to train the model.

In the **Artifacts** tab, you will find the **model.pkl** file, which contains the trained model. In the **Explanations** and **Fairness** tabs, you can view the interpretability results, if they have been generated for the specific model. You will learn more about model interpretability in *Chapter 10, Understanding Model Results*. In the **Datasets** tab, you can see a reference to the specific version of the dataset that you used while configuring the AutoML experiment. This allows you to have lineage between the dataset that was used for training and the models you have deployed.

3.   Once the model has been registered, the deployment wizard creates an endpoint. Back in Azure ML Studio, click on the **Assets | Endpoint** menu item. This will bring you to the **Endpoints** page shown here:

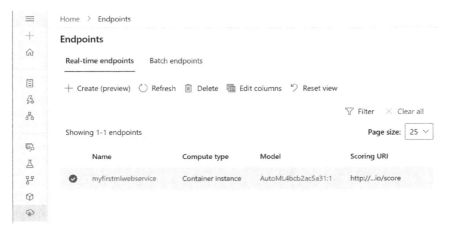

Figure 5.26 – The Endpoints page

This list shows all real-time endpoints you have deployed from this Azure ML workspace. You will notice the **myfirstmlwebservice** endpoint, which you deployed in the previous section. By clicking on its name, you will end up on the endpoint's page, which you saw in *Figure 5.21*.

4. Behind the scenes, this endpoint is a container instance that was deployed in the **resource group** named `packt-azureml-rg`, right next to your Azure ML workspace resource. Navigate to the Azure portal and open the **resource group** named `packt-azureml-rg`. You should have resources similar to the ones shown here:

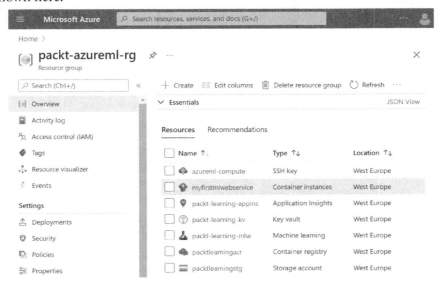

Figure 5.27 – The resources in the packt-azureml-rg resource group of the Azure portal

5. Here, you will see that a **Container instance** has been deployed named **myfirstmllwebservice-<random id>**, which is the name of the endpoint you saw in *Figure 5.26*. This is the engine that is hosting the REST API you deployed in the previous section.

> **Important note**
> Never delete Azure ML workspace artifacts directly from the resource group. This will leave orphan registrations in your workspace, such as an endpoint that points to a deleted container instance.

In this section, you saw what happens behind the scenes when you deploy a model from AutoML. In the next section, you are going to delete the endpoint you deployed to avoid spending money on a real-time endpoint you don't need.

Cleaning up the model deployment

In this section, you will clean up the deployed model. You should remove the deployments of the models that you are not planning to use. Otherwise, you will be paying for unused provisioned resources.

Navigate to Azure ML Studio. Click on the **Assets | Endpoint** menu item. This will bring you to the endpoints list page shown in *Figure 5.26*. Select the `myfirstmlwebservice` endpoint and click on the **Delete** command. Confirm your desire to delete the endpoint by clicking **Delete** in the pop-up window shown here:

Figure 5.28 – Delete real-time endpoint pop-up window

After the confirmation, the endpoint and the container instance you saw back in the Azure portal will get deleted. If you like, you can verify this by visiting the `packt-azureml-rg` **resource group**.

Summary

In this chapter, you learned how to configure an AutoML process to discover the best model that can predict whether a customer will churn or not. First, you used the AutoML wizard of the Azure Machine Learning Studio web experience to configure the experiment. Then, you monitored the execution of the run in the **Experiments** section of the studio interface. Once the training was completed, you reviewed the trained models and saw the information that had been stored regarding the best model. Then, you deployed that machine learning model in an Azure Container Instance and tested that the real-time endpoint performs the requested inferences. In the end, you deleted the deployment to avoid incurring costs in your Azure subscription.

In the next chapter, you will continue exploring the no-code/low code aspects of the Azure Machine Learning Studio experience by looking at the designer, which allows you to graphically design a training pipeline and operationalize the produced model.

Question

You need to train a classification model but only consider linear models during the AutoML process. Which of the following allows you to do that in the Azure Machine Learning Studio experience?

> a) Add all algorithms other than linear ones to the blocked algorithms list.
>
> b) Set the Exit criterion option to a metric score threshold.
>
> c) Disable the automatic featurization option.
>
> d) Disable the deep learning option on the classification task.

Further reading

This section offers additional content as useful web resources:

- Basic concepts regarding AutoML:
- `https://docs.microsoft.com/azure/machine-learning/concept-automated-ml`.
- Deep dive into how to use AutoML: `https://docs.microsoft.com/azure/machine-learning/how-to-use-automated-ml-for-ml-models`.
- Cross-validation in sklearn: `https://scikit-learn.org/stable/modules/cross_validation.html`.
- Understanding the service state of an endpoint: `https://docs.`

microsoft.com/azure/machine-learning/how-to-deploy-and-where?tabs=azcli#understanding-service-state.

- Generating client SDKs from swagger.json files: https://swagger.io/tools/swagger-codegen/.

6
Visual Model Training and Publishing

Azure Machine Learning (AzureML) Studio offers a designer experience when developing a model by allowing you to drag, drop, and configure training and inference pipelines. In this chapter, you will get an overview of the designer. You will then create a training process. Once you have seen the overall flow that's used with the designer, we will close this chapter by creating an inference pipeline and publishing the trained model artifact as a service endpoint.

In this chapter, we will cover the following topics:

- Overview of the designer
- Designing a training process
- Creating a batch and real-time inference pipeline
- Deploying a real-time inference pipeline

Technical requirements

You will need to have access to an Azure subscription. Within that subscription, you will need a **resource group** named packt-azureml-rg. In addition, you will need to have either a Contributor or Owner **access control (IAM)** role at the resource group level. Within that resource group, you should have deployed a **machine learning** resource named packt-learning-mlw, as described in *Chapter 2, Deploying Azure Machine Learning Workspace Resources*.

You will also need to have registered churn-dataset within your workspace, which you created in *Chapter 5, Letting the Machines Do the Model Training*.

Overview of the designer

AzureML Studio offers a graphical designer that allows you to author pipelines visually. As per the definition, a pipeline is an independently executable flow of subtasks that describes a machine learning task. There are three types of pipelines that you can create within the designer:

- **Training pipelines**: These pipelines are used for training models.

- **Batch inference pipelines**: These pipelines are used to operationalize pre-trained models for batch prediction.

- **Real-time inference pipelines**: These pipelines are used to expose a REST API that allows third-party applications to make real-time predictions using pre-trained models.

To create a batch and a real-time pipeline, you need to author a training pipeline. In the following sections, you will learn how to create a training pipeline and then produce a batch and real-time pipeline on top of it. In *Chapter 11, Working with Pipelines*, you will learn how to author similar pipelines through code.

To start authoring pipelines, you will need to visit the **Designer** home page. Click on the **Designer** menu item to navigate to the home page, as shown in the following screenshot:

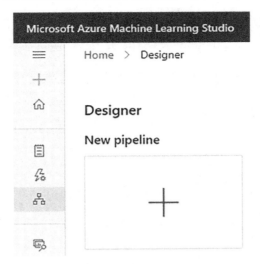

Figure 6.1 – Designer home page

Next to the **New pipeline** + button, you will see several other buttons with different ready-to-use sample pipelines. Please familiarize yourself with these samples later. These samples regularly update to show the latest features of the designer, and it's a great resource to get started.

In this chapter, we will create a new pipeline, starting from scratch. Clicking on the + button will lead you to the authoring screen/view, which we will explore in the next section.

The authoring screen/view

The main page for building a pipeline with the designer looks as follows:

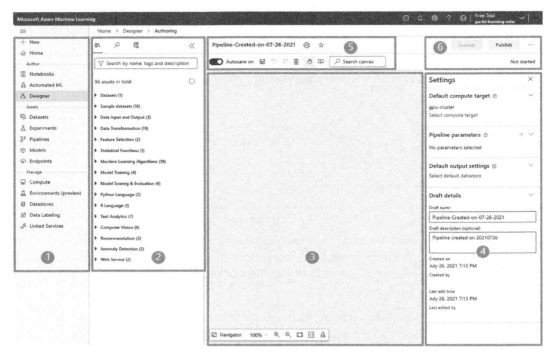

Figure 6.2 – AzureML designer authoring view

We will describe the main page user interface here, and the preceding screenshot serves as a reference:

- By clicking on the hamburger icon (≡) in the top-left corner, you can hide and unhide the AzureML main menu shown in the preceding screenshot as number **1**. From now on, we will assume this area is hidden.

- In the area labeled number **2**, you can find all the assets you can drop onto the canvas, referred to as number **3** in the preceding screenshot. By dropping different assets onto the canvas, you can build a pipeline. You will learn more about this area in the *Understanding the asset library* section of this chapter.

- On the right-hand area marked as **4**, you will find the settings. This area is also referred to as the details page. This view changes depending on what you have selected in the canvas. If you have not chosen any asset in the canvas area, you will see settings for the pipeline you are building, and you can choose a **default compute target** that will run each pipeline step. If you select an asset, you will find various configuration options for the specific asset.

- Area **5** provides a toolbar. You can switch **Autosave** on/off there. You can also change the autogenerated name of the pipeline you are designing. Rename the current pipeline to `test-pipeline`.

- In area **5**, you will also find the **Settings** button (⚙). With that button, you can hide/unhide the **Settings** area marked as **4** in the preceding screenshot. In the same area, you can find additional icons that allow you to save or delete the pipeline and **undo, redo, and search** on the canvas. The **Selection** tool (⧉) is the standard cursor on the canvas. Later, when we work on our pipeline, we will switch to the **Hand** tool (✋) to move selected parts on the canvas. Click on **Settings** to hide area **4** and increase the estate of the canvas.

- The last area, which is marked as **6** in the previous screenshot, provides you with the functionalities to **submit, publish, and clone** the pipeline, which we will discuss in the *Creating a batch and real-time inference pipeline* section.

Before moving on to the next section, you will need to configure the **default compute target** property used by the pipeline to execute all the steps. Open the pipeline settings and select the compute cluster you used in *Chapter 5, Letting the Machines Do the Model Training*.

In the next section, you will explore the area marked as **2**, also known as the *asset library*.

Understanding the asset library

To build a pipeline, you will need to stitch together various assets. In this section, you will look at the different assets available within the asset library of the designer. In *Figure 6.2*, we had 96 of them available. This number depends on how many datasets you have registered in the AzureML workspace, and in a future release of AzureML, you may even be able to create your own coding assets. The following diagram shows the categories that are available in the asset library and a brief explanation of what type of assets (also referred to as modules) they contain:

Datasets	All registered datasets in the AzureML workspace
Samples Dataset	AzureML sample datasets
Custom Module	Self-developed modules registered in the AzureML workspace
Data Input and Output	Enter manually data, import, export of data
Data Transformation	Modules for data manipulation
Feature Selection	Modules to help you select the most useful features to train your model
Statistical Functions	Descriptive statistics reports
Machine Learning Algorithms	Various untrained models for Regression, Clustering and Classification
Model Training	Modules that train models
Model Scoring & Evaluation	Modules for scoring and evaluation of the trained model
Python Language	Modules that allow you to execute Python code
R Language	Module that allow you to execute R code
Text Analytics	Modules related to text processing
Computer Vision	Modules related to image processing
Recommendation	Modules related to recommendation engines
Anomaly Detection	Modules supporting anomaly detection
Web Services	Module for deploying a model as a real-time web service

Figure 6.3 – Categories in the AzureML designer asset library

There are three types of assets in this library:

- Datasets and modules for manual input
- Untrained models
- Modules that perform certain operations on the data

You will be dragging and dropping components from this asset library while building your first end-to-end machine learning training pipeline in the designer. In the next section, you will see what each asset looks like and how you can connect various assets between them.

Exploring the asset's inputs and outputs

Each asset we drop from the asset library is a module of the pipeline we are building. A module looks similar to this sample module shown in the following screenshot:

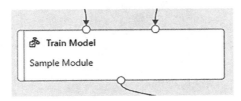

Figure 6.4 – A sample module with two inputs and one output

Let's describe this module from top to bottom:

- Zero, one, or more input ports at the top: The sample module in the preceding screenshot accepts two inputs. You can connect the output of another module to the input of the next one.

- In the middle of the module, the name describes the functionality of the module. Our example is a **Train Model** module, which trains an untrained model passed in the left input port with the data given in the right input port.

- If you select the module in the canvas, the module's detail page will appear in the area marked as **4** in *Figure 6.2*. This page is different for each module. You can configure various options, such as its short description or the compute target that will execute the specific module.

- Under the module name, you can read the description text of that module. You can edit this description by selecting the module and editing the text on the module's detail page. The module description in our example shows the text **Sample Module**.

- At the bottom of the module, there are one or more **output ports** that you can drag and connect to the next module.

In this section, you explored the various aspects of AzureML Studio's designer. In the next section, you will start authoring your first training pipeline.

Building the pipeline with the designer

In this section, we will create a training pipeline to train a machine learning model against the **churn** dataset you used in the previous chapter.

When you start designing a training pipeline, we recommend leveraging the *7 Steps of Machine Learning* approach shown in the following diagram, which contains all the steps needed to create a machine learning model:

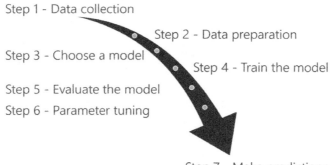

Figure 6.5 – 7 Steps of Machine Learning

This 7-step journey is a valuable checklist for real-life end-to-end scenarios to ensure you are not missing anything. In this journey, you will need various components, transformations, and models, which you can find in the asset library. To keep things simple, we will skip a couple of steps in the pipeline that you are going to design. In this section, you will start with a dataset that you will prepare to train a model. You will then evaluate the model and store it. In the next section, you will use that model to create a batch and a real-time pipeline that utilize the model to make predictions.

Let's start by acquiring the data that will be used to train the model, something you will do in the next section.

Acquiring the data

The first step is selecting the dataset that you will use to train the model:

1. In the asset library, expand the **Datasets** category by clicking on the arrow next to its name. You should see **churn-dataset** there, which you created in *Chapter 5, Letting the Machines Do the Model Training*:

▼ Datasets (1)

☐ **churn-dataset**
Dataset to create a model which can predict the churn of customers

Figure 6.6 – churn-dataset under the Datasets category

2.   Drag **churn-dataset** onto the canvas:

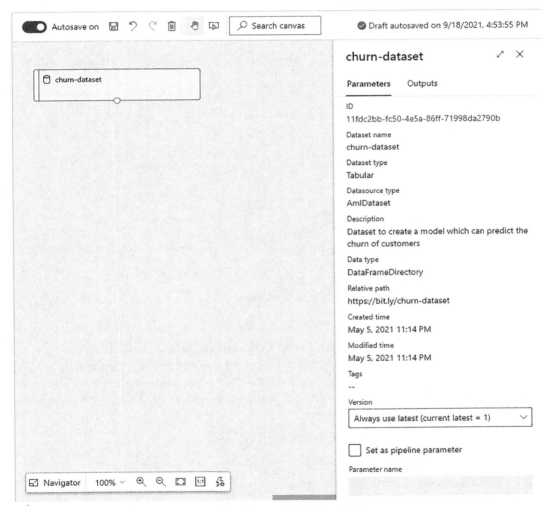

Figure 6.7 – Canvas with churn-dataset

With that, you have just completed the **Data collection** step, which means you can move on to step number 2 of the *7 Steps of Machine Learning*.

3. The next step is **Data preparation**. Add a processing step to the pipeline by dragging the **Select Columns in Dataset** module, which can be found under the **Data Transformation** category in the asset library, onto the canvas.

4. You will now need to create a flow between the dataset and the module. You can do that by pulling from the dataset's **output port**, the small circle at the bottom of this **dataset**, to the dataset's **input port**, the small circle at the top of the **Select Columns in Dataset** module, as shown in the following screenshot:

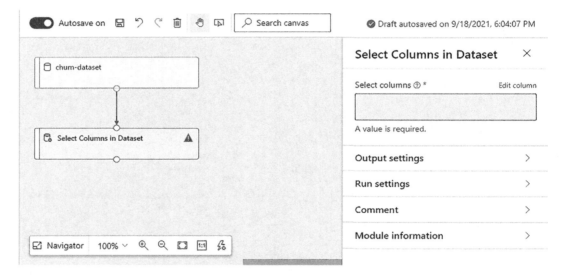

Figure 6.8 – Creating a flow between the dataset and the processing module

5. The next step is to configure the **Select Columns in Dataset** module. With the module selected in the canvas, click on the **Edit column** link on the details pane, which is on the right of the canvas, as shown in the preceding screenshot. The **Select columns** dialog will appear. See the following screenshot for the final configuration of this popup.

6. In that popup, select **All columns** from the dropdown.

7. Add a second line by clicking on the + button.

8. Select **Exclude** from the dropdown.

9. Choose **Column names** from the second dropdown.

10. Select the **id** column from the last dropdown.

The dialog page should look as follows:

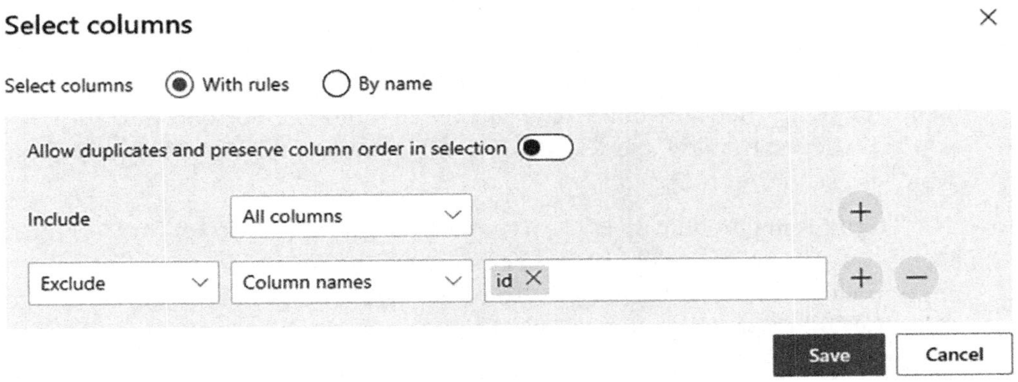

Select columns   ✕

Select columns   ⦿ With rules   ◯ By name

Allow duplicates and preserve column order in selection ⬤

Include   All columns   ⌄   +

Exclude   ⌄   Column names   ⌄   id ✕   +   —

                                                     Save   Cancel

Figure 6.9 – Select columns dialog

11. Click on **Save** to close the popup.

So far, you have selected the dataset that you will use to train the model, and you have prepared the data by removing the **id** column, which you will not need for the training process. In the next section, you will finalize your training pipeline by adding the untrained model, the module that will train the model, and the module for scoring and evaluating the trained model.

Preparing the data and training the model

Now, you will choose the model that you will train. In *Chapter 5*, *Letting the Machines Do the Model Training*, you identified a **voting ensemble** as the best performing model for the given data. This type of model is a combination of different models, including **Random Forest**. To keep this example simple, you will use a **Two-Class Decision Forest** model, similar to **Random Forest**. Let's get started:

1. Navigate to the **Machine Learning Algorithms** category in the asset library. You will notice a couple of subcategories, including **Classification**. From that subcategory, drag and drop the **Two-Class Decision Forest** module onto the canvas.

2. For the model training, you will need two additional modules: the **Split Data** module, which you can find in the asset library under the **Data Transformation** category, and the **Train Model** module, which can be found in the **Model Training** category. Drag and drop both modules onto the canvas.

3. You will need to extend the data flow you created in the previous section to pass the data through the new modules. Pull an **output port** from the **Select Columns in Dataset** module to an **input port** of the **Split Data** module.

4. You will need to configure the **Split Data** module on the module's details pane, as shown in the following screenshot. Set **Fraction of rows in the first output dataset** to **0.7**. By doing that, 70% of the data will be sent on the **left output port** area, which is used to train the model, and 30% will be sent to the **right output port** area, which is used for testing.

5. The **Train Model** module accepts two inputs. On the **left input port** area, you need to pass an untrained model that will be trained with the data given on the **right input port** area. Pull an **output port** from the **Two-Class Decision Forest** module to the **left input port** area of the **Train Model** module.

6. Drag the **left output port** area of the **Split Data** module to the **right input port** area of **Train Model**. Your canvas should look as follows:

Figure 6.10 – The Train Model module is missing some configuration

7. In the preceding screenshot, there is an orange exclamation mark in the **Train Model** module. This mark indicates that something is misconfigured in that module. So far, you have configured which model to train and what data to use for the model's training. However, you have not defined which column the model should predict yet. This column is referred to as **Label column**. To configure **Label column**, select the module in the canvas and click on the **Edit column** link. This will open the **Label column** dialog shown in the following screenshot. Select the **churned** column from the drop-down list and click **Save**:

Figure 6.11 – Selecting the column that the model will predict

So far, the training pipeline is performing the first four steps of the *7 Steps of Machine Learning*. The next step is to evaluate the model.

8. Drag and drop the **Score Model** module onto the canvas, which can be found in the asset library under the **Model Scoring & Evaluation** category. This module accepts a trained model in the **left input port** area and a dataset on the **right input port** area. The output of this module is a dataset that contains the inferences made by the model against the incoming dataset.

9. Connect the **right output port** area of the **Split Data** module to the **right input port** area of the **Score Model** module. This will create a data flow that will bring the 30% part of the original data into the **Score Model** module.

10. Connect the **output port** area of the **Train Model** module to the **left input port** area of the **Score Model** module. The **Score Model** module will use the trained model to perform inferences against the incoming data.

11. Drag and drop the **Evaluate Model** module onto the canvas, which can be found in the asset library under the **Model Scoring & Evaluation** category. This module will compare the predictions that the model made against the values stored in the **churned** column.

12. Connect the **output port** area of the **Score Model** module to the **left input port** area of the **Evaluate Model** module.

If you have followed all the steps so far, your canvas should look as follows:

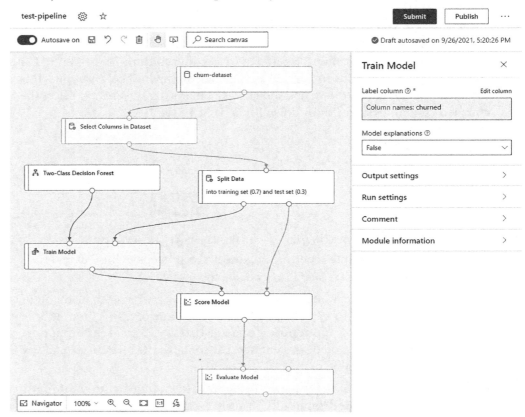

Figure 6.12 – The completed training pipeline

So far, you have authored a training pipeline that performs the following actions:

- Removes the **id** column from the dataset.

- Splits the data into a training dataset and a validation one. The training dataset contains 70% of the original data. The validation dataset contains the remaining 30%.

- Trains **Two-Class Decision Forest** using the training dataset.

- Scores the validation dataset using the trained model.

- Evaluates the performance of the model by examining the results in the scored dataset. You will be able to review the metrics of the trained model in the **Evaluate Model** module.

In the next section, you are going to execute this pipeline to train the model.

Executing the training pipeline

In the previous section, you created a complete training pipeline that you will now execute by creating a new pipeline run. Let's get started:

1. Click on the **Submit** button in the top-right corner. The **Set up pipeline run** dialog will open, as shown in the following screenshot.

2. You will need to create a new experiment and name it **test-pipeline**. Select the **Create new** radio button and then type in this name.

3. Notice that the pipeline will execute in the default **compute target** you selected in the *The authoring screen/view* section. Click on the **Submit** button to start executing the training pipeline:

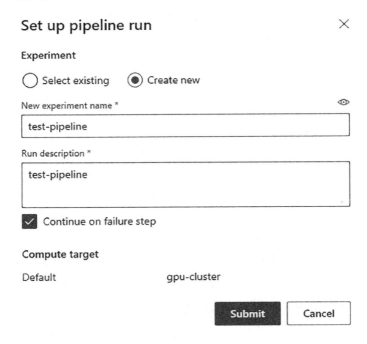

Figure 6.13 – Preparing to execute the training pipeline

Once the pipeline finishes executing, the designer will look similar to the following:

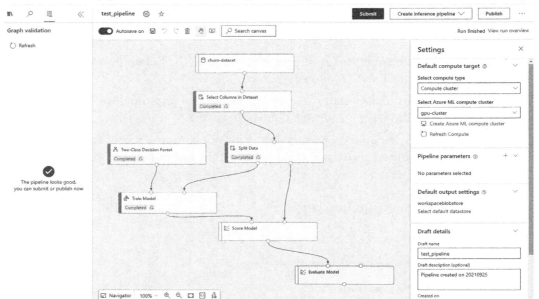

Figure 6.14 – Successfully running the pipeline

With that, you have successfully finished developing and training your first pipeline. When the execution of the pipeline is completed, the **Create inference pipeline** button will appear. The following section describes the different options you have when it comes to creating an inference pipeline.

Creating a batch and real-time inference pipeline

This section will discuss the two options of deploying an inference pipeline from the designer: **batch** and **real time**:

- With batch predictions, you asynchronously score large datasets.

- With real-time prediction, you score a small dataset or a single row in real time.

When you create an inference pipeline, either batch or real time, AzureML takes care of the following things:

- AzureML stores the trained model and all the trained data processing modules as an asset in the asset library under the **Datasets** category.

- It removes unnecessary modules such as **Train Model** and **Split Data** automatically.

- It adds the trained model to the pipeline.

Especially for real-time inference pipelines, AzureML will add a **web service input** and a **web service output** in the final pipeline.

Let's start by creating a batch pipeline, something you will do in the next section.

Creating a batch pipeline

In this section, you will create a batch inference pipeline. Let's get started:

1. Click on the **Create inference pipeline** dropdown next to the **Submit** button and select **Batch inference pipeline**. This action will create the **Batch inference pipeline** tab, as shown in the following screenshot:

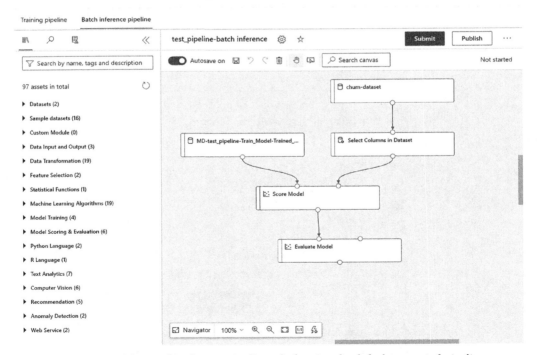

Figure 6.15 – The Batch inference pipeline tab showing the default generated pipeline

2. By adding a pipeline parameter, you will be able to change the behavior of the pipeline at runtime. In our case, we want to parameterize which dataset to use to make predictions. To parameterize the input dataset, click on **churn-dataset** and select the **Set as pipeline parameter** checkbox in the details pane on the right.

3. Change the default parameter name in the **Parameter name** text box to **batchfile**.

4. Click on the **Publish** button to bring up the **Set up published pipeline** dialog shown in the following screenshot.

5. Select the **Create new** radio button to define a new pipeline endpoint. This endpoint is used to trigger the pipeline that you are about to publish.

6. Keep the default value of the **New PipelineEndpoint name** field as is. It should read **test-pipeline-batch inference**.

7. You can add a description to your published endpoint by filling in the **PipelineEndpoint description (optional)** field. Write **Test of a batch pipeline parameter name batchfile** in that field.

8. Keep all the other settings as is. The completed dialog page should look as follows:

Figure 6.16 – Published pipeline dialog page

9. Click on the **Publish** button.

Once the pipeline's endpoint has been successfully published, the message shown in the following screenshot will appear in the designer. The **test-pipeline-batch inference** link will direct you to the published pipeline:

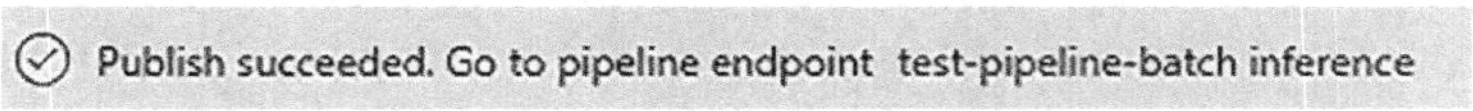

⊘ Publish succeeded. Go to pipeline endpoint test-pipeline-batch inference

Figure 6.17 – Publish succeeded

Now that you have published a batch inference pipeline, you can trigger it through the AzureML Studio interface. In *Chapter 11*, *Working with Pipelines*, in the *Publishing a pipeline to expose it as an endpoint* section, you will learn more about these pipelines and how you can integrate them with third-party applications.

In the next section, we will create a real-time pipeline based on the training pipeline.

Creating a real-time pipeline

In this section, you will create a real-time inference pipeline. Let's get started:

1. Select the **Training pipeline** tab in the designer, which is visible on the top-left corner in *Figure 6.15*.

2. Click on the **Create inference pipeline** dropdown next to the **Submit** button and select **Real-time inference pipeline**. This will generate the default **real-time inference pipeline** shown in the following screenshot:

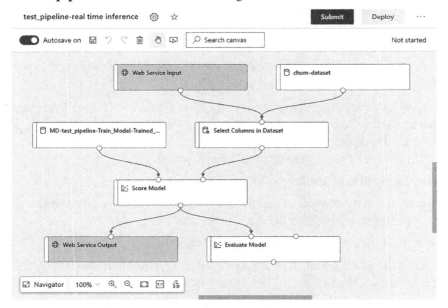

Figure 6.18 – The default real-time inference pipeline

Before we deploy this pipeline, we will need to make a couple of changes.

3. Click on the **Select Columns in Dataset** module and click on the **Edit column** link in the details pane on the right-hand side.

4. Add a new row to the **Select columns** dialog by clicking on the plus (+) icon.

5. Select **Exclude** and **Column names** from the corresponding dropdowns and enter **churned** as the column's name to exclude. The dialog page should look as follows:

Figure 6.19 – Excluding both the id and churned columns from the incoming dataset

6. From the **Data Transformation** category in the asset library, drag the **Apply SQL Transformation** module onto the canvas. Place it above the **Webservice Output** module.

7. Connect the **output port** area of the **Score Model** module to the **left input port** area of the **Apply SQL Transformation** module.

8. Delete the connection between the **Score Model** module and the **Web Service Output** model. To do that, select the connection between those two modules by clicking on it. When highlighted, select the trash icon or press the *Delete* button on your keyboard. The connector should be removed.

9. Delete the **Evaluate Model** module from the canvas.

10. Connect the **output port** area of the **Apply SQL Transformation** module to the **input port** area of the **Web Service Output** module.

11. Select the **Apply SQL Transformation** module.

12. Click on the **Edit code** link in the **Apply SQL Transformation** detail pane and replace the default query with the following one:

```
select [Scored Labels] from t1
```

This SQL transformation only selects the predicted value, which is stored in the **Scored Labels** column.

13. Press the **Save** button. The changed pipeline should look like the one shown in the following screenshot.

14. To ensure that the pipeline you have designed executes properly, you will need to run it once using the **Submit** button. The **Set up published pipeline** dialog will appear.

15. You will need to execute the pipeline within an experiment. Select the **Create new** radio button.

16. Use **test-pipeline-real-time-inference** as **New experiment name**.

17. Keep the default values as is for the rest of the fields and press **Submit**.

Your pipeline should execute, and the canvas should look as follows:

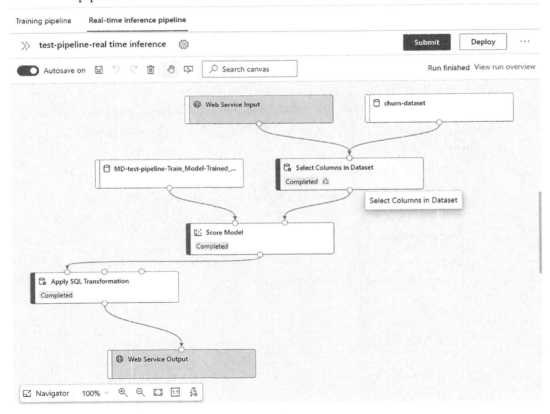

Figure 6.20 – Modified real-time inference pipeline

After verifying that the pipeline can execute without any issues, you can deploy it as a real-time endpoint. You have two options regarding the infrastructure that will host your real-time endpoint. You can deploy either in an **Azure Container Instance** (**ACI**) or **Azure Kubernetes Service** (**AKS**) cluster. The **ACI** infrastructure is useful for testing purposes, while the **AKS** infrastructure supports better production environments. In our case, we will deploy to **ACI**, something you will read about in the next section.

Deploying a real-time inference pipeline

In this section, you will deploy the sample real-time inference pipeline you created in the **Real-time inference pipeline** designer tab. Let's get started:

1. Click on the **Deploy** button. This will bring up the **Set up real-time endpoint** popup shown in the following screenshot.

2. On the **Set up real-time endpoint** popup, select the **Deploy new real-time endpoint** radio button option.

3. In the **Name** text field, enter **first-real-time-endpoint**.

4. In the **Description** text field, enter **Container Deployment of the first real-time pipeline**.

5. Click on the **Compute type** drop-down list and select **Azure Container Instance**.

6. You won't need to modify the **Advanced** settings. The completed popup should look as follows:

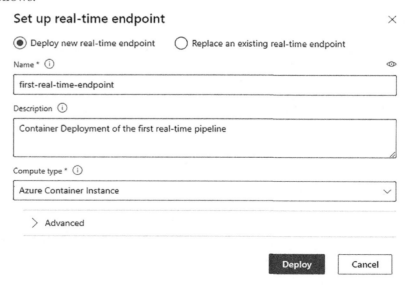

Figure 6.21 – Set up real-time endpoint popup

7. Click on the **Deploy** button to provision your real-time endpoint. This will take a couple of minutes.

After successfully deploying the pipeline, you will find the newly deployed pipeline under **Assets | Endpoints** of AzureML Studio. The endpoint you just deployed is the same as the one you deployed in *Chapter 5, Letting the Machines Do the Model Training*. You can test it through the web interface. You will deep dive into how to use similar endpoints in *Chapter 12, Operationalizing Models with Code*. Before moving on, you should delete the real-time endpoint to avoid being charged. Follow the instructions in the *Cleaning up the model deployment* section of *Chapter 5, Letting the Machines Do the Model Training*, to delete the endpoint you just deployed.

Summary

This chapter introduced the pipeline designer, which allows us to create AzureML pipelines via drag and drop. You built your first training pipeline based on the churn dataset and the **Two-Class Decision Forest** model. We discussed three pipeline types, authored the training pipeline, created a batch pipeline, and developed and deployed a real-time pipeline.

This chapter concludes the no-code, low-code features that AzureML provides. In the next chapter, you will start working on the AzureML Python SDK. The AzureML Python SDK allows you to train models and create machine learning pipelines through code, which is critical for the DP-100 exam.

Question

What are the options for deploying real-time pipelines?

- **Azure Container Instances** only
- **Azure Container Instances** and **Azure Kubernetes Services**
- **Azure Container Instances** and **Azure Virtual Machines**
- **Azure Virtual Machines** only

Further reading

This section offers a list of helpful web resources to help you augment your AzureML designer knowledge:

- Configuring data splits and cross-validation in automated machine learning: `https://docs.microsoft.com/azure/machine-learning/how-to-configure-cross-validation-data-splits`

- Running batch predictions using the AzureML designer: `https://github.com/MicrosoftDocs/azure-docs/blob/master/articles/machine-learning/how-to-run-batch-predictions-designer.md`

- Tutorial: Designer – deploying a machine learning model: `https://docs.microsoft.com/azure/machine-learning/tutorial-designer-automobile-price-deploy`

- What is the AzureML designer? `https://docs.microsoft.com/azure/machine-learning/concept-designer`

- Tutorial: Designer – training a no-code regression model: `https://docs.microsoft.com/azure/machine-learning/tutorial-designer-automobile-price-train-score`

- Tutorial: Designer – deploying a machine learning model: `ttps://docs.microsoft.com/azure/machine-learning/tutorial-designer-automobile-price-deploy`

Section 3: Advanced data science tooling and capabilities

In this section, you will dive into the **Azure Machine Learning (AzureML)** Python SDK. The SDK allows you to configure your workspace and orchestrate the end-to-end data science process with Python code. Here, you will gain more insights into how the AzureML platform works, which is crucial for passing the DP-100 exam.

This section comprises of the following chapters:

- *Chapter 7, The AzureML Python SDK*
- *Chapter 8, Experimenting with Python Code*
- *Chapter 9, Optimizing the ML Model*
- *Chapter 10, Understanding Model Results*
- *Chapter 11, Working with Pipelines*
- *Chapter 12, Operationalizing Models with Code*

7
The AzureML Python SDK

In this chapter, you will understand how the AzureML Python **Software Development Kit (SDK)** is structured and how to work with it, something that is key for the DP-100 exam. You will learn how to work with the **Notebooks** experience that is built into the AzureML Studio web portal, a tool that boosts coding productivity. Using the notebook editor, you will write some Python code to gain a better understanding of how to manage the compute targets, datastores, and datasets that are registered in the workspace. Finally, you are going to revisit the Azure CLI we looked at in *Chapter 2, Deploying Azure Machine Learning Workspace Resources*, to perform workspace management actions using the AzureML extension. This will allow you to script and automate your workspace management activities.

In this chapter, we are going to cover the following main topics:

- Overview of the Python SDK
- Working with AzureML notebooks
- Basic coding with the AzureML SDK
- Working with the AzureML CLI extension

Technical requirements

You will need to have access to an Azure subscription. Within that subscription, you will need a **resource group** named packt-azureml-rg. You will need to have either a Contributor or Owner **Access control (IAM)** role at the resource group level. Within that resource group, you should have already deployed a **machine learning** resource named packt-learning-mlw, as described in *Chapter 2, Deploying Azure Machine Learning Workspace Resources*.

You will also need to have a basic understanding of the **Python** language. The code snippets in this chapter target Python version 3.6 or later. You should know the basics of how a Jupyter notebook works and how the variables that you defined in one cell exist in the execution context of others.

You can find all the notebooks and code snippets for this chapter on GitHub at http:// bit.ly/dp100-ch07.

Overview of the Python SDK

The AzureML **SDK** is a Python library that allows you to interact with the AzureML services. It also provides you with data science modules that will assist you in your machine learning journey. The AzureML SDK is available in the R programming language through a Python to R interoperability package.

The SDK consists of several packages that group different types of modules you can import into your code base. All the Microsoft-supported modules are placed within packages that start with azureml, such as azureml.core and azureml.train. hyperdrive. The following diagram offers a broad overview of the AzureML SDK's most frequently used packages, as well as the key modules that you will see in this book and the exam:

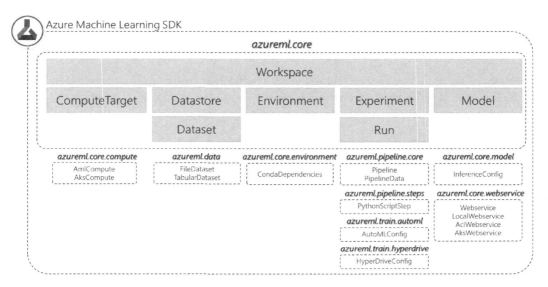

Figure 7.1 – The AzureML SDK modules and important classes

Note that all the key classes that exist in the `azureml.core` package can also be imported from the corresponding child module. For example, the `Experiment` class can be imported in either way, as follows:

```
from azureml.core import Experiment
from azureml.core.experiment import Experiment
```

Both snippets will load the same class and you only need to use one of them. The first one loads the class from the `azureml.core` package, while the second one loads it from the `experiment` module (a file named `experiment.py`), which is part of the `azureml.core` package. Do not be surprised if you notice this type of difference in various code samples you may read through.

> **Important note**
>
> For exam purposes, you will not need to memorize the packages, but you will have to select the appropriate one from a drop-down list. For example, you may be asked to complete some code that refers to `AutoMLConfig`, and you may have to select between the `azureml.automl` package and the `azureml.pipeline` one, a choice that will become even more obvious when you finish reading the next few chapters. The code samples throughout this book import all the required packages on top of the script to help you become familiar with the location of the classes.

In this chapter, you will focus on the SDK classes that allow you to control the AzureML workspace, as well as the compute resources that are deployed in the workspace, the datastores, and the datasets that you can register in the workspace.

In the next section, you will learn how to utilize the **Notebooks** experience that is built into AzureML Studio to write Python scripts.

Working in AzureML notebooks

AzureML Studio offers integration with a couple of code editors that allow you to edit notebooks and Python scripts. These editors are powered by the **compute instance** you provisioned in *Chapter 4, Configuring the Workspace*. If you have stopped that compute instance to save on costs, navigate to **Manage | Compute** and start it. From this view, you can open all third-party coding editors AzureML Studio integrates with, as shown in the following screenshot:

Compute

Compute instances	Compute clusters	Inference clusters	Attached computes

+ New   ⊙ Start   ⊡ Stop   ⟳ Restart   🗑 Delete   ↻ Refresh   ▦ Edit columns   ⋯

🔍 Search   ▽ Filter   ✕ Clear all

◯	Name	State	Applications
◯	my-compute-instance	⊙ Running	JupyterLab Jupyter VS Code RStudio Terminal

Figure 7.2 – List of third-party code editor experiences Azure Studio integrates with

The most widely known open source data science editors are Jupyter Notebook and its newer sibling, JupyterLab. You can open those editing environments by clicking on the respective links shown in the preceding screenshot. This will open a new browser tab, as shown in the following screenshot:

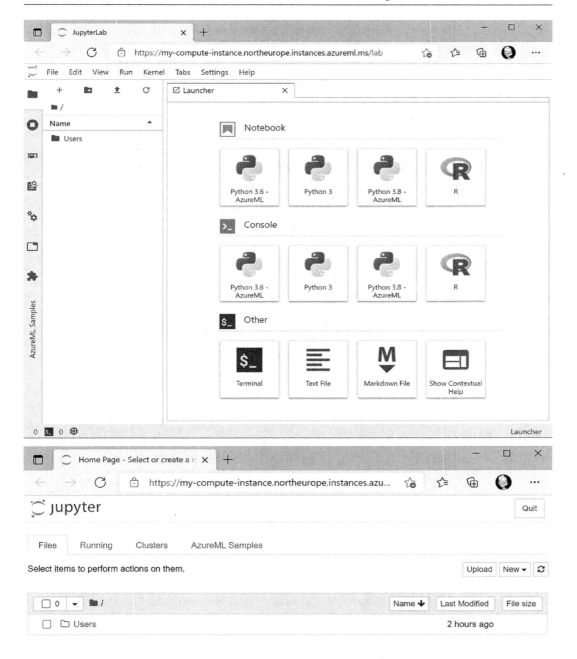

Figure 7.3 – JupyterLab and Jupyter editing experiences provided by the compute instance

Besides these third-party code editing experiences, AzureML Studio offers a built-in enhanced notebook editor that allows you to edit, share, and collaborate within the Studio interface, as shown in the following screenshot. This editor is created on top of the Jupyter Notebook service but offers a much more improved code editing experience, such as inline error highlighting, automatic code completion, popups with parameter information for the method you are about to invoke, and other features that are referred to as **IntelliSense**:

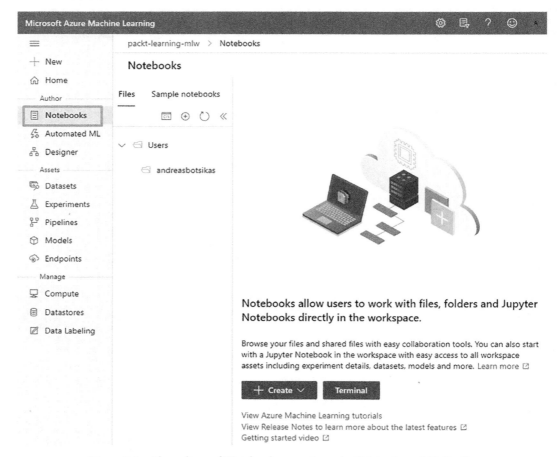

Figure 7.4 – The enhanced Notebooks experience built into AzureML Studio

The notebook editor comes with an embedded sample library that contains an up-to-date catalog of notebooks that demonstrate almost all the capabilities of the latest AzureML SDK. Once you have found a related notebook, you can review its contents and if you want to modify it, you can clone it in your workspace, an action that will copy both the Jupyter notebook and the accompanying scripts and data that relate to that notebook, as shown in the following screenshot:

Notebooks

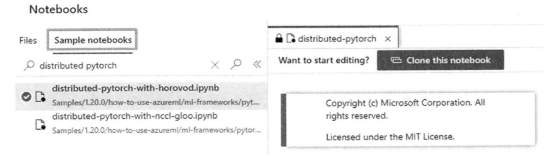

Figure 7.5 – Sample notebooks to help you ramp up the AzureML SDK's capabilities

> **Important note**
> These notebooks are up to date with the latest version of the AzureML
> SDK. The code repository where these notebooks are hosted can
> be found on GitHub at `https://github.com/Azure/`
> `MachineLearningNotebooks/`. You can use GitHub to file an issue
> or search for a code snippet using GitHub's search experience.

Every AzureML workspace comes with a storage account, as mentioned
in *Chapter 2, Deploying Azure Machine Learning Workspace Resources*. This storage
account contains a **file share** prefixed with **code-** that hosts all the notebooks and scripts
available within the workspace, as shown in the following screenshot. The files in that
folder share location are the ones that you saw previously within the Studio experience,
in the **Files** tab:

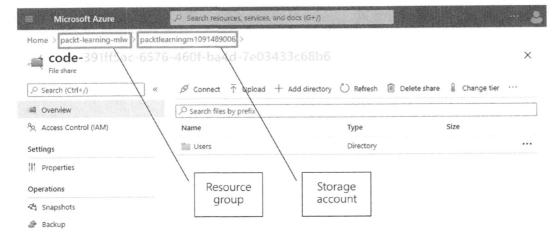

Figure 7.6 – The Azure portal view of the file share that hosts all
the code files in the AzureML workspace

Each user gets a separate folder under the **Users** folder where they can organize their files. All the files can be accessed by all users that have access to the specific AzureML workspace. This makes sharing code very easy. You can point to someone who has access to the AzureML workspace to a file by opening the file in your browser; then, you can share the URL from the browser navigation bar.

In this section, you will create a notebook where you will write and execute the code snippets in this chapter. To work with your files, navigate to the **Files** tab of the **Notebooks** section of AzureML Studio. To keep the code snippets organized by chapter, you must create a folder named `chapter07` and then create a notebook named `chapter07.ipynb`.

Click on the three dots next to your username, as shown in the following screenshot. From there, you can create folder structures and upload files from your local computer. Click on the **Create new folder** option, as shown in the following screenshot:

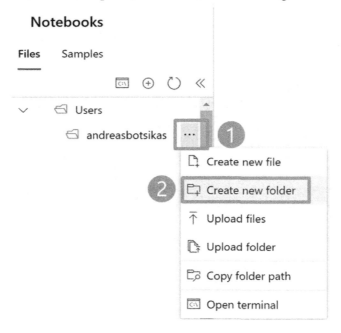

Figure 7.7 – The Create new folder option in the Notebooks experience area of AzureML Studio

Fill in the pop-up dialog that appears to create a folder named `chapter07`. Select that folder and click on the three dots. Then, select the **Create new file** option shown in the following screenshot. In the popup that appears, under **File location**, you should see `Users/<username>/chapter07`, which means that this file will be placed in the newly created folder. Regarding **File type**, you can select from an ever-growing list of types such as notebooks, Python or R script files, text files, and other popular formats. If none of these options fit the file you want to create, you can just select **Other** from the drop-down menu. In the **File name** field, type `chapter07.ipynb` and click on the **Create** button, as shown in the following screenshot:

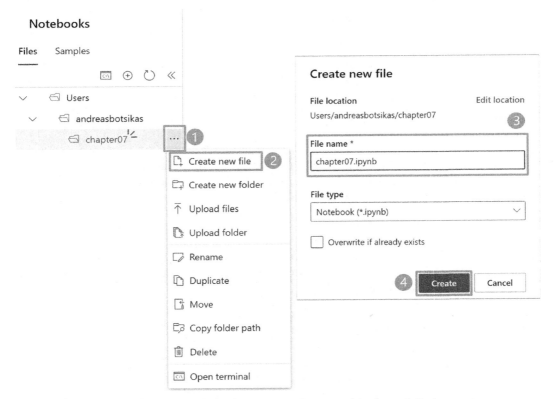

Figure 7.8 – Creating a notebook to write and execute this chapter's Python scripts

This will create two files in your folder: the notebook file, which will open in the editor pane, and a .amlignore file, a file you will read about in *Chapter 8, Experimenting with Python Code*:

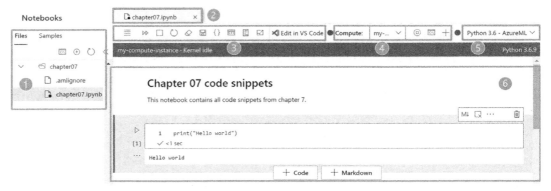

Figure 7.9 – Editing a notebook within AzureML Studio

Starting from the left-hand side of the preceding screenshot, the Notebooks experience offers the following:

1. The **Files** explorer, where you can create or upload new files and delete, download, rename, or move existing files you or your colleagues have created in this workspace.

2. The name of the open file. Note that if you see an asterisk next to the name – for example, * **chapter07.ipynb** – this means that the file hasn't been saved yet. You can save the file by using the *Ctrl + S* shortcut for Windows and Linux or the *Cmd + S* shortcut for macOS. Alternatively, you can select the **Save** option from the **File options** menu, which you will read about next.

3. The **File options** menu, where you have options such as the **Save** operation and **Focus mode**, which expands the editor pane to occupy most of the browser tab space. This is a dynamic menu that's based on the file type you are currently editing. In the preceding screenshot, a notebook is open, and the menu is offering additional operations such as clearing outputs, restarting the Python kernel, or examining the variables that are currently loaded in the Python kernel. You can also edit the same file in Jupyter or JupyterLab by clicking on the menu icon, which is the icon with the four vertical lines, and selecting the corresponding editor from the **Editors** option. Especially for VS Code, a very popular free cross-platform code editor, the **Edit in VS Code** option is available in the main bar.

4. The ability to manage the compute instance where you are currently editing the specific file. From this section, you can quickly create a new compute instance or start/stop an existing one.

5. The ability to select the environment to execute the notebook in. By default, the AzureML Python kernel is selected, which is the environment where the AzureML SDK is already installed. You can change the kernel to an R one if you are editing an R file, or you can create your own kernels if you want to customize the environment you are working in.

6. The main editor pane. This is where you can modify the selected file.

   In your case, the editor pane will be empty, and a single empty cell will be visible, as shown in the following screenshot. Each cell can either contain **Markdown**-formatted text or Python code. You can convert a cell into a code one by clicking on the pop-up menu and selecting the **M↓** icon:

Figure 7.10 – An empty code cell

7. Click on the **M↓** icon and then hit the **edit** icon to add the following Markdown text in the cell:

```
# Chapter 07 code snippets
This notebook contains all code snippets from chapter 7.
```

8. Hit *Shift + Enter* on your keyboard to finish editing, execute the cell, which in this case will render the formatted text, and move the cursor to the next cell. By default, the next cell will be a code one. Add the following Python code inside the cell:

```
print('Hello world')
```

Note that while you start typing, a popup will appear containing code suggestions that you can select using the arrow keys. You can confirm your selection by hitting the *Enter* button on your keyboard. The list is an intelligent one in that it shows classes that start with what you have typed. It also shows frequently used classes that you may have misspelled or forgot to type some letters in for. For example, the following screenshot shows the `PermissionError` class because you may have forgotten to type the **e** and **m** letters. Also, note that while the `print` statement is incomplete, a wavy underline will indicate a syntax error in that portion of the code. To execute a code cell, you can hit the *Shift + Enter* key combo, or you can click on the round button on the left-hand side of the cell:

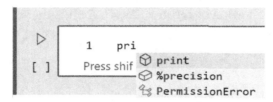

Figure 7.11 – IntelliSense suggesting methods and classes that fit the current script's scope

If an error occurs in the code cell you are executing, the error message will appear at the bottom of the cell and the Traceback will appear in the output section of the cell, as shown in the following screenshot. You can update the cell's content and rerun the cell to fix this error:

```
    1    # Error message output
    2    invalid_result = 0/0
[2]    ⊗ <1 sec - ZeroDivisionError: division by zero
```

```
---------------------------------------------------------------------
ZeroDivisionError                         Traceback (most recent call last)
<ipython-input-2-ef835df9276d> in <module>
      1 # Error message output
----> 2 invalid_result = 0/0

ZeroDivisionError: division by zero
```

Figure 7.12 – Script error during notebook cell execution

In this section, you learned how to use the built-in Notebooks experience to author Python scripts. In the next section, you will start writing code fragments that utilize the AzureML SDK.

Basic coding with the AzureML SDK

The first class you will work with is the AzureML `Workspace`, a class that gives you access to all the resources within your workspace. To create a reference to your workspace, you will need the following information:

- **Subscription ID**: The subscription where the workspace is located. This is a **Globally Unique Identifier** (**GUID**, also known as a **UUID**) that consists of 32 hexadecimal (0-F) digits; for example, `ab05ab05-ab05-ab05-ab05-ab05ab05ab05`. You can find this ID in the Azure portal in the **Properties** tab of the subscription you are using.

- **Resource group name**: The resource group that contains the AzureML workspace components.

- **Workspace name**: The name of the AzureML workspace.

You can store this information in variables by running the following assignments:

```
subscription_id = '<Subscription Id>'
resource_group = 'packt-azureml-rg'
workspace_name = 'packt-learning-mlw'
```

The first approach to creating the reference to the workspace is to instantiate the `Workspace` class, as shown in the following snippet:

```
from azureml.core import Workspace
ws = Workspace(subscription_id, resource_group, workspace_name)
```

This is the code snippet that you saw in *Chapter 4, Configuring the Workspace*, when you created a dataset and explored the **Consume** tab of that dataset.

Important note

This book assumes that you will be writing the code in the notebook you created in the previous section, and that you will be editing the notebook using the **Notebook** experience within Studio. When you open a notebook for the first time you will notice a banner asking you to authenticate. This is an once off process that you need to perform. If you are allowed to install software components on your local computer, you can execute the same scripts on your local machine on a local Jupyter server, so long as you install the `azureml-sdk` package by issuing the `pip install azureml-sdk` command. In that case, you will be prompted to authenticate your device using an interactive authentication, something you will read about in the next section.

Another approach to creating the reference to the AzureML workspace is to use the `get()` method of the `Workspace` class, as shown in the following snippet:

```
from azureml.core import Workspace
ws = Workspace.get(name=workspace_name,
                   subscription_id=subscription_id,
                   resource_group=resource_group)
```

Here, regarding the `ws` variable, you assigned a reference to the AzureML workspace that matches the `name`, `subscription_id`, and `resource_group` values that you specified in the `workspace_name`, `subscription_id`, and `resource_group` variables at the beginning of this section.

> **Important note**
>
> In Python, you can invoke functions by passing arguments either by name or by position. In the previous examples, we invoked `Workspace.get()` by passing arguments by name – that is, we explicitly specified that for the `name` argument, we are passing the `workspace_name` variable as its value. When using this approach, the order of the arguments is not important. In the example before that, we instantiated the `Workspace` class by passing arguments by position. You did not use the `workspace_name=workspace_name` assignment. This means that you assigned values to the parameters of the `Workspace` class's constructor based on the order they were declared in. In this book, as well as in the exam, you will see both ways of performing assignments.

The previous two ways of getting the AzureML workspace reference are identical. The main issue with them, however, is that they hardcode the workspace where the script is connecting to. Imagine that you want to share a notebook with a friend, and you have hardcoded the subscription ID, resource name, and workspace name in that notebook. Your friend would have to manually go and edit that cell. This problem becomes even more obvious when you want to write a script that runs in multiple environments, such as the development environment, the quality assurance environment, and the production environment.

The `Workspace` class offers the `from_config()` method to address this issue. This method searches the folder tree structure for the `config.json` file, which is in the following format and includes all the information that was mentioned at the beginning of this section:

```
{
    "subscription_id": "<Subscription Id>",
    "resource_group": "packt-azureml-rg",
    "workspace_name": "packt-learning-mlw"
}
```

In the case of the compute instance, this file is located in the root folder (`/config.json`) and was automatically created there when you provisioned the compute instance within the AzureML workspace. If you want to run the same script from your local computer, you can create a similar file, place it next to the Python script you are editing, and write the following code to get a reference to the AzureML workspace:

```
from azureml.core import Workspace
ws = Workspace.from_config()
print(f"Connected to workspace {ws.name}")
```

If you want to spin up a new AzureML workspace, you can provision one using the `Workspace.create()` method. The following code snippet creates an AzureML workspace in the West Europe region:

```
from azureml.core import Workspace
new_ws = Workspace.create(
                name='packt-azureml-sdk-mlw',
                subscription_id=subscription_id,
                resource_group='packt-azureml-sdk-rg',
                create_resource_group=True,
                location='westeurope')
```

This snippet will create an AzureML workspace named `packt-azureml-sdk-mlw`, in the subscription with the ID specified by the `subscription_id` variable. This resource will be deployed in the `packt-azureml-sdk-rg` resource group, which will be created if it does not already exist.

> **Important note**
> You will need to have the required permissions at the Azure subscription level to be able to create the resource group if it does not exist already. Otherwise, you will get an error stating **Azure Error: AuthorizationFailed**. This can be either a custom role, a `Contributor` role, or an even more privileged role such as `Owner`. To get past that error, you may try to deploy the new workspace within the `packt-azureml-rg` resource group instead of `packt-azureml-sdk-rg` by modifying the preceding code snippet. You will need to have at least a `Contributor` role at the resource group level to be able to deploy the AzureML workspace with the SDK.

To delete the workspace you just deployed, you can use the following code snippet:

```
new_ws.delete(delete_dependent_resources=True)
```

This code deletes the workspace being referenced by the `new_ws` variable and removes the dependent resources, which are the storage account, the key vault, and the Application Insights resources that were deployed with the AzureML workspace.

In this section, you learned how to get a reference to and manipulate the workspace resource through Python code. This section assumed that you have been using the built-in notebook editor of the studio web UI, so you did not have to authenticate. If you wanted to run the same code on your computer, you would have to authenticate to be able to access the resources, which is something we will look at in the next section.

Authenticating from your device

In March 2020, the **Notebooks** experience in AzureML Studio requests you to authenticate to the compute instance. This is a process you have to do only once and it is as simple as clicking the **Authenticate** button that will be visible in the Notebooks experience. If you are running the same code from your local computer, or if you are trying to execute a Python script within a terminal in a compute instance for the very first time, you must run an AzureML SDK command. A prompt will ask you to authenticate, as shown in the following screenshot:

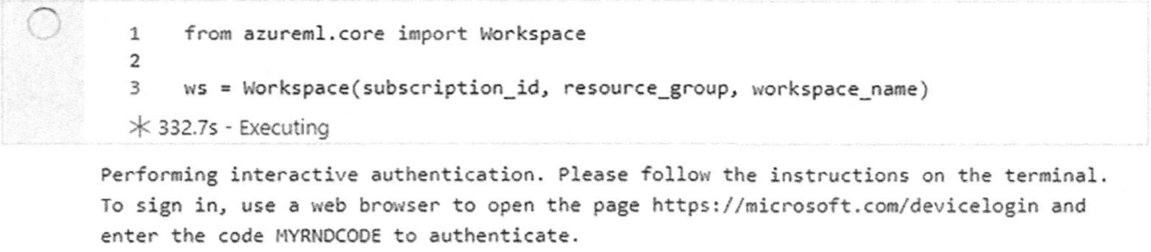

```
1    from azureml.core import Workspace
2
3    ws = Workspace(subscription_id, resource_group, workspace_name)
* 332.7s - Executing

Performing interactive authentication. Please follow the instructions on the terminal.
To sign in, use a web browser to open the page https://microsoft.com/devicelogin and
enter the code MYRNDCODE to authenticate.
```

Figure 7.13 – Interactive authentication requested during the first command's execution

If you see this message, navigate to the link provided, where you will be asked to input the request code displayed in the prompt. In this case, this is **MYRNDCODE**. This code is a unique identifier for a request to log in using your identity from your computer's location. Select the account you are planning to use to access the various Azure resources, including the AzureML workspace. The following figure shows the overall interactive authentication flow:

Figure 7.14 – Using interactive login to authenticate in a compute instance

> **Important note**
> The request code is a short-lived one and it expires in 15 minutes. If you fail to complete the process within that time frame, an error will occur, and you will have to start over.

If your account has access to multiple **Azure Active Directories** (**AADs**), for example, your personal AAD from the trial subscription and your company's one, you may need to manually indicate which AAD tenant to authenticate to. This can be done by invoking the interactive authentication process manually using the following snippet:

```
from azureml.core.authentication import \
                        InteractiveLoginAuthentication

InteractiveLoginAuthentication(tenant_id="<AAD tenant id>")
```

This code initiates the device authentication flow shown in the preceding figure. <AAD tenant id> is a GUID that you can get from the Azure portal by visiting the AAD resource.

In this section, you learned about interactive authentication, which allows you to access your AzureML workspace from any device. This authentication method should be used when you try to execute a script on a remote computer or if you are trying to execute an Azure CLI command. Once authenticated, a token is stored within the computer you are executing `InteractiveLoginAuthentication` on and you will not be prompted for another login until that token has expired.

In the next section, you will start using the authenticated reference to your workspace to deploy compute targets you can use to execute scripts remotely.

Working with compute targets

As we mentioned in *Chapter 4, Configuring the Workspace*, in the *Provisioning compute resources* section, compute resources are machines that allow you to execute scripts remotely. The AzureML SDK allows you to list the existing compute targets you may have in your workspace or provision new ones if needed.

To enumerate the compute targets that you have provisioned or attached to your workspace, you can use the reference to the AzureML workspace that you assigned to the `ws` variable using `ws = Workspace.from_config()`. The workspace object has an attribute named `compute_targets`. This is a Python dictionary that has all the compute instance names as keys and a reference to that compute instance as a value. To enumerate and print out this list, you can use the following code:

```
for compute_name in ws.compute_targets:
    compute = ws.compute_targets[compute_name]
    print(f"Compute {compute.name} is a {type(compute)}")
```

The output should list at least the `ComputeInstance` area where you are executing the script and potentially the `AmlCompute` cluster you created in *Chapter 4, Configuring the Workspace*. You will notice that all the compute types are defined within the modules of the `azureml.core.compute` package.

Important note

This code assumes that you have initialized the `ws` variable, something you did earlier on the notebook by following the instructions in the *Basic coding with the AzureML SDK* section. If you close the compute instance, the kernel will stop, and all the variables you defined by executing the notebook cells will be lost. If you want to continue working on a notebook, the easiest approach is to rerun all the cells, which will ensure that you have initialized all the variables.

Another way to get a reference to a compute target is to use the `ComputeTarget` constructor. You need to pass in the `Workspace` reference and the name of the compute target you are looking for. If the target does not exist, a `ComputeTargetException` exception will be raised that you have to handle in your code base, as shown in the following script:

```
from azureml.core import ComputeTarget
from azureml.exceptions import ComputeTargetException

compute_name = 'gpu-cluster'
compute = None
try:
    compute = ComputeTarget(workspace=ws, name=compute_name)
    print(f"Found {compute_name} which is {type(compute)}")
except ComputeTargetException as e:
    print(f"Failed to get compute {compute_name}. Error: {e}")
```

The `ComputeTarget` class offers the `create()` method, which allows you to provision various compute targets, including compute instances (the `ComputeInstance` class), compute clusters (the `AmlCompute` class), and Azure Kubernetes Service (the `AKSCompute` class) targets.

> **Important note**
> Whenever you are deploying a compute instance or compute cluster from the AzureML Studio web UI, the Azure CLI, or the SDK, the compute target will be provisioned in the same resource group and the same Azure Region that your machine learning workspace is located.

To provision a compute target, you will need to create a configuration object that inherits from the `ComputeTargetProvisioningConfiguration` abstract class. In the following example, the script is trying to locate a compute cluster named `cpu-sm-cluster`. If the cluster exists, it assigns a reference to the cluster to the `cluster` variable. If the cluster does not exist, the script creates an instance of the `AmlComputeProvisioningConfiguration` class, which is assigned to the `config` variable. This instance is created through the `provisioning_configuration()` method of the `AmlCompute` class. This `config` is used to create the cluster and wait for the registration in the workspace to complete, showing the creation logs:

```
from azureml.core.compute import ComputeTarget, AmlCompute
compute_name = 'cpu-sm-cluster'
```

```
cluster = None
if compute_name in ws.compute_targets:
    print('Getting reference to compute cluster')
    cluster = ws.compute_targets[compute_name]
else:
    print('Creating compute cluster')
    config = AmlCompute.provisioning_configuration(
                    vm_size='Standard_D1',
                    max_nodes=2)
    cluster = ComputeTarget.create(ws, compute_name, config)
    cluster.wait_for_completion(show_output=True)
print(f"Got reference to cluster {cluster.name}")
```

This script specifies the virtual machine's size (the vm_size argument). The virtual machine is going to be Standard_D1, which is a **D-Series** one, also known as general-purpose compute. This means that it does not have any GPU capabilities. This is in contrast to **N-Series**, which are also known as GPU-enabled virtual machines. Examples of **N-Series** virtual machine sizes are Standard_NC6, Standard_NV24s_v3, and Standard_ND40rs_v2. Notice how all the sizes start with **N**.

The script is only specifying the maximum nodes (the max_nodes argument) that the compute cluster will have. If you do not specify the minimum nodes (the min_nodes argument), the argument will be the default value of 0. This means that by default, the cluster will scale down to 0 nodes, inflicting no compute costs when no job is running. You can find all the default values for all the arguments of the provisioning_configuration() method on Microsoft's official Python SDK reference page, as shown in the following screenshot, or by using the Python help command by executing help(AmlCompute.provisioning_configuration):

provisioning_configuration

Create a configuration object for provisioning an AmlCompute target.

Python	Copy

```python
provisioning_configuration(vm_size='', vm_priority='dedicated',
min_nodes=0, max_nodes=None, idle_seconds_before_scaledown=None,
admin_username=None, admin_user_password=None, admin_user_ssh_key=None,
vnet_resourcegroup_name=None, vnet_name=None, subnet_name=None, tags=None,
description=None, remote_login_port_public_access='NotSpecified',
identity_type=None, identity_id=None)
```

Figure 7.15 – Documentation for the provisioning_configuration method of the AmlCompute class

One of the drawbacks of having 0 minimum nodes in a compute cluster is that you will have to wait for the compute nodes to be allocated before the job you submitted gets executed. To save this slack time, it is common to scale up the minimum and even the maximum nodes of the cluster during workdays, and then change those values after business hours to save on costs. To change the number of nodes of a compute cluster, you can use the AzureML Studio web UI or the Azure CLI, or even update the min_nodes attribute of the compute cluster using the following code:

```python
from azureml.core.compute import AmlCompute
for ct_name, ct in ws.compute_targets.items():
    if (isinstance(ct, AmlCompute)):
        print(f"Scalling down cluster {ct.name}")
        ct.update(min_nodes=0)
```

> **Important note**
> Changing the number of minimum and maximum nodes of a compute cluster can be done through the AzureML Studio web portal, the CLI, the SDK, and ARM templates. Before October 2020, you could also change the number of nodes through the Azure portal, a functionality that has been removed since.

In this section, you learned how to create or get a reference to a compute target that you can use to execute scripts. In the next section, you will learn how to attach to various data sources through the SDK.

Defining datastores

As we mentioned in *Chapter 4, Configuring the Workspace,* in the *Connecting to datastores* section, datastores are the engines where your data resides and provide access to anyone authorized to do so. The AzureML SDK allows you to attach existing datastores to access the underlying data.

In this section, you are going to attach the blob container of a storage account to your workspace. Imagine that you have a storage account named **mydatastg**. This storage account has a blob container named **existing-container** that contains the CSV files you want to analyze and then train models against, as shown in the following screenshot:

Figure 7.16 – The container in the mydatastg storage account, as seen in the Azure portal

> **Important note**
> Provisioning new storage accounts and adding containers from the Azure portal is an easy task and is outside the scope of the exam. Note that storage accounts have unique names. This means that you will probably not be able to provision a storage account named **mydatastg** because it belongs to someone else. You can use the existing storage account that was provisioned with your AzureML workspace to follow these steps. You can add the **existing-container** container to that storage account through the Azure portal or you can use the **azureml** container that already exists.

To register this container as a new datastore in your AzureML workspace, you will need to follow these steps:

1. Before going into your notebook, you will need the storage account name and the account key. This information is located in the Azure portal, in the **Settings | Access keys** tab of the storage account resource, as shown in the following screenshot:

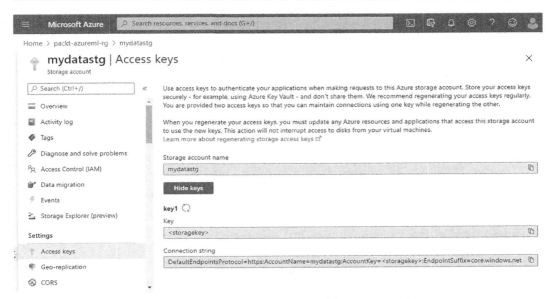

Figure 7.17 – Storage account name and key required to connect to the storage account

2. Go to your `chapter07.ipynb` notebook and in a new code cell, assign that information to the following Python variables:

```
storage_name = 'mydatastg'
storage_key = '<storagekey>'
storage_container = 'existing-container'
```

3. To register the blob container as a new datastore named `my_data_store`, you can use the `register_azure_blob_container()` method of the `Datastore` class, as shown in the following snippet:

```
from azureml.core import Datastore
dstore = Datastore.register_azure_blob_container(
    workspace=ws,
    datastore_name="my_data_store",
    container_name=storage_container,
    account_name=storage_name,
    account_key=storage_key,
    create_if_not_exists=False
)
```

As expected, the method requires a reference to the `Workspace` area where the new datastore will be created as an argument. Also, note that the `create_if_not_exists` argument is set to `False`, something that will make the method raise an `AzureMissingResourceHttpError` exception with an error code of `ContainerNotFound` if that the blob container does not exist.

Similar to the blob container, you can register all supported data storage types through the AzureML SDK's `Datastore` class, as shown in the following screenshot. For example, you can use the `register_azure_data_lake_gen2()` method to connect to an Azure Data Lake Generation 2 datastore or the `register_azure_sql_database()` method to connect to an Azure SQL database:

Supported data storage service types

Datastores currently support storing connection information to the storage services listed in the following matrix.

Storage type	Authentication type	Azure Machine Learning studio ⬀	Azure Machine Learning Python SDK	Azure Machine Learning CLI
Azure Blob Storage	Account key SAS token	✓	✓	✓
Azure File Share	Account key SAS token	✓	✓	✓
Azure Data Lake Storage Gen 1	Service principal	✓	✓	✓
Azure Data Lake Storage Gen 2	Service principal	✓	✓	✓
Azure SQL Database	SQL authentication Service principal	✓	✓	✓
Azure PostgreSQL	SQL authentication	✓	✓	✓
Azure Database for MySQL	SQL authentication		✓*	✓*
Databricks File System	No authentication		✓**	✓ **

* MySQL is only supported for pipeline DataTransferStep
** Databricks is only supported for pipeline DatabricksStep

Figure 7.18 – Supported data storage service types from the official documentation page

4. To get a reference to the connected datastore, you can use the `Datastore` class constructor, as shown in the following snippet:

```
from azureml.core import Datastore
dstore = Datastore.get(ws,"my_data_store")
```

5. In *Chapter 4*, *Configuring the Workspace*, in the list of datastores, you learn how to set one of the registered datastores to the default one for the AzureML workspace. The `Workspace` class offers a shortcut that gives a reference to that store using the `get_default_datastore()` method:

```
dstore = ws.get_default_datastore()
```

In the rest of this book, you will be using the default datastore to store data.

6. Datastores that refer to Azure blob containers (the `AzureBlobDatastore` class) or Azure file shares (the `AzureFileDatastore` class) can upload and download files through the SDK. The following snippet loads the **scikit-learn** diabetes dataset into a pandas `DataFrame`, which is then stored as a local CSV file. Once the file has been stored, the script gets a reference to the default datastore of the `Workspace` area, which is referenced in the ws variable, and uploads that file to `/samples/diabetes/v1/rawdata.csv` using the `upload()` method:

```
from sklearn.datasets import load_diabetes
import pandas as pd

features, target = load_diabetes(return_X_y=True)
diabetes_df = pd.DataFrame(features)
diabetes_df['target']= target
diabetes_df.to_csv('rawdata.csv', index=False)

dstore = ws.get_default_datastore()
dstore.upload_files(
            files=['rawdata.csv'],
            target_path="/samples/diabetes/v1",
            overwrite=True,
            show_progress=True)
```

7. This file will appear in the storage account that was created with your AzureML workspace. You can find it in the Azure portal by navigating to the storage account, selecting the blob container with the name that starts with **azureml-blobstore-**, and navigating through the **samples / diabetes / v1** folders, as shown in the following screenshot:

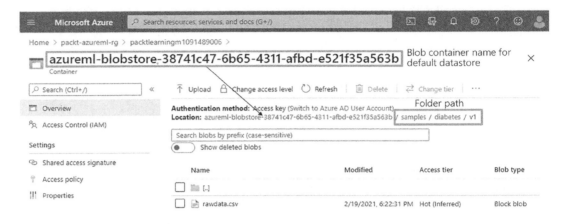

Figure 7.19 – Uploaded data in the blob container that is registered as the default datastore

In this section, you learned how to attach an existing Azure blob container to a new datastore within your AzureML workspace. You also learned how to easily get a reference to the workspace's default datastore, and then you uploaded a CSV file to that datastore. In the next section, you will learn how to define datasets, a construct that will help you work with your data independently from where it's stored.

Working with datasets

As we mentioned in *Chapter 4, Configuring the Workspace*, in the *Working with datasets* section, datasets are an abstraction layer on top of the data that you use for training and inference. They contain references to the physical data's location and provide a series of metadata that helps you understand their shape and statistical properties. They *do not copy* the data that resides within the datastores. AzureML offers two types of datasets:

- `FileDataset` allows you to reference a single file or multiple files in one or multiple datastores. A common example of `FileDataset` is images that are being used to train a computer vision model.

- `TabularDataset` allows you to reference tabular structured data that can be stored in a single file or multiple files within datastores or may be stored directly in relational datastores such as SQL servers. The diabetes **pandas** `DataFrame` that you loaded in the previous section is a typical tabular dataset. You can create `TabularDataset` by parsing various files, including CSV, TSV, Parquet, and JSON files. If your data contains a column/feature that has a timestamp, or the files are stored in a folder structure that contains a date pattern such as `/<year>/<month>/file.csv`, you can enable the time series trait of `TabularDataset`, something that allows you to perform time-based filtering of the dataset.

To get some hands-on experience with this, you can define a `FileDataset` that references the CSV file you uploaded in the default datastore in the previous section. Although CSV represents tabular data, it is also a file, something that `FileDataset` can referenc:.

1. In a new cell in your notebook, type the following code:

```
from azureml.core import Dataset
dstore = ws.get_default_datastore()
file_paths = [
    (dstore, "/samples/diabetes/v1")
]
file_ds = Dataset.File.from_files(
    path = file_paths, validate=True
)
print("Files in FileDataset:")
print(file_ds.to_path())
```

In this code snippet, there is a reference to the default datastore of the workstation.

2. Now, you can create an array of tuples of `Datastore` and its relative paths. Each tuple references a file or a folder within a specific `Datastore`. In this case, you are referencing the `samples/diabetes/v1` folder within the default `Datastore`. You can use the wildcard character, `*`, to load multiple subfolders or partial filenames if you want. For example, the following array of tuples loads all the CSV files of all the months in 2021 of the weather data that's stored in `/weather/<year>/<month>/<day>.csv`:

```
file_paths = [
    (dstore, "/weather/2021/*/*.csv")
]
```

3. If you wanted to explicitly load the data for the first day (01.csv) of January (01), February (02), and March (03) only, then you would use the following array of tuples:

```
file_paths = [
    (dstore, "/weather/2021/01/01.csv"),
    (dstore, "/weather/2021/02/01.csv"),
    (dstore, "/weather/2021/03/01.csv")
]
```

It is advised to keep the array's size to less than 100 data path references per dataset for performance reasons.

4. Returning to the code snippet at the beginning of this section, you can now create an unregistered FileDataset using the from_files() method. Here, you must pass the array of data paths as an argument. You must also validate whether the data can be loaded or not via the method. If the folder did not exist or the datastore was protected with private endpoints and was not directly accessible from the compute that is executing the code, you will get DatasetValidationError. The default value of the validate argument is True, and you can disable that validation by passing False in that argument.

5. Once you have created FileDataset, you can get a list of files that were referenced by invoking the to_path() method. The output of these two prints should look as follows:

```
1   from azureml.core import Dataset
2
3   dstore = ws.get_default_datastore()
4   file_paths = [
5       (dstore, "/samples/diabetes/v1")
6   ]
7
8   file_ds = Dataset.File.from_files(
9       path = file_paths, validate = True
10  )
11
12  print("Files in FileDataset:")
13  print(file_ds.to_path())
```
✓ <1 sec

```
Files in FileDataset:
['/rawdata.csv']
```

Figure 7.20 – Unregistered FileDataset referencing a single CSV file

6. For the CSV files, a far better approach would be to define a `TabularDataset` that could parse the file and provide us with a pandas `DataFrame`. To do so, copy the following code in a new cell:

```
tabular_dataset = Dataset.Tabular.from_delimited_files(
    path=file_paths, validate=False)
df = tabular_dataset.to_pandas_dataframe()
print(len(df))
```

In this snippet, you are reusing the `file_paths` properties that you used while creating `FileDataset`. This time, you are creating an unregistered `TabularDataset` using the `from_delimited_files()` method. Also, note that you explicitly skip the validation so that the data can be loaded from the current compute (`validate=False`), speeding up the declaration process.

Datasets do not load the data by default unless you are explicitly invoking a method that requires the actual data. In this case, your code will reach out to the datastore, load the data in memory as a pandas `DataFrame`, and assign it to the `df` variable when you invoke the `to_pandas_dataframe()` method. Upon calling the `len()` method, you get the number of rows that `DataFrame` has.

7. So far, the datasets that you have created have been unregistered, meaning that they did not register within the AzureML workspace, nor were they listed in the **Datasets** section of the studio web portal. If you want to reuse a dataset in multiple experiments, you can register it in the workspace using the `register()` method:

```
tabular_dataset.register(
    workspace=ws,
    name="diabetes",
    description="The sklearn diabetes dataset")
```

> **Important note**
> If you have already registered a dataset with the same name, you will not be able to rerun this cell. To register a new version of the dataset you must use the `create_new_version` argument as follows: `tabular_dataset.register(workspace=ws, name="diabetes", create_new_version=True)`

This method requires you to specify the workspace where you want to register `TabularDataset` and the name of the registration. Optionally, you can pass a description, tags, and whether to create a new version of the dataset with the specific name that is already registered in the workspace. Once the dataset has been registered, you can review the registration information in the Studio web UI, as shown in the following screenshot:

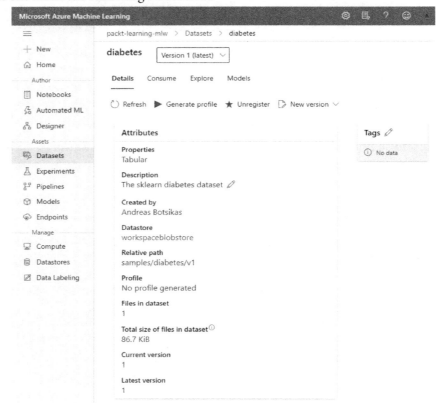

Figure 7.21 – Registered tabular dataset in the workspace

8. If, instead of `TabularDataset`, you have a pandas `DataFrame` that you want to register, you can use the `register_pandas_dataframe()` method, as shown in the following code snippet:

```
Dataset.Tabular.register_pandas_dataframe(
    dataframe=df,
    target=(dstore,"/samples/diabetes"),
    name="diabetes",
    description="The sklearn diabetes dataset")
```

Note that in this snippet, you are passing the `df` pandas `DataFrame` reference and that you are requesting to store that `DataFrame` in the default datastore that is referenced by the `dstore` variable, in the `/samples/diabetes` folder. This method will create a new folder with a GUID name and store the data in Parquet file format. Since the dataset has already been registered and points to a different path, the command will create a new version of the dataset. In the Studio experience, you will notice that **Version 2** of the dataset was registered. This version has a different **relative path**, as shown here:

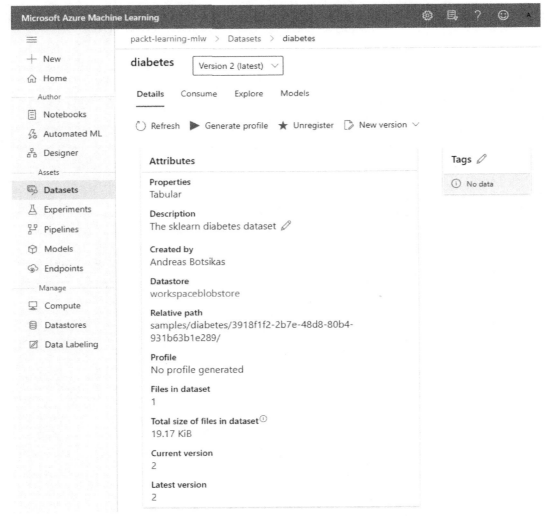

Figure 7.22 – New version of the diabetes dataset, registered directly from a pandas DataFrame

Note that the Parquet file format is a compressed one, which leads to smaller files compared to the CSV file you used for the first version of the dataset.

9. Once you have registered a dataset, either `FileDataset` or `TabularDataset`, you can retrieve it using the `get_by_name()` method of the `Dataset` class using the following code snippet:

```
from azureml.core import Dataset
diabetes_dataset = Dataset.get_by_name(
    workspace=ws,
    name='diabetes')
```

Optionally, you can specify the `version` argument, which is `latest` by default.

10. The preceding code snippet returns an instance of a `TabularDataset` class, but the data hasn't been loaded yet. You can load the dataset partially using various methods of the `TabularDataset` class, as shown in the following code snippet:

```
partial_dataset = diabetes_dataset \
    .skip(10) \
    .take(2) \
    .keep_columns(['0','target'])
```

11. `partial_dataset` is a `TabularDataset` instance that was created from `diabetes_dataset`. This dataset skips the first 10 rows of `diabetes_dataset`, keeps two rows, and then drops all the columns other than the columns named `0` and `target`. No data was loaded during the execution of this multiline statement. Having this unregistered `partial_dataset` dataset defined, you can load the data into a pandas `DataFrame` using the following code:

```
df = partial_dataset.to_pandas_dataframe()
df.head()
```

This will display a small table that consists of two rows and two columns, as shown in the following screenshot:

	0	target
0	-0.096328	101.0
1	0.027178	69.0

Figure 7.23 – Small DataFrame loaded from a sliced tabular dataset

This lazy loading capability of the AzureML dataset classes gives you the flexibility to slice and dice huge datasets without having to load them in memory.

So far, you have learned how to work with the Python SDK to deploy compute targets, define datastores, and create datasets. In the next section, you will learn how to perform similar actions using the Azure CLI tool you saw in *Chapter 2, Deploying Azure Machine Learning Workspace Resources*, in the *Using the Azure CLI* section.

Working with the AzureML CLI extension

In *Chapter 2, Deploying Azure Machine Learning Workspace Resources*, you learned how to use the Azure CLI and how to install the `azure-cli-ml` extension. This extension uses the Python SDK you saw in this chapter to perform various operations. To work with the Azure CLI, you can do one of the following:

1. Open the cloud shell in the Azure portal, as you did in *Chapter 2, Deploying Azure Machine Learning Workspace Resources*.

2. Open a terminal in the compute instance you have been working on in this chapter.

3. Use the shell assignment feature of Jupyter notebooks, which allows you to execute commands using the underlying shell by using an exclamation mark (**!**), also known as **bang**.

In this section, you will use the notebook, something that will allow you to store the steps and repeat them if you need them in the future:

1. The first thing you will need to do is install the `azure-cli-ml` extension in the Azure CLI of the compute instance you are currently working on. Create a new code cell in the notebook you have been editing so far and add the following code:

```
! az extension add -n azure-cli-ml
```

Note that in *Chapter 2, Deploying Azure Machine Learning Workspace Resources*, you executed the same command, without the exclamation prefix. The output of this command should be similar to the following:

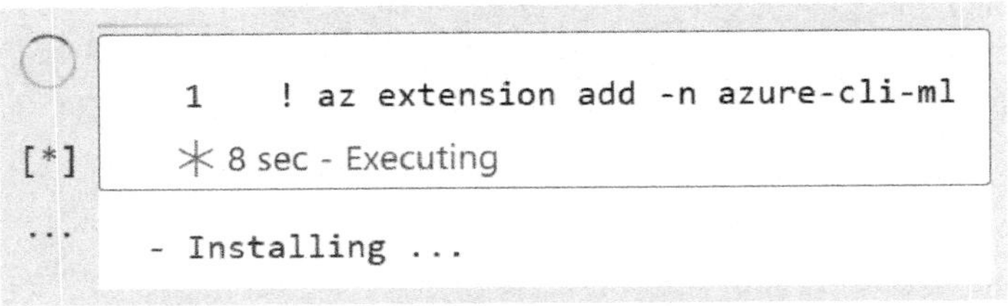

Figure 7.24 – Installing the AzureML extension

2. Then, you will need to log in using the `az login` command. This command will trigger a device authentication process, similar to the one you used at the beginning of this chapter when you first tried to connect to the workspace through the SDK. Run the following command:

```
! az login
```

3. If you have access to multiple Azure subscriptions, you will need to select the one you are targeting using the following code snippet:

```
! az account set --subscription "<subscription id>"
```

From this point on, you can use the AzureML CLI to perform operations against the workspace.

> **Important note**
> If you have multiple AzureML workspaces within your subscription, you will need to specify which workspace and in which resource group you are targeting each AzureML CLI command. To do that, you will need to use the `-g` and `-w` parameters, which we looked at in *Chapter 2*, *Deploying Azure Machine Learning Workspace Resources*.

4. To list all the compute targets in your workspace, use the following code snippet:

```
! az ml computetarget list -g packt-azureml-rg -w packt-learning-mlw -o table
```

5. You can then update `cpu-sm-cluster` so that it has 0 minimum nodes using the following command:

```
! az ml computetarget update amlcompute --name cpu-sm-cluster --min-nodes 0 -g packt-azureml-rg -w packt-learning-mlw
```

6. To get the default datastore that is registered in the workspace, you can use the following command:

```
! az ml datastore show-default -g packt-azureml-rg -w packt-learning-mlw
```

7. Finally, you can list the datasets registered in the workspace using the following snippet:

```
! az ml dataset list -g packt-azureml-rg -w packt-learning-mlw -o table
```

The results of this command should be similar to the following:

```
 1   ! az ml dataset list -g packt-azureml-rg -w packt-learning-mlw -o table
 ✓ 4.2s

Description                                     Name                  Version
--------------------------------------------    ------------------    ---------
The sklearn diabetes dataset                    diabetes              2
This is the inferences done by the model        survey-drift-target   1
                                                survey-drift-base     1
```

Figure 7.25 – Table-formatted output of the datasets listing within the AzureML CLI

The AzureML CLI offers full access to the SDK options, including the ability to create and detach compute targets, datastores, and even define datasets. For the exam, you won't need to memorize the commands, so long as you have understood that the CLI is using the SDK under the hood and that most of the things you can do with the SDK have an equivalent CLI command.

Summary

In this chapter, you learned how the AzureML Python SDK is structured. You also discovered the AzureML notebook editor, which allows you to code Python scripts. You then worked with the SDK. You started your coding journey by managing the compute targets that are attached to the AzureML workspace. You then attached new datastores and got a reference to existing ones, including the default datastore for the workspace. Then, you worked with various files and tabular-based datasets and learned how to reuse them by registering them in the workspace.

Finally, you worked with the AzureML CLI extension, which is a client that utilizes the Python SDK you explored in this chapter.

In the next chapter, you will build on top of this knowledge and learn how to use the AzureML SDK during the data science experimentation phase. You will also learn how to track metrics on your data science experiments, as well as how to scale your training into bigger computes, by running scripts in compute clusters.

Questions

Please answer the following questions to check your knowledge of the topics that were discussed in this chapter:

1. What is the default minimum number of nodes for an AzureML compute cluster?

   a. 0

   b. 1

   c. Equal to the maximum number of nodes

2. You upload a CSV file to the default datastore that contains credit card transaction details. Which of the following methods should you use to create a dataset reference?

   a. `Dataset.File.from_files()`

   b. `Dataset.Tabular.from_delimited_files()`

   c. `Workspace.from_csv_files()`

   d. `Datastore.from_csv_files()`

3. How can you force the creation of a blob container during the registration process of an Azure blob-based datastore?

   a. Pass the `force_create=True` parameter to the `Datastore.register_azure_blob_container()` method.

   b. Pass the `create_if_not_exists=True` parameter to the `Datastore.register_azure_blob_container()` method.

   c. Pass the `force_create=True` parameter to the `Datastore.register_container()` method.

   b. Pass the `create_if_not_exists=True` parameter to the `Datastore.register_container()` method.

Further reading

This section offers a list of useful web resources that will help you augment your knowledge of the AzureML SDK and the various third-party libraries that were used in this chapter:

- Supported data storage service types in AzureML: `https://docs.microsoft.com/en-us/azure/machine-learning/how-to-access-data#supported-data-storage-service-types`

- Reference to the **pandas** DataFrame API: `https://pandas.pydata.org/pandas-docs/stable/reference/api/pandas.DataFrame.html`

- Reference to the diabetes dataset that was loaded from the scikit-learn library: `https://scikit-learn.org/stable/modules/generated/sklearn.datasets.load_diabetes.html`

- AzureML SDK Python API browser, which lists all packages, classes, and methods: `https://docs.microsoft.com/en-us/Python/api/?view=azure-ml-py`

- Reference to the AzureML CLI extension: `https://docs.microsoft.com/cli/azure/ml(v1)?view=azure-cli-latest`

- Free e-book – Learn Python Programming – Second Edition: `https://www.packtpub.com/free-ebook/learn-Python-programming-second-edition/9781788996662`

8
Experimenting with Python Code

In this chapter, you will understand how to train **Machine Learning** (**ML**) models with code. You will start with a simple ML model using the **Python** `scikit-learn` library, which is commonly referred to as `sklearn`. You will understand how you can keep track of the training metrics using the **Azure Machine Learning (AzureML) SDK** and **MLflow**. Then, you will see how you can scale out the training process in compute clusters.

In this chapter, we are going to cover the following topics:

- Training a simple `sklearn` model within notebooks
- Tracking metrics in Experiments
- Scaling the training process with compute clusters

Technical requirements

You will need to have access to an Azure subscription. Within that subscription, you will need a **resource group** named packt-azureml-rg. You will need to have either a Contributor or Owner **Access control (IAM)** role at the resource group level. Within that resource group, you should have already deployed an Azure ML resource named packt-learning-mlw. These resources should be already available to you if you followed the instructions in *Chapter 2, Deploying Azure Machine Learning Workspace Resources*.

You will also need to have a basic understanding of the Python language. The code snippets target Python 3.6 or newer versions. You should also be familiar with working in the notebook experience within AzureML Studio, which was covered in the previous chapter.

This chapter assumes you have registered the scikit-learn diabetes dataset in your AzureML workspace and you have created a compute cluster named cpu-sm-cluster, as described in the *Defining datastores*, *Working with datasets*, and *Working with compute targets* sections in *Chapter 7, The AzureML Python SDK*.

You can find all notebooks and code snippets for this chapter in GitHub at http://bit.ly/dp100-ch08.

Training a simple sklearn model within notebooks

The goal of this section is to create a Python script that will produce a simple model on top of the diabetes dataset that you registered in *Working with datasets* in *Chapter 7, The AzureML Python SDK*. The model will be getting numeric inputs and will be predicting a numeric output. To create this model, you will need to prepare the data, train the model, evaluate how the trained model performs, and then store it so that you will be able to reuse it in the future, as seen in *Figure 8.1*:

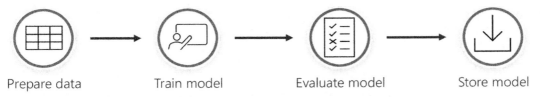

Prepare data   Train model   Evaluate model   Store model

Figure 8.1 – Process to produce the diabetes-predicting model

Let's start by understanding the dataset you will be working with. The `diabetes` dataset consists of data from 442 `diabetes` patients. Each row represents one patient. Each row consists of 10 features (**0** to **9** in *Figure 8.2*) such as age, blood pressure, and blood sugar level. These features have been transformed (mean-centered and scaled), a process similar to the data featurization you saw in automated ML in *Chapter 5*, *Letting The Machines Do the Model Training*. The eleventh column, named `target`, is the quantitative measure of the `diabetes` disease progression 1 year after the features were recorded.

You can explore the dataset further within the AzureML Studio interface as seen in *Figure 8.2*:

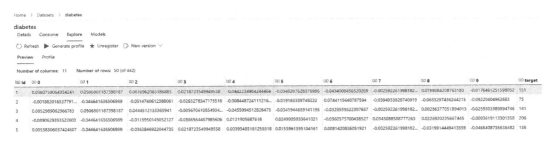

Figure 8.2 – The registered diabetes dataset

Normally in the preparation phase, you load the raw data, curate rows that have missing values, normalize feature values, and then split the dataset into train and validation data. Since the data is already preprocessed, you will just need to load the data and split it into two:

1. Navigate to the **Notebooks** section of your AzureML Studio web interface. Create a folder named chapter08 and then create a notebook named chapter08. ipynb:

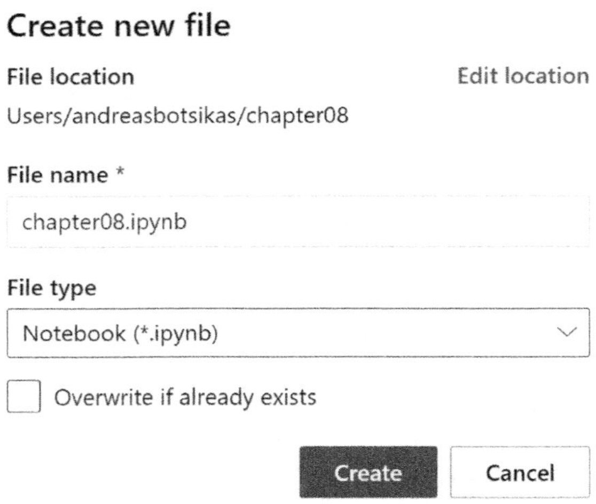

Create new file

File location   Edit location
Users/andreasbotsikas/chapter08

File name *

chapter08.ipynb

File type

Notebook (*.ipynb)   ⌄

☐ Overwrite if already exists

Create   Cancel

Figure 8.3 – Creating the chapter08 notebook you will be working on

2. In the first cell of the notebook, add the following code:

```python
from azureml.core import Workspace
ws = Workspace.from_config()
diabetes_ds = ws.datasets['diabetes']
training_data, validation_data =\
diabetes_ds.random_split(percentage = 0.8)
X_train =\
training_data.drop_columns('target').to_pandas_
dataframe()
y_train =\
training_data.keep_columns('target').to_pandas_
dataframe()
X_validate =\
validation_data.drop_columns('target').to_pandas_
```

```
dataframe()
y_validate =\
validation_data.keep_columns('target').to_pandas_
dataframe()
```

In this code snippet, you get a reference to your workspace and retrieve the dataset named `diabetes`. Then you split it into two `TabularDataset` using the `random_split()` method. The first dataset is `training_data`, which contains 80% of the data, while the `validation_data` dataset references the other 20% of the data. These datasets contain both the features and the label you want to predict. Using the `drop_columns()` and `keep_columns()` methods of `TabularDataset`, you can separate the features from the `label` columns. You then load the data in memory in a **pandas** DataFrame using the `to_pandas_dataframe()` method of `TabularDataset`. You end up with four pandas DataFrames:

- `X_train`: Contains 80% of the rows. Each row has 10 columns (0 to 9).

- `y_train`: Contains 80% of the rows. Each row has 1 column (`target`).

- `X_validate`: Contains 20% of the rows. Each row has 10 columns (0 to 9).

- `y_validate`: Contains 20% of the rows. Each row has 1 column (`target`).

The `diabetes` dataset is very popular in scientific literature. It is used as an example to train *regression* models. The `scikit-learn` library offers a dedicated module named `sklearn.linear_model` containing a lot of linear regression models we can use. Now that you have prepared the data, your next task is to train the model.

3. In this step, you are going to train a `LassoLars` model, which is an abbreviation for **Least Absolute Shrinkage and Selection Operator (LASSO)** model, fit with the **Least-Angle Regression (LARS)** selection algorithm, used in LASSO mode. In a new notebook cell, add the following code:

```
from sklearn.linear_model import LassoLars
alpha = 0.1
model = LassoLars(alpha=alpha)
model.fit(X_train, y_train)
```

In *line 3* of this code block, the constructor of the `LassoLars` class accepts a float parameter named `alpha`, which is known as a *regularization parameter* or *penalty term*. Its primary purpose is to protect the model from overfitting to the training dataset. Since this parameter controls the training process, it is referred to as being a *hyperparameter*. This parameter cannot be changed once the model has been trained. In this code block, you are instantiating an untrained model, setting `0.1` for the `alpha` parameter. In the next chapter, *Chapter 9, Optimizing the ML Model*, you will tune this parameter and try to locate the best value for your dataset.

Then, you are using the `X_train` and `y_train` DataFrames to fit() the model, which means you are training the model against the training dataset. After this process, the `model` variable references a trained model that you can use to make predictions.

4. The next task is to evaluate the model you produced based on a metric. The most common metrics to evaluate a regression model are as follows:

- Mean or median absolute error.

- Mean squared error or log error. Another common variation of this metric is the **Root Mean Squared Error (RMSE)**.

- R2, which is known as the coefficient of determination.

- Explained variance.

- Spearman correlation.

You will use the **RMSE** to measure the performance of your model utilizing the `mean_squared_error` method of the `sklearn.metrics` package. A common issue with this metric is that a model trained on data with a larger range of values has a higher rate of error than the same model trained on data with a smaller range. You are going to use a technique called *metric normalization* that basically divides the metric by the range of the data. The resulting metric is known as the **Normalized Root Mean Squared Error (NRMSE)**.

In a new notebook cell, write the following code:

```
from sklearn.metrics import mean_squared_error
predictions = model.predict(X_validate)
rmse = mean_squared_error(predictions, y_validate,
squared = False)
# Range of data using the peak to peak numpy function
range_y_validate = y_validate.to_numpy().ptp()
# Normalize dividing by the range of the data
nrmse = rmse/range_y_validate
print(f"Normalized Root Mean Squared Error: {nrmse}")
```

You start by predicting the values using the X_validate DataFrame. You calculate the RMSE, comparing the predictions with the ground truth stored in the y_validate DataFrame. Then, you calculate the range of values (maximum minus minimum) using the ptp() method of **NumPy**. As the last step, you calculate the NRMSE by dividing the RMSE metric by the range you calculated.

Since you are splitting the data randomly, and the training dataset is not always the same, the calculated NRMSE will differ from one run to another. Its value will be approximately 0.2.

The last step is to store the trained model to be able to reuse it in the future. You are going to create a folder named outputs, and you are going to persist the model to a file. The persistence of a Python object to a file is done using the dump() method of the joblib library.

In a new notebook cell, input the following source code:

```
import os
import joblib
os.makedirs('./outputs', exist_ok=True)
model_file_name = f'model_{nrmse:.4f}_{alpha:.4f}.pkl'
joblib.dump(value=model,
        filename=os.path.join('./outputs/',model_file_
name))
```

You create the `outputs` folder if it does not exist. Then, you store the model in a filename containing the `model_` prefix, followed by the NRMSE metric calculated in *Step 4*, followed by an _, and then the `alpha` parameter used to instantiate the model. You should be able to see the serialized model in the file explorer, as seen in *Figure 8.4*:

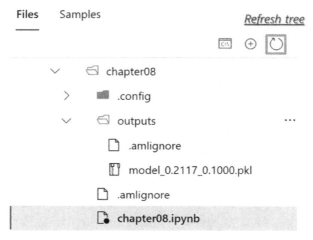

Figure 8.4 – Serialized model stored in the outputs folder

The naming convention you used in *Step 5* helps you keep track of how well the model performs and tracks the parameter you used in this run. The AzureML SDK offers various methods to monitor, organize, and manage your training runs, something you will explore in the next section.

Tracking metrics in Experiments

When you are training a model, you are performing a trial and you are logging various aspects of that process, including metrics such as the NRMSE that you need to compare model performance. The AzureML workspace offers the concept of **Experiments** – that is, a container to group such trials/runs together.

To create a new Experiment, you just need to specify the workspace you will use and provide a name that contains up to 36 letters, numbers, underscores, and dashes. If the Experiment already exists, you will get a reference to it. Add a cell in your `chapter08.ipynb` notebook and add the following code:

```
from azureml.core import Workspace, Experiment
ws = Workspace.from_config()
exp = Experiment(workspace=ws, name="chapter08")
```

You start by getting a reference to the existing AzureML workspace and then create the chapter08 Experiment if it doesn't already exist. If you navigate to the **Assets | Experiments** section of the Studio interface you will notice an empty Experiment appears in the list, as seen in *Figure 8.5*:

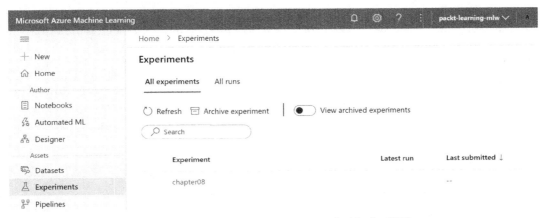

Figure 8.5 – Empty Experiment created with the SDK

To create a run under the chapter08 Experiment, you can add the following code in a new cell:

```
run = exp.start_logging()
print(run.get_details())
```

The run variable gives you access to an instance of the Run class of the AzureML SDK, which represents a single trial of an Experiment. Each run instance has a unique ID that identifies the specific run in the workspace.

> **Important note**
> In the *Scaling the training process with compute clusters* section, you will use the get_context method of the Run class to get a reference to the run instance where the Python script is being executed. The run is normally automatically created when you submit a script to execute under an Experiment. The start_logging method is used rarely and only when you want to manually create a run and log metrics. The most common cases are when you are using notebook cells to train a model or when you are training a model on a remote compute such as your local computer or a **Databricks** workspace.

The `run` class offers a rich logging API. The most frequent method used is the generic `log()` one, which allows you to log metrics with the following code:

```
run.log("nrmse", 0.01)
run.log(name="nrmse", value=0.015, description="2nd measure")
```

In this code, you log the value `0.01` for the `nrmse` metric, and then you log the value `0.015` for the same metric, passing the optional `description` parameter.

If you navigate to the **Experiments** section of the Studio interface and select the `chapter08` Experiment, you will notice there is a single `run` that is currently **Running**. If you open that `run` and navigate to the **Metrics** tab, you will be able to notice the two measurements of the **nrmse** metric, depicted either as a chart or a table, as seen in *Figure 8.6*:

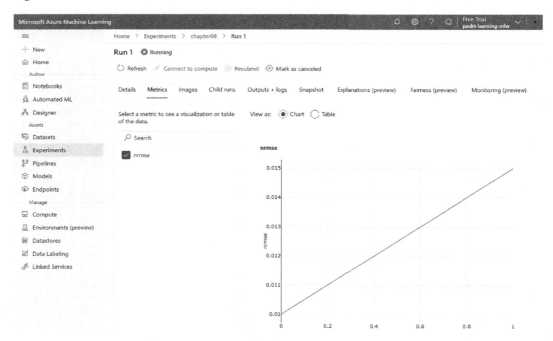

Figure 8.6 – The two measurements of nrmse as seen in the Studio experience

The Run class offers a rich list of logging methods, including the following ones:

- The `log_list` method allows you to log a list of values for the specific metric. An example of this method is the following code:

```
run.log_list("accuracies", [0.5, 0.57, 0.62])
```

This code will produce *Figure 8.7* in the *Metrics* section of the run:

accuracies

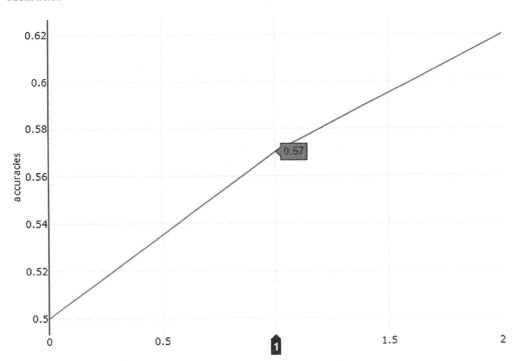

Figure 8.7 – Graph representing three values logged with the log_list method

- The `log_table` and `log_row` methods allow you to log tabular data. Note that, with this method, you can specify the labels in the *x* axis in contrast to the `log_list` method:

```
run.log_table("table", {"x":[1, 2], "y":[0.1, 0.2]})
run.log_row("table", x=3, y=0.3)
```

This code snippet will produce *Figure 8.8* in the *Metrics* section of the run:

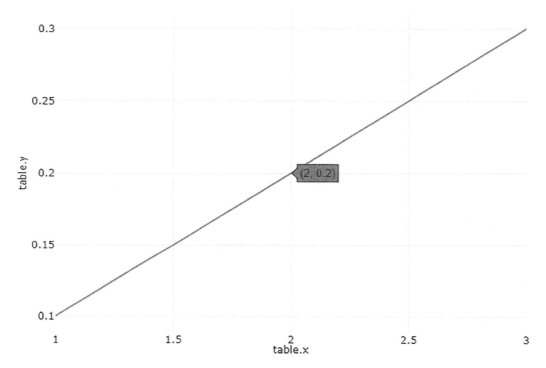

Figure 8.8 – Tabular metric logged using the log_table and log_row methods

- Specialized methods such as `log_accuracy_table`, `log_confusion_matrix`, `log_predictions`, and `log_residuals` provide a custom rendering of the logged data.

- The `log_image` method allows you to log graphs or images from the well-known `matplotlib` Python library or other plotting libraries.

- The `upload_file`, `upload_files`, and `upload_folder` methods allow you to upload Experiment residuals and associate them with the current run. These methods are commonly used to upload various binary artifacts that can be produced during the `run` execution, such as interactive HTML graphs created by open source libraries such as `plotly`.

You can optionally create child runs to isolate a subsection of the trial. Child runs log their own metrics, and you can optionally log in to the parent run as well. For example, the following code snippet creates a child run, logs a metric named `child_metric` (which is only visible within that run), and then logs in the parent's metrics `metric_from_child`:

```
child_run = run.child_run()
child_run.log("child_metric", 0.01)
child_run.parent.log("metric_from_child", 0.02)
```

Once you have completed the run, you need to change its **Running** status. You can use one of the following methods:

- The `complete` method indicates that the run was completed successfully. This method also uploads the `outputs` folder (if it exists) to the `runs` artifacts without needing to explicitly call the `upload_folder` method of the `Run` class.

- The `cancel` method indicates that the job was canceled. You will notice runs being canceled in AutoML Experiments because the timeout period was reached.

- The deprecated `fail` method indicates an error occurred.

The following code snippet cancels the child run and completes the root run, printing the status, which should read **Completed**:

```
child_run.cancel()
run.complete()
print(run.get_status())
```

In this section, you got an overview of the logging capabilities of AzureML. In the next section, you will refactor the code you created in the *Training a simple sklearn model within notebooks* section and add logging capabilities.

Tracking model evolution

In the previous section, you may have noticed that the outputs folder that you created in the *Training a simple sklearn model within notebooks* section of this chapter was automatically uploaded to the run when you executed the complete method. To avoid uploading those stale artifacts, you will need to delete the outputs folder:

1. Add a cell in your chapter08.ipynb notebook and delete the outputs folder using the following code snippet:

```python
import shutil
try:
  shutil.rmtree("./outputs")
except FileNotFoundError:
  pass
```

2. As a next step, you will refactor the training and evaluation code to a single method, passing in the alpha parameter and the training and validation datasets:

```python
from sklearn.linear_model import LassoLars
from sklearn.metrics import mean_squared_error
def train_and_evaluate(alpha, X_t, y_t, X_v, y_v):
    model = LassoLars(alpha=alpha)
    model.fit(X_t, y_t)
    predictions = model.predict(X_v)
    rmse = mean_squared_error(predictions, y_v, squared =
False)
    range_y_validate = y_v.to_numpy().ptp()
    nrmse = rmse/range_y_validate
    print(f"NRMSE: {nrmse}")
    return model, nrmse
trained_model, model_nrmse = train_and_evaluate(0.1,
                      X_train, y_train,
                      X_validate, y_validate)
```

This code is the exact equivalent of the code you wrote in the *Training a simple sklearn model within notebooks* section. You can now train multiple models using train_and_evaluate and passing different values for the alpha parameter, a process referred to as *hyperparameter tuning*. In the last line of this code snippet, you get a reference to the resulting trained model and its NRMSE metric.

> **Important note**
>
> If you get an error as follows: `NameError: name 'X_train' is not defined`, you will need to rerun the cell of your notebook where you defined the `X_train`, `y_train`, `X_validate`, and `y_validate` variables. This is an indication that the Python kernel has restarted, and all the variables have been lost from memory.

So far, you have refactored the existing code and kept the same functionality. To enable logging through the `Run` class you explored in the previous section, you will need to pass the reference to the current run instance to the `train_and_evaluate` method.

3. In a new cell, add the following snippet, which will override the existing declaration of the `train_and_evaluate` method:

```
def train_and_evaluate(run, alpha, X_t, y_t, X_v, y_v):
  model = LassoLars(alpha=alpha)
  model.fit(X_t, y_t)
  predictions = model.predict(X_v)
  rmse = mean_squared_error(predictions, y_v, squared = False)
  range_y_validate = y_v.to_numpy().ptp()
  nrmse = rmse/range_y_validate
  run.log("nrmse", nrmse)
  run.log_row("nrmse over α", α=alpha, nrmse=nrmse)
  return model, nrmse
```

Notice that you are using the `log` and `log_row` methods to log the NRMSE metric of the trained model.

> **Important note**
>
> If you cannot type the α letter shown in the preceding example, you can use the a character instead.

4. Having this `train_and_evaluate` method, you can do a hyperparameter tuning and train multiple models for multiple values of the α (alpha) parameter, using the following code:

```
from azureml.core import Workspace, Experiment
ws = Workspace.from_config()
exp = Experiment(workspace=ws, name="chapter08")
```

```
with exp.start_logging() as run:
    print(run.get_portal_url())
    for a in [0.001, 0.01, 0.1, 0.25, 0.5]:
        train_and_evaluate(run, a,
                            X_train, y_train,
                            X_validate, y_validate)
```

Note that instead of calling the `complete` method, we use the `with .. as` Python design pattern. As the `run` variables move out of scope, it is automatically marked as completed.

5. Using the `get_portal_url` in *Step 4*, you printed the link to the studio's **Experiment** section of the run you just executed. Click on the link and open the run details and then open the **Metrics** section. You should see the metrics you just logged, **nrmse** showing the error increase during the 5 (x axis shows **0** to **4**) `log` method calls, while the **nrmse over α** shows the error increase as we increase the value of the α (`alpha`) parameter, something you logged using the `log_row` method. You should see graphs similar to the ones shown in *Figure 8.9*:

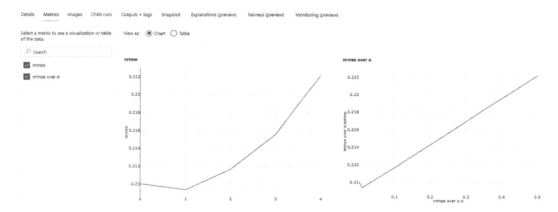

Figure 8.9 – Evolution of the nrmse metric for the diabetes model

---

Important note

In this section, you are just storing the metrics on the Run instance and not the actual trained models. You could have stored the generated models by generating the `.pkl` file and then using the `upload_file` method to upload it in the run's artifacts. In *Chapter 12, Operationalizing Models with Code*, you are going to learn about the model registry capabilities of the AzureML SDK, which provides a superior experience to keep track of the actual models.

In this section, you saw how you can enable metric logging using the AzureML SDK. When it comes to tracking Experiment metrics, the data science community is using a popular open source framework called MLflow. In the next section, you will learn how to use that library to track metrics in the AzureML workspace.

Using MLflow to track Experiments

The MLflow library is a popular open source library for managing the life cycle of your data science Experiments. This library allows you to store artifacts and metrics locally or on a server. The AzureML workspace provides an MLflow server that you can use to do the following:

- Track and log Experiment metrics through the **MLflow Tracking** component.

- Orchestrate code execution on AzureML compute clusters through the **MLflow Projects** component (similar to the pipelines you will see in *Chapter 11, Working with Pipelines*).

- Manage models in the AzureML model registry, which you will see in *Chapter 12, Operationalizing Models with Code*.

In this section, you will focus on the MLflow Tracking component to track metrics. The following snippet uses the MLflow library to track the parameters and the metrics of the diabetes model you have created in the previous section under an Experiment named chapter08-mlflow:

```
import mlflow
def train_and_evaluate(alpha, X_t, y_t, X_v, y_v):
    model = LassoLars(alpha=alpha)
    model.fit(X_t, y_t)
    predictions = model.predict(X_v)
    rmse = mean_squared_error(predictions, y_v, squared = False)
    range_y_validate = y_v.to_numpy().ptp()
    nrmse = rmse/range_y_validate
    mlflow.log_metric("nrmse", nrmse)
    return model, nrmse
mlflow.set_experiment("chapter08-mlflow")
with mlflow.start_run():
    mlflow.sklearn.autolog()
    trained_model, model_nrmse = train_and_evaluate(0.1,
                                    X_train, y_train,
                                    X_validate, y_validate)
```

One of the most well-known features of the MLflow Tracking component is the automatic logging capabilities it provides. Calling the `mlflow.sklearn.autolog()` method before your training code enables automatic logging of `sklearn` metrics, params, and produced models. Similar to the `autolog` method specific to `sklearn`, there are packages for most of the common training frameworks, such as PyTorch, fast.ai, Spark, and others.

Using the `log_metric` method, you explicitly ask the MLflow library to log a metric. In this case, you log the NRMSE metric, which is not captured automatically by the automatic logging capability.

As you can see in *Figure 8.10* the MLflow Tracking component logs all artifacts and the trained model in a folder structure under the `mlruns` folder next to the notebook:

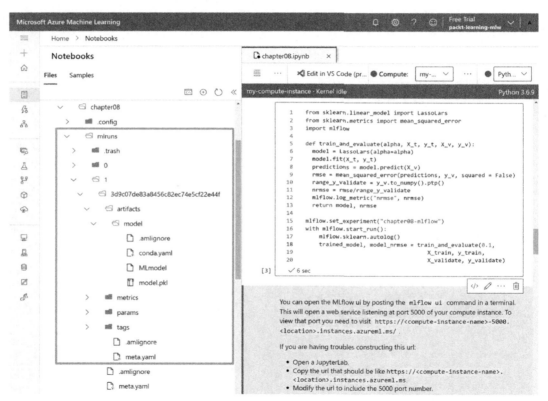

Figure 8.10 – Tracking metrics using the local FileStore mode of the MLflow Tracking component

This is the default setting, referred to as `local FileStore`. You can use the AzureML workspace as a *remote tracking server*. To do so, you need to use the `mlflow.set_tracking_uri()` method to connect to a tracking URI.

To enable the MLflow to AzureML integration, you need to ensure that your environment has the `azureml-mlflow` Python library. This package is already present in the AzureML compute instances. If you were working on a Databricks workspace, you would need to install it manually using the `pip install azureml-mlflow` command.

To get the tracking **URI** and run the same Experiment using AzureML as the remote tracking server, use the following code snippet:

```python
import mlflow
from azureml.core import Workspace
ws = Workspace.from_config()
mlflow.set_tracking_uri(ws.get_mlflow_tracking_uri())
mlflow.set_experiment("chapter08-mlflow")
with mlflow.start_run():
    mlflow.sklearn.autolog()
    trained_model, model_nrmse = train_and_evaluate(0.1,
                                    X_train, y_train,
                                    X_validate, y_validate)
```

The `get_mlflow_tracking_uri` method of the `Workspace` class returns a URL that is valid for 1 hour. If your Experiment takes more than an hour to complete, you will need to generate a new URI and assign it using the `set_tracking_uri` method, as seen in the preceding snippet.

You should be able to see the run and the tracked metrics in the Studio experience, as seen in *Figure 8.11*:

Figure 8.11 – Metrics logged using the MLflow library with AzureML as the remote tracking server

So far, you have been using the compute instance in the AzureML workspace, and you were training ML models in the **Notebook** kernel. This approach works well for small models or rapid prototypes over sample data. At some point, you will need to handle more demanding workloads, either with bigger memory requirements or even distributed training capabilities in multiple computer nodes. This can be achieved by delegating the training process to the compute clusters you created in *Chapter 4, Configuring the Workspace*. In the next section, you will learn how to execute Python scripts in your AzureML compute clusters.

Scaling the training process with compute clusters

In *Chapter 7, The AzureML Python SDK*, you created a compute cluster named cpu-sm-cluster. In this section, you are going to submit a training job to be executed on that cluster. To do that, you will need to create a Python script that will be executed on the remote compute target.

Navigate to the **Notebooks** section of your AzureML workspace and in the **Files** tree view, create a folder named greeter-job under the chapter08 folder you have been working with so far. Add a Python file named greeter.py:

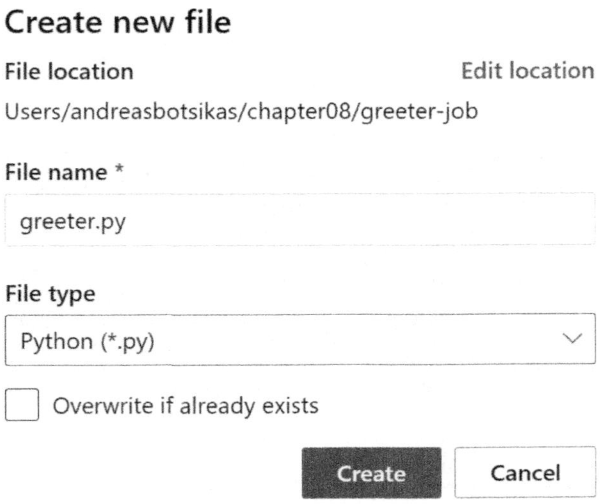

Create new file

File location   Edit location

Users/andreasbotsikas/chapter08/greeter-job

File name *

greeter.py

File type

Python (*.py)   ∨

☐ Overwrite if already exists

Create   Cancel

Figure 8.12 – Adding a simple Python script to execute on a remote compute cluster

Open that file and add the following code in it:

```python
import argparse
parser = argparse.ArgumentParser()
parser.add_argument('--greet-name', type=str,
                    dest='name', help='The name to greet')
args = parser.parse_args()
name = args.name
print(f"Hello {name}!")
```

This script uses the ArgumentParser class from the argparse module to parse the parameters passed to the script. It is trying to locate a --greet-name parameter and assign the discovered value to the name attribute of the object it returns (args.name). Then, it prints a greeting message for the given name. To try the script, open a terminal and type the following:

```
python greeter.py --greet-name packt
```

This command will produce the output seen in *Figure 8.13*:

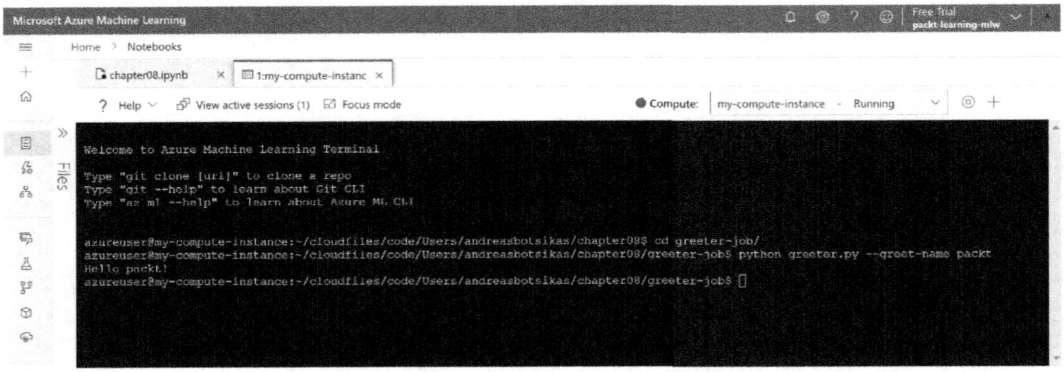

Figure 8.13 – Testing the simple script you will execute on a remote compute

To execute this simple Python script on a remote compute cluster, go back to the chapter08.ipynb notebook, add a new cell, and type the following code:

```python
from azureml.core import Workspace, Experiment
from azureml.core import ScriptRunConfig
ws = Workspace.from_config()
target = ws.compute_targets['cpu-sm-cluster']
script = ScriptRunConfig(
    source_directory='greeter-job',
    script='greeter.py',
    compute_target=target,
    arguments=['--greet-name', 'packt']
)
exp = Experiment(ws, 'greet-packt')
run = exp.submit(script)
print(run.get_portal_url())
run.wait_for_completion(show_output=True)
```

In this code, you are doing the following:

1. Get a reference to the workspace, and then you assign to the target variable a reference to the cpu-sm-cluster cluster.

2. Create a ScriptRunConfig to execute the greeter.py script that is located in the greeter-job folder. This script will execute in the target compute passing the --greet-name and packt arguments, which are going to be concatenated with a space between them.

3. Create an Experiment called `greet-packt`, and you submit the script configuration to execute under this Experiment. The `submit` method creates a new Run instance.

4. You use the `get_portal_url` method to get the portal URL for the specific Run instance. You then call the `wait_for_completion` method, setting the `show_output` parameter to `True`. To wait for the run to complete, turn on verbose logging and print the logs in the output of the cell.

> **Important note**
>
> In the first version of the AzureML SDK, instead of `ScriptRunConfig`, you would have used the `Estimator` class, which is deprecated. Moreover, there are deprecated specialized `Estimator` classes for specific frameworks such as the `TensorFlow` class that provided a way to run TensorFlow-specific code. This approach has been deprecated in favor of the environments you will read about in the *Understanding execution environments* section that follows. Nonetheless, the syntax and the parameters of those deprecated classes are very similar to `ScriptRunConfig`. You should be able to read deprecated code without any issue. Keep that in mind if you see an old question in the certification exam referencing these deprecated classes.

You have successfully completed a remote execution of a run. In the next section, you will explore the logs of the run you just completed and understand better the mechanics of AzureML.

Exploring the outputs and logs of a run

In this section, you are going to explore the outputs of the remote execution you performed in the *Scaling the training process with compute clusters* section. This will give you insights into how the AzureML platform works and help you troubleshoot potential errors you will be facing while developing your training scripts.

Open the link you printed in the previous section using the `get_portal_url` method or navigate to the **Experiments** section of the Studio interface, select the `greet-packt` Experiment, and open **Run 1**. Navigate to the **Outputs + logs** tab of the run:

Figure 8.14 – Outputs + logs tab of an Experiment's run

These outputs are very helpful in troubleshooting potential script errors. The `azureml-logs` folder contains the platform logs. Most of those files are logs from the underlying engine. The log that contains the standard output from your script is `70_driver_log.txt`. This is the log file you will need to look at first to troubleshoot a potential script execution failure. If you have multiple processes, you will see multiple files with a numeric suffix such as `70_driver_log_x.txt`.

The `logs` folder is a special folder you can use in your scripts to output logs. Everything that the script writes in that folder will automatically be uploaded to the run's **logs**, similar to the `outputs` folder you saw in the *Tracking metrics in Experiments* section. AzureML also outputs system logs in that folder under the `azureml` folder you see in *Figure 8.14*.

Navigate to the **Snapshot** tab. AzureML automatically makes a snapshot of the directory you specified in `ScriptRunConfig`. This directory can contain up to 300 MB and up to 2,000 files. If you need more script files, you can use a datastore. If you edited the script file in the **Notebooks** section, you would notice two files in there – the `.py` script and a `.amltmp` file, which is a temporary file used by the notebook editor:

Home > Experiments > greet-packt > Run 1
Run 1
Completed
Refresh
Connect to compute
Resubmit
Cancel
Download snapshot
Details
Metrics
Images
Child runs
Outputs + logs
Snapshot
Explanations
PY greeter.py
greeter.py.amltmp

Figure 8.15 – Temporary file uploaded in the snapshot

To avoid creating snapshots of unwanted files, you can add a `.gitignore` or `.amlignore` file in the folder next to the script and exclude files that follow a specific pattern. Navigate to the **Notebooks** section and add a `.amlignore` file in the `greeter-job` folder, if the file is not already added when you created the folder, as seen in *Figure 8.16*:

Create new file
File location
Edit location
Users/andreasbotsikas/chapter09/greeter-job
File name *
.amlignore
File type
Other
Overwrite if already exists
Create
Cancel

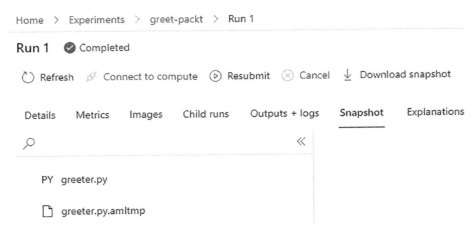

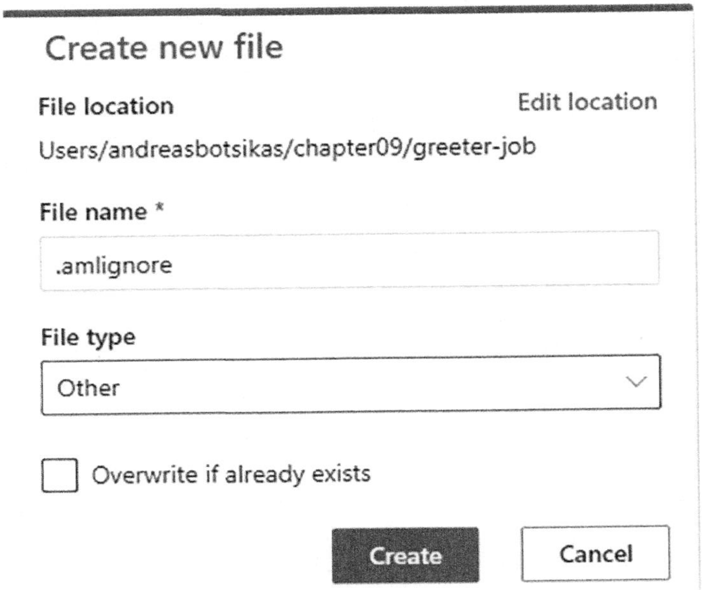

Figure 8.16 – Adding the .amlignore file to exclude temp files from being added to the snapshot

Open the `.amlignore` file and add the following lines in it to exclude all files with a .a mltmp file extension and the `.amlignore` file that you are editing:

```
*.amltmp
.amlignore
```

Open the `chapter08.ipynb` notebook, add a cell, and add the following code to resubmit the script:

```
from azureml.widgets import RunDetails
run = exp.submit(script)
RunDetails(run).show()
```

You are resubmitting the existing instance of the `ScriptRunConfig` you created in the previous step. If you restarted the **Jupyter** kernel, run the previous cell to assign the `exp` and `script` variables once more.

This time, you are using the `RunDetails` widget provided by the AzureML SDK. This is a **Jupyter Notebook** widget used to view the progress of a script execution. This widget is asynchronous and provides updates until the run finishes.

If you want to print the run status, including the contents of the log files, you can use the following code snippet:

```
run.get_details_with_logs()
```

Once the run completes, navigate to the **Snapshot** tab of that run. You will notice that the temp files are gone.

Notice that the execution of this run took significantly less time to complete. Navigate to the run's log. Notice that the `20_image_build_log.txt` file did not appear in the logs this time, as seen in *Figure 8.17*:

Figure 8.17 – Faster run execution and missing the 20_image_build_log.txt file

This is the **Docker** image-building log for the environment used to execute the scripts. This is a very time-consuming process. These images are built and stored in the container registry that got deployed with your AzureML workspace. Since you didn't modify the execution environment, AzureML reused the previously created image in the follow-up run. In the next section, you will understand better what an environment is and how you can modify it.

Understanding execution environments

In the AzureML workspace terminology, an **Environment** means a list of software requirements needed for your scripts to execute. These software requirements include the following:

- The Python packages that your code requires to be installed

- The environment variables that may be needed from your code

- Various pieces of auxiliary software, such as GPU drivers or the **Spark** engine, that may be required for your code to operate properly

Environments are *managed* and *versioned* entities that enable reproducible, auditable, and portable ML workflows across different compute targets.

AzureML provides a list of **curated environments** for you to use for either training or inferencing. For example, the `AzureML-Minimal` curated environment contains just the minimal Python package requirements to enable run tracking you saw in the *Tracking model evolution* section. The `AzureML-AutoML` environment, on the other hand, is a much bigger curated environment and provides the required Python packages for your scripts to be able to run an AutoML Experiment.

> **Important note**
>
> AzureML services are constantly being updated, and old environments are deprecated in favor of newer ones. Even if the `AzureML-Minimal` and `AzureML-AutoML` environments are not visible in the web interface of AzureML Studio, they should be available for you to use. If you encounter any errors, please download the latest code from the GitHub repository of this chapter.

In *Figure 8.18*, you can see how many additional packages are available with the `AzureML-AutoML` environment compared to the minimalistic `AzureML-Minimal` one:

Figure 8.18 – Python package difference between the AzureML-Minimal and AzureML-AutoML environments

Figure 8.18 shows the Conda environment definition for the AzureML-Minimal environment *version 46* versus the AzureML-AutoML environment *version 61*. **Conda** is an open source package management system that allows you to define execution environments, mostly used for Python environments, using a **Yet Another Markup Language (YAML)** format like the one you see in *Figure 8.18*. Conda takes this YAML file and installs Python *version 3.6.2* and the pip requirements listed beneath the - pip: notation. As you can notice, all pip packages have specific versions defined using the ==x.x.x notation. This means that the same Python packages will be installed every time you use this YAML file, something that helps maintain a stable environment for the repeatability of your Experiments.

Installing the packages when you create an environment is a time-consuming process. This is where the Docker technology you saw in the previous section comes in handy. Docker is an open source project for automating the deployment of applications as portable, self-sufficient containers. This means that instead of creating a new environment every time you want to run a script, you can create a Docker container image, also referred to as a Docker image, where all Python dependencies are *baked in* the image once. You can reuse the image from that point on to start a container and execute your scripts. In fact, all the AzureML-curated environments are available as Docker images in the viennaglobal.azurecr.io container registry.

> **Important note**
> Although it is common to create Docker images for your environments, it is not always required. If you are running the Experiments on your local computer or locally on the AzureML compute instance, you can use an existing Conda environment and avoid using a Docker image. If you are planning to use a remote compute, for example, an AzureML compute cluster, a Docker image is required because otherwise, you cannot ensure that the provisioned machine will have all the software components needed by your code to execute.

To better understand what you have read so far, you will rerun the previous greeter.py script using the AzureML-Minimal environmen:.

1. In your notebook, add a new cell and add the following code:

```
from azureml.core import Environment
minimal_env =\
Environment.get(ws, name="AzureML-Minimal")
print(minimal_env.name, minimal_env.version)
print(minimal_env.Python.conda_dependencies.serialize_to_
string())
```

This code retrieves the `AzureML-Minimal` environment, defined in the AzureML workspace referenced by the `ws` variable, which was initialized earlier in the notebook. Then, it prints the name and the version of the environment and the `Conda` environment YAML definition you saw in *Figure 8.18*.

2. Add a new cell and type the following:

```
from azureml.core import Experiment, ScriptRunConfig
target = ws.compute_targets['cpu-sm-cluster']
script = ScriptRunConfig(
    source_directory='greeter-job',
    script='greeter.py',
    environment=minimal_env,
    compute_target=target,
    arguments=['--greet-name', 'packt']
)
exp = Experiment(ws, 'greet-packt')
run = exp.submit(script)
print(run.get_portal_url())
run.wait_for_completion(show_output=True)
```

The only difference from the code you typed in the previous section is the definition of the `environment` argument in the `ScriptRunConfig` constructor.

Observe the output of the run's execution. If you look closer, you will see the following line:

```
Status: Downloaded newer image for viennaglobal.azurecr.io/
azureml/azureml_<something>:latest
```

This line is part of the `55_azureml-execution-something.txt` file in `azureml-logs`. The line informs you that it is pulling a Docker image from the `viennaglobal` container registry, which **Microsoft** owns. In contrast to that, in the previous section, in the run where you didn't specify a curated environment, the image was pulled from your own container registry – the one provisioned with your AzureML workspace, as seen in *Figure 8.19*:

Figure 8.19 – Image pulled from your own container registry
in the execution without using a curated environment

This observation brings us to the next type of AzureML-supported environment, the system-managed one – something you will explore in the next section.

Defining a system-managed environment

System-managed environments allow you to define your code's dependencies by using either a `Conda` environment definition or a simple `pip requirements.txt` file. In the previous section, where you didn't define the `environment` argument in the `ScriptRunConfig` constructor, a default `Conda` environment definition file was used to create the system-managed environment that was stored in your **Azure Container Registry** associated with your AzureML workspace. Let's explicitly create a system-managed environment to use with your code:

1. Navigate to the **Notebooks** section of your AzureML workspace and the **Files** tree view.

2. Click on the three dots of the `greeter-job` folder to open the context menu (or just right-click on the name) and select the **Duplicate** action. Name the new folder `greeter-banner-job`, as seen in the following screenshot:

Figure 8.20 – Duplicating the greeter-job folder as a new one named greeter-banner-job

3. Open the `greeter.py` file in the new folder and change the code to the following:

```python
import argparse
from asciistuff import Banner
import os
parser = argparse.ArgumentParser()
parser.add_argument('--greet-name', type=str,
                    dest='name', help='The name to
greet')
args = parser.parse_args()
name = args.name
```

```
greet_header = os.environ.get('GREET_HEADER','Message:')
print(greet_header)
print(Banner(f"Hello {name}!"))
```

The modified code imports the `Banner` method from the `asciistuff` open source Python package. This method is used in the last print. This will output a fancy **ASCII** banner you will see in *Figure 8.21*. The code also imports the `os` module, which allows you to read the environment variables using the `os.environ.get()` method. The code tries to read the environment variable named GREET_HEADER, and if it is not defined, the default value, `Message:`, is assigned to the `greet_header` variable, which is printed before the banner message.

> **Important note**
>
> If you try to execute the modified `greeter.py` in a terminal within your AzureML *compute instance*, it will fail because you don't have the `asciistuff` package installed. To install it in your compute instance, you can use the `pip install asciistuff` command.

4. The `asciistuff` package is a pip package that you will need to install in your executing environment for your code to work. To define that code dependency, you are going to create a `Conda` environment definition file. In the `chapter08` folder, add a new file named `greeter-banner-job.yml`. Add the following content to it:

```
name: banner-env
dependencies:
- python=3.6.2
- pip:
  - asciistuff==1.2.1
```

This YAML file defines a new `Conda` environment named `banner-env`, which is based on Python *version 3.6.2* and installs the *1.2.1* version of the `pip` package, `asciistuff`.

5. To create an AzureML environment based on the `Conda` environment you just defined, you need to go to the `chapter08.ipynb` notebook, add a cell, and type the following code:

```
from azureml.core import Environment
banner_env = Environment.from_conda_specification(
```

```
              name = "banner-env",
              file_path = "greeter-banner-job.yml")
banner_env.environment_variables["GREET_HEADER"] = \
                              "Env. var. header:"
```

This code snippet creates an AzureML environment named `banner-env` using the `from_conda_specification()` method of the `Environment` class. The `banner_env` variable contains the newly defined environment. In the follow-up line, you define the `GREET_HEADER` environment variable, and you assign the `Env. var. header:` value. This environment is not registered in the workspace, and it doesn't need to be registered in order to use it. If you do want to save it in the workspace to be able to reference it in the same way you reference the curated environments and you want to keep versions of it, you can use the `register()` method, using the `banner_env.register(ws)` code where you pass as an argument a variable that points to the workspace where the Environment will be registered.

> **Important note**
>
> If you plan to start working on your local computer and then scale out on more powerful compute clusters, you should consider creating and registering a system-managed environment that includes all your required Python packages. This will allow you to reuse it in both local and remote executions.

6. To use this newly defined environment, add a new cell in the notebook and type the following code:

```
script = ScriptRunConfig(
    source_directory='greeter-banner-job',
    script='greeter.py',
    environment=banner_env,
    compute_target=target,
    arguments=['--greet-name', 'packt']
)
exp = Experiment(ws, 'greet-packt')
run = exp.submit(script)
print(run.get_portal_url())
run.wait_for_completion(show_output=True)
```

Note that there are a couple of minor differences compared to the last `ScriptRunConfig::`

- The source directory has changed to point to the `greeter-banner-job` folder, which contains the updated script.

- The environment argument is specified, passing your very own defined `banner_env` environment.

The output of this Experiment should look like the one depicted in *Figure 8.21*:

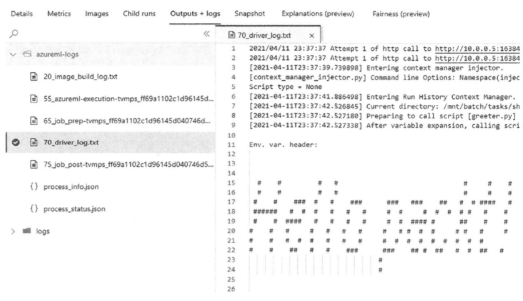

Figure 8.21 – Header text read from an environment variable and banner-based hello greeting

As you noticed, in the system-managed environment you just created, you didn't specify anything about the base operating system (for example, whetherit's **Ubuntu** *16.04* or Ubuntu *20.04*). You assumed that Conda is already installed in the base system. You just specified the Conda dependencies that got installed. If you want even bigger flexibility, you can explicitly configure the environment and install all your software requirements manually. These environments are referred to as **user-managed** environments. Most often, these user-managed environments are custom-made Docker images that encapsulate all the required dependencies. For example, you may need a custom build of the PyTorch framework or even a custom build version of Python. In these cases, you are responsible for installing the Python packages and configuring the entire environment. For the purposes of this book, you will be working with either curated or system-managed environments.

So far, you have explored how to execute a simple greeter Python application on a remote compute. In the next section, you will resume your `diabetes` model training and see how you can train that model on a remote compute cluster.

Training the diabetes model on a compute cluster

In the previous section, you learned how you can run a script on a remote compute cluster by calling the `exp.submit(script)` method from within a notebook, as seen in *Figure 8.22*:

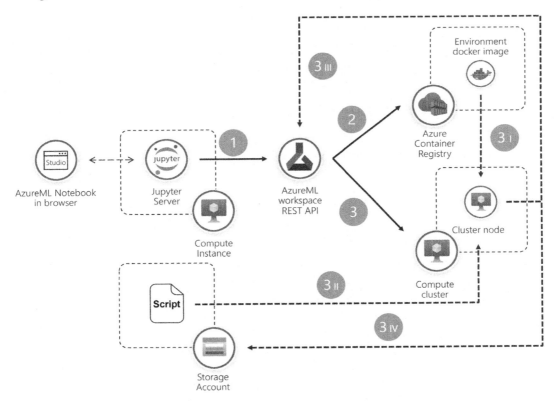

Figure 8.22 – Executing a script on a compute cluster

When you called the `submit` method, the following actions happened behind the scenes:

1. The AzureML SDK made a **REST** API call to the AzureML workspace to trigger the `ScriptRunConfig` execution.

2. The AzureML workspace checked whether a Docker image of the `Environment` already exists. If it didn't exist, it was created within Azure Container Registry.

3. The job is submitted to the compute cluster, which scales up to allocate a compute node. The following operations are performed within the newly allocated compute node:

I. The Docker image with the Environment is pulled to the compute node.

II. The script referenced by `ScriptRunConfig` is loaded in the running Docker instance.

III. Metrics and metadata are stored in the AzureML workspace.

IV. Outputs are stored back in the storage account.

In the *Training a simple sklearn model with notebooks* section, you created a training script within the `chapter08.ipynb` notebook. The training was happening within the Jupyter server's process, inside your compute instance. To run the same training in a compute cluster, you will need to do the following:

1. Move the code to a Python script file.

2. Create an AzureML environment to run the training.

3. Submit `ScriptRunConfig` in an Experiment.

In the next sections, you will see how to transform the script you used in the *Tracking model evolution* section to be able to execute it on a remote compute cluster.

Moving the code to a Python script file

If you look at the script you created in the *Tracking model evolution* section, in the code that was doing the training, you used the `run` variable to log metrics. This variable was referencing the Run object you got when you called `exp.start_logging()`. In the previous section, you learned about `ScriptRunConfig`, which you submitted in an Experiment and returned an instance of the Run class. This instance is created within the notebook of the compute instance. How will the script file that is executing on a remote cluster get access to the same Run object?

AzureML's Run class provides a method called `get_context()`, which returns the current service execution context. In the case of `ScriptRunConfig`, this execution context is the same Run that was created when you called `exp.submit(script)`:

```
from azureml.core.run import Run
run = Run.get_context()
```

Further to the run variable, in the training script, you had the ws variable, which was a reference to the AzureML workspace. You used that variable to get access to the diabetes dataset. You got a reference to the workspace by calling the from_config method. The issue with this approach is that the first time you called that method, you needed to manually authenticate and authorize the compute to access the workspace on your behalf. This will not be feasible to do on the remote compute.

The run variable gives you access to the corresponding workspace by navigating in the Experiment attribute and then to the workspace attribute of that Experiment:

```
ws = run.experiment.workspace
```

There is one caveat for these lines of code, though. Your code assumes that the Python script was submitted through ScriptRunConfig. If you run the Python script locally in a terminal, using the following command line, you will get an error:

```
python training.py --alpha 0.1
```

The get_context() method will return an object of the _OfflineRun class, which inherits from the Run class. This class provides all logging capabilities you saw in the *Tracking metrics in Experiments* section, but instead of uploading the metrics or the artifacts to the workspace, it just prints out the attempt in the terminal. Obviously, there is no Experiment associated with that run and this is going to cause the script to throw an error. Thus, you need to retrieve the workspace reference using the from_config() method you have been using so far. Since the terminal is part of the compute instance, the script will execute passing your credentials and will not prompt you to authenticate, as you will see later in this section. If you run this code on your local computer, you will need to authenticate your device, as you saw in the *Authenticating from your device* section of *Chapter 7, The AzureML Python SDK*.

The complete code that allows you to run both offline in a terminal and submitted in a compute cluster is the following:

```
from azureml.core import Workspace
from azureml.core.run import Run, _OfflineRun
run = Run.get_context()
ws = None
if type(run) == _OfflineRun:
    ws = Workspace.from_config()
else:
    ws = run.experiment.workspace
```

These are the only changes you will need to make to your script to submit it for remote execution and take advantage of the AzureML SDK capabilities.

> **Important note**
>
> Python developers commonly use an _ as a prefix for classes, attributes, or methods that they want to mark as internal. This means that the marked code is for consumption by classes within the SDK library and shouldn't be used by external developers. The marked code may change in the future without any warning. It is considered a bad practice to use classes that start with the _ prefix. Nonetheless, the _OfflineRun class is extensively used in the public samples of the AzureML SDK and is safe to use.

Let's make those changes in your workspace. In the file tree, create a folder under chapter08 named diabetes-training and add a training.py file in there, as seen in *Figure 8.23*:

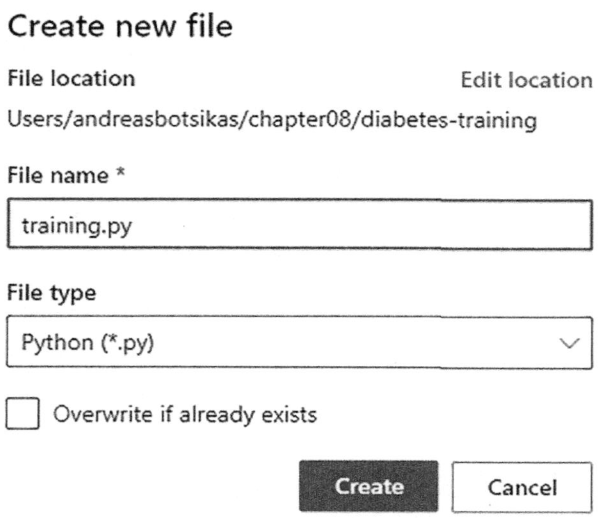

Create new file

File location   Edit location

Users/andreasbotsikas/chapter08/diabetes-training

File name *

training.py

File type

Python (*.py)

☐ Overwrite if already exists

Create   Cancel

Figure 8.23 – Creating the training script for the remote diabetes model training

Add the following code blocks in the training.py script. Instead of typing all this code, you can download it directly from the GitHub repository mentioned in the *Technical requirements* section of this chapter:

```
from sklearn.linear_model import LassoLars
from sklearn.metrics import mean_squared_error
from azureml.core import Workspace
```

```
from azureml.core.run import Run, _OfflineRun
import argparse
import os
import joblib
```

These are all the imports you will need within the script file. It is a good practice to have all your `import` statements on the top of your script files to easily discover the required modules needed for your code to execute properly. If you use `flake8` to lint your code base, it will complain if you don't follow this best practice:

```
parser = argparse.ArgumentParser()
parser.add_argument('--alpha', type=float,
                    dest='alpha', help='The alpha parameter')
args = parser.parse_args()
```

This script file expects an `--alpha` parameter to be passed to it. In this code block, this parameter is parsed using the `argparse` module you saw in the *Scaling the training process with compute clusters* section, and the `float` value is assigned to the `args.alpha` variable, as it is specified in the `dest` argument. The `parse_args` method will throw an error if you pass non-defined arguments to the script. Some people prefer using `args, unknown_args = parser.parse_known_args()` instead of the fourth line of this code block, which allows the script to execute even if it receives more than the expected arguments, assigning the unknown ones in the `unknown_args` variable:

```
run = Run.get_context()
ws = None
if type(run) == _OfflineRun:
    ws = Workspace.from_config()
else:
    ws = run.experiment.workspace
```

In this code block, you get a reference to the `Run` object and the `Workspace` using the snippet you saw at the beginning of this section. Once you get the reference to the `Workspace`, you can load the `diabetes` dataset, as seen in the next script block:

```
diabetes_ds = ws.datasets['diabetes']
training_data, validation_data = \
            diabetes_ds.random_split(
                        percentage = 0.8, seed=1337)
X_train = training_data.drop_columns('target') \
```

```
                            .to_pandas_dataframe()
y_train = training_data.keep_columns('target') \
                            .to_pandas_dataframe()
X_validate = validation_data.drop_columns('target') \
                            .to_pandas_dataframe()
y_validate = validation_data.keep_columns('target') \
                            .to_pandas_dataframe()
```

In this block, you get a reference to the diabetes dataset and split it to the required X_train, y_train, X_validate, and y_validate pandas DataFrames you saw in the *Training a simple sklearn model within notebooks* section of this chapter. Note that you specify the seed parameter in the random_split method. This seed parameter is used to initialize the state of the underlying random function used by the split method to randomly select the rows from the dataset. By doing that, the random function will generate the same random numbers every time it is invoked. This means that training_data and validation_data will be the same every time you run the script. Having the same training and validation dataset will assist in properly comparing multiple executions of the same script with different alpha parameters:

```
def train_and_evaluate(run, alpha, X_t, y_t, X_v, y_v):
    model = LassoLars(alpha=alpha)
    model.fit(X_t, y_t)
    predictions = model.predict(X_v)
    rmse = mean_squared_error(predictions, y_v, squared=False)
    range_y_validate = y_v.to_numpy().ptp()
    nrmse = rmse/range_y_validate
    run.log("nrmse", nrmse)
    run.log_row("nrmse over α", α=alpha, nrmse=nrmse)
    return model, nrmse
```

In this code block, you define the train_and_evaluate method, which is the same one used in the *Tracking model evolution* section of this chapter:

```
model, nrmse = train_and_evaluate(run, args.alpha,
                X_train, y_train, X_validate, y_validate)
```

After the method definition, you invoke the training process passing all the required arguments:

```
os.makedirs('./outputs', exist_ok=True)
model_file_name = 'model.pkl'
joblib.dump(value=model, filename=
            os.path.join('./outputs/',model_file_name))
```

The last code block stores the model in the `outputs` folder next to the script's location.

You can run the script on your local compute instance, and you will notice that the model trains as expected and the metrics are logged in the terminal, as seen in *Figure 8.24*. This is the expected behavior of the `_OfflineRun` class you read about before:

```
azureuser@my-compute-instance:~/cloudfiles/code/Users/andreasbotsikas/chapter09/diabetes-training$ python training.py --alpha 0.001
Attempted to log scalar metric nrmse:
0.1825470156126569
Attempted to log row metric nrmse over α:
{'α': 0.001, 'nrmse': 0.1825470156126569}
```

Figure 8.24 – Running the training script locally

So far, you have created the training script. In the next section, you will create the AzureML environment that will contain all the required dependencies to execute that script on a remote compute.

Creating the AzureML environment to run the training script

The training script you created in the *Tracking model evolution* section uses the `scikit-learn` library, also known as `sklearn`. The Jupyter kernel that you are using in the notebook experience already has the `sklearn` library installed. To see the version that is currently installed in your kernel, go to the `chapter08.ipynb` notebook and add the following code snippet in a new cell:

```
!pip show scikit-learn
```

This command will use Python's `pip` package manager to show the details of the currently installed `scikit-learn` package, as seen in *Figure 8.25*:

```
 ▷        1    !pip show scikit-learn
          ✓ 2 sec

    Name: scikit-learn
    Version: 0.22.2.post1
    Summary: A set of python modules for machine learning and data mining
    Home-page: http://scikit-learn.org
    Author: None
    Author-email: None
    License: new BSD
    Location: /anaconda/envs/azureml_py36/lib/python3.6/site-packages
    Requires: numpy, scipy, joblib
    Required-by: sklearn, sklearn-pandas, skl2onnx, shap, pmdarima, nimbusml, lightgbm,
    interpret-community, fairlearn, azureml-train-automl-runtime, azureml-datadrift, azureml-
    automl-runtime
```

Figure 8.25 – Package information for the installed scikit-learn library

> **Important note**
> If you are unsure of the library name, you can use the `pip freeze` command to get a full list of installed packages in the current Python environment.

You can also find the version of the installed library within a Python script using the `sklearn.__version__` attribute (note the two underscores). In a new notebook cell, add the following lines of Python code:

```
import sklearn
print(sklearn.__version__)
```

You should be able to see exactly the same version printed in the output. Most of the Python SDKs and libraries have this `__version__` attribute, such as the PyTorch and the TensorFlow frameworks.

There are two ways to install the `scikit-learn` package; as a `Conda` package or as a `pip` package. `Conda` offers a curated list of Python packages, and it is the recommended approach. In the *Understanding execution environments* section, you saw how to create an environment using a `Conda` specification file. In this section, you will learn a different approach where you create the environment within the Python code. Add a new cell in the `chapter08.ipynb` notebook and type the following:

```
from azureml.core import Environment
from azureml.core.conda_dependencies import CondaDependencies
```

```
import sklearn
diabetes_env = Environment(name="diabetes-training-env")
diabetes_env.Python.conda_dependencies = CondaDependencies()
diabetes_env.Python.conda_dependencies.add_conda_package(
                f"scikit-learn=={sklearn.__version__}")
diabetes_env.python.conda_dependencies.add_pip_
package("azureml-dataprep[pandas]")
```

In the preceding code snippet, you create a new system-managed environment and then use add_conda_package to add the specific version of scikit-learn. You also use add_pip_package to add the azureml-dataprep[pandas] package, which is required in order to use the to_pandas_dataframe method within the training. py script. You could have added additional pip packages such as the asciistuff package you installed before. Instead of adding one package at a time using the add_ pip_package method, you can use the create method of the CondaDependencies class, as seen in the following snippet:

```
diabetes_env.Python.conda_dependencies = \
CondaDependencies.create(
    conda_packages=[
                f"scikit-learn=={sklearn.__version__}"],
    pip_packages=["azureml-defaults", "azureml-
dataprep[pandas]"])
```

You can request for multiple packages to be present in the environment by adding them in the conda_packages and pip_packages arrays. Note that since you do not append packages to the default CondaDependencies, you need to manually include the azureml-defaults package needed for the training.py script to access the azureml.core module.

You may be wondering why we haven't defined joblib in the Python dependencies. The scikit-learn package depends on the joblib package, and it will automatically be installed in the environment. If you want, you can explicitly specify it in the list of dependencies with the following code:

```
import joblib
diabetes_env.Python.conda_dependencies.add_pip_
package(f"joblib=={joblib.__version__}")
```

> **Important note**
> Although it is not mandatory to specify the version of the packages you want to add to the environment, it is a good practice. If you wrote `add_conda_package("scikit-learn")`, skipping to specify the version of the package, AzureML would assume you are referring to the latest version. The first time you would have used the environment in AzureML, the Docker image would have been created, installing whatever was the newest version of the `scikit-learn` package at the time of the Docker image creation. That version may have been more recent than the one you used to create your script, and it may be incompatible with the code you wrote. Although minor version differences may not affect your code, major versions may introduce breaking changes, as was done when TensorFlow moved from *version 1* to *2*.

If you don't want to create a new environment with your code dependencies, you can use one of the AzureML-curated environments. You can select either the highly specialized GPU-based `AzureML-Scikit-learn0.24-Cuda11-OpenMpi4.1.0-py36` environment or you can use the more generic `AzureML-Tutorial` curated environment, which contains the most used data science libraries such as `scikit-learn`, `MLflow`, and `matplotlib`.

So far, you have written the training script and you defined the AzureML environment with the required `sklearn` library. In the next section, you are going to kick off the training on a compute cluster.

Submitting ScriptRunConfig in an Experiment

Once you have the script and the AzureML environment definition, you can submit `ScriptRunConfig` to execute on the remote compute cluster. In a new cell in the `chapter08.ipynb` notebook, add the following code:

```python
from azureml.core import Workspace, Experiment
from azureml.core import ScriptRunConfig
ws = Workspace.from_config()
target = ws.compute_targets['cpu-sm-cluster']
script = ScriptRunConfig(
    source_directory='diabetes-training',
    script='training.py',
    environment=diabetes_env,
    compute_target=target,
    arguments=['--alpha', 0.01]
)
```

```
exp = Experiment(ws, 'chapter08-diabetes')
run = exp.submit(script)
run.wait_for_completion(show_output=True)
```

This code is the same one used to submit the `greeter.py` scripts in the previous sections. You get a reference to the AzureML workspace and the compute cluster where you will execute the job. You define a `ScriptRunConfig` object where you define the location of the script to execute, the environment you defined in the previous section, and the target compute. You also pass the `alpha` argument to the script. In the last bit of code, you create an Experiment and submit `ScriptRunConfig` to execute.

With this piece of code, you triggered the flow you saw in *Figure 8.22* in the *Training the diabetes model on a compute cluster* section earlier in the chapter.

Once the training is complete, you will be able to navigate to the Experiment, select the run, and observe the collected metrics from the training process, as seen in *Figure 8.26*:

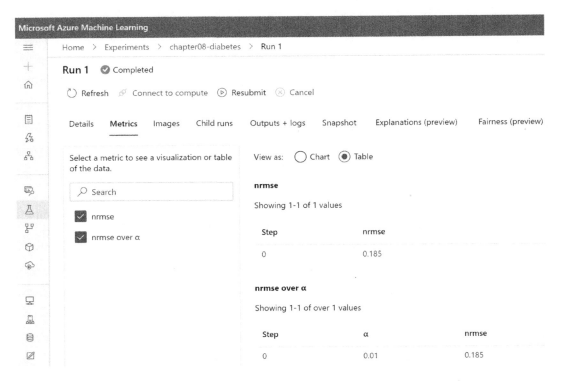

Figure 8.26 – Logged metrics from a script running on a remote compute cluster

So far, you have managed to execute the `diabetes` model training script in a single node on a remote compute cluster, and you have logged the metrics and the trained model in the AzureML Experiment's run.

In the next section, you will discover different ways to scale out your computational efforts and take advantage of more than a single node on the compute cluster.

Utilizing more than a single compute node during model training

As you saw in the *Compute clusters* section of *Chapter 4, Configuring the Workspace*, a cluster can scale from 0 compute nodes to as many as you like. There are a couple of reasons why you would need more than a single node in a cluster during the model training phase. They are as follows:

- **Parallel execution of unrelated model training instances**: When you are working in a team, it is common to have multiple Experiments running in parallel. Each job can run on a single node, as you did in the previous section.

- **Parallel training of a single model, also known as distributed training**: This is an advanced scenario where you are using frameworks such as the **Apache Horovod** distributed deep learning training framework that PyTorch and TensorFlow use. There are two types of distributed training options:

  - **Data parallelism**: Where the training data is split into partitions equal to the amount of compute nodes you have. Each node performs a training batch of the model against the assigned data, and then all nodes synchronize the updated model parameters before moving to the next batch.

  - **Model parallelism**: Where you are training bits of the model on different compute nodes. Each node is responsible for training only a small segment of the entire model, and the synchronization between nodes occurs every time a propagation step is needed.

- **Parallel training of multiple instances of the same model to select the best alternative**: Models may accept parameters when they are initialized, such as the `alpha` parameter of the `LassoLars` model you trained in the previous section. You may want to explore multiple values for those parameters to select the model that performs best on the training dataset. This is a process called hyperparameter tuning, and you will learn more about it in *Chapter 9, Optimizing the ML Model*.

- **Parallel training of multiple models to select the best alternative**: This is the AutoML process you already discovered in *Chapter 5, Letting the Machines Do the Model Training*. You will also see this method again in *Chapter 9, Optimizing the ML Model*, in the *Running AutoML Experiments with code* section.

In this section, you learned about different approaches to utilize multiple nodes in a compute cluster. You will deep dive into the last two methods in *Chapter 9, Optimizing the ML Model*.

Summary

In this chapter, you got an overview of the various ways you can create an ML model in the AzureML workspace. You started with a simple regression model that was trained within the Jupyter notebook's kernel process. You learned how you can keep track of the metrics from the models you train. Then, you scaled the training process into the `cpu-sm-cluster` compute cluster you created in *Chapter 7, The AzureML Python SDK*. While scaling out to a remote compute cluster, you learned what the AzureML environments are and how you can troubleshoot remote executions by looking at the logs.

In the next chapter, you will build on this knowledge and use multiple computer nodes to perform a parallelized *hyperparameter tuning* process, which will locate the best parameters for your model. You will also learn how you can completely automate the model selection, training, and tuning using the AutoML capabilities of the AzureML SDK.

Questions

In each chapter, you will find a couple of questions to check your understanding of the topics discussed:.

1. You want to log the number of validation rows you will use within a script. Which method of the `Run` class will you use?

    a. `log_table`

    b. `log_row`

    c. `log`

2. You want to run a Python script that utilizes `scikit-learn`. How would you configure the AzureML environment?

    a. Add the `scikit-learn Conda dependency`.

    b. Add the `sklearn Conda dependency`.

    c. Use the AzureML `Azure-Minimal` environment, which already contains the needed dependencies.

3. You need to use `MLflow` to track the metrics generated in an Experiment and store them in your AzureML workspace. Which two pip packages do you need to have in your Conda environment?

    a. `mlflow`

    b. `azureml-mlflow`

    c. `sklearn`

    d. `logger`

4. You need to use `MLflow` to track the value `0.1` for the `training_rate` metric. Which of the following code achieves this requirement? Assume all classes are correctly imported at the top of the script:

    a. `mlflow.log_metric('training_rate', 0.1)`

    b. `run.log('training_rate', 0.1)`

    c. `logger.log('training_rate', 0.1)`

Further reading

This section offers a list of web resources to help you augment your knowledge of the AzureML SDK and the various code snippets used in this chapter:

- Source of the diabetes dataset: `https://www4.stat.ncsu.edu/~boos/var.select/diabetes.html`

- *LassoLars* model documentation on *scikit-learn* website: `https://scikit-learn.org/stable/modules/linear_model.html#lars-lasso`

- The *plotly* open source graphing library: `https://github.com/plotly/plotly.py`

- MLflow Tracking API reference: `https://mlflow.org/docs/latest/quickstart.html#using-the-tracking-api`

- Syntax for the `.amlignore` and `.gitignore` files: `https://git-scm.com/docs/gitignore`

- **Flake8** for code linting: `https://flake8.pycqa.org`

9
Optimizing the ML Model

In this chapter, you will learn about two techniques you can use to discover the optimal model for your dataset. You will start by exploring the **HyperDrive** package of the AzureML SDK. This package allows you to fine-tune the model's performance by tweaking the parameters it exposes, a process also known as **hyperparameter tuning**. You will then explore the **Automated ML (AutoML)** package of the AzureML SDK, which allows you to automate the model selection, training, and optimization process through code.

In this chapter, we are going to cover the following main topics:

- Hyperparameter tuning using HyperDrive
- Running AutoML experiments with code

Technical requirements

You will need to have access to an Azure subscription. Within that subscription, you will need a **resource group** named `packt-azureml-rg`. You will need to have either a `Contributor` or `Owner` **Access control (IAM)** role on the resource group level. Within that resource group, you should have already deployed a **machine learning** resource named `packt-learning-mlw`, as described in *Chapter 2, Deploying Azure Machine Learning Workspace Resources*.

You will also need to have a basic understanding of the **Python** language. The code snippets target Python version 3.6 or newer. You should also be familiar with working in the notebook experience within AzureML Studio, something that was covered in *Chapter 8, Experimenting with Python Code*.

This chapter assumes you have registered the **scikit-learn** diabetes dataset in your AzureML workspace and that you have created a compute cluster named **cpu-sm-cluster**, as described in the sections *Defining datastores*, *Working with datasets*, and *Working with compute targets* in *Chapter 7, The AzureML Python SDK*.

You can find all notebooks and code snippets of this chapter in GitHub at the URL `http://bit.ly/dp100-ch09`.

Hyperparameter tuning using HyperDrive

In *Chapter 8, Experimenting with Python Code*, you trained a `LassoLars` model that was accepting the `alpha` parameter. In order to avoid overfitting to the training dataset, the `LassoLars` model uses a technique called **regularization**, which basically introduces a penalty term within the optimization formula of the model. You can think of this technique as if the linear regression that we are trying to fit consists of a normal linear function that is being fitted with the least-squares function plus this penalty term. The `alpha` parameter specifies how important this penalty term is, something that directly impacts the training outcome. Parameters that affect the training process are referred to as being **hyperparameters**. To understand better what a **hyperparameter** is, we are going to explore the hyperparameters of a decision tree. In a decision tree classifier model, like the `DecisionTreeClassifier` class located in the `scikit-learn` library, you can define the maximum depth of the tree through the **hyperparameter** `max_depth`, which is an integer. In the same model, you can control the maximum amount of leaf nodes by specifying a numeric value to the `max_leaf_nodes` **hyperparameter**.

These hyperparameters control the size of the decision tree, as depicted in *Figure 9.1*:

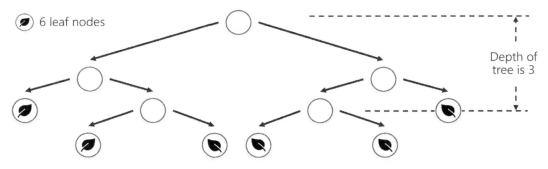

Figure 9.1 – Decision tree hyperparameters

Hyperparameter tuning is the process of finding the optimal values for the **hyperparameters** that produce the best-performing model against the data you are using for training. To be able to evaluate the performance of each **hyperparameter** combination, the model must be trained, and the performance metric must be evaluated. In the case of the diabetes model in *Chapter 8, Experimenting with Python Code*, you were evaluating the models using the **Normalized Root Mean Squared Error** (**NRMSE**) metric.

The AzureML SDK offers the HyperDriveConfig class , which allows you to perform **hyperparameter tuning** for your models, parallelizing the search for the best **hyperparameter** combination by performing model training and evaluation at each node of the compute cluster in parallel. HyperDriveConfig is a wrapper to the ScriptRunConfig class you used in *Chapter 8, Experimenting with Python Code*. This means that you need to pass in the run_config parameter the ScriptRunConfig that you want to use to train your model. You also need to specify the metric that your code is logging and what your goal is for that metric. In the diabetes case, you are trying to minimize the **NRMSE** metric. You can then kick off a **hyperparameter tuning** process with the same submit method you saw in *Chapter 8, Experimenting with Python Code*. The pseudo-code that shows the end-to-end process, where the script variable refers to the ScriptRunConfig object that defines which training script you are going to use, is the following:

```
hd_config = HyperDriveConfig(
            run_config=script,
            primary_metric_name="nrmse",
            primary_metric_goal=PrimaryMetricGoal.MINIMIZE
            ,...)
experiment = Experiment(ws, "chapter09-hyperdrive")
hyperdrive_run = experiment.submit(hd_config)
```

Besides `ScriptRunConfig`, you will need to pass the **hyperparameter** sampling configuration that `HyperDriveConfig` will use. **Hyperparameters** can accept either discrete or continuous values:

- A typical example of discrete values is integers or string values. For example, in the **TensorFlow** framework, you can select the activation function to use by passing a string value to the `activation` **hyperparameter**. These string values represent the built-in activation functions that the **TensorFlow** framework supports. You can select values like `selu` for the **Scaled Exponential Linear Unit (SELU)** or `relu` for the **Rectified Linear Unit (ReLU)**.

- A typical example of continuous values is float values. The `alpha` parameter in the `LassoLars` model you have been training is a **hyperparameter** that accepts float values.

When you are exploring the possible **hyperparameter** combinations, you need to specify the search space that you are going to explore. The AzureML SDK offers a couple of functions that allow you to define the search space you are about to explore. These functions are part of the `azureml.train.hyperdrive.parameter_expressions` module.

In the case of discrete **hyperparameters**, you can use the `choice` function, which allows you to specify the list of options the **hyperparameter** can take. For example, you could have defined the search space for the discrete string values of the `activation` **hyperparameter** you saw previously with the following script:

```
choice('selu','relu')
```

This script will try both the `selu` and `relu` activation functions while looking for the optimal model.

> **Important note**
> If you are interested in working with neural networks, you will probably need to understand these activation functions better. There are great books that can help you get started in neural network design. For the DP-100 exam, you will not need this knowledge.

Note that even in the case of the continuous `alpha` **hyperparameter** of the `LassoLars` model, you can still use the `choice` method to define discrete values to explore. For example, the following use of `choice` is the equivalent of what you did back in the *Tracking model evolution* section of *Chapter 8, Experimenting with Python Code*:

```
choice(0.001, 0.01, 0.1, 0.25, 0.5)
```

You can also define the probability distribution for the samples that you will be getting while you are exploring the search space. For example, if you want to provide an equal chance to all values, you will use a uniform distribution. On the other hand, you can use a normal distribution to focus the search area on the center of the search space. The AzureML SDK offers a couple of methods you can use, such as `uniform(low, high)`, `loguniform(low, high)`, `normal(μ,σ)`, and `lognormal(μ, σ)`. You can use the q prefixed equivalents for discrete values, such as `quniform(low, high, q)`, `qloguniform(low, high, q)`, `qnormal(μ, σ, q)`, and `qlognormal(μ, σ, q)`, where the q parameter is the quantization factor that converts continuous values into discrete ones.

On the GitHub page of this book, you can find the code that plots 1,000 samples being generated with the distributions of these functions. The results can be seen in *Figure 9.2*:

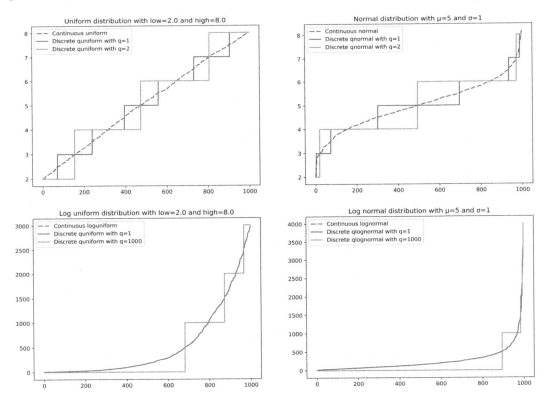

Figure 9.2 – Advanced discrete and continuous hyperparameter value distributions.
Sample values are ordered. The x axis shows the ordered value's index number

> **Important note**
>
> In *Figure 9.2*, in the `loguniform` and `lognormal` plots, the line of the discrete function with quantization factor 1 overlaps with the one from the continuous function. Therefore, you can only see two lines.

Once you have defined the search space, you need to specify the sampling strategy that you will use to select each **hyperparameter** combination that you are going to be testing. The AzureML SDK supports the following methods for sampling the search space defined in the `azureml.train.hyperdrive` module:

- **Grid sampling**: This method supports *only* discrete **hyperparameter** values that are defined using the `choice` method you saw above. The Azure ML SDK will search all possible **hyperparameter** combinations of those discrete values. Imagine that you wanted to explore the following four parameter combinations:

  - a=0.01 and b=10

  - a=0.01 and b=100

  - a=0.5 and b=10

  - a=0.5 and b=100

  The following code snippet defines the search space for these four combinations:

  ```
  from azureml.train.hyperdrive import
  GridParameterSampling
  from azureml.train.hyperdrive import choice
  param_sampling = GridParameterSampling( {
          "a": choice(0.01, 0.5),
          "b": choice(10, 100)
      }
  )
  ```

- **Random sampling**: This technique is implemented in the `RandomParameterSampling` class. It allows you to randomly select **hyperparameter** values from the available options. It supports both discrete and continuous **hyperparameters**.

- **Bayesian sampling**: This method picks samples based on how the previous samples performed. It requires at least 20 iterations x the number of **hyperparameter** parameters you are fine-tuning. This means that if you have two parameters you are fine-tuning, you will need at least 20 x 2 = 40 runs in the `max_total_runs` you will read about next. It supports both discrete and continuous **hyperparameters**.

Let's put everything you have learned so far into action:

1. Navigate to the **Author | Notebooks** section of your AzureML Studio web interface.

2. Create a folder named `chapter09`.

3. You will need to create a `diabetes-training` folder in the **chapter09** folder you just created and add a `training.py` script. The script is the same as the one used in *Chapter 8*, *Experimenting with Python Code*, in the section *Moving the code to a Python script file*. You can copy the contents from there. The final **Files** tree is depicted in *Figure 9.3*.

4. Create a notebook named **chapter09.ipynb** within the **chapter09** folder. *Figure 9.3* shows what the final **Files** tree will look like:

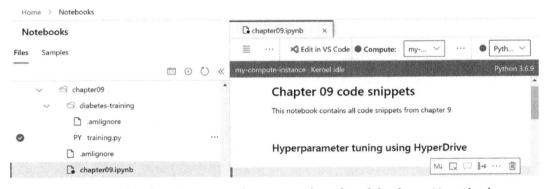

Figure 9.3 – The Files tree structure that contains the code and the chapter09 notebook

5. Add the following initialization code in the first cell:

```
from azureml.core import (
    Workspace, Environment
)
from azureml.core.conda_dependencies import \
    CondaDependencies
import sklearn

ws = Workspace.from_config()

diabetes_env = Environment(name=»diabetes-training-env»)
diabetes_env.python.conda_dependencies = \
    CondaDependencies.create(
      conda_packages=[
            f"scikit-learn=={sklearn.__version__}"],
        pip_packages=["azureml-defaults",
                      "azureml-dataprep[pandas]"])
target = ws.compute_targets['cpu-sm-cluster']
```

This is a code similar to the one you used in *Chapter 8*, *Experimenting with Python Code*. The only difference is that you are using the `create` method instead of adding the packages one by one.

6. In a new cell, define the `ScriptRunConfig` object that will execute the `training.py` script:

```
from azureml.core import ScriptRunConfig

script = ScriptRunConfig(
    source_directory='diabetes-training',
    script='training.py',
    environment=diabetes_env,
    compute_target=target
)
```

This `ScriptRunConfig` object is almost identical to the one you created in the *Training the diabetes model on a compute cluster* section of *Chapter 8, Experimenting with Python Code*. The only difference is that you do not pass the `arguments` parameter. In particular, you don't specify the `--alpha` argument. This argument will automatically be appended by the `HyperDriveConfig` object you will configure in the next step.

7. Add and execute the following code in a new cell:

```python
from azureml.train.hyperdrive import HyperDriveConfig
from azureml.train.hyperdrive import (
    RandomParameterSampling, uniform, PrimaryMetricGoal
)

param_sampling = RandomParameterSampling({
        'alpha': uniform(0.00001, 0.1),
    }
)

hd_config = HyperDriveConfig(
                run_config=script,
                hyperparameter_sampling=param_sampling,
                primary_metric_name="nrmse",
                primary_metric_goal=
                        PrimaryMetricGoal.MINIMIZE,
                max_total_runs=20,
                max_concurrent_runs=4)
```

In this code, you define a `RandomParameterSampling` approach to explore uniformly distributed values, ranging from 0.00001 to 0.1, for the `alpha` argument that will be passed to the training script you created in *step 3*. This training script accepts the `--alpha` argument, which is then passed to the `alpha` **hyperparameter** of the `LassoLars` model.

You assign this `RandomParameterSampling` configuration to the `hyperparameter_sampling` argument of `HyperDriveConfig`.

You have also configured the `run_config` property of `HyperDriveConfig` to use the `ScriptRunConfig` object you defined in *step 6*. Note that the `RandomParameterSampling` class will be passing the `alpha` parameter needed by the script.

You then define that the produced models will be evaluated using the **NRMSE** metric that the training script is logging (the `primary_metric_name` parameter). You also specify that you are trying to minimize that value (the `primary_metric_goal` parameter), since it's the error you want to minimize.

The last two parameters, `max_total_runs` and `max_concurrent_runs`, control the resources you are willing to invest in finding the best model. The `max_total_runs` parameter controls the maximum number of experiments to run. This can be between 1 and 1,000 runs. This is a required parameter. `max_concurrent_runs` is an optional parameter and controls the maximum concurrency of the conducted runs. In this case, you defined *4*, which means that only four nodes will be provisioned in the **cpu-sm-cluster** cluster that you are using for `ScriptRunConfig`. This means that the cluster will still have one unprovisioned node, since the maximum number of nodes it can scale up to is five, as you defined in the section *Working with compute targets* of *Chapter 7, The AzureML Python SDK*. There is one more optional parameter you can use to limit the amount of time you are searching for the optimal **hyperparameter** combination. The `max_duration_minutes` parameter, which you did not specify in the sample above, defines the maximum duration in minutes to run the **hyperparameter tuning** process. After that timeout, all subsequent scheduled runs are automatically canceled.

8. In a new cell, add the following code:

```
from azureml.core import Experiment

experiment = Experiment(ws, "chapter09-hyperdrive")
hyperdrive_run = experiment.submit(hd_config)

hyperdrive_run.wait_for_completion(show_output=True)
```

In this code, you submit `HyperDriveConfig` to execute under the **chapter09-hyperdrive** experiment. The `hyperdrive_run` variable is an instance of `HyperDriveRun`, which inherits from the normal `Run` class.

9. You can review the results of the process in the Studio web UI. Navigate to the **Experiments** tab of AzureML Studio and select that **chapter09-hyperdrive** experiment. You will see **Run 1** or something similar in the list of runs. This run consists of multiple child runs; each child run is a single **hyperparameter** combination. In this case, since you only have a single **hyperparameter**, each child run has a different value for the `alpha` hyperparameter. You can visually explore the effect the various values of the `alpha` parameter have regarding the **nrmse** metric, as seen in *Figure 9.4*:

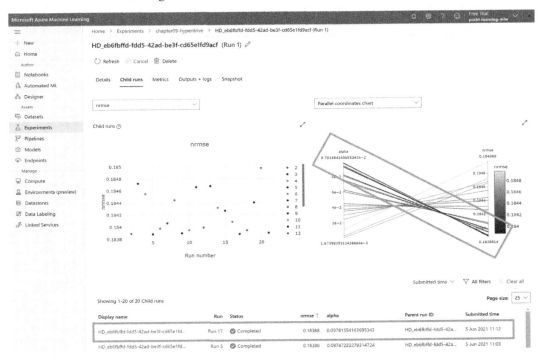

Figure 9.4 – Effect of the alpha parameter on the nrmse metric

Note that the best **nrmse** value will be different in your execution. In this case, it is **0.18388**. That value was achieved with an `alpha` value of **0.09781554163695343**. Don't worry if you cannot read the values from the charts or the table. You can get the exact values by selecting the best run. In this case, it's run 17, while it may be a different number in your case. Clicking on the link that reads **Run 17** will open the details view of the specific run, and you can review the logs and the metrics of that run. If you clicked to view the details of the child run, navigate back to `HyperDriveRun` (**Run 1**).

> **Important note**
>
> Run numbers may be different in your executions. Every time you execute the cells, a new run number is created, continuing from the previous number. So, if you execute code that performs one hyperdrive run with 20 child runs, the last child run will be run 21. The next time you execute the same code, the hyperdrive run will start from run 22, and the last child will be run 42. The run numbers referred to in this section are the ones shown in the various figures, and it is normal to observe differences, especially if you had to rerun a couple of cells.

10. Navigate to the **Outputs + logs** tab of the completed **Run 1** run. You will notice that there is a single file under the **azureml-logs** folder named **hyperdrive.txt**, as shown in *Figure 9.5*:

Figure 9.5 – Log file in HyperDriveRun, picking up the first four jobs from
the hyperparameter space that will be executed in parallel

This file contains all the jobs that were scheduled to complete the hyperparameter tuning process. The actual run logs and the stored model are stored within the child runs. If you need to debug a code issue, you will have to open one of them to see the script errors.

11. You can also get the best model's run and the corresponding **nrmse** value through the AzureML SDK. In the **chapter09.ipynb** notebook, add a new cell and type the following code:

```
best_run = hyperdrive_run.get_best_run_by_primary_
metric()

best_run_metrics = best_run.get_metrics(name='nrmse')

parameter_values = best_run.get_details()[
                        'runDefinition']['arguments']

print('Best Run Id: ', best_run.id)

print('- NRMSE:', best_run_metrics['nrmse'])

print('- alpha:', parameter_values[1])
```

The `get_best_run_by_primary_metric` method retrieves the best run of `HyperDriveRun` that the `hyperdrive_run` variable references. From there, you can read the **NRMSE** metrics using the `get_metrics` method of the `Run` object, and you can get the details of the execution using the `get_details` method. In those details, there is a `runDefinition` object that contains an `arguments` list, as shown in *Figure 9.6*:

```
35 ∨    "runDefinition": {
36           "script": "training.py",
37           "command": "",
38           "useAbsolutePath": false,
39 ∨         "arguments": [
40               "--alpha",
41               "0.09984301913536056"
42           ],
43           "sourceDirectoryDataStore": null,
44           "framework": "Python",
45           "communicator": "None",
46           "target": "cpu-sm-cluster",
```

Figure 9.6 – Demystifying the best_run.get_details()['runDefinition']['arguments'] code

In this section, you saw how to run a **hyperparameter tuning** process to find the optimal value for your model's **hyperparameters**. In the next section, you will see how you can optimize the time you search for the best values by using an early termination policy.

Using the early termination policy

One of the parameters of the `HyperDriveConfig` constructor is the `policy` one. This argument accepts an `EarlyTerminationPolicy` object, which defines the policy with which runs can be terminated early. By default, this parameter has a `None` value, which means that the `NoTerminationPolicy` class will be used, allowing each run to execute until completion.

To be able to use an early termination policy, your script must be performing multiple iterations during each run.

In the **Files** view, add a folder named **termination-policy-training** and add a **training.py** file to it, as shown in *Figure 9.7*:

Figure 9.7 – Adding a training script that performs multiple epochs

Add the following code in the training script:

```
from azureml.core.run import Run
import argparse
import time
parser = argparse.ArgumentParser()
parser.add_argument("--a", type=int, dest="a", help="The alpha parameter")
parser.add_argument("--b", type=int, dest="b", help="The beta parameter")
args = parser.parse_args()
if (args.a > 2):
    args.a = 0
run = Run.get_context()
def fake_train(run, a, b):
    time.sleep(5)
    metric = a + b
    run.log("fake_metric", metric)
```

```
for epoch in range(20):
    fake_train(run, args.a * epoch, args.b)
```

The script gets two parameters, a and b, and then calls the `fake_train` method 20 times. In data science literature, people refer to those 20 times as 20 **epochs**, which are the training cycles over the entire training dataset.

In every epoch, the a parameter is multiplied by the iteration number, which is an integer value from *0* all the way to *19*, and the `fake_train` method is invoked. The `fake_train` method sleeps for 5 seconds to simulate a training process and then adds the modified a value to the b parameter. The result is logged in the `fake_metric` metric.

Moreover, in *line 8*, the code checks the a parameter passed to the script. If it is greater than *2*, it changes to value *0*. This means that the fake model you are training will be performing better as the a value increases to value *2*, and then its performance will drop, as shown in *Figure 9.8*.

Note that you don't need to read any dataset and, thus, you do not need the reference to `Workspace`. This is why *line 10* in the code above doesn't need to check if this is an `_OfflineRun` object or not, as you did in the section *Moving the code to a Python script file* in *Chapter 8, Experimenting with Python Code*.

If you were to run `HyperDriveConfig` with grid search on all values between *1* and *4* for the **hyperparameters**, you would get 16 runs. The output of those runs is shown in *Figure 9.8*. On the left side of the figure, the diagram shows the `fake_metric` evolution over the epochs. On the right side of the figure, you can see how the `fake_metric` is affected by the various values of the a and b **hyperparameters**. On the right side of *Figure 9.8*, you can see that the models trained with values *1* and *2* on the **hyperparameter** a perform better than the models trained with a parameter *3* and *4*, regarding the `fake_metric`:

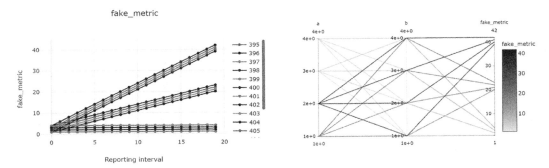

Figure 9.8 – Hyperparameter tuning without early termination policy

Ideally, you would like to reduce the amount of time waiting for all the runs to complete. `EarlyTerminationPolicy` allows you to monitor the jobs that are running, and if they are performing poorly compared to the rest of the jobs, cancel them early. The resulting output would be like the one in *Figure 9.9*, where you can see that some of the jobs were terminated before reaching the twentieth reported interval (the graph starts counting from 0), saving time and compute resources:

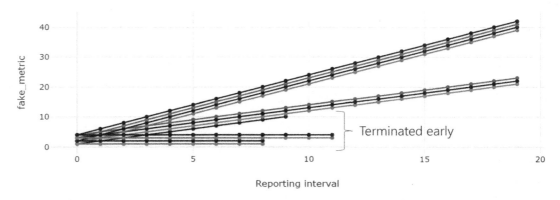

Figure 9.9 – Hyperparameter tuning with aggressive early termination policy

The AzureML SDK offers a few built-in `EarlyTerminationPolicy` implementations, located in the `azureml.train.hyperdrive` module:

- `NoTerminationPolicy`: This is the default stopping policy that allows all runs to complete.

- `MedianStoppingPolicy`: The median stopping policy computes the running averages across all runs. It then cancels runs whose best performance is worse than the median of the running averages. You can think of this policy as comparing the performance of each run against the average performance of the previous runs. The nice thing about this policy is that it considers all runs that have happened so far and does not just compare the current run with the best runs so far. This feature allows the median stopping policy to avoid being trapped in local optimum values.

- `BanditPolicy`: The bandit policy computes the distance between the current run and the best-performing one and then terminates it based on some slack criteria. You can define either the absolute distance (the `slack_amount` parameter) or the maximum allowed ratio (the `slack_factor` parameter) allowed from the best performing run.

- TruncationSelectionPolicy: The truncation selection policy is the most aggressive policy, which cancels a certain percentage (the truncation_ percentage parameter) of runs that rank the lowest for their performance on the primary metric. When ranking a relatively young run, at an early iteration, the policy compares them with the equivalent iteration performance of the older runs. Thus, this policy strives for fairness in ranking the runs by accounting for improving model performance with training time.

All policies take two optional parameters:

- evaluation_interval: The frequency for applying the policy.
- delay_evaluation: This delays the first policy evaluation for a specified number of intervals, giving time for young runs to reach a mature state.

Let's do hyperparameter tuning on the script you created above using the most recommended policy, MedianStoppingPolicy:

1. Go to the **chapter09.ipynb** notebook and add the following code in a new cell:

```python
from azureml.core import Workspace, ScriptRunConfig
ws = Workspace.from_config()
target = ws.compute_targets["cpu-sm-cluster"]
script = ScriptRunConfig(
    source_directory="termination-policy-training",
    script=»training.py»,
    environment=ws.environments[«AzureML-Minimal»],
    compute_target=target,
)
```

This code establishes the connection to the workspace and defines the ScriptRunConfig object that will be used in the hyperparameter tuning process.

2. In a new cell, add the following code:

```python
from azureml.train.hyperdrive import (
    GridParameterSampling,
    choice,
    MedianStoppingPolicy,
    HyperDriveConfig,
    PrimaryMetricGoal
```

```
)


param_sampling = GridParameterSampling(
    {
        "a": choice(1, 2, 3, 4),
        "b": choice(1, 2, 3, 4),
    }
)
early_termination_policy = MedianStoppingPolicy(
    evaluation_interval=1, delay_evaluation=5
)
hd_config = HyperDriveConfig(
    policy=early_termination_policy,
    run_config=script,
    hyperparameter_sampling=param_sampling,
    primary_metric_name="fake_metric",
    primary_metric_goal=PrimaryMetricGoal.MAXIMIZE,
    max_total_runs=50,
    max_concurrent_runs=4
)
```

This `HyperDriveConfig` object is using `MedianStoppingPolicy` as its policy parameter to evaluate all runs after their first *5* iterations and compares their results on every iteration with the median of the running averages.

3. In a new cell, add the following code to start the execution of the `HyperDriveConfig` object you defined in *step 2*:

```
experiment = Experiment(ws, "chapter09-hyperdrive")
hyperdrive_run = experiment.submit(hd_config)
hyperdrive_run.wait_for_completion(show_output=True)
```

Figure 9.10 shows the results of this `HyperDriveRun` run, where only 8 out of 16 jobs were terminated early:

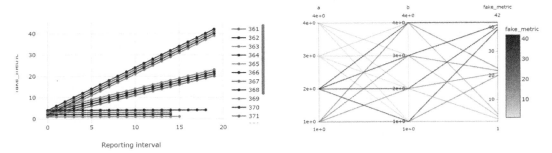

Figure 9.10 – Hyperparameter tuning with median stopping early termination policy

> **Important note**
>
> In the code above, the `max_total_runs` argument has a value of 50. This is the top limit of how many child runs can potentially occur. In this example, you only have 16 combinations. This means that the experiment will run only 16 times and then it will stop, since the whole search area has been searched. If you wanted the `max_total_runs` parameter to have an effect, you should specify a value less than 16.

So far, you have seen how you can optimize a specific model against the data you have. In the next section, you will see how you can search for the best model to run an AutoML experiment through the SDK, similar to what you did in *Chapter 5, Letting the Machines Do the Model Training*, through the studio user interface.

Running AutoML experiments with code

So far, in this chapter, you were fine-tuning a `LassoLars` model, performing a hyperparameter tuning process to identify the best value for the `alpha` parameter based on the training data. In this section, you will use **AutoML** in the AzureML SDK to automatically select the best combination of data preprocessing, model, and hyperparameter settings for your training dataset.

To configure an **AutoML** experiment through the AzureML SDK, you will need to configure an `AutoMLConfig` object. You will need to define the **Task type**, the **Metric**, the **Training data**, and the **Compute budget** you want to invest. The output of this process is a list of models from which you can select the best run and the best model associated with that run, as shown in *Figure 9.11*:

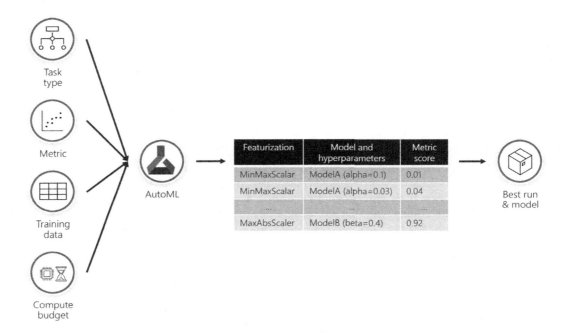

Figure 9.11 – AutoML process

Depending on the type of problem you are trying to model, you must select the `task` parameter, selecting either `classification`, `regression`, or `forecasting`, as shown in *Figure 9.12*:

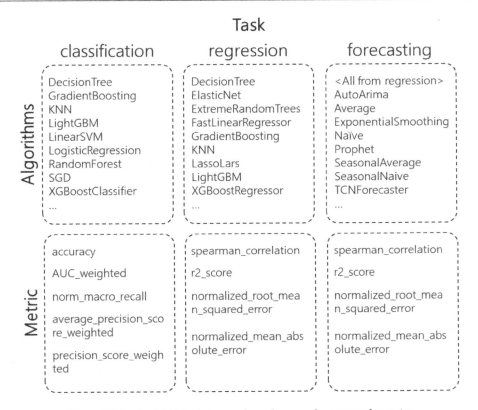

Figure 9.12 – AutoML task types, algorithms, and supported metrics

Figure 9.12 shows only a subset of the supported algorithms that the AzureML SDK supports. The `azureml.train.automl.constants.SupportedModels` package contains the `classification`, `regression`, and `forecasting` classes that list all supported algorithms as attributes. Since forecasting is just a more specialized version of regression, all algorithms from regression can be used. AutoML supports some additional, more specialized, forecasting algorithms, such as the very popular **ARIMA** technique or Facebook's **Prophet** algorithm.

The `primary_metric` parameter determines the metric to be used during model training for optimization. The metrics are the same for both regression and forecasting. Classification algorithms use different metrics, as shown in *Figure 9.12*.

Training data can be provided in the `training_data` parameter, either in the format of a pandas **DataFrame** or through the AzureML native `Dataset` objects. The training data is in tabular format and includes the `target` column. You define the name of the column you want to predict, passing the `label_column_name` parameter. By default, AutoML will use that dataset for both the training and validation of produced models. If the dataset is more than 20,000 rows, the dataset is split, keeping 10% for validation. If the dataset is smaller than 20,000 rows, cross-validation is used. If you want to specify how many folds to create out of `training_data`, you can use the `n_cross_validations` parameter. Another approach is to provide the `validation_size` parameter, which is the percentage (values *0.0* to *1.0*) to hold out of the training data and use as validation. If you want to manually split the data into training and validation data, then you can assign your validation data to the `validation_data` parameter, as you will do later in this section.

Compute budget is the amount of money you are willing to spend to find the best machine learning model out of your training data. It consists of three parts:

- **The compute cluster's node type**: The more capabilities your compute cluster's type has, the bigger the cost per second is when you run the AutoML job. This is a setting you configured when you created the compute cluster, and this cannot change at this point in time unless you create a new cluster.

- **The number of nodes to use for the AutoML job**: You can define the `max_concurrent_iterations` parameter to use up to the maximum number of nodes your compute cluster has. This will allow you to run parallel iterations but increases the cost. By default, this parameter is *1* and allows only a single iteration at a time.

- **The amount of time to search for the best model**: You can either define a literal number of hours to search for the best model using the `experiment_timeout_hours` parameter or you can define the `experiment_exit_score` parameter, which defines the score to achieve and then stop further exploration. Another way to limit your compute spending is to limit the number of different algorithms and parameter combinations to explore. By default, AutoML will explore 1,000 combinations, and you can restrict that by specifying the `iterations` parameter.

Now that you have explored all the options that you need to configure in the `AutoMLConfig` object, navigate to your `chapter09.ipynb` notebook, add a new cell, and type the following code:

```
from azureml.core import Workspace, Dataset
from azureml.train.automl import AutoMLConfig
ws = Workspace.from_config()
```

```
compute_target = ws.compute_targets["cpu-sm-cluster"]

diabetes_dataset = Dataset.get_by_name(workspace=ws,
name='diabetes')
train_ds,validate_ds = diabetes_dataset.random_
split(percentage=0.8, seed=1337)
experiment_config = AutoMLConfig(
    task = "regression",
    primary_metric = 'normalized_root_mean_squared_error',
    training_data = train_ds,
    label_column_name = "target",
    validation_data = validate_ds,
    compute_target = compute_target,
    experiment_timeout_hours = 0.25,
    iterations = 4
)
```

In this code, you get the reference to the workspace, your compute cluster, and the `diabetes` dataset, which you are splitting into a training one and a validation one. You then create an `AutoMLConfig` object that will do **regression**, using the **NRMSE** metric that you used in this chapter in the section *Hyperparameter tuning using HyperDrive*. You specify the training data and configure that you are looking to predict the `target` column. You also specify the `validation_data` parameter.

> **Important note**
> Instead of splitting the dataset, you could have passed the entire dataset in the `training_data` parameter and skipped the `validation_data` parameter. Since the dataset consists of only 442 rows, AutoML would have split the training dataset into 10 folds, which would have been used to perform the cross-validation technique.

You then define the `compute_target` experiment to use for this training and determine your computation budget by allowing the experiment to run for a quarter of an hour (the `experiment_timeout_hours` parameter), which is 15 minutes, and exploring only 4 model and parameter combinations (the `iterations` parameter). In your case, the `iterations` parameter will probably be the reason that will terminate the **AutoML** experiment.

> **Important note**
>
> For forecasting, you would need to specify `forecasting_parameters` in addition to the regression parameters you defined previously. The `ForecastingParameters` class has the following parameters that are commonly used:
>
> 1) `time_column_name`: The column that represents the time dimension of the time series.
>
> 2) `max_horizon`: The desired forecast horizon in units of the time-series frequency. This is by default *1*, meaning that your model will be able to forecast a single slot in the future. The slot is the frequency your dataset uses. If your dataset has 1 row for every hour and you want to forecast for 7 days, `max_horizon` needs to be 7 days x 24 slots per day = 168.

So far, you have created `experiment_config`, which contains the configuration of the **AutoML** experiment you are about to perform. Add a new cell and add the following code to kick off the AutoML training process:

```
from azureml.core.experiment import Experiment
my_experiment = Experiment(ws, 'chapter09-automl-experiment')
run = my_experiment.submit(experiment_config,
                           show_output=True)
```

The `run` variable contains a reference to the `AutoMLRun` object that was created using the `submit` method. After a couple of minutes, the process will be complete. To get the current best run and best model, you can use the `get_output()` method, as shown in the following snippet:

```
best_run, best_model = run.get_output()
```

Alternatively, you can directly access the best run and the best model using the corresponding `Tuple` index, as shown in the following snippet:

```
best_run = run.get_output()[0]
best_model = run.get_output()[1]
```

In every automated machine learning experiment, your data is automatically scaled or normalized to help algorithms perform well. This data transformation is becoming part of the trained model. This means that your data is passing through a data transformer first, and then the model is being trained with new feature names that are not directly visible to you. You will see an example of `sklearn.composeColumnTransformer` in *Chapter 10, Understanding Model Results*. To review the actual steps that are embedded within the AutoML model, you can use the `steps` attribute of the produced model:

```
best_model.steps
```

The first step is named `datatransformer` and contains the imputers used for our `diabetes` dataset. This step is named `datatransformer` for both regression and classification tasks. For forecasting tasks, this step is named `timeseriestransformer`, and it contains additional date-based transformations. To get a list of transformations and the names of engineered features, you can use the following code snippet:

```
print(best_model.named_steps['datatransformer'] \
                .get_featurization_summary())
feature_names=best_model.named_steps['datatransformer'] \
                .get_engineered_feature_names()
print("Engineered feature names:")
print(feature_names)
```

In this section, you searched for the best model against the diabetes regression problem using **AutoML**. This concludes the most frequently used ways you can optimize a machine learning model given a specific dataset.

Summary

In this chapter, you explored the most-used approaches in optimizing a specific model to perform well against a dataset and how you can even automate the process of model selection. You started by performing parallelized **hyperparameter tuning** using the `HyperDriveConfig` class to optimize the `alpha` parameter of the `LassoLars` model you have been training against the `diabetes` dataset. Then, you automated the model selection, using AutoML to detect the best combination of algorithms and parameters that predicts the `target` column of the `diabetes` dataset.

In the next chapter, you will build on top of this knowledge, learning how to use the AzureML SDK to interpret the model results.

Questions

1. You want to get the best model trained by an **AutoML** run. Which code is correct?

   a. `model = run.get_output()[0]`

   b. `model = run.get_output()[1]`

   c. `model = run.get_outputs()[0]`

   d. `model = run.get_outputs()[1]`

2. You want to run a forecasting **AutoML** experiment on top of data you receive from a sensor. You receive one record every day from the sensor. You want to be able to predict the values for 5 days. Which of the following parameters should you pass to the `ForecastingParameters` class?

   a. *forecast_horizon = 5 * 1*

   b. *forecast_horizon = 5 * 24*

   c. *forecast_horizon = 5 * 12*

Further reading

This section offers a list of helpful web resources that will help you augment your knowledge of the AzureML SDK and the various code snippets used in this chapter:

- The `HyperDriveConfig` class: `https://docs.microsoft.com/en-us/python/api/azureml-train-core/azureml.train.hyperdrive.hyperdriveconfig?view=azure-ml-py`

- The `AutoMLConfig` class: `https://docs.microsoft.com/en-us/Python/api/azureml-train-automl-client/azureml.train.automl.automlconfig.automlconfig`

- Data featurization in automated machine learning: `https://docs.microsoft.com/en-us/azure/machine-learning/how-to-configure-auto-features`

- Auto-train a forecast model: `https://docs.microsoft.com/en-us/azure/machine-learning/how-to-auto-train-forecast`

- Reference to the diabetes dataset that was loaded from the scikit-learn library: `https://scikit-learn.org/stable/modules/generated/sklearn.datasets.load_diabetes.html`

10
Understanding Model Results

In this chapter, you will learn how to analyze the results of your machine learning models to interpret why the model made the inference it did. Understanding why the model predicted a value is the key to avoiding black box model deployments and to be able to understand the limitations your model may have. In this chapter, you will learn about the available interpretation features of Azure Machine Learning and visualize the model explanation results. You will also learn how to analyze potential model errors and detect cohorts where the model is performing poorly. Finally, you will explore tools that will help you assess your model's fairness and allow you to mitigate potential issues.

In this chapter, we're going to cover the following topics:

- Creating responsible machine learning models
- Interpreting the predictions of the model
- Analyzing model errors
- Detecting potential model fairness issues

Technical requirements

You will need to have access to an Azure subscription. Within that subscription, you will need a **resource group** named `packt-azureml-rg`. You will need to have either a `Contributor` or `Owner` **Access Control (IAM)** role on the resource group level. Within that resource group, you should have already deployed a **machine learning** resource named `packt-learning-mlw`. These resources should be available to you if you followed the instructions in *Chapter 2, Deploying Azure Machine Learning Workspace Resources*.

You will also need to have a basic understanding of the **Python** language. The code snippets in this chapter target Python version 3.6 or later. You should also be familiar with working in the notebook experience within Azure Machine Learning Studio, something that was covered in the previous chapters.

This chapter assumes you have created a compute cluster named `cpu-sm-cluster`, as described in the *Working with compute targets* section of *Chapter 7, The AzureML Python SDK*.

You can find all the notebooks and code snippets for this chapter in this book's repository at `http://bit.ly/dp100-ch10`.

Creating responsible machine learning models

Machine learning allows you to create models that can influence decisions and shape the future. With great power comes great responsibility, and this is where AI governance becomes a necessity, something commonly referred to as responsible AI principles and practices. Azure Machine Learning offers tools to support the responsible creation of AI under the following three pillars:

- **Understand**: Before publishing any machine learning model, you need to be able to interpret and explain the model's behavior. Moreover, you need to assess and mitigate potential model unfairness against specific cohorts. This chapter focuses on the tools that assist you in understanding your models.

- **Protect**: Here, you put mechanisms in place to protect people and their data. When training a model, data from real people is used. For example, in *Chapter 8, Experimenting with Python Code*, you trained a model on top of medical data from diabetic patients. Although the specific training dataset didn't have any **Personally Identifiable Information (PII)**, the original dataset contained this sensitive information. There are open source libraries such as **SmartNoise** that offer basic building blocks that can be used to implement data handling mechanisms using vetted and mature differential privacy research techniques.

For example, a querying engine built with SmartNoise could allow data scientists
to perform aggregate queries on top of sensitive data and add statistical *noise* in the
results to prevent accidental identification of a single row within the dataset. Other
open source libraries, such as **presidio**, offer a different approach to data protection,
allowing you to quickly identify and anonymize private information such as
credit card numbers, names, locations, financial data, and more. These libraries
are more focused on raw text inputs, inputs you generally use when building
Natural Language Processing (NLP) models. They offer modules you can use to
anonymize your data before using them to train a model. Another approach to
protecting people and their data is to encrypt the data and perform the entire model
training process using the encrypted dataset without decrypting it. This is feasible
through **Homomorphic Encryption (HE)**, which is an encryption technique that
allows certain mathematical operations to be performed on top of the encrypted
data without requiring access to the private (decryption) key. The results of the
computations are encrypted and can only be revealed by the owner of the private
key. This means that using **HE**, you can add two encrypted values, **A** and **B**, and get
the value **C**, which can only be decrypted by the private key that encrypted values
A and **B**, as shown in the following diagram:

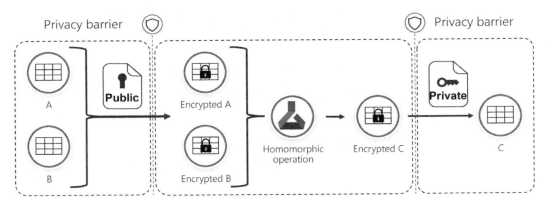

Figure 10.1 – Using HE to perform operations on top of encrypted data

- **Control**: Controlling and documenting the end-to-end process is an essential principle in all software engineering activities. DevOps practices are commonly used to ensure end-to-end process automation and governance. One of the key practices in DevOps is to document the right information in each step of the process, allowing you to make responsible decisions at each stage. An Azure Machine Learning workspace allows you to tag and add descriptions to the various artifacts you create in your end-to-end machine learning process. The following diagram shows how you can add a description to the **AutoML** run you performed in *Chapter 9, Optimizing the ML Model*:

Figure 10.2 – Adding descriptions to runs to document them

Similar to adding descriptions to runs, you can add tags to the various artifacts you produce, such as the models. Tags are key/value pairs, such as `PyTorch` being the value of the `Framework` tag key. You might want to document the following information as part of a model **datasheet**:

- The intended use of the model

- The model architecture, including the framework used

- Training and evaluation data used

- Trained model performance metrics

- Fairness information, which you will read about in this chapter

This information can be part of tags, and the **datasheet** can be a Markdown document that's automatically generated through these tags.

In this section, you got an overview of the tools and the technologies that can help you create responsible AI. All three pillars are equally important, but for the DP100 exam, you will focus on the tools in the understand category, starting with model interpretability, which you will learn more about in the next section.

Interpreting the predictions of the model

Being able to interpret the predictions of a model helps data scientists, auditors, and business leaders understand model behavior by looking at the top important factors that drive the model's predictions. It also enables them to perform what-if analysis to validate the impact of features on predictions. The Azure Machine Learning workspace integrates with **InterpretML** to provide these capabilities.

InterpretML is an open source community that provides tools to perform model interpretability. The community contains a couple of projects. The most famous ones are as follows:

- **Interpret** and **Interpret-Community** repositories, which focus on interpreting models that use tabular data, such as the diabetes dataset you have been working on within this book. You are going to work with the interpret-community repository in this section.

- **interpret-text** extends the interpretability efforts into text classification models.

- **Diverse Counterfactual Explanations (DiCE)** for machine learning allows you to detect the minimum number of changes that you need to perform in a data row to change the model's output. For example, suppose you have a loan approval model that just rejected a loan application. The customer asks what can be done to get the loan approved. **DiCE** could provide the minimum changes to approve the loan, such as reducing the number of credit cards or increasing the annual salary by 1%.

There are two approaches when it comes to interpreting machine learning models:

- **Glassbox models**: These are self-explanatory models, such as decision trees. For example, the **sklearn** `DecisionTreeClassifier` offers the `feature_importances_` attribute, which allows you to understand how features affect the model's predictions. The **InterpretML** community provides a couple more advanced **glassbox** model implementations. These models, once trained, allow you to retrieve an explainer and review which feature is driving what result, also known as **interpretability results**. Explainers for these models are lossless, meaning that they explain the importance of each feature accurately.

- **Black box explanations**: If the model you are training doesn't come with a native explainer, you can create a black box explainer to interpret the model's results. You must provide the trained model and a test dataset, and the explainer observes how the value permutations affect the model's predictions. For example, in the loan approval model, this may tweak the age and the income of a rejected record to observe whetherthat changes the prediction. The information that's gained by performing these experiments is used to produce interpretations of the feature's importance. This technique can be applied to any machine learning model, so it is considered model agnostic. Due to their nature, these explainers are lossy, meaning that they may not accurately represent each feature's importance. There are a couple of well-known black-box techniques in the scientific literature, such as **Shapley Additive Explanations (SHAP)**, **Local Interpretable Model-Agnostic Explanations (LIME)**, **Partial Dependence (PD)**, **Permutation Feature Importance (PFI)**, **feature interaction**, and **Morris sensitivity analysis**. A subcategory of the black box explainers is the **gray box explainers**, which utilize information regarding the model's structure to get better and faster explanations. For example, there are specialized explainers for tree models (**tree explainer**), linear models (**linear explainer**), and even deep neural networks (**deep explainer**).

Model explainers can provide two types of explanations:

- **Local-** or **instance-level feature importance** focuses on the contribution of features for a specific prediction. For example, it can assist in answering why the model denied a particular customer's loan. Not all techniques support local explanations. For instance, **PFI**-based ones do not support instance-level feature importance.

- **Global-** or **aggregate-level feature importance** explains how the model performs overall, considering all predictions done by the model. For example, it can answer which feature is the most important one regarding loan approval.

Now that you have the basic theory behind model interpretation, it is time for you to get some hands-on experience. You will start by training a simple **sklearn** model.

Training a loans approval model

In this section, you will train a classification model against a loans approval dataset that you will generate. You will use this model in the upcoming sections to analyze its results. Let's get started:

1. Navigate to the **Notebooks** section of your Azure Machine Learning Studio web interface. Create a folder called `chapter10` and then create a notebook called `chapter10.ipynb`, as shown here:

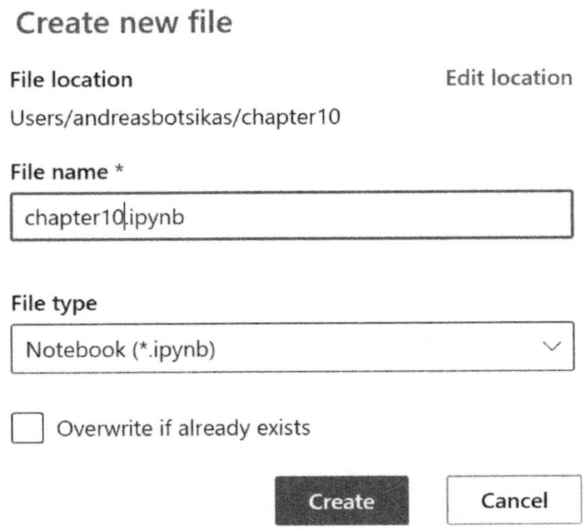

    ### Create new file

    File location   Edit location

    Users/andreasbotsikas/chapter10

    File name *

    | chapter10.ipynb |

    File type

    | Notebook (*.ipynb)   ∨ |

    ☐ Overwrite if already exists

    | Create | | Cancel |

    Figure 10.3 – Creating the chapter10 notebook in the chapter10 folder

2. You will need to install the latest packages of the `interpret-community` library, Microsoft's responsible AI widgets, and **Fairlearn** and restart the Jupyter kernel. Add the following code in the first cell:

    ```
    !pip install --upgrade interpret-community
    !pip install --upgrade raiwidgets
    !pip install --upgrade fairlearn
    ```

Once installed, restart the Jupyter kernel to ensure that the new packages will be loaded. To do so, select **Kernel operations | Restart kernel** from the notebook menu, as shown in the following screenshot. It is also advised that you comment out the contents of this cell to avoid rerunning them every time you want to revisit this notebook. Prefix each line with a # or delete the cell:

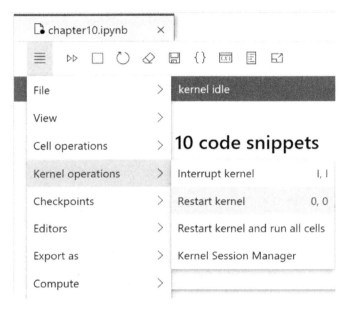

Figure 10.4 – Restarting the Jupyter kernel after installing the necessary packages

3. After restarting you kernel, add a new cell in the notebook. Generate a loans dataset using the following code:

```
from sklearn.datasets import make_classification
import pandas as pd
import numpy as np
features, target = make_classification(
    n_samples=500, n_features=3, n_redundant=1, shift=0,
    scale=1,weights=[0.7, 0.3], random_state=1337)
def fix_series(series, min_val, max_val):
    series = series - min(series)
    series = series / max(series)
    series = series * (max_val - min_val) + min_val
    return series.round(0)
features[:,0] = fix_series(features[:,0], 0, 10000)
```

```
features[:,1] = fix_series(features[:,1], 0, 10)
features[:,2] = fix_series(features[:,2], 18, 85)
classsification_df = pd.DataFrame(features, dtype='int')
classsification_df.set_axis(
    ['income','credit_cards', 'age'],
    axis=1, inplace=True)
classsification_df['approved_loan'] = target
classsification_df.head()
```

This code will generate a dataset with the following normally distributed features:

- income with a minimum value of 0 and a maximum value of 10000.

- credit_cards with a minimum value of 0 and a maximum value of 10.

- age with a minimum value of 18 and a maximum value of 85.

The label you will be predicting is approved_loan, which is a Boolean, and only 30% (weights) of the 500 samples (n_samples) are approved loans.

4. Later in this chapter, you are going to run an **AutoML** experiment against this dataset. Register the dataset, as you saw in *Chapter 7, The AzureML Python SDK*. Add the following code in your notebook:

```
from azureml.core import Workspace, Dataset
ws = Workspace.from_config()
dstore = ws.get_default_datastore()
loans_dataset = \
Dataset.Tabular.register_pandas_dataframe(
    dataframe=classsification_df,
    target=(dstore,"/samples/loans"),
    name="loans",
    description="A genarated dataset for loans")
```

If you visit the registered dataset, you can view the profile of the dataset, as shown here:

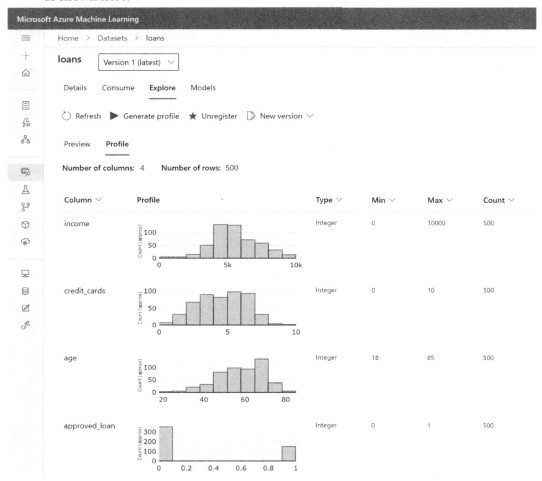

Figure 10.5 – Generated dataset profile

5. To be able to train and evaluate the model, you will need to split the dataset into train and test datasets. Use the following code to do so:

```
from sklearn.model_selection import train_test_split
X = classsification_df[['income','credit_cards', 'age']]
y = classsification_df['approved_loan'].values
x_train, x_test, y_train, y_test = \
        train_test_split(X, y,
                        test_size=0.2, random_state=42)
```

First, you split the dataset into two, one with the features and one with the label you are trying to predict. Then, you use the **sklearn** `train_test_split` method to split the 500-sample data into one that contains 500 * 0.2 = 100 test records and the train set, which contains the remaining 400 samples.

6. The next step is to initialize the model and fit it against the training dataset. In *Chapter 9, Optimizing the ML Model*, you learned how Azure Machine Learning's **AutoML** transforms the data that is going to become part of the trained model. This is done using **sklearn** pipelines, where you can chain various transformations and feature engineering steps into a model. You can create a simplified version of what **AutoML** does using the following code:

```python
from sklearn.compose import ColumnTransformer
from sklearn.preprocessing import MinMaxScaler
from sklearn.pipeline import Pipeline
from sklearn.ensemble import RandomForestClassifier
datatransformer = ColumnTransformer(
    transformers=[
        ('scale', MinMaxScaler(), x_train.columns)])
model_pipeline = Pipeline(steps=[
                ('datatransformer', datatransformer),
                ('model', RandomForestClassifier())])
model_pipeline.fit(x_train, y_train)
```

This code creates a pipeline with two steps:

- The `datatransformer` step is a `ColumnTransformer` that applies `MinMaxScaler` to all features. This transformer scales each feature's values.

- The `model` step is the actual model you are training, which is a `RandomForestClassifier`.

Then, you must call the `fit` method of the instantiated pipeline to train it against the training dataset.

> **Important note**
>
> You do not need to use `Pipeline` to benefit from the interpretability features discussed in this chapter. Instead of creating a pipeline, you could have used the model directly by assigning it to the `model_pipeline` variable; for example, `model_pipeline=RandomForestClassifier()`. The addition of the `datatransformer` step was done to help you understand how AutoML constructs its pipelines. Using `MinMaxScaler` also increases the accuracy of the resulting model. Feel free to try different scalers to observe the differences in the resulting model.

7. Now that you have a trained model, you can test it. Let's test against three fictional customers:

   - A 45-year-old who has two credit cards and a monthly income of 2000

   - A 45-year-old who has nine credit cards and a monthly income of 2000

   - A 45-year-old who has two credit cards and a monthly income of 10000

   To do that, use the following code in a new notebook cell:

   ```
   test_df = pd.DataFrame(data=[
       [2000, 2, 45],
       [2000, 9, 45],
       [10000, 2, 45]
   ], columns= ['income','credit_cards', 'age'])
   test_pred = model_pipeline.predict(test_df)
   print(test_pred)
   ```

   The printed result is [0 1 1], which means that the first customer's loan will be rejected while the second and the third ones will be approved. This indicates that the `income` and `credit_cards` features may play an important role in the prediction of the model.

8. Since the trained model is a decision tree and belongs to the glassbox model category, you can get the importance of the features that were calculated during the training process. Use the following code in a new notebook cell:

   ```
   model_pipeline.named_steps['model'].feature_importances_
   ```

This code gets a reference to the actual `RandomForestClassifier` instance and invokes a **sklearn** attribute called `feature_importances_`. The output of this is something like `array([0.66935129, 0.11090936, 0.21973935])`, which shows that `income` (the first value) is the most important feature, but it seems that `age` (the third value) is more important than `credit_cards` (the second value) in contrast to the observations we made in *Step 7*.

> **Important note**
>
> The model's training process is not deterministic, meaning that your results will be different from the results seen in this book's examples. The numbers should be similar but not the same.

In this section, you trained a simple **sklearn** decision tree and explored the native capabilities that the **glassbox** models offer. Unfortunately, not all models offer this `feature_importances_` attribute. In the next section, you will use a more advanced technique that allows you to explain any model.

Using the tabular explainer

So far, you have used the capabilities of the **sklearn** library to train and understand the results of the model. From this point on, you will use the interpret community's package to interpret your trained model more accurately. You will use **SHAP**, a black box technique that tells you which features play what role in moving a prediction from **Rejected** to **Approved** and vice versa. Let's get started:

1. In a new notebook cell, add the following code:

```
from interpret.ext.blackbox import TabularExplainer
explainer = TabularExplainer(
            model_pipeline.named_steps['model'],
            initialization_examples=x_train,
            features= x_train.columns,
            classes=["Reject", "Approve"],
            transformations=
            model_pipeline.named_
steps['datatransformer'])
```

This code creates a `TabularExplainer`, which is a wrapper class around the SHAP interpretation techniques. This means that this object will select the best SHAP interpretation method, depending on the passed-in model. In this case, since the model is a tree-based one, it will choose the **tree explainer**.

2. Using this explainer, you are going to get the **local** or **instance-level feature importance** to gain more insights into why the model gave the results it did in *Step 7* of the *Training a loans approval model* section. In a new notebook cell, add the following code:

```
local_explanation = explainer.explain_local(test_df)
sorted_local_values = \
    local_explanation.get_ranked_local_values()
sorted_local_names = \
    local_explanation.get_ranked_local_names()
for sample_index in range(0,test_df.shape[0]):
    print(f"Test sample number {sample_index+1}")
    print("\t", test_df.iloc[[sample_index]]
                            .to_dict(orient='list'))
    prediction = test_pred[sample_index]
    print("\t", f"The prediction was {prediction}")
    importance_values = \
        sorted_local_values[prediction][sample_index]
    importance_names = \
        sorted_local_names[prediction][sample_index]
    local_importance = dict(zip(importance_names,
                                importance_values))
    print("\t", "Local feature importance")
    print("\t", local_importance)
```

This code produces the results shown in the following screenshot. If you focus on **Test sample number 2**, you will notice that it shows that the **credit_cards** feature was the most important reason (see the **0.33** value) for the specific sample to be predicted as **Approved** (**The prediction was 1**). The negative values for **income** (whose value is approximately **-0.12**) in the same sample indicate that this feature was pushing the model to **reject** the loan:

```
Test sample number 1
        {'income': [2000], 'credit_cards': [2], 'age': [45]}
        The prediction was 0
        Local feature importance
        {'income': 0.07305237747416485, 'credit_cards': 0.06541726235173884, 'age': -0.06524463982590316}
Test sample number 2
        {'income': [2000], 'credit_cards': [9], 'age': [45]}
        The prediction was 1
        Local feature importance
        {'credit_cards': 0.33099611360048775, 'age': 0.049964937051777014, 'income': -0.12418605065226368}
Test sample number 3
        {'income': [10000], 'credit_cards': [2], 'age': [45]}
        The prediction was 1
        Local feature importance
        {'income': 0.5366698153798725, 'age': 0.03689012384842224, 'credit_cards': -0.10678493922829496}
```

Figure 10.6 – Local importance features show the importance of each feature for each test sample

3. You can also get the **global** or **aggregate-level feature importance** to explain how the model performs overall against a test dataset. Add the following code in a new cell in your notebook:

```
global_explanation = explainer.explain_global(x_test)
print("Feature names:",
        global_explanation.get_ranked_global_names())
print("Feature importances:",
        global_explanation.get_ranked_global_values())
print(f"Method used: {explainer._method}")
```

Using this code, you can retrieve the features in an order based on their importance. In this case, it is income, age, and then credit_cards, whose corresponding importance values are approximately 0.28, 0.09, and 0.06, respectively (the actual values may differ in your execution). Note that these values are not the same as the ones you got in *Step 8* of the *Training a loans approval model* section, although the order remains the same. This is normal since **SHAP** is a black box approach and generates the feature's importance based on the samples provided. The last line prints Method used: shap.tree, which indicates that TabularExplainer interpreted the model using the **tree explainer**, as mentioned in *Step 1* of this section.

4. Finally, you must render the explanation dashboard to review the `global_explanation` results you generated in *Step 3*. Add the following code in your notebook:

```
from raiwidgets import ExplanationDashboard
ExplanationDashboard(global_explanation, model_pipeline,
dataset=x_test, true_y=y_test)
```

This will render an interactive widget that you can use to understand your model's predictions against the test dataset that you provided. Clicking on the **Aggregate feature importance** tab, you should see the same results you saw in *Step 3*:

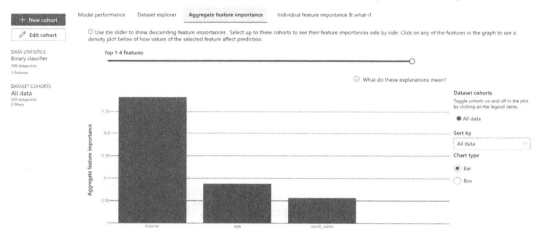

Figure 10.7 – The explanation dashboard provided by the interpret community

You will explore this dashboard in more detail in the *Reviewing the interpretation results* section.

So far, you have trained a model and used the **SHAP** interpretation technique to explain the feature importance of your model's predictions, either at a global or local level for specific inferences. In the next section, you will learn more about the alternative interpretation techniques available in the Interpret-Community package.

Understanding the tabular data interpretation techniques

In the previous section, you used the tabular explainer to automatically select one of the available **SHAP** techniques. Currently, the interpret community supports the following SHAP explainers:

- **Tree explainer** is used to explain decision tree models.

- **Linear explainer** explains linear models and can also explain inter-feature correlations.

- **Deep explainer** provides approximate explanations for deep learning models.

- **Kernel explainer** is the most generic and the slowest one. It can explain any function's output, making it suitable for any model.

An alternative to the **SHAP** interpretation techniques is to build an easier-to-explain surrogate model, such as the **glassbox** models that the interpret community offers, to reproduce the output of the given black box and then explain that surrogate. This technique is used by the **Mimic** explainer, and you need to provide one of the following glass box models:

- **LGBMExplainableModel**, which is a **LightGBM** (a fast, high-performance framework based on decision trees) explainable model

- **LinearExplainableModel**, which is a linear explainable model

- **SGDExplainableModel**, which is a stochastic gradient descent explainable model

- **DecisionTreeExplainableModel**, which is a decision tree explainable model

If you wanted to use Mimic explainer in *Step 1* of the previous section, the code for this would look like this:

```
from interpret.ext.glassbox import (
    LGBMExplainableModel,
    LinearExplainableModel,
    SGDExplainableModel,
    DecisionTreeExplainableModel
)
from interpret.ext.blackbox import MimicExplainer
mimic_explainer = MimicExplainer(
        model=model_pipeline,
        initialization_examples=x_train,
```

```
explainable_model= DecisionTreeExplainableModel,
augment_data=True,
max_num_of_augmentations=10,
features=x_train.columns,
classes=["Reject", "Approve"],
model_task='classification')
```

You can select any surrogate model from the `import` statement you can see in *line 1*.
In this sample, you are using the `DecisionTreeExplainableModel` one. To get the
global explanations, the code is the same as the code you wrote in *Step 3* and looks
like this:

```
mimic_global_explanation = \
       mimic_explainer.explain_global(x_test)
print("Feature names:",
       mimic_global_explanation.get_ranked_global_names())
print("Feature importances:",
       mimic_global_explanation.get_ranked_global_values())
print(f"Method used: {mimic_explainer._method}")
```

Although the order of the feature importance is the same, the calculated feature
importance values are different, as shown here:

```
Feature names: ['income', 'age', 'credit_cards']
Feature importances: [3.333978677937333, 0.597888625850212, 0.2614772174180758]
Method used: tree
```

Figure 10.8 – Mimic explainer feature importance calculated using the decision tree glassbox model

Similar to the **global** or **aggregate-level feature importance**, you can use the same
`mimic_explainer` to calculate **local** or **instance-level feature importance** using
the same code as in *Step 2* in the previous section. The explanations can be seen in the
following screenshot:

```
Test sample number 1
        {'income': [2000], 'credit_cards': [2], 'age': [45]}
        The prediction was 0
        Local feature importance
        {'credit_cards': 0.12837847785808038, 'income': 0.02227639452295829, 'age': -2.8787573983603227}
Test sample number 2
        {'income': [2000], 'credit_cards': [9], 'age': [45]}
        The prediction was 0
        Local feature importance
        {'income': 0.7705360860152681, 'credit_cards': 0.15764917819076013, 'age': -1.2656336786434985}
Test sample number 3
        {'income': [10000], 'credit_cards': [2], 'age': [45]}
        The prediction was 1
        Local feature importance
        {'income': 5.578514559752732, 'age': -0.0024538612376400716, 'credit_cards': -0.836632973341428}
```

Figure 10.9 – Local feature importance calculated using the decision
tree glassbox model of the Mimic explainer

The last interpretation technique offered by the interpret community is the one based on
PFI. This technique permutates the values of each feature and observes how the model's
predictions change. To create a PFI explainer to interpret your model, you will need the
following code:

```
from interpret.ext.blackbox import PFIExplainer
pfi_explainer = PFIExplainer(model_pipeline,
                             features=x_train.columns,
                             classes=["Reject", "Approve"])
```

Getting the global explanations requires passing in the `true_labels` parameter, which
is the ground truth for the dataset, which are the actual values:

```
pfi_global_explanation = \
        pfi_explainer.explain_global(x_test,
                                     true_labels=y_test)
print("Feature names:",
        pfi_global_explanation.get_ranked_global_names())
print("Feature importances:",
        pfi_global_explanation.get_ranked_global_values())
print(f"Method used: {pfi_explainer._method}")
```

The result of this code can be seen here. Due to the way **PFI** works, the `credit_cards` and `age` features may be the other way around in your results, since they have very similar feature importance values:

```
3it [00:00, 86.23it/s]
Feature names: ['income', 'credit_cards', 'age']
Feature importances: [0.3600000000000001, 0.050000000000000044, 0.040000000000000036]
Method used: pfi
```

Figure 10.10 – Global feature importance calculated by the PFI explainer

> **Important note**
>
> Due to the nature of the **PFI** explainer, you *cannot* use it to create **local** or **instance-level feature importance**. Keep that in mind if, during the exam, you are asked whether this technique could provide local explanations.

In this section, you looked at all the interpretation techniques that are supported by the Interpret-Community package. In the next section, you will explore the capabilities that the explanation dashboard offers and how this dashboard is embedded within Azure Machine Learning Studio.

Reviewing the interpretation results

Azure Machine Learning offers rich integration with the interpret community's efforts. One of those integration points is the explanation dashboard, which is embedded in every run. You can use `ExplanationClient` from the `azureml.interpret` package to upload and download model explanations to and from your workspace. To upload the global explanations that you created using `TabularExplainer` in the *Using the tabular explainer* section, navigate to the **Author | Notebooks** section of your Azure Machine Learning Studio web interface, open the `chapter10.ipynb` notebook, and add a new cell at the end of the file with the following code:

```
from azureml.core import Workspace, Experiment
from azureml.interpret import ExplanationClient
ws = Workspace.from_config()
exp = Experiment(workspace=ws, name="chapter10")
run = exp.start_logging()
client = ExplanationClient.from_run(run)
client.upload_model_explanation(
    global_explanation, true_ys= y_test,
    comment='global explanation: TabularExplainer')
```

```
run.complete()
print(run.get_portal_url())
```

This code starts a new run within the chapter10 experiment. From that run, you create an ExplanationClient, which you use to upload the model explanations you generated and the ground truth (true_ys), which helps the dashboard evaluate the model's performance.

If you visit the portal link that this code prints out, you will navigate to a run, where, in the **Explanations** tab, you will need to select **Explanation ID** on the left and then review the explanation dashboard by visiting the **Aggregate feature importance** tab, as shown here:

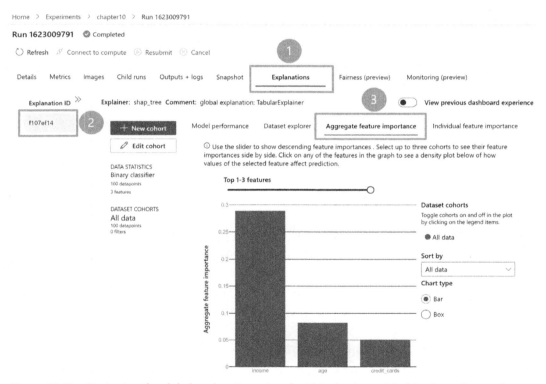

Figure 10.11 – Reviewing the global explanations stored within the Azure Machine Learning workspace

`ExplanationClient` is used by Azure Machine Learning's **AutoML** capability to explain the best model found, as you read about in *Chapter 5, Letting the Machines Do the Model Training*. To kick off **AutoML** training against the loans dataset that you registered in the previous section, go back to your `chapter10.ipynb` notebook and add the following code block in a new cell:

```
from azureml.core import Workspace, Dataset, Experiment
from azureml.train.automl import AutoMLConfig
ws = Workspace.from_config()
compute_target = ws.compute_targets["cpu-sm-cluster"]
loans_dataset = Dataset.get_by_name(
                        workspace=ws, name='loans')
train_ds,validate_ds = loans_dataset.random_split(
                        percentage=0.8, seed=1337)
```

This code looks very similar to the code you used in *Chapter 9, Optimizing the ML Model*, in the *Running AutoML experiments with code* section. In this code block, you are getting a reference to the Azure Machine Learning workspace, the `loans` dataset, and then you are splitting the dataset into training and validation sets.

In the same or a new cell, add the following code block:

```
experiment_config = AutoMLConfig(
    task = "classification",
    primary_metric = 'accuracy',
    training_data = train_ds,
    label_column_name = "approved_loan",
    validation_data = validate_ds,
    compute_target = compute_target,
    experiment_timeout_hours = 0.25,
    iterations = 4,
    model_explainability = True)
automl_experiment = Experiment(ws, 'loans-automl')
automl_run = automl_experiment.submit(experiment_config)
automl_run.wait_for_completion(show_output=True)
```

In this code block, you are kicking off **AutoML** training for a classification task, you are using accuracy as the primary metric, and you are explicitly setting `model_explainability` (which is `True` by default). This option schedules a model explanation of the best model once the **AutoML** process concludes. Once the run completes, navigate to the run's UI and open the **Models** tab, as shown here:

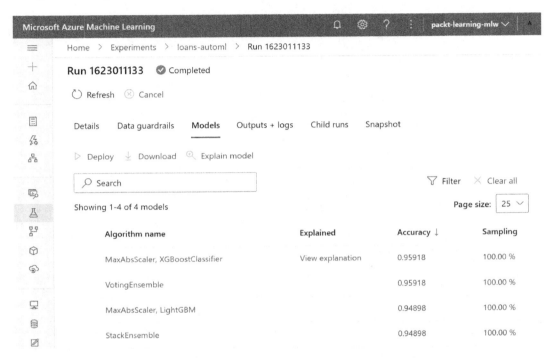

Figure 10.12 – Explanations become available for the best model in the AutoML run

Click on the **View explanation** link of the best model to navigate to the **Explanations** tab of the child run that trained the specific model. Once you land in the **Explanations** tab, you will notice that **AutoML** stored two global explanations: one for the raw features and one for the engineered features. You can switch between those two explanations by selecting the appropriate ID on the left-hand side of the screen, as shown in the following screenshot. Raw features are the ones from the original dataset. Engineered features are the ones you get after preprocessing. The engineered features are the internal inputs to the model. If you select the lower **explanation ID** and visit the **Aggregate feature importance** area, you will notice that **AutoML** has converted the credit card number into a categorical feature. Moreover, the model's input is 12 features compared to the three features you produced in your model training.

You can review those features and their corresponding feature importance here:

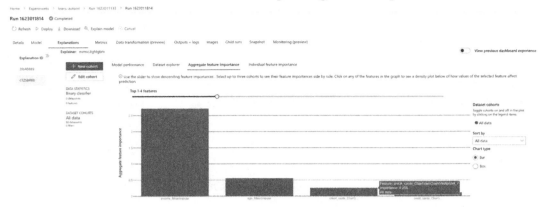

Figure 10.13 – Global explanations for engineered features

Since the engineered features are more difficult to understand, go to the top **explanation ID**, which is where you have the three raw features you have worked with so far. Navigate to the **Dataset explorer** tab, as shown here:

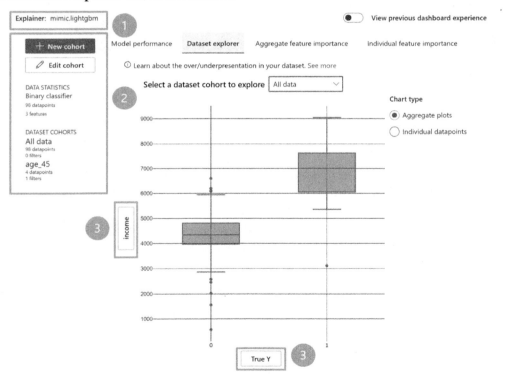

Figure 10.14 – Dataset explorer in the raw features explanations

Here, we can see the following:

1. The **Mimic** explainer was used to explain the specific model (which is an **XGBoostClassifier**, as seen in *Figure 10.12*). The **glassbox** model that was used as a surrogate model was an **LGBMExplainableModel**, as shown at the top left of the preceding screenshot.

2. You can edit the cohorts or define new ones to be able to focus your analysis on specific subgroups by selecting them from the **Select a dataset cohort to explore** dropdown. To define a new cohort, you need to specify the dataset filtering criteria you want to apply. For example, in the preceding screenshot, we have defined a cohort named **age_45**, which has a single filter (age == 45). There are **4 datapoints** in the test dataset that are used by this explanation dashboard.

3. You can modify the *x*-axis and *y*-axis fields by clicking on the highlighted areas marked as **3** in the preceding screenshot. This allows you to change the view and get insights about the correlations of the features with the predicted values or the ground truth, the correlation between features, and any other view that makes sense for your model understanding analysis.

In the **Aggregate feature importance** tab, as shown here, you can view the feature importance for all the data or for the specific cohorts you have defined:

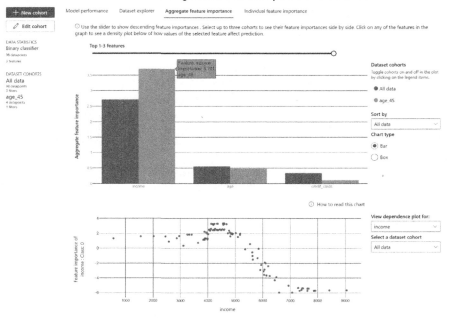

Figure 10.15 – Aggregate feature importance for the raw features with the cohorts and dependency of the rejected loans based on income

In this example, the **income** feature is more important for the **age_45** cohort than the general public, which is represented by **All data**. If you click on a feature importance bar, the graph below updates to show you how this feature is affecting the model's decision to reject a loan request (**Class 0**). In this example, you can see that incomes that are from 0 up to a bit more than 5,000 *push* the model to reject the loan, while incomes from 6,000 onward have a negative impact, which means that they try to *push* the model to approve the loan.

There are plenty of features in the explanation dashboard, and new features appear all the time as contributions to the interpret community. In this section, you reviewed the most important features of the dashboard, which have helped you understand why the model makes the predictions it does and how to potentially debug corner cases where it performs poorly.

In the next section, you will learn about error analysis, which is part of Microsoft's overall responsible AI widgets package. This tool allows you to understand the blind spots of your models, which are the cases where your model is performing poorly.

Analyzing model errors

Error analysis is a model assessment/debugging tool that enables you to gain a deeper understanding of your machine learning model errors. Error analysis helps you identify cohorts within your dataset with higher error rates than the rest of the records. You can observe the misclassified and erroneous data points more closely to investigate whether any systematic patterns can be spotted, such as whether no data is available for a specific cohort. Error analysis is also a powerful way to describe the current shortcomings of the system and communicate that to other stakeholders and auditors.

The tool consists of several visualization components that can help you understand where the errors appear.

Navigate to the **Author | Notebooks** section of your Azure Machine Learning Studio web interface and open the `chapter10.ipynb` notebook. From **Menu**, in the **Editors** sub-menu, click **Edit in Jupyter** to open the same notebook in Jupyter and continue editing it there, as shown here:

Figure 10.16 – Editing a notebook in Jupyter for better compatibility with the widget

> **Important note**
>
> At the time of writing this book, the error analysis dashboard doesn't work on the Notebooks experience due to security restrictions imposed by the Notebooks experience that prevent certain features from working properly. If you try to run it within Notebooks, it doesn't produce the necessary visualizations. This is why you are going to open the notebook in Jupyter, something that may not be needed by the time you read this book.

In the Jupyter environment, add a new cell at the end of the file with the following code:

```
from raiwidgets import ErrorAnalysisDashboard
ErrorAnalysisDashboard(global_explanation, model_pipeline,
                       dataset=x_test, true_y=y_test)
```

Notice that this code is very similar to the code you used to trigger the explanation dashboard.

> **Important note**
>
> Make sure that you close the notebook from any other editing experience you may have, such as the Notebooks experience within Azure Machine Learning Studio. If the file is modified accidentally from another editor, you may lose some of your code.

The tool opens in the global view, as shown here:

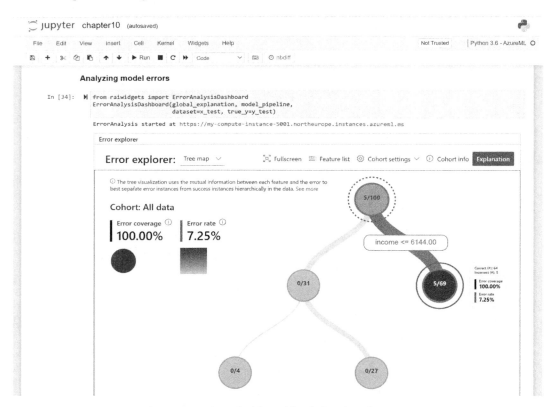

Figure 10.17 – The error analysis dashboard loaded within the Jupyter environment

In this view, you are looking at the model's error rates on overall data. In this view, you can see a binary tree that depicts data partitions between interpretable subgroups, which have unexpectedly high or low error rates. In our example, all the errors of the model occur for incomes less than or equal to **6144**, which accounts for a **7.25%** error rate, meaning that **7.25%** of the loans with monthly incomes less than **6144** were misclassified. Error coverage is the portion of all errors that fall into the node, and in this case, all the errors are located in this node (**100%**). The numbers within the node show the data representation. Here, **5** samples were wrong out of **69** records that belong in that node.

Once you have selected a node in **Tree map**, you can click on **Cohort settings** or **Cohort info** and save those records as a cohort of interest. This cohort can be used in the explanation dashboard. By clicking on the **Explanation** button, you will be taken to the **Data explorer** view, as shown here:

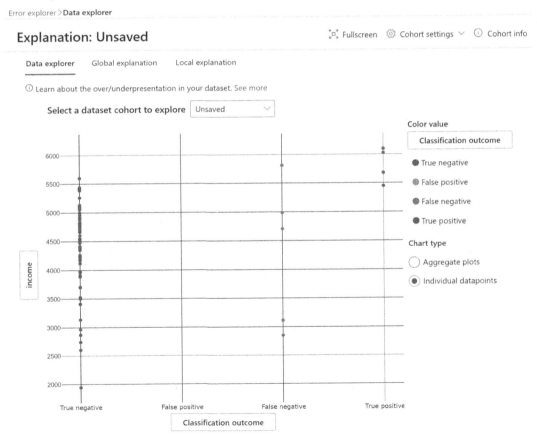

Figure 10.18 – The data explorer for the specific cohort selected in the tree map

This view has preselected the node's cohort. It has similar functionality to the explanation dashboard, such as seeing the feature importance that impacts the overall model predictions for a selected cohort. This view also offers the **Local explanation** tab, which allows you to understand individual error records and even perform what-if analysis to understand when the model would classify that record correctly.

By clicking on the **Error explorer** link at the top-left corner of the widget, you will navigate back to the **Tree map** view. From the **Error explorer:** dropdown, select **Heat map** instead of **Tree map**, which is currently selected. This will lead you to the error heat map view, as shown here:

Figure 10.19 – Error heat map view

This view slices the data in a one- or two-dimensional way based on the features selected on the top left-hand side. The heat map visualizes cells with higher errors with a darker red color to bring the user's attention to regions with high error discrepancies. The cells with stripes indicate that no samples were evaluated, potentially indicating hidden pockets of errors.

In this section, you were provided with an overview of the capabilities of the error analysis dashboard and how it can help you understand where your model is making errors. This tool can help you identify those error pockets and mitigate them by designing new features, collecting better data, discarding some of the current training data, or performing better hyperparameter tuning.

In the next section, you will learn about Fairlearn, a tool that will help you assess your model's fairness and mitigate any observed unfairness issues.

Detecting potential model fairness issues

Machine learning models can behave unfairly due to multiple reasons:

- Historical bias in society may be reflected in the data that was used to train the model.

- The decisions made by the developers of the model may have been skewed.

- Lack of representative data used to train the model. For example, there may be too few data points from a specific group of people.

Since it is hard to identify the actual reasons that cause the model to behave unfairly, the definition of a model behaving unfairly is defined by its impact on people. There are two significant types of harm that a model can cause:

- **Allocation harm**: This happens when the model withholds opportunities, resources, or information from a group of people. For example, during the hiring process or the loan lending example we have been working on so far, you may not have the opportunity to be hired or get a loan.

- **Quality-of-service harm**: This happens when the system doesn't offer everyone the same quality of service. For example, it has reduced accuracy in terms of face detection for specific groups of people.

Based on that, it is evident that model fairness issues cannot be solved automatically because there is no mathematical formulation. **Fairlearn** is a toolkit that provides tools that help assess and mitigate the fairness of the predictions of classification and regression models.

In our case, if we treat age groups as a sensitive feature, we can analyze the model's behavior based on its accuracy with the following code:

```
from fairlearn.metrics import MetricFrame
from sklearn.metrics import accuracy_score
y_pred = model_pipeline.predict(x_test)

age = x_test['age']
model_metrics = MetricFrame(accuracy_score, y_test,
                            y_pred, sensitive_features=age)
print(model_metrics.overall)
print(model_metrics.by_group[model_metrics.by_group < 1])
```

This code gets the predictions of the model you trained in the *Training a loans approval model* section and creates the predictions for the x_test dataset. Then, it assigns all values from the x_test['age'] feature to the age variable. Then, by using MetricFrame, we can calculate the accuracy_score metric of the model either for the entire test dataset, which is stored in the overall attribute, or the accuracy by group, which is stored in the by_group attribute. This code prints the overall accuracy score and the accuracy score for the groups with less than 1. The results are shown in the following screenshot:

```
Found 35 subgroups. Evaluation may be slow
0.96
age
48      0.666667
60           0.8
63          0.75
65           0.5
Name: accuracy_score, dtype: object
```

Figure 10.20 – The model has a 0.96 accuracy but for 65-year-olds its accuracy is 0.5

Although the dataset was generated, you can see that the model's accuracy for 65-year-olds is only 50%. Note that although the model was trained with ages 18 to 85, only 35 subgroups were detected in the dataset, indicating that we may not be testing it accurately.

Similar to ExplanationDashboard and ErrorAnalysisDashboard, the responsible AI widgets (raiwidgets) package offers a FairnessDashboard, which can be used to analyze the fairness of the model results.

> **Important note**
>
> At the time of writing this book, `FairnessDashboard` works in
> Jupyter. In the Notebooks experience, there are some technical glitches.
> Open your notebook in Jupyter to get the best experience out of
> `FairnessDashboard`.

In a new cell, add the following code to invoke the fairness dashboard using the
age-sensitive feature you defined in the preceding code:

```
from raiwidgets import FairnessDashboard
FairnessDashboard(sensitive_features=age,
                  y_true=y_test, y_pred=y_pred)
```

After the launch, the widget will guide you through the fairness assessment process, where
you will need to define the following:

- **Sensitive features**: Here, you must configure the sensitive features. Sensitive
  features are used to split your data into groups, as we saw previously. In this case,
  it will prompt you to create five bins for the age groups (18-29, 30-40, 41-52, 53-64,
  and 64-75), and you can modify the binning process or even request it to treat each
  age on its own by selecting the **Treat as categorical** option it provides.

- **Performance metrics**: Performance metrics are used to evaluate the quality of your
  model overall and in each group. In this case, you can select accuracy as we did
  previously. You can change this even after the wizard finishes.

- **Fairness metrics**: Fairness metrics represent either the difference or ratio between
  the extreme values of a performance metric, or simply the worst value of any group.
  An example of such a metric is **Accuracy score ratio**, which is the minimum ratio
  accuracy score between any two groups. You can change this even after the
  wizard finishes.

The resulting dashboard allows you to drill through your model's impact on the subgroups. It consists of two areas – the summarization table and the visualization area – where you can select different graphical representations, as shown here:

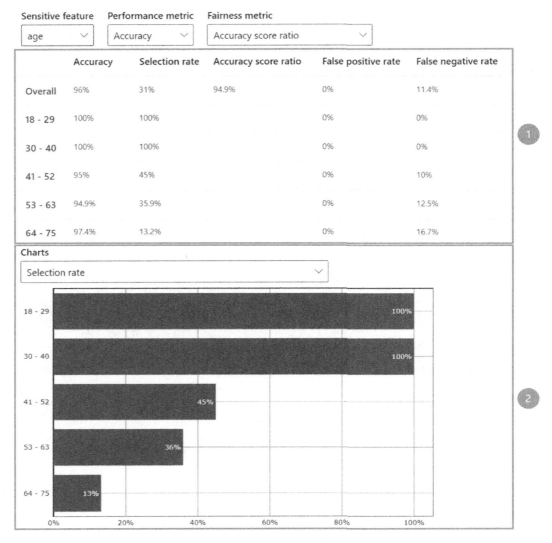

Figure 10.21 – Fairness dashboard showing the accuracy of the model in various age groups

Once you have identified a fairness issue with your model, you can use the **Fairlearn** library to mitigate them. The **Fairlearn** library offers two approaches:

- **Postprocessing**: These algorithms, similar to `ThresholdOptimizer`, adjust the output of the underlying model to achieve an explicit constraint, such as the constrain of equalizing odds. Equalizing odds in our binary classification model means that true-positive and false-positive rates should match across groups.

- **Reduction**: This approach reweights and relabels the input data based on a constraint and then fits the underlying model by passing the `sample_weight` parameter that the `fit` **sklearn** method accepts.

Using these techniques, you can balance the fairness of your model by sacrificing some of your model's performance to meet the needs of your business.

The **Fairlearn** package is constantly evolving and has been integrated within the Azure Machine Learning SDK and the Studio web experience, enabling data scientists to upload model fairness insights into the Azure Machine Learning run history and observe the **Fairlearn** dashboard within Azure Machine Learning Studio.

In this section, you learned how to detect potential unfair behaviors that your model may have. You also read about the possible mitigation techniques that can be implemented within the **Fairlearn** package. This concludes the tools provided by the Azure Machine Learning workspace and the open source communities that allow you to understand your models and assist you in creating AI.

Summary

In this chapter, you were given an overview of the various tools that can help you understand your models. You started with the Interpret-Community package, which allows you to understand why the model is making its predictions. You learned about the various interpretation techniques and explored the explanation dashboard, which provides views such as feature importance. You then saw the error analysis dashboard, which allows you to determine where the model is performing poorly. Finally, you learned about the fairness evaluation techniques, the corresponding dashboard that enables you to explore potentially unfair results, and the methods you can use to mitigate potential fairness issues.

In the next chapter, you will learn about Azure Machine Learning pipelines, which allow you to orchestrate model training and model results interpretation in a repeatable manner.

Questions

In each chapter, you will find a couple of questions to help you conduct a knowledge check regarding the topics that have been discussed in each chapter:

1. You are using `TabularExplainer` to interpret a **sklearn** `DecisionTreeClassifier`. Which underlying SHAP explainer will be used?

   a. `DecisionTreeExplainer`

   b. `TreeExplainer`

   c. `KernelExplainer`

   d. `LinearExplainer`

2. You want to interpret a **sklearn** `DecisionTreeClassifier` using `MimicExplainer`. Which of the following models can you use for the `explainable_model` parameter?

   a. `LGBMExplainableModel`

   b. `LinearExplainableModel`

   c. `SGDExplainableModel`

   d. `DecisionTreeExplainableModel`

   e. All of the above

3. Can you use `PFIExplainer` to produce local feature importance values?

   a. Yes

   b. No

Further reading

This section offers a list of useful web resources that will help you augment your knowledge of the Azure Machine Learning SDK and the various code snippets that were used in this chapter:

- **The SmartNoise** library for differential privacy: `https://github.com/opendp/smartnoise-core`

- HE resources: `https://www.microsoft.com/en-us/research/project/homomorphic-encryption/`

- Deploying an encrypted inference web service: `https://docs.microsoft.com/en-us/azure/machine-learning/how-to-homomorphic-encryption-seal`

- **Presidio**, the data protection and anonymization API: `https://github.com/Microsoft/presidio`

- Sample repository for aDevOps process in data science projects, also known as **MLOps**: `https://aka.ms/mlOps`

- **Model Cards for Model Reporting**: `https://arxiv.org/pdf/1810.03993.pdf`

- The **InterpretML** website, with links to the GitHub repository of the community: `https://interpret.ml/`

- The **Error Analysis** home page, including guides on how to use the toolkit: `https://erroranalysis.ai/`

- The **Fairlearn** home page: `https://fairlearn.org/`

11
Working with Pipelines

In this chapter, you will learn how you can author repeatable processes, defining pipelines that consist of multiple steps. You can use these pipelines to author training pipelines that transform your data and then train models, or you can use them to perform batch inferences using pre-trained models. Once you register one of those pipelines, you can invoke it using either an HTTP endpoint or through the SDK, or even configure them to execute on a schedule. With this knowledge, you will be able to implement and consume pipelines by using the **Azure Machine Learning** (**AzureML**) SDK.

In this chapter, we are going to cover the following main topics:

- Understanding AzureML pipelines
- Authoring a pipeline
- Publishing a pipeline to expose it as an endpoint
- Scheduling a recurring pipeline

Technical requirements

You will need to have access to an Azure subscription. Within that subscription, you will need a **resource group** named `packt-azureml-rg`. You will need to have either a `Contributor` or `Owner` **Access control (IAM)** role on the resource group level. Within that resource group, you should have already deployed a **machine learning** resource named `packt-learning-mlw`, as described in *Chapter 2, Deploying Azure Machine Learning Workspace Resources*.

You will also need to have a basic understanding of the **Python** language. The code snippets target Python version 3.6 or newer. You should also be familiar with working in the notebook experience within AzureML studio, something that was covered in *Chapter 8, Experimenting with Python Code*.

This chapter assumes you have registered the **loans** dataset you generated in *Chapter 10, Understanding Model Results*. It is also assumed that you have created a compute cluster named **cpu-sm-cluster**, as described in the *Working with compute targets* section in *Chapter 7, The AzureML Python SDK*.

You can find all the notebooks and code snippets for this chapter in GitHub at the following URL: `http://bit.ly/dp100-ch11`.

Understanding AzureML pipelines

In *Chapter 6, Visual Model Training and Publishing*, you saw how you can design a training process using building boxes. Similar to those workflows, the AzureML SDK allows you to author `Pipelines` that orchestrate multiple steps. For example, in this chapter, you will author a `Pipeline` that consists of two steps. The first step pre-processes the **loans** dataset that is regarded as raw training data and stores it in a temporary location. The second step then reads this data and trains a machine learning model, which will be stored in a blob store location. In this example, each step will be nothing more than a Python script file that is being executed in a specific compute target using a predefined `Environment`.

> **Important note**
>
> Do not confuse the **AzureML** `Pipelines` with the **sklearn** `Pipelines` you read in *Chapter 10, Understanding Model Results*. The **sklearn** ones allow you to chain various transformations and feature engineering methods to transform the data that the model is fed. These transformations are performed every time you try to pass any data to the model, either during training or at inference time. You can think of the **sklearn** `Pipelines` as a wrapper around the actual model class that you want to train and use for inferences.

The AzureML SDK offers quite a few building blocks that you can use to construct a `Pipeline`. *Figure 11.1* contains the most popular classes that you may encounter in the exam and real-life code:

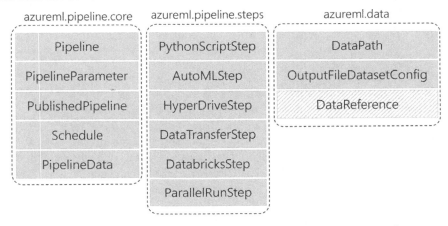

Figure 11.1 – Classes available in the AzureML SDK to author your pipelines

The **Pipeline** is the core class that defines a workflow that stitches together multiple steps. You can pass in parameters to a pipeline by defining them using the **PipelineParameter** class. These parameters can be references in one or more steps within the **Pipeline**. Once you have finished defining a pipeline, you can publish it to register it in the AzureML workspace as a versioned object that can be referenced using the **PublishedPipeline** class. This published pipeline has an endpoint that you can use to trigger its execution. If you want, you can define a **Schedule** and have this **PublishedPipeline** class triggered at a specific time interval. **PipelineData** defines temporary storage where one step can drop some files for the next one to pick them up. The data dependency between those two steps creates an implicit execution order in the **Pipeline**, meaning that the dependent step will wait for the first step to complete. You will be using all these classes in this chapter.

In the **azureml.pipeline.steps** module, you will find all the available steps you can use. The most commonly used steps are the following:

- **PythonScriptStep**: This step allows you to execute a Python script. You will be using this step in this chapter.

- **AutoMLStep**: This step encapsulates an automated ML run. It requires the `AutoMLConfig` object you saw in *Chapter 9, Optimizing the ML Model*.

- **HyperDriveStep**: This step allows you to run a hyperparameter tuning, passing the `HyperDriveConfig` parameter you saw in *Chapter 9, Optimizing the ML Model*.

- **DataTransferStep**: A **Pipeline** step that allows you to transfer data between AzureML-supported storage options.

- **DatabricksStep**: This allows you to execute a DataBricks notebook, Python script, or JAR file in an attached DataBricks cluster.

- **ParallelRunStep**: This step allows you to process large amounts of data in parallel. You will be using this step in the next chapter, *Chapter 12, Operationalizing Models with Code*, where you will be creating a batch inference pipeline.

> **Important note**
>
> In the past, AzureML provided an `Estimator` class that represented a generic training script. Some framework-specific estimators inherited from that generic `Estimator` class, such as `TensorFlow` and `PyTorch`. To incorporate one of those estimators in your pipelines, you would have used an `EstimatorStep`. The whole `Estimator` class and its derivatives have been deprecated in favor of `ScriptRunConfig`, which you have used in the previous chapters. If, during the exam, you see a deprecated reference to an `EstimatorStep`, you can treat it as a `PythonScriptStep`.

The last major piece of a **Pipeline** is the data that flows through it.

- **DataPath** allows you to reference a path in the data store. For example, in *Chapter 7, The AzureML Python SDK*, in the *Working with datasets* section, you used the `(dstore, "/samples/diabetes")` tuple to indicate where you wanted to store the data when you called the `register_pandas_dataframe` method of a `TabularDataset`. Instead of that tuple, you could have passed the equivalent `DataPath(datastore=dstore, path_on_datastore="/samples/diabetes")`.

- **OutputFileDatasetConfig** configures the datastore location where you want to upload the contents of a local path that resides within a compute target that executes a specific test. In *Chapter 8, Experimenting with Python Code*, in the *Tracking metrics in experiments* section, you saw how the `outputs` folder was automatically uploaded to a `Run` execution. Similar to that folder, you can define additional local folders that will be automatically uploaded to a target path in a target datastore. In this chapter, you will be using this class to store the produced model in a specific location within the default blob storage account.

- **DataReference** represents a path in a datastore and can be used to describe how and where data should be made available in a run. It is no longer the recommended approach for data referencing in AzureML. If you encounter it in an obsolete exam question, you can treat it as a **DataPath** object.

In this section, you learned about the building blocks you can use to construct an AzureML **Pipeline**. In the next section, you will get some hands-on experience of using those classes.

Authoring a pipeline

Let's assume that you need to create a repeatable workflow that has two steps:

1. It loads the data from a registered dataset and splits it into training and test datasets. These datasets are converted into a special construct needed by the **LightGBM** tree-based algorithm. The converted constructs are stored to be used by the next step. In our case, you will use the **loans** dataset that you registered in *Chapter 10, Understanding Model Results*. You will be writing the code for this step within a folder named step01.

2. It loads the pre-processed data and trains a **LightGBM** model that is then stored in the /models/loans/ folder of the default datastore attached to the AzureML workspace. You will be writing the code for this step within a folder named step02.

    Each step will be a separate Python file, taking some arguments to specify where to read the data from and where to write the data to. These scripts will utilize the same mechanics as the scripts you authored in *Chapter 8, Experimenting with Python Code*. What is different in this chapter is that instead of invoking each Python script separately, you will create a Pipeline that will invoke those steps one after the other. In *Figure 11.2*, you can see the overall inputs and outputs each script is going to have, along with the parameters you will need to configure for each step to execute:

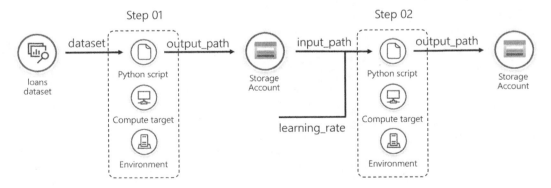

Figure 11.2 – Inputs and outputs of each pipeline step

Based on *Figure 11.2*, for each step, you will need to define the compute target and the `Environment` that will be used to execute the specific Python script. Although each step can have a separate compute target and a separate `Environment` specified, you will be running both steps using the same `Environment`, and the same compute target to simplify the code. You will be using the out-of-the-box **AzureML-Tutorial** `Environment`, which contains standard data science packages, including the **LightGBM** library that your scripts will require. You will be executing the steps in the **cpu-sm-cluster** cluster you created in *Chapter 7, The AzureML Python SDK*.

You will start by authoring the `Pipeline`, and then you will author the actual Python scripts required for each step. Navigate to the **Notebooks** section of your AzureML studio web interface. In your user folder, create a folder named `chapter11` and then create a notebook named `chapter11.ipynb`, as seen in *Figure 11.3*:

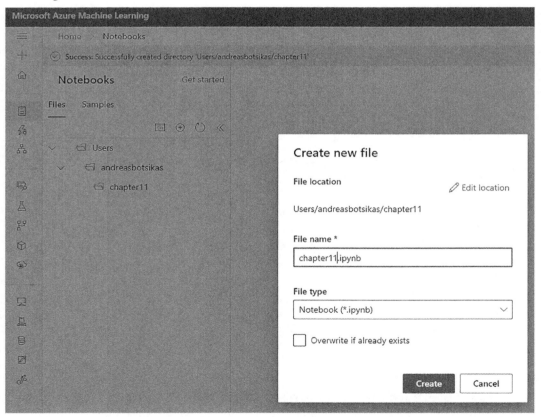

Figure 11.3 – Adding the chapter11 notebook to your working files

Open the newly created notebook and follow the steps to author an AzureML pipeline using the AzureML SDK:

1. You will start by getting a reference to your workspace. Then you will get references to the `loans` dataset and the `cpu-sm-cluster`. Add the following code to a cell in your notebook:

```
from azureml.core import Workspace

ws = Workspace.from_config()
loans_ds = ws.datasets['loans']
compute_target = ws.compute_targets['cpu-sm-cluster']
```

If you are having difficulties understanding this code snippet, please review *Chapter 7, The AzureML Python SDK*.

2. You will need to create a configuration object that will dictate the use of the **AzureML-Tutorial** `Environment` when each step gets executed. To do that, you will need to create a `RunConfiguration` using the following code:

```
from azureml.core import RunConfiguration

runconfig = RunConfiguration()
runconfig.environment = ws.environments['AzureML-Tutorial']
```

In this code, you create a new `RunConfiguration` object, and you assign the predefined **AzureML-Tutorial** `Environment` to its `environment` attribute. To help you understand how this `RunConfiguration` object relates to the work you have been doing in *Chapter 8, Experimenting with Python Code*, the `ScriptRunConfig` you have been using in that chapter had an optional `run_config` parameter where you could have passed this `RunConfiguration` object you defined in this cell.

3. You will then need to define a temporary storage folder where the first step will drop the output files. You will use the `PipelineData` class using the following code:

```
from azureml.pipeline.core import PipelineData

step01_output = PipelineData(
    "training_data",
    datastore= ws.get_default_datastore(),
    is_directory=True)
```

In this code, you are creating an intermediate data location named `training_data`, which is stored as a folder in the default datastore that is registered in your AzureML workspace. You should not care about the actual path of this temporary data, but if you are curious, the actual path of that folder in the default storage container is something like `azureml/{step01_run_id}/training_data`.

4. Now that you have all the prerequisites for your pipeline's first step, it is time to define it. In a new cell, add the following code:

```
from azureml.pipeline.steps import PythonScriptStep


step_01 = PythonScriptStep(
    'prepare_data.py',
    source_directory='step01',
    arguments = [
        "--dataset", loans_ds.as_named_input('loans'),
        "--output-path", step01_output],
    name='Prepare data',
    runconfig=runconfig,
    compute_target=compute_target,
    outputs=[step01_output],
    allow_reuse=True
)
```

This code defines a `PythonScriptStep` that will be using the source code in the `step01` folder. It will execute the script named `prepare_data.py`, passing the following arguments:

- `--dataset`: This passes the `loans_ds` dataset ID to that variable. This dataset ID is a unique **GUID** representing the specific version of the dataset as it is registered within your AzureML workspace. The code goes one step further and makes a call to the `as_named_input` method. This method is available in both `FileDataset` and `TabularDataset` and is only applicable when a `Run` executes within the AzureML workspace. To invoke the method, you must provide a name, in this case, `loans`, that can be used within the script to retrieve the dataset. The AzureML SDK will make the `TabularDataset` object available within the `prepare_data.py` script in the `input_datasets` dictionary of the run object. Within the `prepare_data.py` script, you can get a reference to that dataset using the following code:

```
run = Run.get_context()
loans_dataset = run.input_datasets["loans"]
```

- --output-path: This passes the PipelineData object you created in *Step 3*. This parameter will be a string representing a path where the script can store its output files. The datastore location is mounted to the local storage of the compute node that is about to execute the specific step. This mounting path is passed to the script, allowing your script to transparently write the outputs directly to the datastore.

Coming back to the arguments you pass to the PythonScriptStep initialization, you define a name that will be visible in the visual representation of the pipeline seen in *Figure 11.6*. In the runconfig parameter, you pass the RunConfiguration object that you defined in *Step 2*. In the compute_target parameter, you pass the reference to the cpu-sm-cluster cluster that you got in *Step 1*.

In the outputs parameter, you pass an array of outputs to which this step will be posting data. This is a very important parameter to define the right execution order of the steps within the pipeline. Although you are passing the PipelineData object as an argument to the script, the AzureML SDK is not aware of whether your script will be writing or reading data from that location. By explicitly adding the PipelineData object to the outputs parameter, you mark this step as a producer of the data stored in the PipelineData object. Thus, anyone referencing the same object in the corresponding inputs parameter will need to execute after this PythonScriptStep.

The allow_reuse Boolean parameter allows you to reuse the outputs of this PythonScriptStep if the inputs of the script and the source code within the step01 folder haven't changed since the last execution of the pipeline. Since the only input of this step is a specific version of the **loans** TabularDataset, it cannot change. Although you did not specify a particular version when you referenced the TabularDataset, the latest version was automatically selected. This version was pinned to the pipeline's definition at creation time. The pipeline will keep executing on the pinned version, even if you create a new version of the TabularDataset. Moreover, since the allow_reuse parameter is set to True, this step will run only once, and from there on, the results will be automatically reused. At the end of this section, you will see how this affects the pipeline execution time when you rerun the same pipeline.

> **Important note**
> If you wanted to force the pipeline to read the latest version of the **loans** dataset, you could re-register the pipeline after creating the new version of the dataset. The authoring code would be exactly the same, only this time, the `loans_ds` variable would reference the latest version of the `TabularDataset`. At the end of this section, you will also learn how you can pass the training dataset as a `PipelineParameter`.

5. Now that you have defined the `PythonScriptStep`, it is time to add the missing Python script to your files. Next to your notebook, under the `chapter11` folder you are currently working on, add a new folder named `step01`. Within that folder, add a new Python script file named `prepare_data.py`. The final folder structure should be similar to the one shown in *Figure 11.4*:

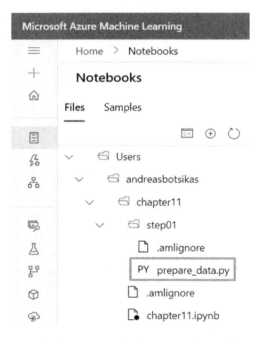

Figure 11.4 – Folder structure for the prepare_data.py script that will be executed in your pipeline

6. Add the following code blocks within the `prepare_data.py` file. Instead of typing all this code, you can download it directly from the GitHub repository mentioned in the *Technical requirements* section of this chapter:

```
import argparse
from azureml.core.run import Run
```

```
from sklearn.model_selection import train_test_split
import lightgbm as lgb
import os
```

These are all the imports you will need within the script file. You are going to create the training and test datasets using the `train_test_split` method for the **sklearn** library. Moreover, you are going to be referring to the `lightgbm` library with the `lgb` short alias:

```
parser = argparse.ArgumentParser()
parser.add_argument("--dataset", type=str,
dest="dataset")
parser.add_argument("--output-path", type=str,
    dest="output_path",
    help="Directory to store datasets")
args = parser.parse_args()
```

This script creates an `ArgumentParser` that parses the arguments you passed when you defined the `PythonScriptStep` in *Step 4*. As a reminder, the `--dataset` parameter is going to contain the dataset ID that the script will need to process, and the `--output-path` parameter will be the local path location where the script is supposed to write the transformed datasets:

```
run = Run.get_context()
loans_dataset = run.input_datasets["loans"]
```

Right after parsing the arguments, you are getting a reference to the `Run` context. From there, you get a reference to the `loans` dataset, something that becomes available to you because you called the `as_named_input` method as discussed in *Step 4*. Later in this section, you will read about how you could have rewritten this code block to be able to run the same script in your local computer without a Run context:

```
print(f"Dataset id: {loans_dataset.id}")
```

This code block prints the ID of the dataset that your code picked as a reference. If you print the ID passed to the `--dataset` parameter, and which is stored in the `args.dataset` variable, you will notice that these two values are identical:

```
loans_df = loans_dataset.to_pandas_dataframe()


x = loans_df[["income", "credit_cards", "age"]]
y = loans_df["approved_loan"].values
```

```
feature_names = x.columns.to_list()
x_train, x_test, y_train, y_test = train_test_split(
    x, y, test_size=0.2, random_state=42, stratify=y
)
```

In this code block, you load the dataset into memory and use the **sklearn** `train_test_split` method to split the dataset into training and test features (`x_train` and `x_test`) and training and test labels (`y_train` and `y_test`):

```
train_data = lgb.Dataset(x_train, label=y_train, feature_name=feature_names)
test_data = lgb.Dataset(x_test, label=y_test, reference=train_data)
```

The features and the labels are then converted into `train_data` and `test_data`, which are **LightGBM** `Dataset` objects. **LightGBM** requires a special `Dataset` format for training and validation. Note that the validation dataset stored in the `test_data` variable needs to reference the training data (`train_data`). This is a failsafe mechanism embedded by **LightGBM** to prevent the accidental passing of incompatible validation data. **LightGBM** constructs the validation dataset using the reference dataset as a template and then populates the actual validation data. This process ensures that all categorical values are available in both the training and the validation dataset structures. If you don't do this, you will end up with the cryptic *Cannot add validation data, since it has different bin mappers with training data* error message when you attempt to train the **LightGBM** model:

```
output_path = args.output_path
if not os.path.exists(output_path):
    os.makedirs(output_path)

train_data.save_binary(os.path.join(output_path, "train_dataset.bin"))
test_data.save_binary(os.path.join(output_path, "validation_dataset.bin"))
```

In the last code block of the script, you create the `output_path` folder, if it doesn't already exist, and then use the native `save_binary` method of the **LightGBM** `Dataset` to serialize the dataset into a binary file that is optimized for storing and loading.

In contrast to the scripts you created in *Chapter 8, Experimenting with Python Code*, the prepare_data.py file cannot execute on your local computer as an _OfflineRun. This is because you have a dependency on the input_datasets dictionary that is only available if the Run is executing within the AzureML workspace. If you wanted to test this file locally before using it within the Pipeline, you could use the following code instead:

```
run = Run.get_context()
loans_dataset = None
if type(run) == _OfflineRun:
    from azureml.core import Workspace, Dataset
    ws = Workspace.from_config()
    if args.dataset in ws.datasets:
        loans_dataset = ws.datasets[args.dataset]
    else:
        loans_dataset = Dataset.get_by_id(ws, args.dataset)
else:
    loans_dataset = run.input_datasets["loans"]
```

This code checks whether this is an offline run. In that case, it first gets a reference to the workspace as you saw in *Chapter 8, Experimenting with Python Code*, and then it checks whether the --dataset parameter stored in the args.dataset variable is a dataset name. If it is, the latest version of the dataset is assigned to the loans_dataset variable. If it is not a name, the script assumes it is a GUID, which should represent the ID of a specific dataset version. In that case, the script tries the get_by_id method to retrieve the specific dataset or throw an error if the value passed is not a known dataset ID. If the run is online, you can still use the input_datasets dictionary to retrieve the dataset reference.

7. Back to your notebook, you will start defining the prerequisites for the second step, the model training phase of your Pipeline. In *Figure 11.2*, you saw that this step requires a parameter named learning_rate. Instead of hardcoding the learning rate hyperparameter of the **LightGBM** model within your training script, you will use a PipelineParameter to pass in this value. This parameter will be defined at Pipeline level, and it will be passed to the training script as an argument, as you will see in *Step 9*. To create such a parameter, use the following code:

```
from azureml.pipeline.core import PipelineParameter
```

```
learning_rate_param = PipelineParameter( name="learning_
rate", default_value=0.05)
```

This code defines a new `PipelineParameter` named `learning_rate`.
The default value will be `0.05`, meaning that you can omit to pass this parameter
when you execute the pipeline, and this default value will be used. You will see
later in *Step 13* how you can execute the `Pipeline` and specify a value other
than the default.

8. You will store the trained model in the `/models/loans/` folder of the default
    datastore attached to the AzureML workspace. To specify the exact location where
    you want to store the files, you will use the `OutputFileDatasetConfig` class.
    In a new notebook cell, add the following code:

```
from azureml.data import OutputFileDatasetConfig

datastore = ws.get_default_datastore()
step02_output = OutputFileDatasetConfig(
    name = "model_store",
    destination = (datastore, '/models/loans/'))
```

In this script, you are getting a reference to the default datastore. Then, you create
an `OutputFileDatasetConfig` object, passing a tuple to the `destination`
parameter. This tuple consists of the datastore you selected and the path within that
datastore. You could have selected any datastore you have attached in the AzureML
workspace. This `OutputFileDatasetConfig` object defines the destination to
copy the outputs to. If you don't specify the `destination` argument, the default `/
dataset/{run-id}/{output-name}` value is used. Note that `destination`
allows you to use placeholders while defining the path. The default value uses both
the `{run-id}` and `{output-name}` placeholders that are currently supported.
These placeholders will be replaced with the corresponding values at the
appropriate time.

9. Now that you have all the prerequisites defined, you can define the second step of your `Pipeline`. In a new cell in your notebook, add the following code:

```
step_02 = PythonScriptStep(
    'train_model.py',
    source_directory='step02',
    arguments = [
        "--learning-rate", learning_rate_param,
        "--input-path", step01_output,
        "--output-path", step02_output],
    name='Train model',
    runconfig=runconfig,
    compute_target=compute_target,
    inputs=[step01_output],
    outputs=[step02_output]
)
```

Similar to the `step_01` folder you created in *Step 4*; this code defines a `PythonScriptStep` that will invoke the `train_model.py` script located in the `step02` folder. It will populate the `--learning-rate` argument using the value passed to the `PipelineParameter` you defined in *Step 7*. It will also pass the output of `step_01` to the `--input-path` argument. Note that `step01_output` is also added to the list of inputs of this `PythonScriptStep`. This forces `step_02` to wait for `step_01` to complete in order to consume the data stored in `step01_output`. The last script argument is `--output-path`, where you pass the `OutputFileDatasetConfig` object you created in the previous step. This object is also added to the list of outputs of this `PythonScriptStep`.

10. Let's create the Python script that will be executed by step_02. Next to your notebook, under the chapter11 folder you are currently working on, add a new folder named step02. Within that folder, add a new Python script file named train_model.py. The final folder structure should be similar to the one shown in *Figure 11.5*:

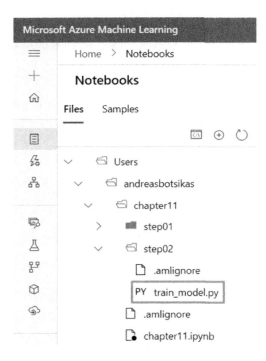

Figure 11.5 – The training script that will be executed in the step02 folder of your pipeline

11. Open the train_model.py file and add the following code blocks to it. Instead of typing all this code, you can download it directly from the GitHub repository mentioned in the *Technical requirements* section of this chapter:

```
import argparse
import os
import lightgbm as lgb
import joblib
parser = argparse.ArgumentParser()
```

This block imports all modules you will need in the file and creates an `ArgumentParser` to read the arguments you will be passing to this script. If you so wished, you could have used another famous library for script parameter parsing called **click**. You can learn more about this library in the *Further reading* section:

```
parser.add_argument(
    "--learning-rate",
    type=float,
    dest="learning_rate",
    help="Learning date for LightGBM",
    default=0.01,
)
```

In this block, you define the `learning_rate` argument. Note that this is a float with a default value different from the value you defined in *Step 7*, an example that shows that those two default values do not need to be the same. When executing the pipeline, `PipelineParameter` will be the one defining the actual value:

```
parser.add_argument(
    "--input-path",
    type=str,
    dest="input_path",
    help="Directory containing the datasets",
    default="../data",
)
parser.add_argument(
    "--output-path",
    type=str,
    dest="output_path",
    help="Directory to store model",
    default="./model",
)
args = parser.parse_args()
```

You then parse `input_path` and `output_path`, which are string values that point to local folders within the compute where this script is executing. The last line parses the incoming arguments and assigns the results to the `args` variable:

```
print(f"Loading data from {args.input_path}")
train_data = lgb.Dataset(os.path.join(args.input_path,
"train_dataset.bin"))
```

```
validation_data = lgb.Dataset(os.path.join(args.input_
path, "validation_dataset.bin"))
```

After parsing the script arguments, the training and validation datasets are loaded:

```
param = {
    "task": "train",
    "objective": "binary",
    "metric": "auc",
    "num_leaves": 5,
    "learning_rate": args.learning_rate
}
model = lgb.train(
    param,
    train_set = train_data,
    valid_sets = validation_data,
    early_stopping_rounds = 5
)
```

In this code block, a binary classification training process is configured that will use the **Area Under Curve** (auc) metric to evaluate the training progression. **LightGBM** uses an iterative training approach where the model will train until the validation score stops improving for the last **5** iterations, as you specified when passing in the early_stopping_rounds parameter:

```
output_path = args.output_path
if not os.path.exists(output_path):
    os.makedirs(output_path)


joblib.dump(value=model, filename=os.path.join(output_
path, "model.joblib"))
```

Once the training is complete, the model is serialized using the joblib library and stored in the output_path folder.

12. Back to the notebook, it's time you defined the actual `Pipeline` you have been building so far. In a new cell, add the following code:

```
from azureml.pipeline.core import Pipeline

pipeline = Pipeline(workspace=ws, steps=[step_01,
step_02])
```

You define a new `Pipeline` object, passing in a list with all the steps you want to include. Note that the order of the steps is not important since the real execution order is defined by the `step01_output` `PipelineData` dependency you specified between those two steps.

13. To execute the pipeline, you will need to submit it in an `Experiment`. In a new notebook cell, add the following code:

```
from azureml.core import Experiment

experiment = Experiment(ws, "chapter-11-runs")
pipeline_run = experiment.submit(
    pipeline,
    pipeline_parameters= {
        "learning_rate" : 0.5
    }
)
pipeline_run.wait_for_completion()
```

This code defines a new `Experiment` named `chapter-11-runs` and submits the pipeline to run, passing the value of `0.5` to the `learning_rate` parameter you defined in *Step 7*.

One of the first outputs of the pipeline execution is the link to the AzureML portal. Clicking on that link will get you to the pipeline execution run, as seen in *Figure 11.6*:

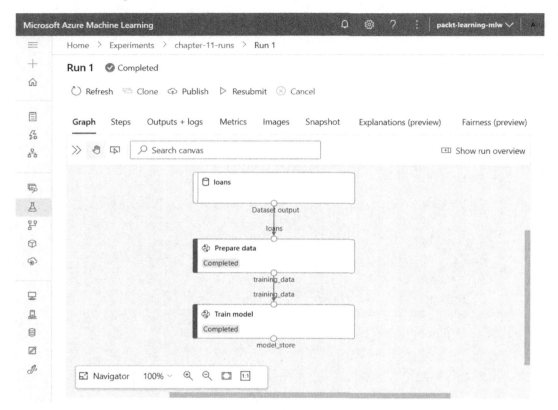

Figure 11.6 – A graphical representation of the pipeline you authored in this section

Suppose you try to rerun the pipeline by executing the code you wrote in *Step 13* for a second time. In that case, you will notice that the execution will be almost instant (just a few seconds compared to the minute-long execution you should have seen the first time). The pipeline detected that no input had changed and reused the outputs of the previously executed steps. This demonstrates what the `allow_reuse=True` in *Step 4* does, and it also proves that even though we didn't specify that parameter in *Step 9*, the default value is `True`. This means that, by default, all steps will reuse previous executions if the inputs and the code files are the same as the ones of an earlier execution. If you want to force a retrain even if the same `learning_rate` variable is passed to the pipeline, you can specify `allow_reuse=False` in *Step 9*.

> **Important note**
>
> If you wanted to pass the training dataset as a `PipelineParameter`, you would have to use the following code:
>
> ```
> from azureml.data.dataset_consumption_config
> import DatasetConsumptionConfig
>
> ds_pipeline_param =
> PipelineParameter(name="dataset ", default_
> value=loans_ds)
>
> dataset_consumption =
> DatasetConsumptionConfig("loans", ds_pipeline_
> param)
> ```
>
> Using this code and passing the `dataset_consumption` object in *Step 4* instead of `loans_ds.as_named_input('loans')` would allow you to select the input dataset and its version while submitting a pipeline to execute.

So far, you have defined a pipeline that executes two Python scripts. `step_01` pre-processes the training data and stores it in an intermediate data store for `step_02` to pick up. From there, the second step trains a **LightGBM** model and stores it in the `/models/loans/` folder of the default datastore attached to the AzureML workspace. If you have followed the steps accurately, the pipeline will have been completed successfully. In real life, though, coding issues creep in, and your pipeline may fail to complete. In the next section, you will learn how to troubleshoot potential pipeline runtime issues.

Troubleshooting code issues

So far, your code has worked like a charm. What happens if a script has a coding issue or if a dependency is missing? In that case, your pipeline will fail. In the graphical representation you saw in *Figure 11.6*, you will be able to identify the failing step. If you want to get the details of a specific child step, you will have to first locate it using `find_step_run` of the `pipeline_run` object you got when you executed the pipeline. In a new cell within your notebook, add the following code:

```
train_step_run = pipeline_run.find_step_run("Train model")[0]
train_step_run.get_details_with_logs()
```

This code finds all steps with the name **Train model**, and you select the first result located on the 0 index. This retrieves a StepRun object, which is for the step_02 folder you defined in the previous section. StepRun inherits from the base Run class, exposing the get_details_with_logs method that is also available in the ScriptRun class you were using in *Chapter 8, Experimenting with Python Code*. This method is handy in troubleshooting potential issues with your dependencies or your script code. It produces a lot of helpful information regarding the execution of the script, including the log files.

If you prefer the AzureML studio web experience, you can navigate to the Pipeline run. In the graphical representation of the pipeline, select the step you want to see the logs for. View the logs in the **Outputs + logs** tab, as shown in *Figure 11.7*:

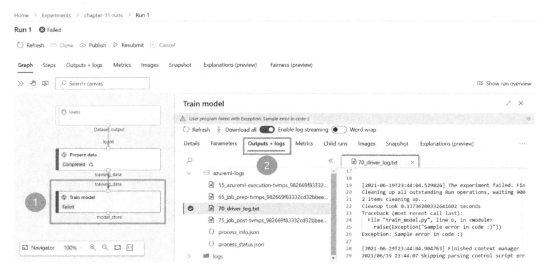

Figure 11.7 – Viewing the logs of the Train model step in the web portal

So far, you have learned how to author a Pipeline and how to troubleshoot potential runtime errors. The Pipeline you created is not yet registered within your workspace, something you will do in the next section.

Publishing a pipeline to expose it as an endpoint

So far, you have defined a pipeline using the AzureML SDK. If you had to restart the kernel of your Jupyter notebook, you would lose the reference to the pipeline you defined, and you would have to rerun all the cells to recreate the pipeline object. The AzureML SDK allows you to publish a pipeline that effectively registers it as a versioned object within the workspace. Once a pipeline is published, it can be submitted without the Python code that constructed it.

In a new cell in your notebook, add the following code:

```
published_pipeline = pipeline.publish(
    "Loans training pipeline",
    description="A pipeline to train a LightGBM model")
```

This code publishes the pipeline and returns a `PublishedPipeline` object, the versioned object registered within the workspace. The most interesting attribute of that object is the `endpoint`, which returns the REST endpoint URL to trigger the execution of the specific pipeline.

To invoke the published pipeline, you will need an authentication header. To acquire this security header, you can use the `InteractiveLoginAuthentication` class, as seen in the following code snippet:

```
from azureml.core.authentication import
InteractiveLoginAuthentication

auth = InteractiveLoginAuthentication()
aad_token = auth.get_authentication_header()
```

Then you can use the Python `requests` package to make a `POST` request to the specific endpoint using the following code:

```
import requests
response = requests.post(published_pipeline.endpoint,
            headers=aad_token,
            json={"ExperimentName": "chapter-11-runs",
            "ParameterAssignments": {"learning_rate" : 0.02}})

print(f"Made a POST request to {published_pipeline.endpoint}
and got {response.status_code}.")
```

```
print(f"The portal url for the run is {response.json()
['RunUrl']}")
```

This code only needs the URL and not the actual pipeline code. If you ever lose the endpoint URL, you can retrieve it by code through the `list` method of the `PublishedPipeline` class, which enumerates all the published pipelines registered in the workspace. The preceding script invokes the REST endpoint using the HTTP POST verb and passing the value `0.02` as the `learning_rate` parameter.

> **Important note**
> If you are unfamiliar with the **Hyper Text Transfer Protocol (HTTP)** and the `POST` method, also referred to as a verb, you can learn more in the *Further reading* section.

The resulting object from this HTTP request contains information about the execution of the pipeline, including `RunUrl`, which allows you to visit the AzureML studio portal to monitor the pipeline execution.

When you publish the pipeline, the registered object becomes available in the AzureML studio portal. If you navigate to **Endpoints | Pipeline endpoints**, you will find a list of all your published pipeline endpoints, as seen in *Figure 11.8*:

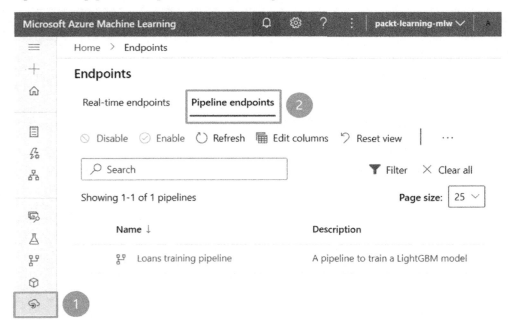

Figure 11.8 – The published pipeline endpoint

Once you select a pipeline, you can trigger it using a graphical wizard that allows you to specify the pipeline parameters and the experiment under which the pipeline will execute.

In this section, you saw how you can publish a pipeline to be able to reuse it without having the pipeline definition code. You saw how you can trigger the registered pipeline using the REST endpoint. In the next section, you will learn how to schedule the pipeline to schedule monthly retraining.

Scheduling a recurring pipeline

Being able to invoke a pipeline through the published REST endpoint is great when you have third-party systems that need to invoke a training process after a specific event has occurred. For example, suppose you are using **Azure Data Factory** to copy data from your on-premises databases. You could use the **Machine Learning Execute Pipeline** activity and trigger a published pipeline, as shown in *Figure 11.9*:

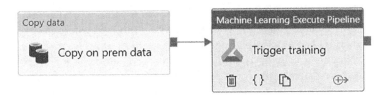

Figure 11.9 – Sample Azure Data Factory pipeline triggering an AzureML
published pipeline following a copy activity

If you wanted to schedule the pipeline to be triggered monthly, you would need to publish the pipeline as you did in the previous section, get the published pipeline ID, create a ScheduleRecurrence, and then create the Schedule. Return to your notebook where you already have a reference to published_pipeline. Add a new cell with the following code:

```
from azureml.pipeline.core.schedule import ScheduleRecurrence,
Schedule
from datetime import datetime
recurrence = ScheduleRecurrence(frequency="Month",
                                interval=1,
                                start_time = datetime.now())
schedule = Schedule.create(workspace=ws,
              name="chapter-11-schedule",
              pipeline_id=published_pipeline.id,
              experiment_name="chapter-11-scheduled-run",
```

```
                        recurrence=recurrence,
                        wait_for_provisioning=True,
                        description="Schedule to retrain model")
print("Created schedule with id: {}".format(schedule.id))
```

In this code, you define a `ScheduleRecurrence` with monthly frequency. By specifying the `start_time = datetime.now()`, you are preventing the immediate execution of the pipeline, which is the default behavior when creating a new `Schedule`. Once you have the recurrence you want to use, you can schedule the pipeline execution by calling the `create` method of the `Schedule` class. You are passing in the ID of the `published_pipeline` you want to trigger, and you specify the experiment name under which each execution will occur.

Important note

Scheduling the execution of the specific pipeline doesn't make any sense as no additional training will ever happen since both steps have `allow_reuse=True`. If you wanted to retrain every month, you would probably want this setting to be `False` and force the execution of both steps when the pipeline schedule was invoked. Moreover, in a scheduled pipeline, it is common that the very first step fetches new data from various sources attached to the AzureML workspace and then transforms the data and trains the model.

If you want to disable a scheduled execution, you can use the `disable` method of the `Schedule` class. The following code disables all scheduled pipelines in your workspace:

```
from azureml.pipeline.core.schedule import Schedule


schedules = Schedule.list(ws, active_only=True)
print("Your workspace has the following schedules set up:")
for schedule in schedules:
    print(f"Disabling {schedule.id} (Published pipeline:
{schedule.pipeline_id}")
    schedule.disable(wait_for_provisioning=True)
```

This code lists all active schedules within the workspace and then disables them one by one. Make sure you don't accidentally disable a pipeline that should have been scheduled in your workspace.

Summary

In this chapter, you learned how you can define AzureML pipelines using the AzureML SDK. These pipelines allow you to orchestrate various steps in a repeatable manner. You started by defining a training pipeline consisting of two steps. You then learned how to trigger the pipeline and how to troubleshoot potential code issues. Then you published the pipeline to register it within the AzureML workspace and acquire an HTTP endpoint that third-party software systems could use to trigger pipeline executions. In the last section, you learned how to schedule the recurrence of a published pipeline.

In the next chapter, you will learn how to operationalize the models you have been training so far in the book. Within that context, you will use the knowledge you acquired in this chapter to author batch inference pipelines, something that you can publish and trigger with HTTP or have it scheduled, as you learned in this chapter.

Questions

In each chapter, you will find a couple of questions to validate your understanding of the topics discussed in this chapter.

1. What affects the execution order of the pipeline steps?

    a. The order in which the steps were defined when constructing the `Pipeline` object.

    b. The data dependencies between the steps.

    c. All steps execute in parallel, and you cannot affect the execution order.

2. True or false: All steps within a pipeline need to execute within the same compute target and `Environment`.

3. True or false: `PythonScriptStep`, by default, reuses the previous execution results if nothing has changed in the parameters or the code files.

4. You are trying to debug a child run execution issue. Which of the following methods should you call in the `StepRun` object?

    a. `get_file_names`

    b. `get_details_with_logs`

    c. `get_metrics`

    d. `get_details`

5. You have just defined a pipeline in Python code. What steps do you need to make to schedule a daily execution of that pipeline?

Further reading

This section offers a list of helpful web resources to help you augment your knowledge of the AzureML SDK and the various code snippets used in this chapter.

- Documentation regarding the **LightGBM** framework used in this chapter: `https://lightgbm.readthedocs.io`

- HTTP request methods: `https://www.w3schools.com/tags/ref_httpmethods.asp`

- Requests Python library for making HTTP requests: `https://docs.Python-requests.org`

- Executing an AzureML pipeline through **Azure Data Factory**: `https://docs.microsoft.com/en-us/azure/data-factory/transform-data-machine-learning-service`

- The **click** Python library for script parameter parsing and the creation of **Command-Line Interface (CLI)** applications: `https://click.palletsprojects.com/`

12
Operationalizing Models with Code

In this chapter, you are going to learn how to operationalize the machine learning models you have been training, in this book, so far. You will explore two approaches: exposing a real-time endpoint by hosting a REST API that you can use to make inferences and expanding your pipeline authoring knowledge to make inferences on top of big data, in parallel, efficiently. You will begin by registering a model in the workspace to keep track of the artifact. Then, you will publish a REST API; this is something that will allow your model to integrate with third-party applications such as **Power BI**. Following this, you will author a pipeline to process half a million records within a couple of minutes in a very cost-effective manner.

In this chapter, we are going to cover the following topics:

- Understanding the various deployment options
- Registering models in the workspace
- Deploying real-time endpoints
- Creating a batch inference pipeline

Technical requirements

You will require access to an Azure subscription. Within that subscription, you will need a **resource group** named `packt-azureml-rg`. You will need to have either a `Contributor` or `Owner` **Access control (IAM)** role on the resource group level. Within that resource group, you should have already deployed a machine learning resource, named `packt-learning-mlw`. These resources should be already available to you if you followed the instructions in *Chapter 2, Deploying Azure Machine Learning Workspace Resources.*

Additionally, you will require a basic understanding of the **Python** language. The code snippets in this chapter target Python version 3.6 or later. You should also be familiar with working with notebooks within AzureML studio; this is something that was covered in *Chapter 7, The AzureML Python SDK.*

This chapter assumes you have registered the **loans** dataset that you generated in *Chapter 10, Understanding Model Results*. It also assumes that you have created a compute cluster, named **cpu-sm-cluster**, as described in the *Working with compute targets* section of *Chapter 7, The AzureML Python SDK.*

> **Important note**
>
> AzureML is constantly being updated. If you face any issues with the code samples in this book, try upgrading your AzureML SDK by adding the following code into a new notebook cell:
>
> ```
> !pip install --upgrade azureml-core azureml-sdk[notebooks]
> ```
>
> Then, restart the Jupyter kernel, as you learned in the *Training a loans approval model* section of *Chapter 10, Understanding Model Results*. Additionally, try downloading the latest version of the notebooks from the GitHub page of this book. If the problem persists, feel free to open an issue on this book's GitHub page.

You can find all of the notebooks and code snippets for this chapter on GitHub at `http://bit.ly/dp100-ch12`.

Understanding the various deployment options

We have been working with Python code since *Chapter 8, Experimenting with Python Code*. So far, you have trained various models, evaluated them based on metrics, and saved the trained model using the `dump` method of the **joblib** library. The AzureML workspace allows you to store and version those artifacts by registering them in the model registry that we discussed in *Chapter 5, Letting the Machines Do the Model Training*. Registering the model allows you to version both the saved model and the metadata regarding the specific model, such as its performance according to various metrics. You will learn how to register models from the SDK in the *Registering models in the workspace* section.

Once the model has been registered, you have to decide how you want to operationalize the model, either by deploying a real-time endpoint or by creating a batch process, as displayed in *Figure 12.1*:

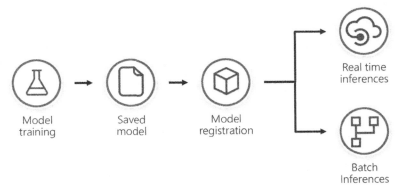

Figure 12.1 – A path from training to operationalization

There are two main categories in terms of how a model processes incoming data:

- **Real-time inferences**: Let's suppose that you trained an anti-fraud model that a web banking application will use. This model will score each transaction and block those that are at high risk. In this scenario, the model needs to be up and running all of the time. Usually, the web banking application will make an HTTP request to your model's endpoint and send the transaction data for the model to evaluate. Then, the model will respond with the probability of that record being fraudulent, perhaps by invoking the `predict_proba` method of the classifier you trained. You will read more about this scenario in the *Deploying real-time endpoints* section of this chapter.

- **Batch inferences**: In *Chapter 5*, *Letting the Machines Do the Model Training*, you trained an AutoML model to churn customer predictions. The model was trained using features such as the consumer's activity over the last 6 to 12 months. Let's suppose that you wanted to evaluate all of your customers and drive a marketing campaign for those who are likely to churn. You would have to run a once-off process that reads all of your customer information, calculates the required features, and then invokes the model for each of them to produce a prediction. The result can be stored in a CSV file to be consumed by the marketing department. In this approach, you only need the model for a short period of time, that is, only while making the predictions. You do not require a real-time endpoint, such as the one you deployed in *Chapter 5*, *Letting the Machines Do the Model Training*, as you do not need the model to make ad hoc inferences. You can read more about this scenario in the *Creating a batch inference pipeline* section of this chapter.

All models can be used in either real-time or batch inferences. It is up to you to decide whether you require ad hoc model inferences or a scheduled process that produces and stores the inference results. Operationalizing models in batch mode tends to be more cost-effective, as you can utilize low-priority compute clusters to perform inferences. In that scenario, you do not need to pay to have a real-time endpoint infrastructure waiting to make live inferences.

In the next section, you will start the path to operationalization by training and registering the model that you will be using throughout the rest of the chapter.

Registering models in the workspace

Registering a model allows you to keep different versions of the trained models. Each model version has artifacts and metadata. Among the metadata, you can keep references to experiment with runs and datasets. This allows you to track the lineage between the data used to train a model, the run ID that trained the model, and the actual model artifacts themselves, as displayed in *Figure 12.2*:

Dataset   Run Id   Model

Figure 12.2 – Building the lineage from the training dataset all the way to the registered model

In this section, you will train a model and register it in your AzureML workspace. Perform the following steps:

1. Navigate to the **Notebooks** section of your AzureML studio web interface.

2. Create a folder, named `chapter12`, and then create a notebook named `chapter12.ipynb`, as shown in *Figure 12.3*:

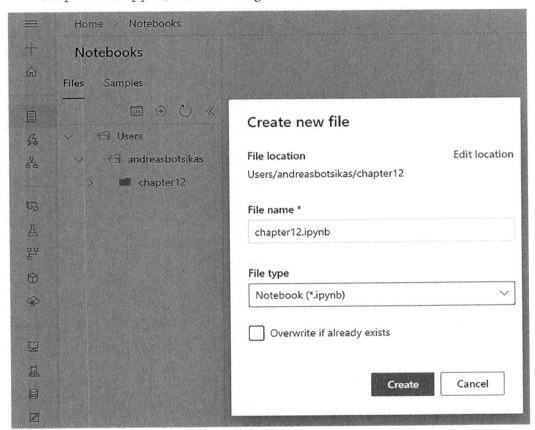

Figure 12.3 – Adding the chapter12 notebook to your working files

3. Add and execute the following code snippets in separate notebook cells. You will start by getting a reference to the workspace resources:

```python
from azureml.core import Workspace, Experiment

ws = Workspace.from_config()
loans_ds = ws.datasets['loans']
experiment = Experiment(ws, "chapter-12-train")
```

In the preceding code, you get a reference to a workspace, that is, the **loans** dataset that you generated in *Chapter 10*, *Understanding Model Results*, along with a reference to an experiment named `chapter-12-train`.

4. Split the dataset into training and validation using the following code:

```
training_data, validation_data = loans_ds.random_split(
                        percentage = 0.8, seed=42)
X_train = training_data.drop_columns('approved_loan') \
            .to_pandas_dataframe()
y_train = training_data.keep_columns('approved_loan') \
            .to_pandas_dataframe().values.ravel()


X_validate = validation_data.drop_columns('approved_
loan') \
                    .to_pandas_dataframe()
y_validate = validation_data.keep_columns('approved_
loan') \
                    .to_pandas_dataframe().values.ravel()
```

The code splits the dataset into 80% training data and 20% validation data. The `seed` argument initializes the internal random state of the `random_split` method, allowing you to hardcode the data split and generate the same `training_data` and `validation_data` every time you invoke this code.

Here, `X_train` is a pandas `DataFrame` that contains the `income`, `credit_cards`, and `age` features (that is, all of the columns besides `approved_loan`).

In comparison, `y_train` contains the values you want to predict. First, you load a pandas `DataFrame` that only contains the `approved_loan` column. Then, you convert that DataFrame into a **NumPy** array using the `values` attribute. This array has a single element array for each row. For example, *[[0],[1]]* represents two records: a not-approved loan with a value of *0* and an approved one with a value of *1*. Following this, you call the `ravel` method to flatten the array, which converts the given example into *[0, 1]*. Although you could have used the pandas `DataFrame` directly to train the model, a warning message will inform you that an automatic convention has occurred, prompting you to use the `ravel` method that you observed in this cell.

The same process repeats for the `X_validate` DataFrame and the `y_validate` array that will be used to evaluate the model's performance.

5. Train a model and log the achieved accuracy using the following code:

```
from sklearn.linear_model import LogisticRegression
from sklearn.metrics import accuracy_score

run = experiment.start_logging()

sk_model = LogisticRegression()
sk_model.fit(X_train, y_train)

y_predicted = sk_model.predict(X_validate)
accuracy = accuracy_score(y_validate, y_predicted)

print(accuracy)
run.log("accuracy", accuracy)

run.complete()
```

Here, you start with a run in the experiment, as defined in *Step 3*. You will use this run to register the metrics, logs, and artifacts of the model training process. Then, you train a LogisticRegression model, and you use the accuracy_score function to calculate the accuracy of the trained model. Following this, you print the calculated accuracy and log it as a metric in the run. In the end, you complete the run to finalize its execution.

6. Now that you have a trained model referenced by the sk_model variable, you are going to save it using the following code:

```
import os
import joblib

os.makedirs('./model', exist_ok=True)
joblib.dump(value=sk_model,
            filename=
                os.path.join('./model/','model.joblib'))
```

First, you create a folder named model. The name of that folder is not important. In that folder, you dump the trained model using the joblib library. The model is stored in a file named model.joblib.

> **Important note**
>
> The `.joblib` filename extension is not standard, and you can use whatever you like as long as you are consistent. Some people use the `.pkl` filename extension instead, which was used in the past because we were serializing Python object structures using Python's built-in `pickle` module. Nowadays, the `joblib` library is the recommended way that is proposed by **scikit-learn** because it is more efficient in serializing large NumPy arrays, which is very common with the trained models.

7. Now that you have the artifacts ready, you can register the model using the following code:

```
from sklearn import __version__ as sk_version
from azureml.core import Model


run.upload_folder("model", "./model")
model = run.register_model(
        model_name="chapter12-loans",
        model_path="./model/",
        tags={ "accuracy": accuracy},
        properties={ "accuracy": accuracy},
        model_framework= Model.Framework.SCIKITLEARN,
        model_framework_version= sk_version,
        datasets=[("training", loans_ds)]
)
```

In the first line, you import the `__version__` variable of the `sklearn` package, which is a string showing the version currently loaded in your environment. Then, you create an alias for that variable (using the `as` statement), and you reference it inside your code as `sk_version`. This is the version of the `sklearn` library that you used to train the model. Additionally, you import the `Model` class from the AzureML SDK to use it as a reference in the following lines.

After importing your references, you upload the contents of the local `./model` folder, which you created in *Step 6*, to the run's outputs, underneath a folder named `model`. This allows AzureML to have access to the artifacts that you are about to register; otherwise, you will receive an `ModelPathNotFoundException` error.

Having all of the prerequisites ready, you can register the model. The model will be named `chapter12-loans` (the `model_name` argument) using the artifacts that just got uploaded in the `model` folder (the `model_path` argument) of the run's outputs. You specify the accuracy as both a tag (the `tags` argument) and a property (the `properties` argument) of that model. You indicate that you used the `SCIKITLEARN` framework (the `model_framework` argument) to train the model, and you specify which version of the framework you used (the `model_framework_version` argument). In the last line, you specify that you used the `loans_ds` dataset as a `training` dataset (the `datasets` argument).

> **Important note**
>
> If you try to rerun the same cell, a *Resource Conflict* error will occur because you cannot override files that already exist in the run's outputs folder. If you comment out the `upload_folder` line by using # as a line prefix and rerun the cell, you will register a new version of the same model, using the artifacts that already exist in the specific run.

8. Navigate to **Assets | Models** from AzureML studio's menu on the left-hand side. You will reach the model list you saw in *Chapter 5, Letting the Machines Do the Model Training*. Select the **chapter12-loans** model that you just registered. You should see something similar to *Figure 12.4*:

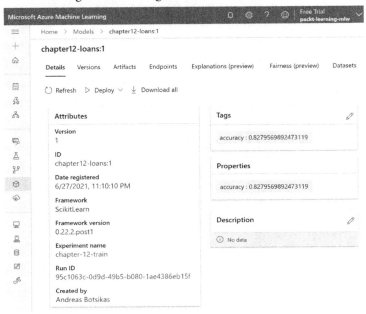

Figure 12.4 – The registered model in AzureML studio

Notice that all of the information you logged is available on this page, including links to the run that trained the model and the dataset you used for training (underneath the **Datasets** tab). Here, **accuracy** is logged both as a tag and a property of the model. The difference between the two is that you can modify the tags (by clicking on the pencil icon in the UI or from the code), while the properties cannot change. If you click on **Deploy** from this screen, you will get the deployment wizard that you saw in *Chapter 5, Letting the Machines Do the Model Training*. The wizard will automatically deploy a real-time endpoint for this model because you used a supported framework (Model.Framework.SCIKITLEARN). This type of deployment is considered a no-code deployment, which is a capability that AzureML offers for supported frameworks. Otherwise, you need to specify a scoring file; this is something that we will cover in the *Deploying real-time endpoints* section.

9. If you want to register a pretrained model that you downloaded from the internet, you will not have a Run object to call the register_model method. You can use the register method of the Model class, as demonstrated in the following code snippet:

```
from azureml.core import Model
offline_model = Model.register(
        ws,
        model_name="chapter12-pre-trained-loans",
        model_path="./model/",
        properties={"accuracy": 0.828},
        model_framework= "ScikitLearn",
        model_framework_version= "0.22.2.post1"
)
```

In the preceding code, you register, in your AzureML workspace (the ws variable), the artifacts that are located inside the *local* model folder (the model_path argument) as a model named chapter12-pre-trained-loans (the model_ name argument). This is a model trained using version 0.22.2.post1 (the model_framework_version argument) of the sklearn library (the model_ framework_version argument). Additionally, its accuracy, which is 0.828, is stored as a model property.

10. If you had a process to train new models, such as the scheduled pipeline that you created in *Chapter 11, Working with Pipelines*, you will have to verify whether the newly trained model has better metrics than the one already registered. Then, if it is better, proceed with the registration of the model. To do that, you can use code similar to the following:

```
from sklearn.linear_model import RidgeClassifier


new_model = RidgeClassifier(solver='svd')
new_model.fit(X_train, y_train)
y_predicted = new_model.predict(X_validate)
accuracy = accuracy_score(y_validate, y_predicted)


registered_model = Model(ws, name="chapter12-loans")
r_version = registered_model.version
r_acc = float(registered_model.properties['accuracy'])
if accuracy > r_acc:
    print(f"New model has better accuracy {accuracy}")
else:
    print(f"Registered model with version {r_version}" \
          " has better accuracy {r_acc}")
```

In the preceding code, you train a `RidgeClassifier`-based model that uses **Singular Value Decomposition (SVD)** to compute the ridge coefficients of the model. The code is similar to the one that you used in *Step 5*. Then, you get a reference to the latest version of the workspace's registered model, named `chapter12-loans`, which you registered in *Step 7*. The `registered_model` variable has the same reference as the `model` variable you got in *Step 7*; only, this time, you create that reference using the `Model` class and not by registering a model. From that model, you read the `version` attribute and the `accuracy` property. You could retrieve the accuracy from the `tags` dictionary instead of the `properties` dictionary of the model. You convert the accuracy value into a float because tags and properties store their values as strings. Following this, you then compare the new model's accuracy to the one that has already been registered (which is stored in the `r_acc` variable). If the new model is better than the registered one, you print a message. In this case, you repeat *Step 6* and *Step 7* to store the model and then register the new, improved version of the model.

> **Important note**
> To register a new model version, you just need to register the new model with the same name. By registering a new model with the same name, AzureML will automatically create a new version for you.

11. Optionally, as a last step, delete the locally stored model using the following code:

```
import shutil
shutil.rmtree('./model',ignore_errors=True)
```

This code deletes the `model` folder that you created in *Step 6*, including the serialized model you no longer need. The `ignore_errors` parameter allows you to run this cell even if the folder doesn't exist without raising any errors.

In this section, you trained a model in your notebook within the Jupyter kernel. Then, you registered the model inside your workspace. You could have used the same registration code in the `train_model.py` script, which you authored in *Step 11* of the *Authoring a pipeline* section of *Chapter 11*, *Working with Pipelines*, to register the **LightGBM** model that you were training within the pipeline. You would need to get a reference to the execution context using the `run=Run.get_context()` method, and then you would need to upload the serialized model and register the model, as you did in *Step 7*. As an additional activity, try to modify the `train_model.py` script and `chapter11.ipynb` to create a pipeline that registers the model that is being trained within the pipeline. A potential solution to this activity is available in the `train_model_and_register.py` script. This can be found in the `step02` folder of the GitHub repository at `http://bit.ly/dp100-ch11`.

In the next section, you will start operationalizing the model that you registered in this section by deploying it as a web service that will serve real-time inferences.

Deploying real-time endpoints

Let's imagine that you have an e-banking solution that has a process for customers to request loans. You want to properly set the expectations of the customer and prepare them for potential rejection. When the customer submits their loan application form, you want to invoke the model you registered in the *Registering models in the workspace* section, that is, the model named **chapter12-loans**, and pass in the information that the customer filled out on the application form. If the model predicts that the loan will not be approved, a message will appear on the confirmation page of the loan request, preparing the customer for the potential rejection of the loan request.

Figure 12.5 shows an oversimplified architecture to depict the flow of requests that start from the customer to the real-time endpoint of the model:

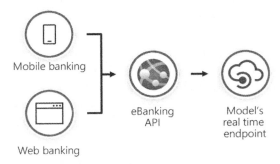

Figure 12.5 – An oversimplified e-banking architecture showing the flow
of requests from the customer to the model

The easiest way to deploy a model is via the no-code deployment approach that AzureML offers for specific machine learning frameworks, including **TensorFlow**, **ONNX**, and the `sklearn` library that you used in the previous section. Perform the following steps:

1. Go to the `chapter12.ipynb` notebook, and add the following code to get a reference to the last version of the **chapter12-loans** model that you created in the previous section:

```
from azureml.core import Workspace, Model
ws = Workspace.from_config()
model = Model(ws, name="chapter12-loans")
```

2. To deploy a real-time endpoint, use the following code:

```
no_code_service = Model.deploy(ws, "no-code-loans",
                               [model])
no_code_service.wait_for_deployment(show_output=True)
```

This code deploys a new real-time endpoint service, named `no-code-loans`, and then waits for the deployment to complete.

3. To get the scoring URI for the newly deployed endpoint, use the following code:

```
print(no_code_service.scoring_uri)
```

This is a URL in the format of `http://guid.region.azurecontainer.io/score`, which accepts **POST** requests with a **JSON** payload, as follows:

```
{"data": [[2000,2,45]]}
```

This payload will trigger an inference request for a customer with a monthly income of 2,000, who has 2 credit cards and is 45 years old. You can use tools such as **Postman** or **curl** to craft such an HTTP request and invoke the endpoint.

4. Instead of making an HTTP request using a tool such as `curl`, you can use the `no_code_service` reference and invoke the `run` method by passing in the JSON payload that you would normally send to the service:

```
import json
input_payload = json.dumps({
    'data': [[2000, 2, 45], [2000, 9, 45]],
    'method': 'predict'
})
output = no_code_service.run(input_payload)
print(output)
```

The preceding code imports the `json` library, which helps you to serialize objects into JSON strings. You create the payload using the `dumps` method. Note that the payload is slightly different from the simple version you saw in *Step 3*. Instead of passing a single customer's information, in this example, you pass the information of two customers: the one you passed before and another one who has *9* credit cards instead of *2*. Moreover, you are specifying which method to invoke. By default, the method name of the model is `predict`, which is the one you have been using in the previous chapters to make inferences. Finally, you print the output, which should appear similar to the following:

```
{'predict': [0, 1]}
```

The preceding result shows that the first loan will be rejected, while the second one will be approved.

Most of the classification models offer another method called `predict_proba`, which returns an array with the probabilities of each label. In the `loans` approval case, this array will only contain 2 probabilities that sum to 1, that is, the probability of the loan getting approved and the probability of it getting rejected. If you change the method name from `predict` to `predict_proba` and re-execute the cell, you will get the following result:

```
{'predict_proba': [[0.998, 0.002], [0.173, 0.827]]}
```

The preceding result shows that the model is 99.8% confident that the first loan will be rejected and 82.7% confident that the second loan will be approved.

5. Optionally, navigate to **Assets | Endpoints** to view the **no-code-loans** endpoint that you just deployed. Note that the compute type is a container instance, as displayed in *Figure 12.6*:

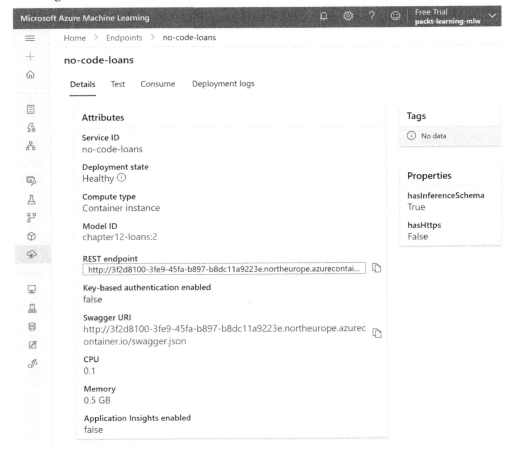

Figure 12.6 – Real-time endpoint information for the endpoint you just deployed

AzureML hosts the web application that is serving the model in **Azure Container Instance (ACI)**, which is similar to the one you deployed in *Chapter 5, Letting the Machines Do the Model Training*. Note that the container instance that was deployed is configured to use **0.1** CPU cores and **0.5 GB** memory. If your model requires more resources, you could specify the size of the ACI service that should be deployed for the specific model. You can do this by passing a `ResourceConfiguration` object to the `resource_configuration` parameter while registering the model, as shown in the following code snippet:

```
from azureml.core import Model
from azureml.core.resource_configuration import
ResourceConfiguration


model = Model.register(workspace=ws,
            model_name="chapter12-demanding-loans",
            model_path="./model/",
            model_framework=Model.Framework.SCIKITLEARN,
            model_framework_version="0.22.2.post1",
            resource_configuration=ResourceConfiguration(
                        cpu=1, memory_in_gb=1.5))
```

In the preceding code, you register a model named `chapter12-demanding-loans`. You specify that it needs 1 CPU and 1.5 GB of RAM. Note that if you deleted the `model` folder in *Step 11* of the *Registering models in the workspace* section, this code would fail to register the new model, as it will not be able to find the model artifact.

6.   To save on costs, you should delete the service using the following code:

```
no_code_service.delete()
```

So far, you have deployed a real-time endpoint using the no-code approach, which deploys the model as a container instance. This is only feasible if the model is trained using specific supported models. In the next section, you will learn how to deploy models using more advanced options.

Understanding the model deployment options

In the previous section, you deployed a model using the no-code approach. Behind the scenes, AzureML used an `environment` with all of the required model dependencies, which, in our case, was `sklearn`, generated a Python script to load the model and make inferences when data arrived at the endpoint, and published an ACI service using an `AciServiceDeploymentConfiguration` class.

If you had a model that was trained with a non-supported framework or if you wanted to get better control of the deployment model, you could deploy the model using the AzureML SDK classes, as depicted in *Figure 12.7*:

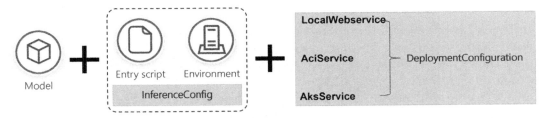

Figure 12.7 – The components required in a real-time endpoint deployment

Here, the **InferenceConfig** class specifies the model dependencies. It requires an entry script that will load the model and process the incoming requests along with an environment in which the entry script will execute. This environment contains all of the dependencies required by the model to load and make inferences.

The entry script should have the following two methods:

- `Init`: During this step, the script loads the trained model into memory. Depending on how you stored the state of the model to the disk, you can use the corresponding method to deserialize the model. For example, if you used the `joblib` library to serialize your model, you can use the `load` method of the same library to load it into memory. Some models provide their own serialization and deserialization methods, but the process remains the same; the state of the trained model is persisted in one file or multiple files, which you can later use to load the trained model into memory. Depending on how big your model is, the initialization phase might require a significant amount of time. Smaller `sklearn` models should load into memory in only a few milliseconds, while larger neural networks might require a couple of seconds to load.

- `run`: This is the method invoked when a dataset is received by the real-time endpoint for inference. In this method, you must use the model loaded in the `init` code to invoke the prediction method it offers to make inferences on the incoming data. As mentioned earlier, most of the models offer the `predict` method, which you can invoke and pass into the data that you want to make an inference. Most of the classification models offer an additional method, called `predict_proba`, which returns the probabilities of each class. The AutoML forecasting models offer the `forecast` method instead of the `predict` method. Neural networks have a different approach when it comes to making predictions. For example, in the first version of TensorFlow, you would have to invoke a prediction method through a `session.run()` method call.

Once you have configured the model dependencies, you need to decide where you want to deploy the model. The AzureML SDK offers three classes: `LocalWebserviceDeploymentConfiguration`, `AciServiceDeploymentConfiguration`, and `AksServiceDeploymentConfiguration`. These allow you to deploy on your local machine into ACI or **Azure Kubernetes Services (AKS)**, as displayed in *Figure 12.8*:

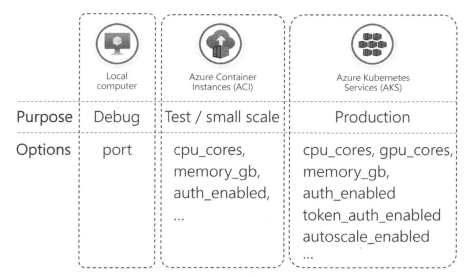

Figure 12.8 – Picking the right compute target for your model

As you might have gathered, in *Figure 12.8*, you can deploy to your local computer by specifying the port you want the service to listen to. This is a nice approach in which to debug any potential loading issues of your model or verify the integration with the remaining systems on your local computer. The next option is to use ACI, which is meant for test environments or small-scale production environments. You can only use CPUs and not GPUs in the `AciServiceDeploymentConfiguration` class. You can protect the endpoint using a key-based authentication by setting the `auth_enabled` parameter to `True`. This authentication method requires you to pass a static key as an **Authorization** header into your HTTP requests.

On the other side, `AksServiceDeploymentConfiguration` deploys the service inside an AKS cluster. This allows you to use GPUs if your model can make use of them and if the cluster you are deploying to has GPU-capable nodes. This deployment configuration allows you to choose between key-based authentication or a token-based one. Token-based authentication requires the end user to acquire an access token from the **Azure Active Directory** that protects the AzureML workspace, which will allow you to access the endpoint deployed within it. This token is short-lived and conceals the caller's identity in contrast to key-based authentication, which is the only available option in ACI. Another production-ready feature of the AKS deployment is the ability to dynamically scale up and down to handle the fluctuation in the number of incoming requests. In the e-banking scenario at hand, customers tend to visit the e-banking solution during working hours, and the system is pretty much idle at night. Moreover, at the end of the month, the incoming traffic peaks. In such a workload, you want to be able to scale your endpoint to accommodate for the increase in traffic when needed. AKS can automatically spin up multiple containers of your model and load balance the traffic among them when the incoming traffic increases significantly. When the traffic returns to normal, it can only keep a single container as a hot standby for potential incoming traffic.

Now that you have a better understanding of the deployment options, you will deploy the same model in ACI using the classes that you saw in *Figure 12.7*:

1. The first thing you will need to create is the entry script. Underneath the **chapter12** folder, create a new folder named **script** and place a **score.py** file inside it, as shown in *Figure 12.9*:

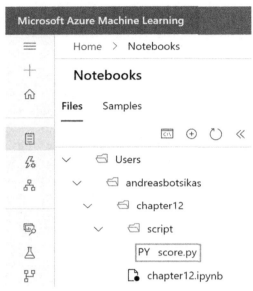

Figure 12.9 – Adding the score.py file for the real-time endpoint

2. In the **score.py** file, add the following code:

```python
import os
import joblib
import json

def init():
    global model
    model_path = \
        os.path.join(os.getenv("AZUREML_MODEL_DIR"),
                    "model/model.joblib")
    print(f"Loading model from {model_path}")
    model = joblib.load(model_path)

def run(raw_data):
```

```
try:
    print(raw_data)
    data = json.loads(raw_data)["data"]
    result = model.predict(data)
    return result.tolist()
except Exception as e:
    error = str(e)
    return error
```

This code implements the two methods that you read about earlier in this section. In the `init` method, you are getting the path of the serialized model using the `AZUREML_MODEL_DIR` environment variable. When AzureML spins up the Docker image that will be serving the model, this variable points to the folder where the model is located; for example, `/tmp/azureml_umso8bpm/chapter12-loans/1` could be the location where you find the first version of the `chapter12-loans` model. In that folder, the actual artifact, named `model.joblib`, is located in the `model` folder, which you uploaded in *Step 5* of the *Deploying real-time endpoints* section. You use `os.path.join` to get the final path of the model, and then you load the model in a `global` variable named `model`. If you want to use the AzureML SDK to get the location of the model, you could use `model_path = Model.get_model_path(model_name, version=version)`, which uses the same environment variable under the hood. However, note that you would need to install the AzureML SDK in your environment to be able to import the `Model` class from it; this is something that is not necessary with the preceding code.

> **Important note**
>
> Note that you are using `print` to write the model path and incoming `raw_data` into the console. You will learn how to view those messages in the *Monitoring with Application Insights* section.

In the `run` method, you are using the `try except` block to catch potential errors while trying to read the request's input. If such an error occurs, the exception is serialized into a string (using the `str()` method), which is returned to the end user. Note that returning the exceptions to the caller is a security anti-pattern, as you might accidentally expose valuable information to a potential attacker, but it is helpful while debugging. Instead of returning the error message, you could use a `print` statement or a more advanced library such as **OpenCensus**, and then review the error within Application Insights, as we will cover in the *Monitoring with Application Insights* section. You can learn more about OpenCensus by following the links in the *Further reading* section of this chapter. Within the `try` block, you deserialize the incoming JSON payload, as demonstrated in *Step 3* of the *Deploying real-time endpoints* section. Then, you call the `predict` method of the `model` object you have loaded in memory through the `init` method. Following this, you return the model results as a list that will be serialized into an array.

> **Important note**
>
> You will never directly invoke either the `init` or the `run` method. There is another piece of code that AzureML will be putting inside the final Docker image, which is the HTTP inference server. This server will be responsible for calling your `init` method when the server boots up and will pass the incoming HTTP data into the `run` method. Moreover, the result that you return in the `run` method will be serialized into a **JSON** and will be returned to the caller.

3. The next thing you need is an `Environment` that has all of the necessary dependencies to run the `score.py` script that you created. Open your `chapter12.ipynb` notebook and add the following code inside a new cell:

```python
from azureml.core import Environment
from azureml.core.conda_dependencies import CondaDependencies
import sklearn


myEnv= Environment(name="sklearn-inference")
myEnv.Python.conda_dependencies = CondaDependencies()
myEnv.Python.conda_dependencies.add_conda_package(
            f"scikit-learn=={sklearn.__version__}")
myEnv.Python.conda_dependencies.add_pip_package(
            "azureml-defaults>=1.0.45")
```

In the preceding code, you created an `Environment` as demonstrated in *Chapter 8, Experimenting with Python Code*. You add the `scikit-learn` **conda** package to the version that is available in the compute where you trained the model. Moreover, you add the `azureml-defaults` pip package, which contains the necessary functionality to host the model as a web service. Because you are building your own `Environment`, you need to add this package and use, at the very least, version 1.0.45. This is the bare minimum environment that you can use to run your scoring script. Additionally, AzureML provides a curated environment that you can use, such as `AzureML-sklearn-0.24.1-ubuntu18.04-py37-cpu-inference`, which contains everything you need to make an inference request using a model trained in `sklearn` version 0.24.1.

4. You have defined everything that is needed by the `InferenceConfig` class. Add a new cell and type in the following code to put everything together:

```
from azureml.core.model import InferenceConfig
inference_config = InferenceConfig(
                        source_directory= "./script",
                        entry_script='score.py',
                        environment=myEnv)
```

This code creates the configuration you will need to make inferences with your model. It uses the `score.py` file that is located inside the `script` folder and executes that file in the `myEnv` environment, which you defined in *Step 3*.

5. Now you have two out of the three components depicted in *Figure 12.7*. In this step, you will create an `AciServiceDeploymentConfiguration` class, and you will deploy the model in ACI. In a new cell, add the following code:

```
from azureml.core.webservice import AciWebservice
deployment_config = AciWebservice.deploy_configuration(
                        cpu_cores=1, memory_gb=1)
service = Model.deploy(ws, "aci-loans", [model],
                    inference_config, deployment_config)
service.wait_for_deployment(show_output=True)
```

Here, we use the `AciWebservice` class to get a deployment configuration for the container instance you want to deploy. In the preceding code, you specify that you require 1 CPU core and 1 GB of RAM. Then, you deploy the model into a new service, named `aci-loans`, and you wait for the deployment to complete.

> **Important note**
>
> If you are running into issues while attempting to deploy the container, you can view the error messages in the printed outputs or use the `service.get_logs()` method. Most likely, it is an issue with your code base within the `score.py` script. You can locally test the code by installing the `azureml-inference-server-http` pip package and running the following command:
>
> **`azmlinfsrv --entry_script score.py`**
>
> This will show you any potential errors when loading your script. Once you have fixed the script, the preceding command should open the web server that is listening to port `5001`. Another approach to debugging such situations is to use `LocalWebservice`, as we will discuss later. If your code is fine, then you might be running into memory issues. This should be visible in the service logs. In that case, refer to the next section to learn how you can profile your model to determine its resource requirements.

6. To test the deployed service, you can use the following code, which is similar to the one that you used in the previous section:

```
import json
input_payload = json.dumps({
    'data': [[2000, 2, 45]]
})
output = service.run(input_payload)
print(output)
```

Note that the `method` property of the payload, which you used in *Step 4* of the *Deploying real-time endpoints* section, will not have any effect on this deployment and is omitted from the payload. If you wanted to support this property, you would have to write the code within the `run` method of the `score.py` file to read that property and call the corresponding method of the model.

7. To save on costs, delete the service when you are done testing it using the following code:

```
service.delete()
```

8. If you want to deploy the same service in your local computer, you can use the following code:

```
from azureml.core.webservice import LocalWebservice
deployment_config = LocalWebservice.deploy_
configuration(port=1337)
```

```
service = Model.deploy(ws, "local-loans", [model],
inference_config, deployment_config)
service.wait_for_deployment()
```

Instead of the `AciWebservice` class, you use the `LocalWebservice` to create a local service that listens to port `1337`. If you are running the notebooks on your local computer, you need to visit `http://localhost:1337` and view the service endpoint's health status. Now that you have run this code within the AzureML notebooks, the local computer is the compute instance you are working on. To view port `1337` of the compute instance named **compute-instance-name**, which is deployed in **region**, please visit `https://compute-instance-name-1337.region.instances.azureml.ms`. This endpoint is only accessible by you since you are assigned to the specific compute instance. Once you are done playing with the locally deployed endpoint, you can delete it by using the `service.delete()` code, as demonstrated in *Step 7*.

Similar to the `AciWebservice` and the `LocalWebservice`, you can use `AksWebservice` to create an `AksServiceDeploymentConfiguration`. While deploying it, you would need to specify an additional parameter in the `Model.deploy` method, that is, the `deployment_target` parameter. This parameter allows you to specify the `AksCompute` inference cluster that you want to deploy the model to.

Aside from the local computer, ACI, and AKS deployment options that you saw earlier, AzureML offers multiple other deployment options. For example, **Azure Functions** allows you to run your models inside a serverless infrastructure, and **Azure App Services** hosts the model as a traditional web application that is always ready to serve incoming requests. On the other hand, you can use **IoT Edge**, which allows you to deploy the service on an Edge device such as a Raspberry Pi or a GPU-based Jetson Nano. Finally, you can even package the model inside a Docker container image, which can be operationalized inside an isolated air gap data center.

In this section, you deployed an ACI real-time inference endpoint requesting 1 CPU core and 1 GB of RAM. In the next section, you will explore how you can optimize your resource requirements by profiling the model's performance.

Profiling the model's resource requirements

Before bringing something into production, it is very common to perform a stress test. Essentially, this test bombards the real-time endpoint with requests and measures the responsiveness and performance of the endpoint. You can do something similar with your models to understand what type of resources you will need in order for them to perform as expected. For example, you might need to ensure that all inferences are performed within 200 ms.

In this section, you are going to create a test dataset that will be used to stress-test the real-time endpoint and observe its performance. Each row in the dataset will contain a single inference request.

Navigate to your `chapter12.ipynb` notebook and perform the following steps:

1. In a new cell, add the following code:

    ```
    loans_ds = ws.datasets['loans']
    prof_df = loans_ds.drop_columns('approved_loan') \
                             .to_pandas_dataframe()
    prof_df['sample_request'] = \
        "{'data':[[" + prof_df['income'].map(str) \
       + ","+ prof_df['credit_cards'].map(str) \
       + "," + prof_df['age'].map(str) + "]]}"
    prof_df = prof_df[['sample_request']]
    prof_df.head()
    ```

    This code loads the `loans` dataset, drops the `approved_loan` column, which we don't need, and loads it inside a `pandas DataFrame`. Following this, you create a new column named `sample_request` that concatenates the columns to produce a string such as the following:

    ```
    {"data": [[2000,2,45]]}
    ```

    Then, you keep only that column and print the top 5 rows to verify that the requests look as expected. Note that it does not matter whether the data is the one we used to train the model. It could even be random records. We only care about the number of requests we will be making and not what the inference result is going to look like.

2. Store the newly created dataset inside the workspace using the following code:

    ```
    from azureml.core import Dataset
    dstore = ws.get_default_datastore()
    loan_req_ds = Dataset.Tabular.register_pandas_dataframe(
        dataframe=prof_df,
        target=(dstore,"/samples/loans-requests"),
        name="loans-requests",
        description="Sample requests for the loans model")
    ```

The preceding code registers the DataFrame as the `loans-requests` dataset. The data is stored inside `/samples/loans-requests` of the default datastore. The `loans_req_ds` variable has a reference to the newly registered `tabular Dataset`.

3. Now that you have the necessary data, you can start the model profiling process using the following code:

```
profile = Model.profile(ws,
              'chapter12-loan',
              [model], inference_config,
              input_dataset=loan_req_ds,
              cpu=2, memory_in_gb=1)
profile.wait_for_completion(True)
print(profile.get_details())
```

Note that the profile method requires the `model` and the `inference_config` that you used during model deployment in the previous section. Additionally, you need to specify your ACI size to use to perform the analysis. In the preceding code, you request 2 CPUs and 1 GB of RAM. The analysis could take a long time, sometimes, more than 20 minutes. After the analysis completes, you will view the results, including the 1 CPU as the `recommendedCpu` and 0.5 GB of RAM as the `recommendedMemoryInGB` value.

> **Important note**
> The name of the model profile should be unique within the workspace.
> An error will occur if you try to rerun the code of *Step 3* without changing the name.

Behind the scenes, an experiment named **chapter12-loan-ModelProfile** is created. In that experiment, a `ModelProfile` run is executed, which deploys an ACI service with the model. Once the service is up and running, the process sends the 500 requests that you specified in the **loan_req_ds** dataset and records the response time of the model while monitoring the CPU and memory utilization of the deployed container instance. AzureML can suggest the recommended CPU and memory that you should configure for your real-time endpoint based on those statistics.

In the next section, you will use those values to deploy an ACI service. Following this, you will explore how to monitor its performance once deployed in production and log the incoming data using **Application Insights**.

Monitoring with Application Insights

As you learned in *Chapter 2, Deploying Azure Machine Learning Workspace Resources*, when you deploy the AzureML workspace, an Application Insights account named `packtlearningm<random_number>` is deployed in the same resource group. This Azure resource allows you to monitor the performance of your applications. Especially for web applications, such as the real-time endpoint you are deploying, Application Insights allows you to monitor the request and response times, the failure rate of the endpoint, any potential exceptions raised in your code, and even log traces that you want to emit from your code base.

In the *Understanding the model deployment options* section earlier, you created a `score.py` file that contained a couple of `print` statements. These messages were written inside the console of the endpoint and could be found either by calling the `service.get_logs()` method or navigating to the **Deployment logs** tab of the deployment, as shown in *Figure 12.10*:

Figure 12.10 – The model path and incoming raw_data logged in the console of the container instance

The problem with this approach is that the logs do not persist. If you redeploy the container instance, you will lose the logs. Moreover, if you have multiple models deployed, you will need a centralized place to be able to monitor all of them together. These are two of the many benefits that Application Insights brings to your solution.

Go back to your chapter12.ipynb notebook to redeploy the ACI container and enable Application Insights for it. Inside a new cell, add the following code:

```
from azureml.core.webservice import AciWebservice
deployment_config = AciWebservice.deploy_configuration(
    cpu_cores=1, memory_gb=0.5, enable_app_insights= True)
service = Model.deploy(ws, "aci-loans", [model], inference_
config, deployment_config)
service.wait_for_deployment(show_output=True)
```

Notice that you are using the 1 CPU core and 0.5 GB RAM that was recommended in the *Profiling the model resource requirements* section. Additionally, note that you are enabling Application Insights in the deployment configuration by passing the enable_app_insights= True argument. If you had already deployed the service and you wanted to enable Application Insights for it, you could use the following code to update its configuration:

```
service.update(enable_app_insights=True)
```

Let's send a couple of requests to the service to be able to better understand what Application Insights can do for you. Inside a new cell, add the following code:

```
import json
input_payload = json.dumps({'data': [[2000, 2, 45], [2000, 9,
45]]})
for x in range(10):
    print(service.run(input_payload))
```

This code sends *10* identical requests to the service, one after the other, generating some artificial traffic that should be logged in Application Insights. The easiest way to find the URL that is pointing to the Azure portal and directly inside the Application Insights resource is to visit the endpoint's information page, as displayed in *Figure 12.11*:

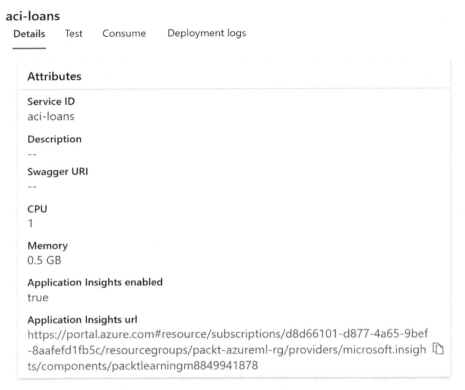

Figure 12.11 – The Application Insights URL that is associated with your AzureML workspace

Note that this **Application Insights url** link is not specific to the **aci-loans** deployment. This link will be the same for all of your real-time endpoints, allowing you to centrally monitor all of your real-time endpoints. Clicking on that link will take you inside Application Insights, as shown in *Figure 12.12*:

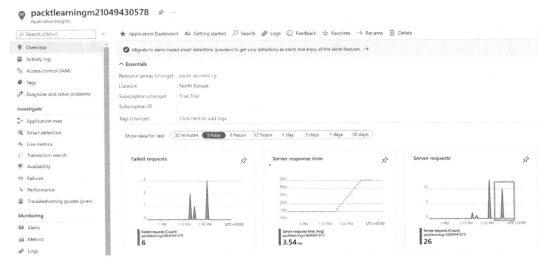

Figure 12.12 – Application Insights showing the 10 requests that you sent with the last code

From this dashboard, you can click on the graphs and drill down to the signal details; or you can view all the traces that your application is writing inside the console. To view them, navigate to **Monitoring | Logs**, click on the **traces**, select a time range that you want to investigate, and click on the **Run** button. You should see all of the **STDOUT** messages appear in the results, and you can drill down into the details, as displayed in *Figure 12.13*:

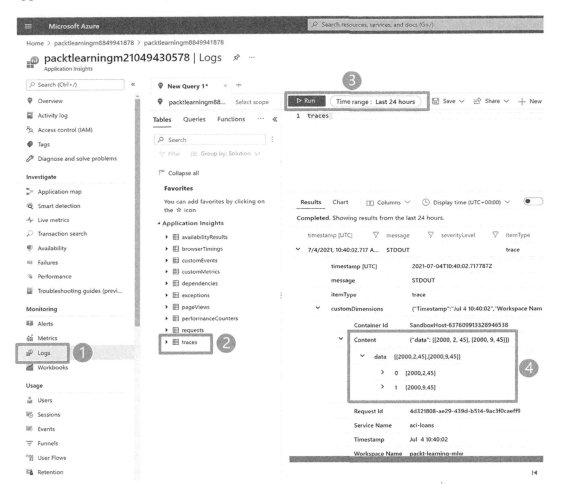

Figure 12.13 – Reading all of the traces emitted by your model's real-time endpoint in Application Insights

You can create complex queries in this **Logs** section using a powerful SQL-like language known as **Kusto**. You can even create automated alerts based on those queries, notifying you, for example, whenever you have had more than 100 loans rejected in the last 30 minutes.

Important note

Application Insights supports the logging of small payloads of up to 64 KB at a time. If you plan to log more than that, for example, a mini-batch input with more than 64 KB of data, you should consider working with the `DataCollector` class of the AzureML SDK. This class allows you to log data directly into a storage account; however, it is only available if you deploy in AKS.

Before moving on to the next section, do not forget to delete the deployed service to prevent any accidental cost charges for the ACI service. You can delete the service from the **Assets | Endpoints** list in the studio experience or via the code using the following line:

```
service.delete()
```

In this section, you learned how to monitor your real-time endpoint once you have it deployed in production. In *Figure 12.12*, you might have noticed that there were a couple of **Failed requests** logged. You can drill down into those errors in Application Insights, or you can look at *Figure 12.10*, where you will see the logs complaining about a missing `swagger` file. In the next section, you will learn how to fix those failed requests and enable rich integration with third-party applications that want to consume the results of your model.

Integrating with third-party applications

So far, you have deployed a web service that accepts an array of arrays as input. This is a cryptic input that you need to explain to whoever wants to consume your real-time endpoint. In *Chapter 5*, *Letting the Machines Do the Model Training*, you read about the `swagger` file that could be used to generate code to automatically consume your endpoints. To produce such a file, you can use the open source `inference-schema` package and decorate your code with metadata that will drive the generation of the `swagger.json` file.

In order to make your model slightly easier to consume by third-party applications, you should accept the following payload:

```
{"data":[{"income": 2000, "credit_cards": 2, "age": 45}]}
```

Here, you will need to create a new version of the scoring file. Instead of cloning and editing the existing scoring file, you can download the modified `score_v2.py` version directly from the GitHub page, as mentioned in the *Technical requirements* section. In the **Notebooks** section, duplicate the **score.py** file located in the **script** folder by right-clicking on it and selecting the **Duplicate** command, as shown in *Figure 12.14*:

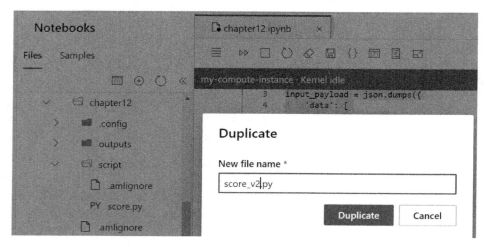

Figure 12.14 – Creating the v2 file of the entry script

Name the clone `score_v2.py`, and modify the code to look like the following code block:

```python
import os
import joblib
from inference_schema.schema_decorators import input_schema, output_schema
import pandas as pd
from inference_schema.parameter_types.pandas_parameter_type import PandasParameterType
import numpy as np
from inference_schema.parameter_types.numpy_parameter_type import NumpyParameterType
```

At the beginning of the script file, you are importing additional helper classes, which will be used later in the code. Notice that you will no longer need the `json` module:

```
def init():
    global model
    model_path = os.path.join(os.getenv(\
"AZUREML_MODEL_DIR"), "model/model.joblib")
    model = joblib.load(model_path)
```

You won't modify the `init` method:

```
data_sample = pd.DataFrame(
    {
        "income": pd.Series([2000.0], dtype="float64"),
        "credit_cards": pd.Series([1], dtype="int"),
        "age": pd.Series([25], dtype="int")
    }
)
output_sample = np.array([0])
```

In the preceding code block, you create a pandas `DataFrame` that will act as the sample for the objects contained in the incoming request's `data` attribute. This `data_sample` object has an `income` feature, which is `float64`, and the `credit_cards` and `age` features, which are integers. Similarly, for the output, you define `output_sample` as a NumPy array or numeric value. You can use the `data_sample` and `output_sample` objects inside the decorators of the following code block:

```
@input_schema("data", PandasParameterType(data_sample))
@output_schema(NumpyParameterType(output_sample))
def run(data):
    try:
        result = model.predict(data)
        return result.tolist()
    except Exception as e:
        error = str(e)
        return error
```

Here, you use the `data_sample` object with the `@input_schema` decorator. Additionally, you use `PandasParameterType`, which indicates that the parameter named **data** will be a pandas `DataFrame` that follows the schema defined by the `data_sample` example. You use the `@output_schema` decorator to specify that your service returns a NumPy array as an output, similar to `output_sample`. Once you have configured these schemas, you will notice that you do not have to deserialize the incoming payload within the `run` method. The `data` object is an already deserialized pandas `DataFrame`.

If you want to process binary files instead of tabular data, for instance, processing an image, you can use the `@rawhttp` directive, which will pass the raw HTTP request to your `run` method. Working with plain HTTP requests gives you greater flexibility, including setting the response headers; this is something required when you configure security features such as **Cross-Origin Resource Sharing (CORS)**. You can find resources to learn more about those advanced scenarios in the *Further reading* section of this chapter.

Now that you have the code of the `score_v2.py` script file ready, you need to publish the real-time endpoint. To create a real-time endpoint for the new scoring function, add the following code inside a cell within your notebook:

```
from azureml.core.model import InferenceConfig
from azureml.core.webservice import AciWebservice
myEnv.Python.conda_dependencies.add_pip_package("inference_
schema[pandas-support]>=1.1.0")
inference_config = InferenceConfig(source_directory= "./
script", entry_script='score_v2.py', environment=myEnv)
deployment_config = AciWebservice.deploy_configuration( cpu_
cores=1, memory_gb=0.5)
service = Model.deploy(ws, "aci-loans", [model], inference_
config, deployment_config)
service.wait_for_deployment(show_output=True)
```

In the preceding code, you append the `inference_schema` pip packages in the `myEnv` dependencies, which you defined in the *Understanding the model deployment options* section earlier. Note that you are installing that package with the `pandas-support` extra, which will include the `pandas` package. The numpy dependency that your `score_v2.py` file depends upon will automatically be installed by pip since it is a dependency of the `pandas` package.

Following this, you specify that you are using the `score_v2.py` entry script and deploy the new service. The new service will have a `swagger.json` file available for third-party applications such as Power BI to read and automatically understand how to invoke your model. You can get the Swagger URI to point to that file on the endpoint's page, as shown in *Figure 12.11*. On the endpoint's page, you should notice that the **Test** tab has been enhanced to guide you on what fields you need to provide to invoke the model. On the code side, you can invoke the model with the following payloads:

```
import json
service = ws.webservices['aci-loans']
input_payload = json.dumps({"data":[
    {"income": 2000,"credit_cards": 2,"age": 45},
    {"income": 2000, "credit_cards": 9,"age": 45}
]})
print(service.run(input_payload))
input_payload = json.dumps({'data': [
    [2000, 2, 45], [2000, 9, 45]
]})
print(service.run(input_payload))
```

Before moving on to the next section, make sure you delete the ACI service you just deployed by using the following code:

```
service.delete()
```

So far, you have been deploying real-time inference endpoints that could fulfill ad hoc inference requests through a REST API. In the next section, you will learn how to deploy a batch inference pipeline that can process big data in parallel using `ParallelRunStep`.

Creating a batch inference pipeline

In *Chapter 11*, *Working with Pipelines*, you learned how to create pipelines that orchestrate multiple steps. These pipelines can be invoked using a REST API, similar to the real-time endpoint that you created in the previous section. One key difference is that in the real-time endpoint, the infrastructure is constantly on, waiting for a request to arrive, while in the published pipelines, the cluster will spin up only after the pipeline has been triggered.

You could use these pipelines to orchestrate batch inference on top of data residing in a dataset. For example, let's imagine that you just trained the `loans` model you have been using in this chapter. You want to run the model against all of the pending loan requests and store the results; this is so that you can implement an email campaign targeting the customers that might get their loan rejected. The easiest approach is to create a single `PythonScriptStep` that will process each record sequentially and store the results in the output folder, as you learned in *Chapter 11, Working with Pipelines*. Instead of doing that, you could break the dataset into multiple batches and then have them processed, in parallel, in multiple processes running inside each node of your cluster, as displayed in *Figure 12.15*:

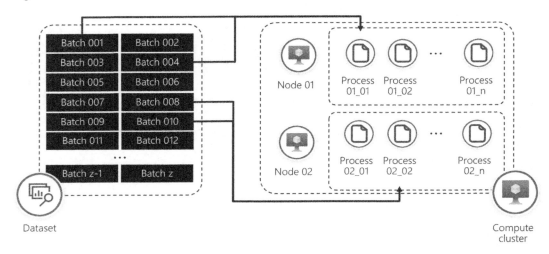

Figure 12.15 – Parallel processing big datasets by splitting them into smaller batches and processing them in parallel

In this section, you will create a batch processing pipeline that will be making inferences using the `chapter12-loans` model you trained in this chapter. You already have a dataset named `loans`, but it is too small to show how `ParallelRunStep` can help you speed up by parallelizing the inferences. You will generate a new dataset that will be 1,024 times bigger by copying the same DataFrame repeatedly. Then, you will create a pipeline similar to the one that you created in *Chapter 11, Working with Pipelines*. This time, you will use the `ParallelRunConfig` and the `ParallelRunStep` classes to parallelize the processing of the dataset. The configuration class requires an entry script, similar to the entry script that you saw in the previous section. Additionally, you need to define the following two methods:

- `init()`: This method loads the model and prepares the process for the incoming batches. No output is expected from this method.

- `run(mini_batch)`: This method does the actual data processing. This method will be invoked multiple times, passing a different `mini_batch` parameter every time. You have to return an array containing one row for each item you managed to process within this function as an output. For example, if the `mini_batch` parameter had 100 rows and you return an array of 98 items, you will indicate that you failed to process 2 of those records. The `mini_batch` parameter could either be a pandas `DataFrame` if you are processing `TabularDataset` or an array that contains the file paths you need to process if you are processing a `FileDataset`.

Navigate to your `chapter12.ipynb` notebook and perform the following steps:

1. Start by getting a reference to the workspace, the dataset, and the compute cluster you are going to use for your pipeline:

```
from azureml.core import Workspace
ws = Workspace.from_config()
loans_ds = ws.datasets['loans']
compute_target = ws.compute_targets['cpu-sm-cluster']
```

The code should be self-explanatory, as you used it in *Chapter 11, Working with Pipelines*.

2. Create a new, bigger dataset based on the `loans` dataset:

```
from azureml.core import Dataset
loans_df = loans_ds.drop_columns('approved_loan') \
                .to_pandas_dataframe()

for x in range(10):
    loans_df = loans_df.append(loans_df)

dstore = ws.get_default_datastore()
pending_loans_ds =\
Dataset.Tabular.register_pandas_dataframe(
    dataframe=loans_df,
    target=(dstore,"/samples/pending-loans"),
    name="pending-loans",
    description="Pending loans to be processed")
```

In the preceding code, you are loading the `loans DataFrame` into memory without the `approved_loan` column. This dataset only contains 500 rows. Then, you append the dataset to itself 10 times. This will create a much bigger dataset containing 512,000 rows, which you register as `pending-loans`.

3. Now, it's time to create the script that will be processing this dataset. In the `chapter12` folder, add a `pipeline_step` folder and then add a `tabular_batch.py` file with the following contents:

```python
from azureml.core import Model
import joblib

def init():
    global model
    model_path = Model.get_model_path("chapter12-loans")
    model = joblib.load(model_path)

def run(mini_batch):
    print(mini_batch.info())
    mini_batch["approved"] = model.predict(mini_batch)
    return mini_batch.values.tolist()
```

This script has two methods, as metioned earlier. In the `init` method, you use the `get_model_path` method of the `Model` class to get the location of the model that you have been using so far. From the script's perspective, the model will reside in a folder on the same computer where the script is running. Then, you use `joblib` to load the model inside a `global` variable named `model`. In the `run` method, you print the size of the incoming DataFrame, and then you create a new column, named *approved*, where you store all of the model inferences. You return a list containing a four-element array for each row you processed, similar to the following records:

```
[7298, 2, 35, 1]
[4698, 7, 70, 0]
```

If you were to process `FileDataset` instead of the `TabularDataset` that you are processing in this section, the corresponding `file_batch.py` file would look like the following:

```python
def init():
    print('Load model here')
```

```
def run(mini_batch):
    output = []
    for file_path in mini_batch:
        output.append([file_path, 0])
    return output
```

You load your model, as usual, inside the `init` method, for example, a neural network that will implement image classification. In the `run` method, the `mini_batch` parameter is an array containing the file paths of the files you need to process. You can loop through those files and make the inferences using your model. As an output, you return the filename and result of the model, as demonstrated in the following example:

```
['/path/sample_cat.jpg', 0]
['/path/sample_dog.jpg', 1]
```

You will observe, in *Step 5*, that those results will be aggregated in a single file defined in `ParallelRunConfig`.

4. You will need to create an environment to execute your pipeline step. Add the following code inside a cell:

```
from azureml.core import Environment
from azureml.core.conda_dependencies import
CondaDependencies
import sklearn

pEnv= Environment(name="sklearn-parallel")
pEnv.Python.conda_dependencies = CondaDependencies()
pEnv.Python.conda_dependencies.add_conda_
package(f"scikit-learn=={sklearn.__version__}")
pEnv.Python.conda_dependencies.add_pip_package("azureml-
core")
pEnv.Python.conda_dependencies.add_pip_package("azureml-
dataset-runtime[pandas,fuse]")
```

You need to install the `scikit-learn` conda package, just as you have been doing so far. For `ParallelRunConfig` to work, you will need to include the `azureml-core` and `azureml-dataset-runtime[pandas,fuse]` pip packages.

5. Next, create the `ParallelRunConfig` class that configures how the run will split the workload and what script to use for data processing. Add the following code inside a new notebook cell:

```
from azureml.pipeline.steps import ParallelRunConfig
parallel_run_config = ParallelRunConfig(
    source_directory='pipeline_step',
    entry_script='tabular_batch.py',
    mini_batch_size='100Kb',
    error_threshold=-1,
    output_action='append_row',
    append_row_file_name="loans_outputs.txt",
    environment=pEnv,
    compute_target=compute_target,
    node_count=1,
    process_count_per_node=2
)
```

Here, you will run the `tabular_batch.py` script located inside the `pipeline_step` folder. You are going to split the dataset into smaller batches of, approximately, 100 KB. If you were processing a `FileDataset`, you would need to specify the number of files to put in each batch. Here, `error_threshold` specifies the number of record or file failures that should be ignored while processing the data. `-1` means you are okay with any number of processing errors. The `output_action` parameter accepts either `append_row` values or `summary_only` values. Using the `append_row` value, you can request all outputs from the `run` method invocations to be appended inside a single output file, the name of which is `parallel_run_step.txt`, unless you override it via the `append_row_file_name` parameter, as demonstrated in the preceding example. The order of the records in that file is not guaranteed since the records are processed in parallel. Usually, you would return the customer ID, or the loan application ID, and the model's inference. Using that ID, you could link back the original record with the model's prediction. In the current example, we don't have any ID; therefore, we return the entire row, just as we did in the `tabular_batch.py` script in *Step 3*.

Following this, you specify the environment and the cluster where this pipeline step will be executed. In the end, you specify that this pipeline step will run in a single node, and it will spin up *two* processes per participating node. If you used two nodes, you would have four processes running in parallel. In the current example, two parallel processes are enough to handle the processing in only a couple of minutes.

If you have a heavy processing script that requires more than 60 seconds to process the `mini_batch_size` parameter you specified, you can increase the timeout value by setting the `run_invocation_timeout` parameter.

6. As a next step, you will define the output location of `append_row_file_name` that you specified earlier:

```
from azureml.data import OutputFileDatasetConfig

datastore = ws.get_default_datastore()
step_output = OutputFileDatasetConfig(
    name= "results_store",
    destination=(datastore, '/inferences/loans/'))
```

You will store that aggregation file in the default datastore, underneath the `/inferences/loans/` folder.

7. Now it's time to create the first and only step of the pipeline, that is, `ParallelRunStep`:

```
from azureml.pipeline.steps import ParallelRunStep

parallel_step = ParallelRunStep(
    name='chapter12-parallel-loans',
    inputs=[pending_loans_ds.as_named_input('loans')],
    output=step_output,
    parallel_run_config=parallel_run_config,
    allow_reuse=False
)
```

Name that step `chapter12-parallel-loans` and pass the `pending_loans_ds` dataset that you registered in *Step 2* earlier. The output is stored in `OutputFileDatasetConfig`, which you created in *Step 6*. Specify that this step should not be reused (`allow_reuse`); this allows you to trigger the pipeline multiple times to always get the latest data in the dataset along with the latest registered model.

8. Create and execute a pipeline using the following code:

```
from azureml.core import Experiment
from azureml.pipeline.core import Pipeline
pipeline = Pipeline(workspace=ws, steps=[parallel_step])
pipeline_run = Experiment(ws, 'chapter12-parallel-run').
submit(pipeline)
```

9. You can watch the execution logs by using the `RunDetails` widget with the following code:

```
from azureml.widgets import RunDetails
RunDetails(pipeline_run).show()
```

Alternatively, you can wait for the execution to complete with the following code:

```
pipeline_run.wait_for_completion(show_output=True)
```

10. From that point on, you can publish and even schedule the pipeline, as discussed in *Chapter 11*, *Working with Pipelines*.

You can visit the pipeline in AzureML studio and observe the outputs and the logs it produced, as shown in *Figure 12.16*. Notice that you will find a single node and two processes. Each process has multiple `run` method invocations. Each time the `run` method was invoked, a DataFrame that required 117.3 KB in memory was passed in, which is close to the 100 KB that you requested in *Step 5* earlier:

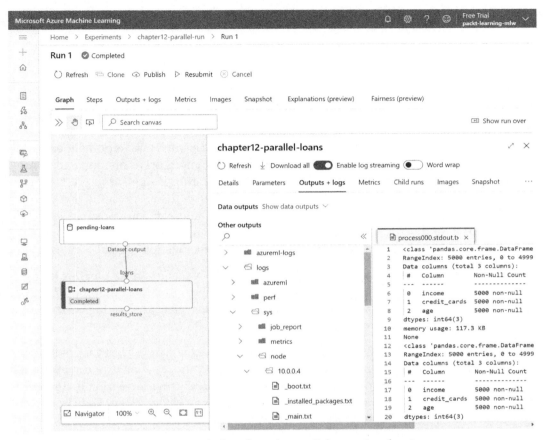

Figure 12.16 – The logs from the parallel execution showing
the information of the mini_batch DataFrame

In this section, you learned how to create a batch processing pipeline that can process
a significant amount of data in parallel. This concludes the operationalization options that
you need to be aware of for the exam, covering both the real-time and batch modes.

Summary

In this chapter, you explored various ways in which to use the machine learning models that you have been training in this book. You can make either real-time inferences or batch process a large number of records in a cost-effective manner. You started by registering the model you would use for inferences. From there, you can either deploy a real-time endpoint in ACI for testing or in AKS for production workloads that require high availability and automatic scaling. You explored how to profile your model to determine the recommended container size to host the real-time endpoint. Following this, you discovered Application Insights, which allows you to monitor production endpoints and identify potential production issues. Through Application Insights, you noticed that the real-time endpoint you produced wasn't exposing a `swagger.json` file that was needed by third-party applications, such as Power BI, to automatically consume your endpoint. You modified the scoring function to include metadata regarding your model's inputs and outputs, thus completing the real-time inference section of this chapter.

Then, you moved on to the batch inferencing side, where you authored a pipeline that can process half a million records, in parallel, in only a few minutes. Combining this parallelization with low-priority computes, you can achieve great cost savings when inferencing larger data volumes.

Congratulations! You have completed your journey of discovering the basic capabilities of the AzureML workspace. Now you can now conduct machine learning experiments in the workspace, and you can operationalize the resulting models using the option that suits the business problem that you are trying to solve. With this knowledge, you should be able to pass the *DP-100* exam, *Designing and Implementing a Data Science Solution on Azure*, with flying colors.

Questions

In each chapter, you will find a number of questions to validate your understanding of the topics that have been discussed:

1. You want to deploy a real-time endpoint that will handle transactions from a live betting website. The traffic from this website will have spikes during games and will be very low during the night. Which of the following compute targets should you use?

    a. ACI

    b. A compute instance

    c. A compute cluster

    d. AKS

2. You want to monitor a real-time endpoint deployed in AKS and determine the average response time of the service. Which monitoring solution should you use?

   a. ACI

   b. Azure Container Registry

   c. Application Insights

3. You have a computer vision model, and you want to process 100 images in parallel. You author a pipeline with a parallel step. You want to process 10 images at a time. Which of the following `ParallelRunConfig` parameters should you set?

   a. `mini_batch_size=10`

   b. `error_threshold=10`

   c. `node_count=10`

   d. `process_count_per_node=10`

Further reading

This section offers a list of helpful web resources to help you augment your knowledge of the AzureML SDK and the various code snippets used in this chapter:

- Model persistence guidance from scikit-learn: `https://scikit-learn.org/stable/modules/model_persistence.html`

- Testing a REST API using Postman: `https://www.postman.com/product/api-client/`

- The **curl** command-line tool to make web requests: `https://curl.se/`

- Monitor Python applications using OpenCensus: `https://docs.microsoft.com/azure/azure-monitor/app/opencensus-python`

- How to use the inference server to test your entry scripts locally: `https://docs.microsoft.com/azure/machine-learning/how-to-inference-server-http`

- Packaging the model inside an autonomous Docker container: `https://docs.microsoft.com/azure/machine-learning/how-to-deploy-package-models`

- The ONNX machine learning format used to store models that can be loaded in multiple platforms: `https://docs.microsoft.com/azure/machine-learning/concept-onnx`

- An introduction to Application Insights: `https://docs.microsoft.com/azure/azure-monitor/app/app-insights-overview`

- An introduction to the Kusto Query Language: `https://docs.microsoft.com/azure/data-explorer/kusto/concepts/`

- The advanced real-time endpoint entry script authoring guide: `https://docs.microsoft.com/azure/machine-learning/how-to-deploy-advanced-entry-script`

- Integrating AzureML models in Power BI: `https://docs.microsoft.com/power-bi/transform-model/dataflows/dataflows-machine-learning-integration#azure-machine-learning-integration-in-power-bi`

- Using the `ParallelRunStep` class to train hundreds of models: `https://github.com/microsoft/solution-accelerator-many-models`

Packt.com

Subscribe to our online digital library for full access to over 7,000 books and videos, as well as industry leading tools to help you plan your personal development and advance your career. For more information, please visit our website.

Why subscribe?

- Spend less time learning and more time coding with practical eBooks and Videos from over 4,000 industry professionals

- Improve your learning with Skill Plans built especially for you

- Get a free eBook or video every month

- Fully searchable for easy access to vital information

- Copy and paste, print, and bookmark content

Did you know that Packt offers eBook versions of every book published, with PDF and ePub files available? You can upgrade to the eBook version at packt.com and as a print book customer, you are entitled to a discount on the eBook copy. Get in touch with us at customercare@packtpub.com for more details.

At www.packt.com, you can also read a collection of free technical articles, sign up for a range of free newsletters, and receive exclusive discounts and offers on Packt books and eBooks.

Other Books You May Enjoy

If you enjoyed this book, you may be interested in these other books by Packt:

Cloud Analytics with Microsoft Azure

Has Altaiar, Jack Lee, Michael Peña

ISBN: 9781839216404

- Explore the concepts of modern data warehouses and data pipelines
- Discover different design considerations while applying a cloud analytics solution
- Design an end-to-end analytics pipeline on the cloud
- Differentiate between structured, semi-structured, and unstructured data
- Choose a cloud-based service for your data analytics solutions

Use Azure services to ingest, store and analyze data of any scale

Cloud Scale Analytics with Azure Data Services

Patrik Borosch

ISBN: 9781800562936

- Implement data governance with Azure services
- Use integrated monitoring in the Azure Portal and integrate Azure Data Lake Storage into the Azure Monitor
- Explore the serverless feature for ad-hoc data discovery, logical data warehousing, and data wrangling
- Implement networking with Synapse Analytics and Spark pools
- Create and run Spark jobs with Databricks clusters
- Implement streaming using Azure Functions, a serverless runtime environment on Azure
- Explore the predefined ML services in Azure and use them in your app

Packt is searching for authors like you

If you're interested in becoming an author for Packt, please visit `authors.packtpub.com` and apply today. We have worked with thousands of developers and tech professionals, just like you, to help them share their insight with the global tech community. You can make a general application, apply for a specific hot topic that we are recruiting an author for, or submit your own idea.

Share Your Thoughts

Now you've finished *Azure Data Scientist Associate Certification Guide*, we'd love to hear your thoughts! Scan the QR code below to go straight to the Amazon review page for this book and share your feedback or leave a review on the site that you purchased it from.

`https://packt.link/r/1-800-56500-3`

Your review is important to us and the tech community and will help us make sure we're delivering excellent quality content.

Index

Printed in Great Britain
by Amazon

21690020R00255